The Oxford Book
of
New Zealand Short Stories

The Oxford Book
of
New Zealand Short Stories

Selected by Vincent O'Sullivan

Auckland
Oxford University Press
Oxford   Melbourne   New York

Oxford University Press, Walton Street, Oxford OX2 6DP
Oxford   New York   Toronto
Delhi   Bombay   Calcutta   Madras   Karachi
Kuala Lumpur   Singapore   Hong Kong   Tokyo
Nairobi   Dar es Salaam   Cape Town
Melbourne   Auckland   Madrid
and associated companies in
Berlin   Ibadan

Oxford is a trade mark of Oxford University Press

Introduction and selection © Vincent O'Sullivan 1992
Setting © Oxford University Press 1992
First published 1992
This edition first published 1994

ISBN 0 19 558291 8

Cover designed by Jacinda Torrance / Paradigm
Typeset in Adobe Ehrhardt by Egan-Reid Ltd
Printed in New Zealand by GP Print Ltd
Published by Oxford University Press
1A Matai Road, Greenlane
PO Box 11–149, Auckland, New Zealand

Contents

Introduction   vii

Acknowledgements   xii

Lady Barker (1831–1911)   From *Christmas Day in New Zealand*   1

Clara Cheeseman (1852–1943)   *Married for His Money*   14

Rudyard Kipling (1865–1936)   *One Lady at Wairakei*   25

Henry Lawson (1867–1922)   *Stiffner and Jim (Thirdly, Bill)*   34

G. B. Lancaster (1873–1945)   *Hantock's Dissertation*   41

Katherine Mansfield (1888-1923)   *The Wind Blows*   45
   An Indiscreet Journey   49

Jean Devanny (1894–1962)   *The Perfect Mother*   62

Greville Texidor (1902–1964)   *Home Front*   75

Frank Sargeson (1903–1982)   *A Great Day*   83
   Old Man's Story   90

Roderick Finlayson (1904–1992)   *Another Kind of Life*   96

Dan Davin (1913–1990)   *Coming and Going*   100

A. P. Gaskell (b. 1913)   *School Picnic*   109

Amelia Batistich (b. 1915)   *A Dalmatian Woman*   119

G. R. Gilbert (b. 1917)   *A Girl with Ambition*   123

Maurice Duggan (1922–1974)   *Along Rideout Road that Summer*   127

Ronald Hugh Morrieson (1922–1972)   *Cross My Heart and Cut My Throat*   143

Janet Frame (b. 1924)   *The Reservoir*   149
   The Bath   161

Barbara Anderson (b. 1926)   *Up the River with Mrs Gallant*   168

Renato Amato (1928–1964)   *One of the Titans*   176

Noel Hilliard (b. 1929)   *Corrective Training*   181

Yvonne du Fresne (b. 1929)   *The Morning Talk*   190

Maurice Gee (b. 1931) *A Glorious Morning, Comrade* 196

Maurice Shadbolt (b. 1932) *The People Before* 203

C. K. Stead (b. 1932) *A New Zealand Elegy* 223

Alexander Guyan (1933–1991) *An Opinion of the Ballet* 247

Russell Haley (b. 1934) *Fog* 250

Joy Cowley (b. 1936) *The Silk* 256

Patricia Grace (b. 1937) *Journey* 264
Between Earth and Sky 276

Vincent O'Sullivan (b. 1937) *Dandy Edison for Lunch* 280

Albert Wendt (b. 1939) *Crocodile* 297

Fiona Kidman (b. 1940) *The Tennis Player* 304

Owen Marshall (b. 1941) *Valley Day* 314
Mumsie and Zip 323

Michael Morrissey (b. 1942) *Jack Kerouac Sat Down Beside the*
Wanganui River and Wept 331

Witi Ihimaera (b. 1944) *Big Brother, Little Sister* 338

Bill Manhire (b. 1946) *The Poet's Wife* 353

Ian Wedde (b. 1946) *The Gringos* 361

Colleen Reilly (b. 1946) *Jim's Elvis* 368

Keri Hulme (b. 1947) *One Whale, Singing* 372

Fiona Farrell (b. 1947) *The Gift* 381

Peter Wells (b. 1953) *Outing* 392

John Cranna (b. 1954) *Archaeology* 398

Lloyd Jones (b. 1955) *Who's That Dancing With My Mother?* 411

Vivienne Plumb (b. 1955) *The Wife Who Spoke Japanese*
in her Sleep 416

Anne Kennedy (b. 1959) *A Veil Dropped from a Great Height* 426

Anthony McCarten (b. 1961) *Baby Clare* 431

Biographical Notes 441

Glossary of Maori and Samoan Words 450

Introduction

Until the 1960s at least, young New Zealanders were likely to come across their first local short stories of any real distinction in either Katherine Mansfield or Frank Sargeson. The pathos of 'the little lamp' in 'The Doll's House', the man plugging his ears and rowing away from the friend he leaves on a reef in 'A Great Day', were the kind of incidents, told in a language that was close to home, that made you see for the first time that fiction might happen as naturally here as anywhere else, even if 'anywhere else' was where you mostly read about. And you then learned fairly early on that these were the two ways New Zealand stories had come to be written—in the perceptively feminine, middle-class, stylish manner of Mansfield, or with the working-class, masculine, no-frills directness of Sargeson.

Both 'approaches', as they were called, were necessary myths for the time, within the larger myth that New Zealand was a country where, as every immigrant forebear dreamed, things eventually did get better, governments more humane, race relations more settled, the community more civil and informed. And it was in the nature of things, in any colonial society, that as life improved so art would perhaps come to tell you more about yourself. Language, as surely as paint and perspective, would gradually take in what was immediate, yet also divergent from whatever arrived in the cultural baggage of the settlers. The new perspective, of course, was not always what its audience most wanted. Mansfield's father may have chucked one of her books into the fireplace, complaining that it didn't even tell a story; Sargeson's narrow Waikato background was not the place where he could expect his readers to be. But Mansfield showed that art could take in her father's commercial world and a good deal else as well, and Sargeson that there was a way of listening to the near inarticulate, and writing of it with tough resilience. All of which may be true, yet rather too simply so, if one looks to where the New Zealand short story began.

Clara Cheeseman's story 'Married for his Money', published in 1878, takes up a conventionally satirical mode to place those comic but rigidly observed social strata that are also so apparent, at the beginnings of our fiction, to Lady Barker's sympathetic and condescending ear. Yet the comedy and the assumed gentility that give so much New Zealand social history its divertingly provincial edge are there rather less in our early fiction than might be expected. From Cheeseman until Mansfield there were numerous magazine stories by men that for the most part played over the stereotypes of ghost story, humorous yarns—often with a heavy racist slant—and outdoor life, and stories by women that were often 'local' merely by virtue of flora and bird-life, native colouring, a hankering in various forms for Britain as repository of what was abidingly Real. To break through such stage-props (as they seem to us) was difficult, as it was to move beyond the magazine conventions of romance and adventure. Where Mansfield moved towards Modernism and into the deft time levels of one of her stories included here, and into the problematic freedom and historical immediacy of the 'new woman' in the other, Sargeson a little later turned to distinctively masculine American models, a necessary turning as he saw it from English dominance if he too was to break free, and, in his case, remain at home.

Yet already in the 1890s, the Australian Henry Lawson had caught how working men talked and behaved, and gave New Zealand as well as his own country the vivid colloquial narrative that carried social commentary even in the casual yarn. Through his dominance in shaping the pre-First World War 'Australasian' voice, Lawson also shaped New Zealand writing rather more than has been acknowledged. He represented male speech and thinking as a secular stoicism that was 'natural' to the society he depicts, and 'mateship' as the essential democratic base.

Politics and war, not surprisingly, dominate the best New Zealand stories from the late 1920s into the 1950s, stories that so often articulate social issues, and frequently worry at the bone of national identity, at finding an appropriate 'discourse' to define ourselves by, as though to solve that adequately would solve so much else as well. They are stories, too, which apart from Jean Devanny's and Greville Texidor's, assume that gender roles are pretty much fixities of nature. In those two decades when New Zealand turned itself from a depressed economy into a humane and quasi-socialist state, and found itself in the throes of a global war, a fairly straightforward realism was the prevailing narrative mode. For a community concerned with both reform and violence, accurately to depict fact was a way of ensuring too the accuracy of intention and response. In Davin's war stories, as well as in his own, Sargeson's, and Gaskell's strongly localized stories at home, one picks up the signals that the metropolitan and the modernist were siren voices that a distinctively Kiwi ethos had no call for. This was reinforced by the first attempts by European New Zealanders to write about Maori on their own terms, to remove them from mere exotic display and to place them, as in fact they always had been, at the centre of national experience. Roderick Finlayson to begin with, and then Noel Hilliard as forcefully as any writer since, set the contemporary Maori in a disruptive urban milieu. (In almost all later writing by Maori as well, the City stands as inveterate enemy to the Tribe; aroha and commercial success are mutually exclusive.) Yet for all the insistence on social decency in the stories from this time, there is often a resisting pressure, an oppressiveness even, that has sometimes and wrongly been laid at the door of social realism as a mode in itself. In so many wartime and post-war stories the individual—and the writer— assumes there is a wall of convention to break through, the calcified layers of a society where ideas move slowly, where difference is construed as danger, where the world at large is as unsettling as the presence of indigenous people. New Zealand resisted all except eugenic immigration following the war, in the official fear that the Mediterranean in particular would contaminate our genetic pool. A fresh foreign voice like Renato Amato's was a rare thing. When the breakthrough to new fictional possibilities did arrive, it was through Maurice Duggan calculatedly opting for European 'stylishness', for the ornate, layered, intricate tutelage of Joyce; and through Janet Frame's even more deliberately courting the invigorating dangers that 'difference' offered her. With both Duggan and Frame, language itself becomes what stories are largely about, and events the material rather than the end of what is told. Modernism was reclaimed through Duggan, and post-modernism anticipated by Frame's longer fiction especially. But her short stories, too, moved in new directions, along veins of imagery and subversion that harried the cherished humanist assumption that language itself was intrinsically redemptive. Her concern was more ambivalent, with 'the Word as monster or angel'.

Perhaps the strongest alternative to Frame's almost constantly negative narratives has come from Maori writers like Grace and Ihimaera, who turn whatever they take from literary traditions towards specifically Maori ends. These are not simply to present Maori experience as no Pakeha could validly claim to do. There is the insistence that Maori values are necessarily of a different kind, shaped by colonial experience certainly, but elusive of any final determination. Ihimaera puts this most vividly in an often quoted incident where an old man explains why *whakapapa*, an abiding concern with ancestry and place, so matters to him: 'Because it gives me unison with the Universe . . . It moves me into a pattern of creation that began at world's creation and will be there at world's end . . . Although I will die, the pattern will not be broken.' There is a deep political implication that might be read in that as well, a drawing of lines that warn against intrusion.

A little before Maori writers claimed their own voice as the best—some would now say the only—that might validly represent them, the generation of Cowley and Shadbolt and Gee were extending different borders. They had begun to take in middle-class urban life—anathema to Frame, the shadowy enemy to Sargeson, the unlikely peacetime bourgeoisie to Davin's soldiers and working class—with fresh perception and sympathy. These writers would see themselves primarily as novelists, but their shorter fiction was central in bringing the genre to where it now stands.

I began this introductory note with the reminder that thirty or so years ago the New Zealand short story was thought to fall, obviously and neatly, into two more or less exclusive modes, although the prevailing opinion was that one was rather more serviceable, rather closer to the grain of New Zealand experience, than the other. (Sargeson wrote to me in the early 1970s about paying too much attention to Mansfield, 'the Karori schoolgirl'.) Anyone coming to the form as it now stands would find prescriptive loading of that earlier kind, or even arguing for an appropriately distinctive New Zealand kind of story, as irrelevant, if not bizarre. Although literary boundary riders from time to time trot out directives on how fiction should proceed, most writers don't seem too fazed. The proliferation in the number of stories written in the last decade or so especially, and the corresponding extension of narrative methods, argues an ear quite as attuned to international writing as it is to closer pressures. Owen Marshall, pre-eminently, shows how much might still be drawn from the mainstream realism of New Zealand fiction, and how richly it may be turned to new ends.

And what of New Zealand short fiction among younger writers? Take four of the last names in this collection and you are directed to as many variations on what a story does, or how it can be told. Antony McCarten's fling with gothic innocence, Vivienne Plumb on the Asian already residing in our subconscious, Fiona Farrell's surreal and domesticated Jesus, and John Cranna's constructing a future that won't be there with the bones of an earlier extinction, all present what a New Zealand reader would recognize and accept as local density. But would one bother to argue, or think it important to argue, that any single one of them, as a narrative method, was necessarily to be opted for? Or better suited to who and where we are? If there has been a shaking down of what once seemed such 'essential' concerns, the gains in diversity and fictional freedom have been immense. In ten years' time, of course, one may well have to say something very different. But for the moment, vigorous uncertainty is not a bad condition for a writer to contend with.

A final, if fairly obvious, word. In reading for this anthology, and in putting it together, I have defined a 'New Zealand story' broadly and, I think, cogently, as one by a born New Zealander, by someone who has chosen to live here, or by a writer who has written specifically from or on New Zealand experience. Kipling or Texidor quite as compellingly meet that definition as do, say, Finlayson or Wells. And I accept what any anthologist accepts as the constriction of his or her brief: because choices have to be made, one's own preferences certainly aren't going to match up with everyone else's. Space is always the silent and implacable co-editor of any collection. I regret having to leave out many stories I admire and like. Those I have included make their own case.

Vincent O'Sullivan
August, 1992

Acknowledgements

For permission to reproduce copyright passages grateful acknowledgement is made to the publishers and copyright holders of the following:

Renato Amato, the Author's estate. Barbara Anderson, *I think we should go into the jungle* (Victoria University Press, 1989). Amelia Batistich, *An Olive Tree in Dalmatia* (Longman Paul, 1963). Joy Cowley, *Heart Attack and Other Stories* (Hodder and Stoughton, 1985). John Cranna, *Visitors* (Random House, 1989). Dan Davin, *Selected Stories* (Victoria University Press, 1981). Yvonne du Fresne, *Farvel and Other Stories* (Victoria University Press, 1980). Maurice Duggan, *Collected Stories* (Auckland University Press, 1981). Fiona Farrell, *The Rock Garden* (Auckland University Press, 1989). Roderick Finlayson, *Brown Man's Burden and later Stories* (Auckland University Press, 1973). Janet Frame, *You Are Now Entering the Human Heart* (Victoria University Press, 1983). A. P. Gaskell, *All Part of the Game* (Auckland University Press, 1978). Maurice Gee, *A Glorious Morning*, Comrade (Auckland University Press, 1975). G. R. Gilbert, *Free to Laugh and Dance* (Caxton Press, 1942). Patricia Grace, *The Dream Sleepers and Other Stories* (Penguin, 1980). Alexander Guyan, the Author. Russell Haley, *Real Illusions* (Victoria University Press, 1984). Noel Hilliard, the Author. Keri Hulme, *Te Kaihau: the Windeater* (Victoria University Press, 1986). Witi Ihimaera, *The New Net Goes Fishing* (Reed, 1977). Lloyd Jones, *Swimming to Australia and Other Stories* (Victoria University Press, 1991). Anne Kennedy, *New Women's Fiction* (New Women's Press, 1988). Fiona Kidman, *Unsuitable Friends* (Random Century, 1988). Anthony McCarten, *A Modest Apocalypse and Other Stories* (Godwit, 1991). Bill Manhire, the Author. Owen Marshall, *Divided World: Selected Stories* (John McIndoe, 1989). Ronald Hugh Morrieson, the Author's estate. Michael Morrissey, *Octavio's Last Invention* (Brick Row, 1991). Vincent O'Sullivan, *Dandy Edison for Lunch* (John McIndoe, 1981). Vivienne Plumb, the Author. Colleen Reilly, *Jim's Elvis* (John McIndoe, 1992). Frank Sargeson, *Collected Stories* (Penguin, 1982). Maurice Shadbolt, *Summer Fires and Winter Country*, the Author. C. K. Stead, *Five For the Symbol* (Longman Paul, 1981). Greville Texidor, *In Fifteen Minutes You Can Say A Lot* (Victoria University Press, 1987). Ian Wedde, *The Shirt Factory and Other Stories* (Victoria University Press, 1981). Peter Wells, *Dangerous Desires* (Reed, 1991). Albert Wendt, *The Birth and Death of the Miracle Man* (Penguin, 1986).

Lady Barker

From CHRISTMAS DAY IN NEW ZEALAND

The question then seriously presented itself to my mind, of how to amuse my twenty stalwart guests from 3 o'clock until 7. I intended them to have tea again about 5, and quantities of plum cake if they could possibly eat it; but there were two hours of broiling heat to be got through, socially speaking, before they could be invited to eat again. After tea I knew there would be athletic games, so soon as Flagpole's mighty shadow had laid a cool patch over the valley. My guests would be affronted if I went away, and yet my presence evidently made them miserable. They all sat in rigid and uncomfortable attitudes, and blushed furiously if I spoke to them, trying hard all the time to persuade themselves and me that they were enjoying themselves. Even the unfailing pipes, which I had insisted on being produced, failed to create an element of contentment, for the smokers suffered incessant anxiety lest the light shifting summer air should send a puff of tobacco-smoke towards me. We were all very polite, but wretched; and I shall never forgive F——'s unkind enjoyment of the horrible dullness of this stage of my party. 'Dear me, this is too exciting,' he would whisper; 'don't let them all talk at once;' or else he would ask me if it was not 'going off' very brilliantly, when all the time it was not going off at all.

I began to grow desperate; my company would not talk or do anything, but sit steadily staring at each other and me. In vain I asked questions about subjects which I thought might interest them. Conversation seemed impossible, and I had firmly resolved to go away in five minutes, and see if they would be more lively without me, when some bold individual started the subject of gold-digging. Everybody's tongue was unloosed as if by magic, and all had some really interesting story to tell about either their own or their 'mate's' experiences at the West Coast gold-diggings. One man described with much humour how he had been in the very first 'rush', and how amazed a lonely settler in the Bush had been at the sudden appearance of a thousand men in the silence and solitude of his hut, which was built up a gully. When the eager gold-seekers questioned him as to whether he had found the 'colour' in the creek which they were bent on tracing to its rich source, he lazily shook his head and said, coolly, pointing over his shoulder, 'Me and the boys' (his equally lazy sons) 'have never earned no wages, no, nor had any money of our own. Whenever we wanted to go to the store'—about twenty miles off, and a wretched track between—'we jest took and we washed a bit among that 'ere dirt, and we allers found as much dust as we wanted.' The bed of that creek contained nearly as many particles of fine flake-gold as of sand; and that lazy old man could have made a fabulous fortune years and years before, if he had taken the trouble to see it, as it rippled past his log hut. He never found a speck of gold in all his life afterwards, for no sooner had he finished his dawdling speech than the diggers had flung themselves into the wealth-bearing streamlet and fought and scrambled for its golden sands, which glided away during the night like a fairy vision. Great boulders were upheaved by the gold-seekers in their first eager rush, so the natural dams being thus removed, when the next morning dawned the water had rushed away into a new channel, bearing its precious freight with it.

The spokesman took from his neck a little wash-leather bag as he finished his story, with the words, 'All gone—clean gone;' and opening it shook a few pinches of the sparkling flaky dust into my lap, saying, 'That's some o' wot I got evenin' before. It's beautiful, ain't it, mum?' I duly admired the shining treasure, and he bade me keep it 'for my Christmas box', and I have it safely put away to this day. But I very nearly lost it, and this is how it happened. A discussion arose as to the most successful method of washing sand for gold, and some new inventions were freely discussed. 'Well, I reckon I got them there nuggets'—the largest no bigger than a small pin's head—'by washin' with a milk dish.' 'How?' I asked. 'I'll show you, mum, if I may get a dish from the gals;' and he strode off towards the house, returning with a large milk-tin in his hands. He then proceeded to the side of the duck-pond, and, in spite of the 'agony of dress' in which he was arrayed, filled the shallow dish with mud and stones and grit of all sorts. At this stage of the proceedings he appeared intent on making a huge dirt-pie. Imagine my dismay when he pounced on the paper packet into which I had just carefully collected my gold-dust, counted the tiny flakes rapidly up to fifteen, and then scattered them ruthlessly over the surface of this abominable mess. He next proceeded to stir it all up with a piece of wooden shingle, and regardless of my face of dismay, said calmly, 'Now we'll wash 'em out.' I should have had no objection to seeing the experiment tried with anybody else's gold dust, but I must say I was very sorry to find that my newly acquired treasure was thus lightly disposed of. 'Lightly won, lightly lost,' I thought to myself, 'for I shall never see it again.'

Pratchard (that was the name of the quondam digger) now marched off to the creek close by, and in spite of the blazing sunshine we all followed him. He stooped down, and, scooping up some water, began shaking his great heavy tin backwards and forwards. By degrees he got rid of the surface mud, then he added more water, until in half an hour or so he had washed and shaken all the materials for his dirt-pie out of the dish, and disclosed my fifteen wee nuggets shining like so many flecks of sunlight at the bottom of the tin vessel. 'Count 'em, mum, if *you* please,' said Pratchard, hot, but triumphant; and so I did, to find not one missing. To me it seemed like a conjuror's trick, but Pratchard and the rest of my company hastened to assure me that it was not possible to wash away gold. It sank and sank, being so much heavier than anything else, until it could be perceived at the bottom of whatever dish or even plate was used to scoop up the dirt among which it was to be found.

We were more sociable now, but hotter than ever, and we returned gladly to the shade of the stable. As things looked more promising at this stage of my party, I suggested that everybody should, in turn, tell a story. Of course they all declared 'they didn't know nothing', but finally I coaxed old Bob, a shepherd, to tell me about one of his early Christmas Days in the colony, and this is his narrative, but not in his own phraseology. I wish I could spell it as he pronounced it.

* * *

'Things are very different now,' said Bob, 'all over the country, though it is not so many years ago, not more than six or seven perhaps. We did not think much of Sunday in the early days; we didn't exactly work, such as digging or such-like on that day, but we did other jobs which had been waiting for a spare moment all the week. We used not to think any harm of breaking a young colt on Sunday, or of riding over to the next run with a draughting notice; or if it was wet we lay in our bunks and smoked, or p'raps we got up and sat on a bucket turned wrong side up, and mended our clothes. As for Christmas Day, we never thought of it beyond wondering what sort of "duff" we were going to have. That's colonial for a pudding, ma'am, you know, don't you? If we had a couple of handfuls of currants and raisins, we shoved them into a lot of flour and sugar, and we put a bit of mutton fat into the middle, and tied it all up together in the sleeve of an old flannel shirt and boiled it, and it used to come out a first-rate plum duff and we thought we had no end of a Christmas if we could manage such a pudding as that.

'But we could not always get even a holiday on Christmas Day, because of the shearing. Shearers were too scarce in those days, and wages too high to miss a day's work, so it often happened that we had to work just as hard, or harder on Christmas than on any other day of the year. I was working then up at Mr Vansittart's ('Vans-start's', Bob called his master), and we had hopes of getting finished by Christmas Eve, and having at all events a good lie-in-bed on Christmas Day; but as ill-luck would have it, a mob of wethers bolted from the flat where Tom Duckworth was watching them, and got right away into the hills at the back of the run. *He* said it was because his dogs were new and wouldn't work properly for him, but I knew better—he done it a-purpose. Tom's sheep were always coming to grief. He couldn't cross 'em over a river without losing half the mob, and never a week passed without his getting boxed. That's mixed-up, ma'am,' explained Bob politely, observing a puzzled expression in my eyes. 'We calls it boxing when your sheep go and join another mob feeding close by, and you can't tell one from another except by the brand or the ear-mark. It's a nasty business is boxing, and *werry* trying to the temper. Even the dogs get out of patience like, and nip the stupid sheep harder than they do at any other time.

'Well, ma'am, as I was saying, Tom Duckworth let a fine mob of young wethers get away the day before Christmas Day, and started to look for them with his precious dogs. They were the very last mob which had to come up to be shorn, so, as he couldn't find 'em—I never expected he could,—there was the skillions standing empty, and the shearers lounging about idling when Christmas Day came; and a werry beautiful day it was, just like this one. The boss, that's Master Vans-start, he was at his wits' ends what to do. He knew right well that if the wethers wasn't in the yards that night, the shearers would be off across the hills to Brown and Wetherby's next morning first thing. You couldn't expect men who had their two pounds a day waiting for them to lose many days, especially as Brown and Wetherby's was an "open shed", where any shearers that came were taken on until there were hands enough, so they knew they might lose the job if they didn't look sharp. The boss managed to keep them quiet on Christmas Day, by pretending he always meant to take a spell on that day. He got the cook to make a stunning duff, and he sent a boy on horseback across the river to Mulready's for some beef; he knew Mulready always killed a bullock about Christmas and he served out some grog, so in that way he kept the shearers well fed and rested all

Christmas Day. He never let them out of his sight, not even down to the creek to wash their shirts, lest any of them should slip away.

'I didn't come in for any of these good things: so far from it, quite the contra-*ry*;' and here Bob paused and took a pull at his pipe, resting his hands on his knees and gazing straight before him with regretful eyes, as the memory of his wrongs rose freshly to his mind. 'Tom Duckworth did, though, the stupid fool! He laid in his bunk on Christmas morning and had his snooze out, and then he got up and eat the best part of a cold leg of mutton for his breakfast, and he came in for the duff, and the grog, and all the rest of it afterwards. But I'll tell you how I spent my Christmas Day, ma'am, and I hope I'll never have to spend another like it.

'As soon as ever it was light, the boss, leastways Master Vans-start, he came into the kitchen where I was sleeping, and he says, "Bob, I must have that mob of wethers by tonight, and that's all about it. They're quite likely to have gone up into the back ranges, but unless they're gone up into the sky I'm bound to have 'em in the skillions tonight." You see, ma'am, when Master Vans-start put it in that way, I knew that mob had got to be found before nightfall, and that he was going to tell me off to find 'em. So I lay there and listened, as was my dooty to. "Bob," says Master Vans-start, "I'll tell you what it is, I'll give you a fiver," — that's a five-pound note, ma'am, you'll understand, — "yes, Bob, a fiver, over and above your year's pay when I draws a cheque for your wages next week, and you can go down to town and spend it, Bob, if you bring me in the whole of that mob of wethers by sundown. Take any body you like with you and the best of the dogs, only you bring them in; for if you don't, I shall be three hundred pounds short in my wool-money this year, and I've got too heavy a mortgage on this run, Bob, to be able to afford to lose that much, and all through Tom Duckworth's sleepy-headedness."

'Well, ma'am, when the boss spoke so feelingly, and put it to me in that way, I knew it had to be done, so I said, "Right you are, sir," and then he only said, "I looks to you, Bob, for them sheep," and he went away. It was barely light enough to see your hand, and I knew that the *mistesses* (that was the way Bob pronounced mists) would be hanging about the hills for a good time yet, so I reached out my hand and I got my pipe and a match and I smoked a bit, whilst I considered which way I should go and who I should take with me. Men, I mean; I didn't want to know what dogs I should take, for if Sharp and Sally couldn't find 'em, all I could say was, they wasn't to be found. I'd a good mind to name Tom Duckworth to come, but I meant to give whoever went with me a pound a-piece, and I didn't want to tip him for giving all this bother;

besides, he was just as likely as not to sit down under the lea of a rock and smoke the moment he got out of my sight. No, I wouldn't take Tom, but I'd take little Joe Smelt, who was as active as a kid on the hills, and Munro, who, although he belonged to the next station, knew every yard of country round, and who had the best head on his shoulders of any man I knew. Besides, Munro had always been a chum of mine, and was such a decent well-spoken fellow, it was a pleasure to have any dealin's with him.

'By the time I had settled all this in my own mind, I thought it was about time to get up, so up I got and I lighted the stove and put the kettle on to boil, and a whole lot of chops on to fry, and I got the pannikins out and the tin plates. I remember well I was so anxious to have a good comfortable breakfast ready before I called Joe and Munro, that I even cleaned up the knives and forks for 'em. How did I do that, is it you want to know, ma'am? Oh, very easy: I just stuck 'em into the soft ground outside the back door, and worked 'em up and down a bit, and they came out fine and clean. Well, as soon as I had got everything ready, I went into the men's hut, and I got out Munro and little Joe Smelt without waking up any of the others; and when they got on their boots and moleskins, saving your presence, ma'am, they come into the kitchen, and I showed 'em the breakfast all ready and smelling uncommon good, and I told 'em what the boss had said, and I lays it before 'em whether they likes to come up the hills with me and earn their pound a-piece, or whether they'd *pre*-fer to loaf about the station all day, whiles I goes out by myself and sticks to the whole of the fiver.

'Munro, he goes on eating his breakfast quite quiet-like—for that matter we was all pegging away pretty tidily—and then, after a bit, he says in his pretty peaceable way—I've told you he was a very well spoken man, ma'am, haven't I?—he says, "Well, Bob, I don't mind if I do come;" and then Joe Smelt says, as well as he can speak for a mouthful of damper, "The same here;" so then I knew it was settled, and I enjoyed my break-fast with the rest. We didn't dawdle too long, though, for it was getting light enough to see, though them mistesses was still too low to please me, but I thought we might be making our way up the river-gorge and smoke our pipes as we went. The sheep had gone up that way, I knew, and there was no way out. Besides, sheep don't like crossing the water oftener than they can help. Nine times we had to cross that there river on that there blessed Christmas morning. Get wet! I should just think we did: leastways I took off my Cookhams and worsted socks at each ford, because I knew right well that if I went up the hills and walked all day in wet things my feet would get that blistered I'd feel like a cat in walnut-shells. Joe Smelt found that out to his cost before the day was over. He started werry cocky and turned up his trouser-legs and walked right through the water, saying he couldn't be bothered to stop and take his boots off and on at each crossing. Munro, he walked through all nine fords in his boots; and then, when we had done with them for that day, he sat down on a big stone and took off his socks and his boots and drew out a nice dry pair of worsted socks, and put 'em on; then he poured the water out of his boots and shook 'em up and down a bit and put 'em on again, and laced 'em up werry tight. But still, long before the day was done, his feet was smartin' and his boots was all out o' shape, and wringing him awful. Joe and I couldn't have managed that way if it had been ever so, for socks wasn't plenty with us in those days. We just used to get one pair at a time from the nighest store, and wear 'em until they got into one big hole all over, and then we chucked 'em away and got another pair. Now, Munro, he had a nice little Scotch wife up at his place, and she was always a-spinning and a-knitting for him, and kept him as comfortable as could be. But Joe and me, we hadn't neither wives, nor socks, nor anything nice about us, but we just pulled through as well as we could.

'Well, ma'am, to come back to that Christmas Day. It was as beautiful a morning as you would wish to see, and not too hot, neither; the sun just beginning to shine, and drinking up them mistesses as if they was grog, till there wasn't one to be seen, and Munro's glass showed him every sheep on every hill within sight as plain as you see your hand now. Lots of sheep there were too, and werry cheerful it sounded their calling to each other, and werry good feed there was for 'em on those hills. But they was all too white for what we wanted. They'd all been *shored*, 'twas easy to see that, and the mob we wanted was still in their wool, and would have looked dirty and much larger among the fresh-shored ones. We could track 'em easy enough by their footmarks up to the head of the gorge, but there we lost all trace, and though we spent a good hour hunting. We felt sure they'd all keep together, for they'd be frightened at the sight of all their fellows so white and so bare, and likely as not travel away from 'em. They wasn't anywhere on the low hills, that was certain; there was no use funking it, we had got to separate and go carefully over the back ranges, and a long hot climb we had before us that Christmas morning; and, not to be too long about it, ma'am, a long hot climb we had if ever there was one in this world. I sent the dogs many and many a time after what I thought might be a part of the mob; but though I hunted as close as ever I could, never a sheep did I see, no, nor a sign of one. Well, ma'am, it was very disheartening, you'll allow that, and I was so vexed I couldn't feel properly hungry even long after dinner-time came, and I kept thinking whatever I should do if they wasn't to be found. You see, I had chosen the most likely place to search in myself, as was but nat'ral, so I never thought that if *I* couldn't find 'em anybody else could. There's where I deceived myself; because when I had worked all round that blessed range and come upon Davis's hut—that was the out-station where we had settled to meet some time in the afternoon—what should I see but Munro and Joe Smelt a-lying on the shady side of the hut as cool and comfortable as you please smoking their pipes, and the whole mob of sheep lying quiet and peaceable on the little flat, with Munro's dog watching 'em. Not that they wanted any watching just then, for sheep always take a good spell in the afternoon of a hot day, and lie down and go to sleep, maybe, until it gets cool enough to make it pleasant to wander about and feed before dark.

'As soon as ever I see that sight I flung up my hat and danced for joy, and I felt desperate hungry all of a minute. I can tell you, my mates, I didn't lose much time getting down that hill, though I come pretty quiet for fear of scaring the sheep.

'When I comes up to the men, before I could speak, Joe Smelt says, first thing, "Munro found 'em; I haven't been long here." And Munro smiles quiet and pleased-like, and says, "I had a mob once served me the same trick, and I thought I knew where to look for 'em, and sure enough they was there, reg'larly hiding; I had to bring 'em down uncommon easy, for it was a nasty place, and I didn't want half of 'em to be smothered in the creek."

'Well, of course I meant to ask and to hear all about it, but I thought it would keep until we had had a bit of dinner, for it was about two o'clock, and you must please to remember, ma'am, that we had breakfasted somewhere about five, and likewise that walking up and down them back ranges is hungry work at the best of times, besides being wearing to the boots. "Where's Davis?" was my first words. "Davis must have gone away altogether for a bit" they said, "for the hut is locked and fastened up until it can't be fastened no more, and unless we reg'larly break into it, we shall never get in it."

'"Drat the fellow!" I cried, "there ain't no bush-rangers about. Why doesn't he just lock his door and hang the key on a nail outside where anybody can see it, as I used to do when I was a back-country shepherd, and wanted to go away for a bit." But it was no manner of use pitching into Davis, not then, because you see, ma'am, he wasn't there to hear himself abused, though we did that same and no mistake. It *was* aggravating—now, ma'am, wasn't it? There was we three, and the dogs, poor things! as hungry as hungry could be; and we knew there'd be flour and tea and sugar, and likely a bit of bacon (for Davis was a good hand at curing a ham of a wild pig), inside the door, if we could only open it. Not a bit of it would stir, though, for all our kicks, and Joe Smelt ran at it with his shoulders until I thought he must burst it open; but no, the lock didn't give one bit. "Tell you what," said Joe, rubbing his shoulder after his last attempt, "Davis has gone and barred this 'ere door up on the inside, and then got out of the window and fastened it up outside afterwards." When we came to look, it seemed quite likely, for the shutter was driven home and kept in its place by good-sized nails; but we got a big stone, and we used our knives, and Munro worked away that patiently that at last down came the shutter, and we had the little bit of a window open in no time after that. We made little Joe get through first, and we laughed and said we felt just like real house-breakers, but we thought we'd keep our jokes until we had had something to eat. Before Joe had well unbarred the door—for it was fastened up as if it was never meant to be opened again—Munro and me had settled that he should make some flap-jacks as soon as ever we could get the fire to burn; that is, supposing there wasn't any bacon or mutton lying about.

"The minute Joe opened the door with a cheery, "Here you are," we looked round us like so many hungry wolves, and the first thing we see is a fine big shoulder of mutton on the floor. Well, it was easy to see how it had got there, for there were marks of rats' teeth and feet too, all over it. Davis hadn't been long gone that was easy to see—not more than a few hours likely, though he plainly intended to be away for some time by the way he'd fastened up everything; but still it was very neglectful of him not to have flung that shoulder of mutton outside before he went because you see, ma'am, in a day or two it would surely be very unpleasant. A neat man was Davis—a very neat man—and when we'd prized open his cupboard made out of old gin-cases, we found his couple of tin-plates and pannikins, and his tea and sugar, and his flour and his matches, and his salt, all as tidy as tidy could be, and there was a big packet of "Vermin Destroyer" too, open and half used. We gave that a wide berth, however, as you may fancy; but we had some sticks in the fire-place and the kettle on to boil before you could say "Jack Robinson." We found half a loaf of bread also in the cupboard, which we concluded to eat, lest it should get stale by the time Davis came back, and we told Munro we'd have his flap–jacks for second course. "Here's a capital Christmas dinner after all," said Joe; and he picked up the meat carefully off the floor, and blew the dust off, and we sat down to the table with that shoulder of mutton before us; and all I can tell you, ma'am, is, that long before the kettle boiled—and it had a good fire under it too—there wasn't a scrap left on the bone. Cooked! in course it was cooked; you don't think we was going to eat raw wittles on Christmas Day. No, no, ma'am, we weren't such cannibals as that! Davis had baked it as nice as could be, but it seemed uncommon funny that he should have taken so much trouble for nothing. However, there it was, or, I *should* say, there it wasn't, for we had eaten it up, every bite; and we told Joe Smelt to get the tea out of the cupboard, and throw a couple of handfuls into the kettle, which was beginning to boil. Joe got up, saying, "I haven't half done yet; I'm just as hungry as ever I can be;" and he went to the cupboard and began to rummage among the things in it. "Don't give us any pison by mistake, Joe," said Munro, joking. Just as he said the words, Joe turned short round, his face looking as white as death underneath all the sunburn and freckles, his very lips white, and his eyes open wider than I thought mortal eyes could open; and he said in a dreadful voice—a sort of whisper, and yet you might have heard it all over the place—"That's where it is, we're pisoned!" With that Munro and I jumped up from the table, and we gasped out, "Pisoned, Joe!" but we needn't to ask—we couldn't speak if we wished. Joe pointed to the bare mutton bone, and held out the half-used paper of the poison in the other, and never a word did he say but, "Rats."

'We guessed it all then. Davis must have been fairly bullied by the impudent hungry critturs, and he had taken the trouble to cook for 'em, as if they had been Christians, and then he'd quite likely as not rubbed an ounce or two of strychnine into that shoulder of mutton, and left it where the rats could get at it, and we'd been and eaten it all up instead o' they. Yes, ma'am, it's all very well to laugh,' said Bob, taking his hat off, and wiping his head with the handkerchief stowed away in its crown, looking into the hat afterwards as if he saw the scene he was describing pictured there—'it was the werry roughest moment of all *my* life. To be pisoned like a rat, and in a lonely gully, where no one would ever pass. Most likely we shouldn't even be found before Davis came back. It was lucky Davis didn't come back, though—not at that moment, I mean— for I'm certain that if he stood in his own doorway just then we'd 'a set on him and killed him without so much as saying "with your leave or by your leave." We couldn't have been whiter than Joe, not if we'd tried; but we was white enough no doubt. Munro was a good man, so he was the bravest of the lot, and he said, or he tried to say, for he couldn't speak very clear, "The will of God be done, my poor Jeanie!" and with that he threw himself down on Davis's bed and hid his face.

'I don't rightly know what poor little Joe did, for I felt desperate mad. I caught sight of half a bar of soap stowed away at the back of the cupboard, and I seized it as if it *had* been a life-buouy, and I'd been drowning man. I couldn't have gripped it harder or held it tighter if it had been a buouy,' said Bob, shaking his head meditatively. 'And I runs down to the creek with it. I don't know why I went there, unless it was to be handy to the water to gulp it down with. Well, ma'am, I had picked up my knife off the table as I passed, and I cut great junks of that bar of soap, and bolted 'em, whole. I seemed to remember having heard some one say that soap was good as a hemetick: and so I found it; for by the time I had swallowed half the bar I felt desperate sick, and joyful I was to feel it, I can tell you; but still I wasn't bad enough to please myself, so I drank some water and had three or four slices more, and that about finished me, and I lay down among the tussocks by the water side; and what with the fright, and the early rising, and the long walk, and the heat of the sun, joined to the murmur like of the creek, I went off into the comfortablest sleep as I ever had, and it wasn't till the sun had got right behind the high hills to the westward that I woke up. I reckon it was the barking of Munro's dog that woke me, for the poor beast found he had more than he could do to manage the mob of sheep. They must have been feeding some time, and now wanted to be off up the hill to their camping ground; for you must know, ma'am, that sheep never settle for the night on low ground. They always travel up as high as they can conveniently get, and camp on the top of a hill.

'The poor beast seemed quite joyful to see it was me coming to help him, as he thought, but I couldn't give my mind to the sheep, not just yet. I was rather empty and a bit weak, but as well as ever I felt in my life. I remember I took off my hat, and looked up to the sky and I thanked God in my own rough fashion for saving my life all along of that bar of soap, and I give you my word, ma'am, I meant it, even when I found out my mistake. I thought I'd look up Munro and the other little chap, but I was more than half frightened to go and see about 'em, for at that time you see, I thought I was wot you may call the sole surwivor. However, the others were surwivors too, and a very good job for 'em *that* was. Munro had pegged away into a bag of salt until he must have reg'larly *cured* his inside in more senses than one, whilst Joe had hemeticked himself by shoving his fingers down his throat. Poor Joe! he must have been desperate bad too. Well, they'd been to sleep as well as me, and there we stood staring at each other, awful pale and haggard-looking, but still safe and well so far.

'Munro was the first to recover himself, and he said, "Them sheep'll be off before we can count ten," so with that we went to help the dog, who was barking hisself off his legs. Joe Smelt hung back a bit at first, for he said he'd heard as how exercise caused pison to work, but Munro called out, "Do your duty Joe, and never mind the pison."

'So we got the sheep together, and we brought 'em down to the homestead, and right glad the boss was to see 'em. When I told him the story of the shoulder of mutton, he went nearly as white as we did, and he said he'd send for the doctor and tell him to bring proper hemeticks along, but we felt we couldn't stand no more not just then, and Joe says, says he, "It wouldn't be no manner of use, sir, not till we'd had some supper." With that the boss laughs and tells the manager to give us each a glass of hot grog; and very comfortin' it was. That's all, ma'am,' concluded Bob, getting up from his hencoop and making me a bow.

'No, no, Bob,' I cried, 'that isn't all; I must know the end.'

'There wasn't no more end than that, ma'am; leastways when Davis turned up, which he did by chance next day, at the home station, we werry nearly made an end to him when he lets out that there never had been no pison on the shoulder of mutton at all. He said he'd cooked it, meaning to take it in his swag for his supper that night, and was fine and mad when he found he'd forgotten it. Mr Vans-start, he said we ought to be downright thankful to Davis when we found he hadn't let us in for his pison, but we couldn't see it in that light no how, and we give Davis, one and all of us, a bit of our minds, and Joe Smelt offered to fight him the very next Sunday for five pounds a side. Poor Davis! he made us mad by the way he laughed and he tried to comfort us by telling us that if the "Vermin Destroyer" did us as little harm as it did the rats, we needn't to have cried out. "Why, they thrive on it," he said. "I lets 'em have it pretty often, and they comes about more than ever arter a dose on it."'

Bob's story took a long time in the telling, for he told it very deliberately, and enjoyed a long word, or any pet expression, such as his life-buouy, so intensely that he repeated it over and over again, rolling the words in his mouth as if they were good to taste. By the time he had finished, the valley was in deep shadow, and the delicious crisp feeling in the air, which always follows a summer's day in our New Zealand hills, made us feel inclined for a change of occupation. The quoits were got out, and the iron pegs stuck in the ground, and some of the shearers were soon hard at work pitching the heavy circlets through the air. Another group were putting the stone or the hammer, whilst a few made themselves very hot by running races or having hopping matches. The constant open-air exercise, keeps men of all grades in New Zealand in such good condition that, even in such rough primitive sports as these were, I have seen far more surprising feats of strength performed by athletes who had had no other training than their daily hill-walks and frugal, wholesome fare, than in the *champ-clos* of a fashionable arena in the old country.

But to-morrow's work must begin with the dawn so whilst there was yet light to see their way home across the rolling downs which stretched like a green sea before us, the good-nights were said. I stood in the porch and shook hands with each guest as he passed, though the performance of this ceremony entailed deep blushes on the part of my stalwart company. 'Here's wishin' you the best o' luck, mum,' was the general adieu; but when they all got to the bottom of the paddock, they consulted together and gave a ringing hearty cheer, which woke up the valley's quiet echoes, may be for the first time since it emerged from the water-world. 'One more for Old Father Christmas,' were the last words I heard, as I turned indoors, leaving the joyous sounds to die gradually away into the deep perfumy silence which hung over that lonely valley of the Malvern Hills.

Clara Cheeseman

MARRIED FOR HIS MONEY

I

Those persons who were fortunate enough to be acquainted with the Repton family, wondered how they lived. Mr Repton could not be exactly described as having no visible means of support; for he received from a grateful country the pension of £200 per annum; but it is well known that such an income is quite inadequate to supply the wants of a fashionable family.

Auckland is supposed to be a cheap place; but even there, to provide several young ladies with three-button kid gloves, and prunella walking shoes alone, without reckoning other equally indispensable articles, is no joke; and then they have also to be taken out to every entertainment of the day, and be present, as a matter of course, at the vice-regal and other balls. All must acknowledge that their parents have managed well if they find their accounts balance at the end of the year. This small sum, however, was all that the Reptons had to depend on, and they contrived to keep their footing in society, or thought they did, which nearly amounts to the same thing. If Mr Repton was sometimes troubled with little bills, or seen in company with a professional money-lender, who had the reputation of charging higher interest than any of his Auckland brethren, it was nobody's business; and if anyone deserved blame it was the niggardly New Zealand Government, whose miserable pittances were not sufficient for the support of a respectable family.

At the time of which we are about to write, Mrs Repton was engaged in projecting an evening party. She very seldom entertained her friends; it was so much cheaper to go out than to receive company in her own house; so the unusual event required considerable thought and preparation.

'I think, my dear,' she observed to Mr Repton, who lay on the sofa, reading a new novel ('A Struggle for Existence'), 'that we had better order the refreshments from Candytuft's this time. You know you have not paid Joffee yet for the last affair.'

'Well, how was I to pay him? I am surprised when I succeed in paying anyone. Thank goodness we are going to get one of the girls off at last! I suppose that Simpelson will come down with something handsome.'

'Don't allude to it so heartlessly,' said Mrs Repton, making a great show of her pockethandkerchief. 'If it were not for our unhappy position, I should be spared the humiliation of seeing my daughter marry beneath her.'

'I see more cause for rejoicing than humiliation, about it. A man with £40,000 does not turn up every day. If you could contrive it, Emily, it would be as well for him to bear the expenses connected with the wedding. I could not borrow another penny now, if I were to tramp Queen-street from morning till night.'

'I have arranged that already,' said Mrs Repton. 'He is a good-natured young man, and easily led. It is quite a charity to relieve him of some of his superfluous cash. Those men who have become suddenly rich are never happy, except when they are spending, and he seemed quite pleased when I just hinted how he could assist us.'

'So much the better; he may please himself in that way as long as he likes. One blessing is that he is fairly presentable, and, so long as he does not open his mouth to say anything, may pass for a gentleman. Give him a hint, if you can, not to wear so much jewelry.'

'I will see about that,' said Mrs Repton, 'but we cannot be too careful. You offended him, you know, last night, by remarking on it. He is improving fast, and after all is not so bad, considering his former station. I was very glad to hear that both his parents are dead, and I cannot learn that he has any relations here. It would be dreadful to have a crowd of vulgar people all claiming relationship with one.'

'I should prefer them to a crowd of debt collectors, my dear,' remarked her husband. 'I believe—yes, there is Simpelson walking down the road. Now, if he is coming here, you might get an advance, you know. If he is going to pay for everything, I don't see why he should not begin to do so at once, and then I will settle with both Candytuft and Joffee, and give something to Pinchbeck, to stop his mouth about that silver service you bought for Mrs Raymond.'

'It is an expensive habit, giving those wedding presents,' said Mrs Repton. 'I wish it would go out of fashion. Simpelson is not coming here, after all.'

Which was true, the object of their hopes did not enter the Repton residence. About a mile further on, he stopped before a very neat little house, with an orchard and vegetable garden attached.

Here, lived a family named Landon, who were not in Mrs Repton's set; Mrs Landon being a dressmaker, and her husband a market gardener. Mrs Landon, however, and her daughter Milly, had sometimes the honour of making the Misses Repton's dresses, and generally waiting a year before they were paid for their work.

On this morning Landon was in his garden, promenading the walks, armed with a large pruning knife, as sharp as a razor, with which, whenever he saw a tree or a shrub presuming to grow too luxuriantly, or not according to orthodox fashion, he immediately cut it down without mercy.

Evidently he was somewhat excited, and did not very well know what he was about, for he kept muttering fiercely to himself, and occasionally, with a more vehement gesture than usual, would savagely brandish his knife, and lop off the greater part of some offending plant.

When he observed Mr Simpelson at the gate, he scowled at him, and retreated to the back of the house. 'I won't speak to the fellow,' he muttered, 'though I should like to have the pleasure of kicking him. A good riddance for Milly, I say,' and a little apricot was cut down almost to the root.

Mr Simpelson looked very downcast as he came up the path to the door. He knocked gently, and was admitted by Mrs Landon, whose greeting was of the shortest and most unassuring kind. Evidently Mr Simpelson, though he might be worth £40,000, was no welcome visitor here.

He was shown into the room where Milly Landon sat at her sewing machine. Now, Miss Milly was a very pretty girl indeed; with hair and eyes as black as jet, and being well skilled in her trade, and very tasteful (which all dressmakers are not), was always the perfection of neatness and good taste in attire, and looked what Mrs Repton would have called 'superior to her station'.

She had been engaged to Simpelson for four years, during which time he had been an unsuccessful searcher for gold at Hokitika. He would have starved there, had it not been for the pecuniary assistance of the Landons, who had forwarded him, from time to time, enough support till something should turn up.

Something did turn up; a rich old grand-uncle was considerate enough to die, and wishing to disappoint his nearer relatives in England, left his property to Simpelson, whom he had never seen. Simpelson became a personage of importance, and wedged his way into higher society than that of the Landons. He was very affectionate to them, at first; but soon began to think that it would be as well to marry into a more stylish family. Milly was very nice-looking and lady-like; but fancy, having old Landon for his father-in–law, a mere market gardener, and who had, worse than that, even been a milkman! The idea was revolting to his noble soul, and when he became acquainted with the Reptons, who quite charmed him by their gracious condescension, the superior acquirements of Miss Blanche Repton decided the question. With such a wife, he might hope to rise in the fashionable world, and then after all, it would be very much better for Milly to marry some one in her own walk of life. She was not fitted to be the mistress of a large establishment, such as he intended to have, and ought to thank him for having discovered this fact.

But these convincing arguments did not seem to give him confidence, when he was in her presence. He looked woefully embarrassed, and presented a most ridiculous appearance. Mr Simpelson had, since the arrival of his fortune, indulged in a style of dress resembling that often affected by lucky diggers, and other suddenly-enriched mortals. Although it was only eleven in the forenoon, he was in full evening costume; his black suit was of superfine cloth, his new boots creaked with every step he took. The jewelry that the misguided young man wore would have realised a small fortune; coral and gold studs, and sleeve links, a gold watch with a guard that was nearly thick and strong enough to be used as a dog chain, and from which were suspended various ornaments, while six rings studded with enormous gems, adorned his fingers. He sat down when invited to do so, and feeling uncommonly nervous, mopped his face with an embroidered cambric handkerchief that diffused a fragrance throughout the room.

Deep silence prevailed. Milly would not speak first, but gazed at the bedizened figure before her, with something like contempt.

At last, Simpelson, having composed a speech, said, 'I suppose you know the object of my visit, Miss Landon?'

'I think you fully explained in your letter,' said Milly.

'I did; but I thought it my duty to call, to thank you, and Mr and Mrs Landon, for what you have done for me, and to make some return. I was afraid you would not understand my motives, and think me ungrateful.'

'I believe we perfectly understand them, Mr Simpelson.'

'Good gracious, Milly!' said the unhappy Simpelson, again mopping his face, 'don't look at me in that way. I am sure I have done all for the best, yet your mother looked at me as if I was a houtcast'—Mr Simpelson occasionally murdered the Queen's English, though he had wonderfully improved, in that respect, since his introduction to the Reptons—'and your father would not speak to me at all. But I'm willing to forgive anything, and I feel sure we made a great mistake. We are so unsuited to each other in every way.'

'I quite agree with you, Mr Simpelson, and feel grateful to you, for having made the discovery in time,' said Milly, her eyes fixed on the gigantic watch-chain.

'But I hope, really now, you'll allow me to do something for you. I've not forgotten how your father helped me at Hokitika. If you will give him this, and accept this for yourself, Milly, I shall be very happy, and you may always depend on me as a friend; I hope you will always think of me as one.'

Milly had been very cool and contemptuous up to this point, but now she flushed scarlet with anger, and wounded pride, as the magnanimous Simpelson drew from a bulky pocket-book, two cheques. One was for the amount that her father had lent him, with interest added, nicely calculated up to the very day, the other was payable to Miss Landon, and for the sum of 200 guineas.

'No, thank you,' she said rising hastily. 'We are fully repaid already, Mr Simpelson, for what we have done for you. All that I desire is, that you will return my letters.'

'I will send them up to-night,' faltered Simpelson. 'I am very sorry, Mil—hem, Miss Landon, that you take such a wrong view of the matter. You are very unjust to me. I—I—I think I'd better be goi—.'

'Wait a moment, if you please.' And Milly swept with dignity into the next room, where she was heard pulling open drawers, and rustling among papers. She returned with an apron full of a most extraordinary collection of articles, and in her hand a parcel containing the jewelry that Simpelson had presented to her, in the first excitement of his newly acquired riches, and before he had been captured by the Reptons.

In the parcel, were seven brooches and lockets, four pairs of earrings, three bouquet holders, six bracelets, and a dozen rings at least.

'I ought never to have taken them,' she observed, handing him the parcel; 'I never should, if I had not been blind and foolish. As for these,' and she indicated the contents of her apron, a mass of lace and silk ties, collars and cuffs, gloves, fans, and many an ill scrawled and spelt letter of Simpelson's, 'I shall dispose of them more easily;' and she threw them passionately into the fire, where they blazed up with such flame and thick black smoke, that neighbours concluded the Landon's chimney had caught fire, and some officious persons rushed to ring the fire-bells.

I fear that Miss Milly's conduct cannot be excused, it was both ridiculous and unladylike, and Mr Simpelson felt more than ever convinced of his wisdom. Miss Blanche, he was sure, would never have behaved in such an unbecoming manner. He ventured to press his cheques on Milly again, who took them this time, and added them to the blazing pile. And then he retired, as quickly as possible, taking the rejected jewelry with him. It would come in very nicely for presents to the bridesmaids, Mrs Repton having already given him a hint of what would be required in that way. As for Milly, she returned to her work, and stitched away very composedly at Miss Blanche's wedding dress, a splendid garment of white satin and lace.

II

That day week, Simpelson dressed himself with unusual care, and repaired to the Reptons. It was the evening of their party, and Mrs Repton had brought together a very select company.

Her intended son-in-law was improving so rapidly in manners and dress, under her tuition, that she did not fear presenting him to anyone.

As, however, the house was small, and the number of guests limited, she displayed great skill in securing the attendance of those whom she considered the very cream of Auckland society.

She had invited Sir John Jennings, Bart., then travelling in New Zealand. He had only been two days in Auckland, but Mrs Repton had heard of him, and determined he should grace her party with his aristocratical presence. It was a pity he was not a Duke, or Earl at the least; but those characters do not come round every day, and in default of something better, a Baronet would do very nicely. Besides this gentleman, also came the Hon. John Sanders Sanderson, Mrs and Miss Sanderson. Mr Sanderson was a member of the Legislative Council, and chiefly remarkable for a golden silence, generally preserved both there and everywhere else. There was also Alexander Rufus Marchmont, Esq., and the Misses Marchmont. He was a Canterbury run holder, and supposed to be immensely wealthy, and having been on a visit to the Lake district, was taking Auckland on his way home. Also there were two M.G.A.'s, a Colonial judge, a distinguished lawyer, and various members of their families; Mr Scampion, an old colonist, whose antecedents were rather shady, but were thickly gilded over by his money, with his showy wife and daughters. Mr Layman, a high and mighty Government officer, and Mrs Layman; and a few bank clerks and young ladies of the neigh-bourhood, added chiefly on account of their extraordinary dancing and conversational powers.

Mr and Mrs Repton received their friends with that politeness and urbanity of manner so natural to them. Simpelson behaved very creditably, and followed Mrs Repton's delicate suggestions, by leaving most of his heavy jewelry at home. Miss Blanche was radiant, and exquisitely dressed, and she and Simpelson looked so well, when they stood up together in the first quadrille, that Mrs Repton thought that after all, her daughter might have done worse.

As she never had an opportunity of doing otherwise, perhaps this reflection was unnecessary. The evening was perfectly charming. Simpelson had been practising dancing with all his energies for a fortnight before, and acquitted himself very well. In fact, he presented such a distinguished appearance, that Mr Scampion, who had heard there was to be a baronet at the party, imagined he must be the great man, and persisted in addressing him as Sir John.

At length the company repaired to the room where supper had been laid. This was the kitchen; but the bare, unlined walls, and the whitewashed chimney, and cooking stove, had been so skilfully concealed with ferns, green boughs, and great masses of white clematis, then in bloom, that no one would have suspected the fact. The supper was sumptuous; for Mr Candytuft, having been paid in advance, was so surprised and gratified at the unusual promptitude of the Reptons, that he had done his very best. Mr and Mrs Repton were beaming with delight, on their assembled friends, when there seemed to be some disturbance in the entrance hall, and voices heard in high altercation.

'Now, just stand out of the way, my good fellow. I know he's in here and it's strange if a man can't speak to his own brother.' Great scuffling followed, then the door was burst open, and in walked a dirty, rough-looking man, without coat or waistcoat, his tall felt hat perched on the back of his head, and his muddy boots leaving many fine impressions on the spotless floor.

On he strode, right up to Mr Simpelson, grasped that gentleman's reluctant hand, and wrung it heartily.

'Well, Jack, my boy, right glad I am to see you! It's sometime since we set eyes on one another, I was working on the railway down at Dunedin, when I heard of your stroke of luck. Thinks I, there's shares for you, Bill Simpelson, Jack won't grudge his brother a slice. You're in good quarters here, old boy, risin' in life I should say."

All this had not taken five seconds. The Reptons were paralysed, and could not have uttered a word, had it been a matter of life and death. Mrs Repton stared at the intruder with fixed and glassy eyes. Simpelson was as white as a sheet, and attempted to gasp out a faint denial.

'My good fellow—er—look here, you must be mistaken, you know; you take me for someone else.'

'Well!' exclaimed Mr W. Simpelson, 'if ever I heard the like of that! Ain't you afraid of the earth opening, and swallowing you up? Oh Jack!' he added, with real emotion, 'I never thought you'd deny your own brother.'

Meanwhile, the others had been making remarks on the occurrence.

'How extraordinary!' said the Hon. J. Sanders Sanderson.

'It reveals the hollowness and corruption of colonial society,' observed the baronet, who was surreptitiously taking copious notes. They were afterwards inserted in his valuable work on the Australian colonies.

'I shall faint soon,' said Miss Theresa Sanderson, 'if that horrid man is not put out. Why don't they put him out, Mr Cashman?'

'Why,' said that young gentleman, a rising bank clerk, 'I suppose they don't like to turn out their future relations.'

'Delightful!' said Mrs Scampion, 'it is evidently the first scene of a charade. What perfect acting! Mrs Repton always has something new and original at her parties.'

'Just look at old Repton,' sneered Mr Scampion, 'I'll bet fifty to one he's thinking how he's to explain it all. Simpelson don't seem over pleased to see his brother again!'

'It serves them richly right,' said Mrs Layman, who before the announcement of Simpelson's engagement, had patronised him most indefatigably, 'I detest such fortune-hunting.'

Mr Repton saw the smiles and glances of his guests, heard some of these remarks, and the suppressed laughter of the bank clerks and young ladies. His indignation was at boiling point; he rose and was about to thunder forth some sentences, when suddenly his countenance changed, he smiled blandly, and said, 'Poor fellow! I see it all. Ladies and gentlemen, you must excuse this little interruption of the harmony of the evening. Simpelson, I am delighted to find that you have such a near relation as a brother living! I hope he will permit me to offer him some refreshment. We require no introduction; Mr William, I think;' and Mr Repton actually extended his lily white hand, which never in all his lifetime had done a hard day's work, and it was grasped in the rough and horny palm of the railway navvy, with a vigour that made him repent his cordiality.

'Any friend of Jack's, sir, is one of mine. Your health, sir; and glad I am to know you!' and the wine-glass was set down again emptied.

Mr Repton now said a word or two in Mr Simpelson's ear. He had been unable, after his last effort, to do anything but sit still, and stare at his brother; but now he rose and whispered something to him.

'Well, Jack,' replied that person audibly, 'I don't care if I do. I'm not exactly of your friends' sort. You have risen to a higher spear, old fellow. Good evening, ladies and gentlemen,' and with an awkward bow, that sent the Misses Marchmont off into convulsions of laughter, he suffered himself to be led from the room.

Mr Repton followed them, but returned after a few minutes. He came in smiling. 'A most laughable affair,' he said, 'if it were not for the sad fact that the poor fellow is a lunatic.'

'A lunatic!' exclaimed Mrs Repton, taking up the cue at once, 'I thought so! His eyes rolled frightfully.'

'I knew it at once, and so thought it best to get him out of the way quietly,' continued Mr Repton. 'He escaped from the asylum this morning, and thought he recognised his brother in Mr Simpelson, who really resembles him very much.'

'So he does,' said Mr Margin, the lawyer, who prided himself on his penetration. 'I saw it as soon as he entered the room.'

'Mr Simpelson,' said Mr Repton, 'had the good sense and presence of mind, after the first shock, not to contradict the assertions the unhappy man made in the aberrations of his intellect. He deserves our thanks; had he lost his temper, as most men would have done, the maniac might have been provoked to some desperate deed. I tremble to think of what might have happened!'

'It is just like him, so unselfish!' said Mrs Repton, 'I can breathe freely now;' which was quite true.

'Really, Repton ought to be in the General Assembly,' whispered Cashman to his next neighbour, 'did you ever hear a more plausible account? It won't do, though, too transparent.'

'Disgraceful,' said Mrs Layman. 'I am perfectly astonished at the effrontery of these people. Not all the gold in the universe would tempt me to admit that Simpelson to my house!'

It was very sad for the Reptons, but the charm of the evening was gone, never to return. Very glad were they when it was over. When their friends had gone, Mrs Repton broke out with, 'I knew it all. I felt sure something would happen of this kind! After this Blanche cannot disgrace herself by marrying such a low fellow. That brother of his would be everlastingly appearing.'

'Mrs Repton,' said Repton, solemnly waving his cigar, 'you are a goose, to use a very mild expression.'

'Of course I am, whenever I do not agree with you,' answered his wife.

'My dear, don't lose your temper. A woman never should; it induces premature age.'

'I know I look old, Mr Repton, living as I do, with all the care and trouble of the family dragging me down.'

'Listen to me,' said Repton. 'This Simpelson, so far as I can make out, taking him all in all, is a very decent fellow. He is steady in his habits; his manners are not amiss; and better than all, he has £40,000. Money, my dear, is of great importance to us. It is not of great importance what our friends who were here to-night, think. Simpelson can give his brother three or four thousand, he will never miss it, and stipulate he is not to show himself again. What can be easier. I thought you were a sensible woman, Emily; now, to-night, if I had not had the spirit to get up that monstrous fib about the asylum, I believe you and Simpelson would have allowed that man to say and do exactly as he liked, and ruined everything.'

'And what good do you think you did? Not one of them believed it.'

'What does that matter?' rejoined her husband; and then, bursting into a loud laugh, he exclaimed—'It was perfectly splendid to see Simpelson wither up when the fellow came in! What does Blanche think of it?'

'Blanche,' said her mother, 'will never suppose that he really was an escaped lunatic. I shall take care of that.'

About three weeks after this, a fashionable wedding took place, at which several clergymen assisted one another, and a numerous crowd of bridesmaids attended the beauteous and richly-attired bride.

Blanche Repton became Mrs Simpelson, and received congratulations and costly presents from more friends than she was aware she possessed; for it was as well to be on good terms with a young couple who started in life with £40,000.

Milly Landon was acquainted with all the fine doings at the Reptons, and saw the hundredweight of bride cake borne triumphantly to the house, uncovered to the vulgar public eye, in a common baker's cart, for which negligence Mrs Repton sharply reprimanded Mr Candytuft.

Milly was even present at the wedding, in a quiet corner of the church, unnoticed by anyone, and did not seem remarkably heart-broken at the spectacle. There is now a Madame Blanchard, milliner and dressmaker, who has a stylish establishment in Auckland. I think that the elegant and polite Madame very much resembles Milly Landon, and she certainly speaks English with great correctness, considering her foreign extraction. There is also a M. Blanchard, and he is very like a certain young Frenchman, a working jeweller by trade, who used to be intimate with the Landons, before Mr Simpelson's frequent visits threw him rather into the shade.

As for Simpelson, he flourished more and more, and so did the Reptons. Mrs Repton always speaks of him in a most touching manner, and declares that he is the best of husbands to her dear Blanche, and that she herself looks upon him with as much affection as if he were her own son. And so she ought, for Simpelson paid all the bills when he became one of the family, and has continued to do so ever since. Mr Repton takes care that he does not waste his money, and as Simpelson has been troubled no more by his affectionate brother, nothing has occurred yet to disturb the happiness of this united family.

Mrs Simpelson has money without end to spend as she likes, is always beautifully dressed (she is the chief customer of Madame Blanchard), and is perfectly happy. She firmly believes that her husband's talents would have raised him to a high position, even had he never inherited forty thousand pounds.

Rudyard Kipling

ONE LADY AT WAIRAKEI

The extraordinary thing about this story is its absolute truth.

All tourists who scamper through New Zealand have in their tours visited the geysers at Wairakei, but none of them have seen there what I have seen. It came about with perfect naturalness. I had wandered from one pool to another, from geyser to mud spout, mud spout to goblin bath, and goblin bath to fairy terrace, till I came to a still pool, where a wild duck sat bobbing on the warm green water, undisturbed by all the noises of the wonderful gorge. A steam jet hidden in the brushwood sighed and was silent, a tiny geyser gobbled, and a big one answered it with snorts. I thrust my stick into the soft ground, and something below hissed, thrusting out a tongue of white steam. A wind moved through the scrub, and all the noises were hushed for an instant. So far there had been nothing uncommon—except geysers and blow-holes—to catch the eye. Therefore I was the more astonished when from the depths of the pool, and so quietly that even the wild duck was not scared, there rose up the head and shoulders of a woman. At first I imagined that I had better get away. But, since I had seen the face, I did not move. The woman flung back her long hair, and said, laughing:

"Well?"

"I—I beg your pardon," I stammered. "But I didn't know—I didn't—I mean—"

"Do you mean to say that you don't know *me*?" she said. "To be sure in your profession I'm more talked about than seen."

"To whom have I the pleasure of speaking?" I said desperately—for it is not seemly to stand on a bank and talk to a woman who is swimming in the water. Besides, I felt sure that she was laughing at me.

"They call me all sorts of things," was the reply; "but my real name is Truth. Haven't you heard that I live in a well? This is it. It communicates directly with the other side of the world, but I generally come here for peace and quiet on a Sunday. I have some friends here." She nodded casually up the gorge, and I heard the geysers bellow.

Natural politeness and a strong desire to see whether she was not a mermaid led me to put the next question. It came rather clumsily.

"Aren't you going to get out?" I asked.

"I can't. You'd die if I did, because I'm the Truth, the Whole Truth, and Nothing but the Truth. No man can see me and live." She swam a few strokes towards the bank, and rested while the steam drifted in clouds across the pool. I sat down and stared again.

"*Some* people," said Truth, "would say they were pleased to meet me."

"I'm not," I replied. "You see, or rather I see, in the first place, that you are too unconventional, and in the second place I never believed in you—much." This was not in the least what I meant to say, but the words came of themselves. Truth laughed.

"Shall I go away?" she said.

"This pool is private property. I've paid to see it. You haven't. What do you think yourself?"

"From your point of view you're quite right, but—you wouldn't care to see a fresh geyser break out just under your feet, would you? or a mud volcano? or a rift in the earth? My friends would be happy to oblige me. Shall I ask them?"

"Truth," I said, jumping up, for the ground was shaking like a boiler-plate, "you know as well as I do that you're making me say unpleasant things, and now you propose to boil me alive for saying them. You're illogical, because you're a woman, and I'm going back to the hotel."

"Wait a minute," said Truth, laughing. "I want to ask you a question, and then I won't be rude any more. How do you like New Zea——?"

"Don't!" I shouted. "*Please* don't! Let me put the answer on paper, at least."

"Tell me now," said Truth, "or I'll splash hot water at you. Tell me the truth."

"Promise me you'll tell me anything I want to know afterwards?" I said, for I felt the answer coming, and it was not a polite answer.

"I promise," she said, and heard my remarks out to the end.

"H'm!" she said, gravely. "One big encumbered estate, is it? Folly to play at party government when the whole population is less than half the German army? All in the hands of the banks, is it? Forty thousand horsepower to drive a hundred-ton yacht, and the country not scratched? Upon my word, you'll get yourself dearly beloved if those are your sentiments, and you say them aloud."

"Well, it *is* absurd, isn't it, if you can run the place with three men and a boy, to start Upper Houses and Lower Houses, and pay a few hundred men to help spend borrowed money?" I persisted. I knew that

I had gone too far to explain.

"I admit nothing. I'm the Truth," she said, "and I merely wished to hear what you considered the truth. It's your turn to ask questions now. I'll give you five minutes to think of them."

"Tell me the truth, the whole truth, and nothing but the truth, about New Zealand," I said promptly.

"Banks—railways—exports—harbour boards, and so forth—eh?" She smiled wickedly. "You will find all that in books."

"No. I want to know how the people live, and what they think, and how they die; and what makes them love and fight and trade in the particular manner in which they fight and love and trade. That isn't in the books."

"No—not yet," said Truth thoughtfully, drawing her pink fingers to and fro through the water. "It will come some day."

"That's just what I want to know, When is it coming?"

"What?"

"The story of the lives of the people here. I want to read it."

"Perhaps they haven't any lives. You said they were all in the hands of the banks. How can you expect an encumbered estate, mortgaged to the hilt, to have a life of its own?"

"Truth, you're prevaricating. You know I didn't mean that. Banks have nothing to do with the inside lives of peoples. I have not the key to the stories myself, but they are here in the country somewhere—thousands of them. When are they going to be written, Truth, and how are they going to be written, and who are going to write them?"

"My young men and my young women. All in good time. You can't fell timber with one hand and write a tale with the other. But they'll come, and when they come—"

"Yes."

"The world will listen to them. Do you remember coming through some dense bush fifty miles down the road? Well, half a mile from the road, down in a gully among the tree ferns, there lies the body of a man under the butt of a great pine tree. He loved a woman at a sheep station— one of the women who serve up the 'colonial goose' to the tourist when he stops at the wooden shanties with the chemists' presentation almanacks on the walls—a red-faced raddled woman who talks about 'ke-ows,' and 'bye-bies.' He was one of three lovers!"

"Whew!" I said. "That sounds like an old story."

"Yes, it *is* an old story—otherwise it wouldn't be new. And that woman in her sloppy, slatternly house among the fern-hills where the sheep live, played with those three lovers as a Duchess might have done; and the drovers and the sheep-men came down the road and said most awful things. She took her sentiment and her heroics out of the bound volumes of the Family Herald and Bow Bells—you've seen the tattered copies in the wooden houses on the tables where the painted kerosene lamp stands, haven't you? But her iniquity was all her own. Two of her lovers were just sheep-men, but the third was a remittance-man, if you know what that is, and he had been a gentleman in England who thought a good deal of himself."

"And she killed him?"

"No, he killed himself. At least, after some things had happened, he went out into the bush and carefully backscarfed a big tree so that it would fall in one particular direction, and stood there when it fell. Now he will become a rata-vine. Remember, he had loved her for three years and put up with everything at her chapped hands."

"So she *did* kill him."

"That comes of knowing too much. He killed himself after a good think, wholly and solely on account of a girl in England whom he had no chance whatever of winning. I think he realised that competing with sheep-men for stolen kisses behind corrugated iron sheds was not nice; and that showed him several other things. So he died, and the husband, of course, had to get a new hand for the shearing. But *she* believes that she killed him and—she is rather proud of it."

"Truth, who is going to tell that story?"

"I don't quite know. Perhaps one of her children, or grandchildren, as soon as the spirit of the fern-hills—they are very lonely, you know— and the snow mountains has entered into his blood. Yes, it shall be one of her children (that is to say, one of *his* children) and he shall lie under wool-drays in summer, and sleep with his back on a salt-bag, and his heels on a bag of harness, and be frozen and sun-tanned, and ride long rides at night, fording rivers, to make love to big, round-faced girls, till he finds that story. Then he will tell it and a hundred thousand things with it, and the world will say, 'This is the truth, because it is written so.'"

"And after?"

"Afterwards he may try to tell other stories as good as the first. If he tries he'll fail, but there are thousands more. Hark! Do you hear nothing?"

Under my very feet there was the dull thud as of a steam-hammer in a mine—a thud that rippled the still waters of the pool and struck the geysers dumb.

"What's that?" I asked, wondering and afraid.

"It's down in the guide-book as a Natural Phenomenon. But you have heard of the Roaring Loom of Time, haven't you? That's the shuttle clicking through the web, and you know who the Weavers are?"

I bowed my head and was silent, having no wish to meet the Fates yet.

"They are busy today," Truth continued. "It is no easy work to weave the souls of men into their surroundings. So far, they have done little. The men don't belong to the mountains and the plains and the swamps and the snow passes and the fiords and the thick fat grazing land—and the women, of course, poor dears, they belong to the men. But in time the men will be of the land, and write of the land and the life of the land as they have seen it and as they know it. Then the people will know themselves, and wonder at their own lives. There is a girl-baby nearly a thousand miles away from here. Her father found a pass through the Southern Alps, and good grazing ground the other side. So he stole people's sheep, drove them through the pass, and was well to do till people found him out and he disappeared. That girl has lived among the mountains and the snow rivers all her days. She knows how the water comes down cold as ice, and chokes men and horses, and tosses them out on the shingle a dozen miles down stream. Some day, I think, she will sing up there among the mountains, and half the world will listen. After her will come others—women—and they will tell how women love men in this country, and all the women all over the world will listen to *that*."

"Won't that be rather an old story?" I demanded.

"Of course it will (Eve loved Adam very much, I remember), but you forget what the hills and the clouds and the winds and the rain and the sun can do. Remember how nearly some parts of this land run into the tropics, and wait till you hear them sing."

I remembered at once and sat corrected.

"But won't they imitate Shelley and Tennyson, and Mrs Browning?"

"At first, naturally. When they belong to their own country you will hear what you will hear."

"And what shall I hear?"

Truth was silent for a while, and then raising one shapely arm from the water, said softly:—"Listen now! Listen and see!" The thud of the loom beneath me ceased, and the dead air became full of voices, thickened into shadows that took form and became men and women, before my amazed eyes.

A man with a shaggy red beard and deep sunk eyes strode forward scowling; and with savage gestures and a hundred hurrying colonial oaths, told a tale of riotous living, risk of life, sorrow, despair, and death. "I have suffered this, and I have suffered that, and my tale is true," he cried. A woman cumbered with many children, but in whose face there were few wrinkles followed, and—"Our lives were very quiet in Christchurch," she said, "as quiet as the river, and— and I thought, perhaps, that if I wrote just our little lives—for the children, you understand . . . But, oh!"—she clutched my arm nervously—"it—it has just been the saving of our house."

Truth laughed tenderly as the woman passed on, gathering her children round her.

"She will be taught through Poverty," said Truth; "but thousands of mothers will laugh and cry over her tale."

The men came next, assured and over-confident some, crippled and doubting others, but each with his tale to tell of the land he knew, the loves he had loved, and the life that lay about him. There were tales of the building of new cities; desperate intrigue for diversions of the local railroad; of railway frauds; local magnate pitted against local magnate, both fighting furiously, first for their own pockets, and next for the interests of their towns; tales of gumdigging under the dusty manuka scrub, and dreams of lost loves and lost hopes in the dead-houses of the country pubs; stories of the breaking of new lands, where the wisdom of men said that there was not feed for a rat; of Toil that began before dawn and lasted far into the starlight, when men, women, and children worked together for the sake of their home, amid the scarred and blackened stumps; stories of unclean politics, swayed by longshore loafers drowzing at wharf-ends, and, in an almost virgin land, clamouring for the aid of a spineless Government; of money paid to three or four hundred of these who dared not work, and for each payment of a thousand pounds twenty times that much capital scared from a land that, on its own confession, was as hopeless as an eight-hundred-year-old island. Lastly, a change sudden and surprising, in the midst of this keen-voiced strife. I heard tales of gentle lives, as sheltered in the midst of the turmoil as the ferns in the gorge—lives of ease, elegance, and utter peace, begun under the trailing willows, where the little children go to school, two and three together, astride of the old bare backed horse, and ended in some well-kept cemetery, looking seaward to America. They were old tales, but upon each lay the stamp, inimitable and indescribable, of a new land and of fresh minds turning the thought, old as Adam, to lights as new as the latest road across the mountains. And, Heavens! how they gambled and swore and drank in the pauses between the crises, thinking no shame of themselves, having no fear, and reverence only for that which was indubitably and provedly stronger than themselves. But there were liars, too, among the crowd, smooth-faced men who shaped their work as they conceived that other folk would best approve, and a few of those unhappy souls whose fate it is to pile up wealth of fact and fiction that stronger people may raid into it at will. I caught one wail of a weak-lipped shadow:—"But I—but *I* wrote all this before, and another has merely re-written my work, and *he* gets the credit. It was I—it was I!"

"He will suffer," said Truth. "With his temperament he will probably die; but it is necessary. Hark to the women now. They tell the old story well."

I listened as the shades went by—of girls too early dead—sterile blossoms whose only fruit was a song; of hard-featured Scotchwomen preaching wittily and wisely with illustrations drawn from the rainy wind-swept South, the fear of the Lord that goes to the making of home; of mothers driven by bitter grief and loss to soothe the grief of others, marvelling in their simplicity that they could so soothe; and of maidens who had never known love, and therefore told his power and his beauty till heartstrings quivered twelve thousand miles away. Since they were women they sang chiefly of the things about their homesteads, the orange-ribbed black velvet of the burnt fern-hills, the windy plains overlooked by the mountains whose scaurs are the faces of dead kings, the jade-green rivers with the oily swirls in them that run through the bush and take away the lives of little children playing at the back of the house, the long breathless days when the iron roof works uneasily over the new wood framing, expanding till noon and contracting till night, when you hear the buzzing of the flies about the face of the sick one under the roof, and outside the rush of the wild horses, their twilled manes flying free over the shoulder point, across the crackling, dried swamp-bed as it reels in the sun-haze. There was always a man in their songs— a man who went away and never came back, a face seen on horseback for a day and lost for evermore, or some treachery of a man with only the black stumps for witness to the sin, or a drowned man brought up from the river-bed at night through the grass that he had planted only that spring—only that spring.

The shades passed, and the click and thud of the unseen loom recommenced.

"Well," said Truth, "you have seen?"

"It is very well," I answered. "But when does it begin?"

"Oh, I forgot that you people die so soon. In five years, in fifty, in five hundred. What does it matter to me?"

"Will it be in my time?" I asked eagerly. I wanted to hear some of the tales again.

"I cannot say. Perhaps—some of it—if you live long enough. Be content to know that it is coming."

"In this country alone, Truth?"

"In every country that has not spoken as yet, and as surely as sunlight follows morning. You have seen the beginnings of it. Have faith. There is such a little time to wait."

Once more Truth was forgetting the limitations of man's life, and I did not care to remind her. I was thinking of the future, and the voices of all those shadows who had told me their tales. The more I meditated, the more magnificent did the prospect appear.

"What are you thinking of?" said Truth. "The banks and the loans again?"

"No. I'm thinking," I responded loftily, for Truth was only a woman, and could not be expected to understand these things, "of the Future of Colonial Literature!"

"What?" said Truth, with a touch of scorn in her voice.

I repeated the words, emphasising the capitals.

"Oh, hear him!" she cried, lifting up her face to the fern-wreathed rocks around. "One short-lived son of Adam, who may die to-morrow, splitting his tiny world into classes, and labelling them, like dead butterflies. What do you mean"—she looked me in the face—"by Colonial Literature?"

"Oh—er—stuff written in the colonies, and all that sort of thing, y'know." I couldn't understand why Truth was so angry. The loom thundered under my feet till the sand by the pool shook.

"Isn't the stuff, as you call it, written by men and women? Do the Weavers down below there at the loom make anything else but men and women? And, until you step off this world can you expect anything more than stories of the lives of men and women written by men and women? What manner of monsters live in your part of the world," she concluded, "that you speak so blindly?"

"Fools," I said, penitently. "Just fools, Truth. I'm one of 'em, and you're right. It's only men and women that we have to think of all the world over. But," I added, remembering another country across the seas, "these people will be quite as foolish as myself when their time comes, won't they?"

"I'm afraid so," said Truth, with a smile, "they will be only men and women."

"Ah!" I said triumphantly, "they will talk rubbish about a Distinctively Colonial Literature, a Freer Air, Larger Horizons, and so forth. They'll vex 'emselves with unholy comparisons between their work and other people's work. They'll flatter each other and write of the Oamaru Shakespeare, and the Timaru Tennyson, and the Dunedin Dryden, and the Thursday Island Thackeray, won't they?"

"They will," said Truth. "(When did you leave America, by the way?) Some of the people here will do all those things, and more also. What else can you expect? They are only men and women, but those who make the noise will not be the people who tell the stories."

"Thanks. That's all I wanted to know. The banks can look after themselves. You are sure that the tales will come?"

"I have said so, and you have heard. Good-bye!"

Truth nodded and disappeared under the water. I watched the ripples stupidly, and not till they died away did I remember that I had a hundred questions to ask. Only the wild duck at the far end of the pool did not look as if it could answer them.

*   *   *

That same afternoon, riding in the buggy with Sam the Maori, across a new land teeming with new stories to which, alas, I had neither clue nor key, it occurred to me that I had largely discounted the future. But when I came to the sea coast and found a ten-thousand-soul town up to its tree-ferns in debt for a quarter-million pound harbour, the sand faithfully following each pile of the futile breakwater, and a sixty-thousand-soul town with municipal offices that might have served Manchester or Liverpool, I perceived that I was in good company.

You see, New Zealand is bound to pay her unwritten debt. Truth said so, and I have seen the assets. They are sufficient securities.

The other things are not of the slightest importance.

Henry Lawson

STIFFNER AND JIM
(THIRDLY, BILL)

We were tramping down in Canterbury, Maoriland, at the time, swagging it—me and Bill—looking for work on the new railway line. Well, one afternoon, after a long, hot tramp, we comes to Stiffner's Hotel—between Christchurch and that other place—I forget the name of it—with throats on us like sun-struck bones, and not the price of a stick of tobacco.

We had to have a drink, anyway, so we chanced it. We walked right into the bar, handed over our swags, put up four drinks, and tried to look as if we'd just drawn our cheques and didn't care a curse for any man. We looked solvent enough, as far as swagmen go. We were dirty and haggard and ragged and tired-looking, and that was all the more reason why we might have our cheques all right.

This Stiffner was a hard customer. He'd been a spieler, fighting man, bush parson, temperance preacher, and a policeman, and a commercial traveller, and everything else that was damnable; he'd been a journalist, and an editor; he'd been a lawyer, too. He was an ugly brute to look at, and uglier to have a row with—about six-foot-six, wide in proportion, and stronger than Donald Dinnie.

He was meaner than a gold-field Chinaman, and sharper than a sewer rat: he wouldn't give his own father a feed, nor lend him a sprat—unless some safe person backed the old man's I.O.U.

We knew that we needn't expect any mercy from Stiffner; but something had to be done, so I said to Bill:

"Something's got to be done, Bill! What do you think of it?"

Bill was mostly a quiet young chap, from Sydney, except when he got drunk—which was seldom—and then he was a lively customer from all round. He was cracked on the subject of spielers. He held that the population of the world was divided into two classes—one was the spielers and the other was the mugs. He reckoned that he wasn't a mug. At first I thought that he was a spieler, and afterwards I thought that he was a mug. He used to say that a man had to do it these times; that he was honest once and a fool, and was robbed and starved in consequence by his friends and relations; but now he intended to take all that he could get. He said that you either had to have or be had; that men were driven to be sharps, and there was no help for it.

Bill said:

"We'll have to sharpen our teeth, that's all, and chew somebody's lug."

"How?" I asked.

There was a lot of navvies at the pub, and I knew one or two by sight, so Bill says:

"You know one or two of these mugs. Bite one of their ears."

So I took aside a chap that I knowed and bit his ear for ten bob, and gave it to Bill to mind, for I thought it would be safer with him than with me.

"Hang on to that," I says, "and don't lose it for your natural life's sake, or Stiffner'll stiffen us."

We put up about nine bob's worth of drinks that night—me and Bill—and Stiffner didn't squeal: he was too sharp. He shouted once or twice.

By-and-by I left Bill and turned in, and in the morning when I woke up there was Bill sitting alongside of me, and looking about as lively as the fighting kangaroo in London in fog time. He had a black eye and eighteen-pence. He'd been taking down some of the mugs.

"Well, what's to be done now?" I asked. "Stiffner can smash us both with one hand, and if we don't pay up he'll pound our swags and cripple us. He's just the man to do it. He loves a fight even more than he hates being had."

"There's only one thing to be done, Jim," says Bill, in a tired, dis-interested tone that made me mad.

"Well, what's that?" I said.

"Smoke!"

"Smoke be damned," I snarled, losing my temper. "You know dashed well that our swags are in the bar, and we can't smoke without them."

"Well, then," says Bill, "I'll toss you to see who's to face the landlord."

"Well, I'll be blessed!" I says. "I'll see you further first. You have got a front. You mugged that stuff away, and you'll have to get us out of the mess."

It made him wild to be called a mug, and we swore and growled at each other for a while; but we daren't speak loud enough to have a fight, so at last I agreed to toss up for it, and I lost.

Bill started to give me some of his points, but I shut him up quick.

"You've had your turn, and made a mess of it," I said. "For God's sake give me a show. Now, I'll go into the bar and ask for the swags, and carry them out on to the verandah, and then go back to settle up. You keep him talking all the time. You dump the two swags together, and smoke like sheol. That's all you've got to do."

I went into the bar, got the swags from the missus, carried them out on to the verandah, and then went back.

Stiffner came in.

"Good morning!"

"Good morning, sir," says Stiffner.

"It'll be a nice day, I think?"

"Yes, I think so. I suppose you are going on?"

"Yes, we'll have to make a move to-day." Then I hooked carelessly on to the counter with one elbow, and looked dreamy-like out across the clearing, and presently I gave a sort of sigh and said: "Ah, well! I think I'll have a beer."

"Right you are! Where's your mate?"

"Oh, he's round at the back. He'll be round directly; but he ain't drinking this morning."

Stiffner laughed that nasty empty laugh of his. He thought Bill was whipping the cat.

"What's yours, boss?" I said.

"Thankee!…Here's luck!"

"Here's luck!"

The country was pretty open round here—the nearest timber was better than a mile away, and I wanted to give Bill a good start across the flat before the go-as-you-can commenced; so I talked for a while, and while we were talking I thought I might as well go the whole hog—I might as well die for a pound as a penny, if I had to die; and if I hadn't I'd have the pound to the good, anyway, so to speak. Anyhow, the risk would be about the same, or less, for I might have the spirit to run harder the more I had to run for—the more spirits I had to run for, in fact, as it turned out—so I says:

"I think I'll take one of them there flasks of whisky to last us on the road."

"Right y'are," says Stiffner. "What'll yer have—a small one or a big one?"

"Oh, a big one, I think—if I can get it into my pocket."

"It'll be a tight squeeze," he said, and he laughed.

"I'll try," I said. "Bet you two drinks I'll get it in."

"Done!" he says. "The top inside coat pocket, and no tearing."

It was a big bottle, and all my pockets were small; but I got it into the pocket he'd betted against. It was a tight squeeze, but I got it in.

Then we both laughed, but his laugh was nastier than usual, because it was meant to be pleasant, and he'd lost two drinks; and my laugh wasn't easy—I was anxious as to which of us would laugh next.

Just then I noticed something, and an idea struck me—about the most up-to-date idea that ever struck me in my life. I noticed that Stiffner was limping on his right foot this morning, so I said to him:

"What's up with your foot?" putting my hand in my pocket.

"Oh, it's a crimson nail in my boot," he said. "I thought I got the blanky thing out this morning; but I didn't."

There just happened to be an old bag of shoemaker's tools in the bar, belonging to an old cobbler who was lying dead drunk on the verandah. So I said, taking my hand out of my pocket again:

"Lend us the boot, and I'll fix it in a minute. That's my old trade."

"Oh, so you're a shoemaker," he said. "I'd never have thought it."

He laughs one of his useless laughs that wasn't wanted, and slips off the boot—he hadn't laced it up—and hands it across the bar to me. It was an ugly brute—a great thick, iron-bound, boiler-plated navvy's boot. It made me feel sore when I looked at it.

I got the bag and pretended to fix the nail; but I didn't.

"There's a couple of nails gone from the sole," I said. "I'll put 'em in if I can find any hobnails, and it'll save the sole," and I rooted in the bag and found a good long nail, and shoved it right through the sole on the sly. He'd been a bit of a sprinter in his time, and I thought it might be better for me in the near future if the spikes of his running-shoes were inside.

"There, you'll find that better, I fancy," I said, standing the boot on the bar counter, but keeping my hand on it in an absent-minded kind of way. Presently I yawned and stretched myself, and said in a careless way:

"Ah, well! How's the slate?"

He scratched the back of his head and pretended to think.

"Oh, well, we'll call it thirty bob."

Perhaps he thought I'd slap down two quid.

"Well," I says, "and what will you do supposing we don't pay you?"

He looked blank for a moment. Then he fired up and gasped and choked once or twice; and then he cooled down suddenly and laughed his nastiest laugh—he was one of those men who always laugh when they're wild—and said in a nasty, quiet tone:

"You thundering, jumped-up crawlers! If you don't (something) well part up I'll take your swags and (something) well kick your gory pants so you won't be able to sit down for a month—or stand up either!"

"Well, the sooner you begin the better," I said; and I chucked the boot into a corner and bolted.

*   *   *

He jumped the bar counter, got his boot, and came after me. He paused to slip the boot on—but he only made one step, and then gave a howl and slung the boot off and rushed back. When I looked round again he'd got a slipper on, and was coming—and gaining on me, too. I shifted scenery pretty quick the next five minutes. But I was soon pumped. My heart began to beat against the ceiling of my head, and my lungs all choked up in my throat. When I guessed he was getting within kicking distance I glanced round so's to dodge the kick. He let out; but I shied just in time. He missed fire, and the slipper went about twenty feet up in the air and fell in a waterhole.

He was done then, for the ground was stubbly and stony. I seen Bill on ahead pegging out for the horizon, and I took after him and reached for the timber for all I was worth, for I'd seen Stiffner's missus coming with a shovel—to bury the remains, I suppose; and those two were a good match—Stiffner and his missus, I mean.

Bill looked round once, and melted into the bush pretty soon after that. When I caught up he was about done; but I grabbed my swag and we pushed on, for I told Bill that I'd seen Stiffner making for the stables when I'd last looked round; and Bill thought that we'd better get lost in the bush as soon as ever we could, and stay lost, too, for Stiffner was a man that couldn't stand being had.

The first thing that Bill said when we got safe into camp was: "I told you that we'd pull through all right. You need never be frightened when you're travelling with me. Just take my advice and leave things to me, and we'll hang out all right. Now——"

But I shut him up. He made me mad.

"Why, you—! What the sheol did *you* do?"

"Do?" he says. "I got away with the swags, didn't I? Where'd they be now if it wasn't for me?"

Then I sat on him pretty hard for his pretensions, and paid him out for all the patronage he'd worked off on me, and called him a mug straight, and walked round him, so to speak, and blowed, and told him never to pretend to me again that he was a battler.

Then, when I thought I'd licked him into form, I cooled down and soaped him up a bit; but I never thought that he had three climaxes and a crisis in store for me.

He took it all pretty cool; he let me have my fling, and gave me time to get breath; then he leaned languidly over on his right side, shoved his left hand down into his left trouser pocket, and brought up a boot-lace, a box of matches, and nine-and-six.

As soon as I got the focus of it I gasped:

"Where the deuce did you get that?"

"I had it all along," he said, "but I seen at the pub that you had the show to chew a lug, so I thought we'd save it—nine-and-sixpences ain't picked up everyday."

Then he leaned over on his left, went down into the other pocket, and came up with a piece of tobacco and half-a-sovereign. My eyes bulged out.

"Where the blazes did you get that from?" I yelled.

"That," he said, "was the half-quid you give me last night. Half-quids ain't to be thrown away these times; and, besides, I had a down on Stiffner, and meant to pay him out; I reckoned that if we wasn't sharp enough to take him down we hadn't any business to be supposed to be alive. Anyway I guessed we'd do it; and so we did—and got a bottle of whisky into the bargain."

Then he leaned back, tired-like, against the log, and dredged his upper left-hand waistcoat pocket, and brought up a sovereign wrapped in a pound-note. Then he waited for me to speak; but I couldn't. I got my mouth open, but couldn't get it shut again.

"I got that out of the mugs last night, but I thought that we'd want it, and might as well keep it. Quids ain't so easily picked up nowadays; and, besides, we need stuff mor'n Stiffner does, and so—— "

"And did he know you had the stuff?" I gasped.

"Oh yes, that's the fun of it. That's what made him so excited. He was in the parlour all the time I was playing. But we might as well have a drink!"

We did. I wanted it.

*   *   *

Bill turned in by-and-by, and looked like a sleeping innocent in the moonlight. I sat up late, and smoked, and thought hard, and watched Bill, and turned in, and thought till near daylight, and then went to sleep, and had a nightmare about it. I dreamed I chased Stiffner forty miles to buy his pub, and that Bill turned out to be his nephew.

Bill divvied up all right, and gave me half-a-crown over, but I didn't travel with him long after that. He was a decent young fellow as far as chaps go, and a good mate as far as mates go; but he was too far ahead for a peaceful, easy-going chap like me. It would have worn me out in a year to keep up to him.

G. B. Lancaster

HANTOCK'S DISSERTATION

> "Oh, the nor'-west rising grimly where the stern hills stand up dimly;
> Oh, the reckless ride of rivers to the sea;
> Oh, the careless sun-kissed reaches, and the fierce white battered
> beaches—
> We are part of you, and all that is To Be."
>
> *In Our Own Right.*

Lane had been giving his men orders for the next day's work, and the Man from England was puzzled at little irregularities connected with the performance. He said so later, from the big chair before the library fire, and Lane laughed, nodding across the open fireplace at Hantock.

"That's the man to go to if you want to find out things about the colonial. Hantock knows 'em from backbone to waistcoat button. Ask him."

"Why," said the Man from England promptly, turning in his chair, "can't a colonial say 'sir,' or touch his hat, or take his hands out of his pockets when he's speaking to his betters? And why does he tacitly suggest the idea that if you called him names he'd knock your head off?"

Hantock was drawing the life into his pipe with a half-smile on his thin lips, and so it was Lane who answered.

"I don't know—unless it is because he would. And, you see, he works hand and foot with so many of his betters that he loses respect for reverence."

"Ah," said Hantock in approval, and the Man from England said that he didn't see. Lane drummed on the chair-rail nervously. He was not a man of words.

"Respect is outward acknowledgment of superiority, I take it. That's English, and we have sloughed it pretty completely. Reverence is inward acknowledgment of superiority. Suppose a man can cut out a steer, or wheel a mob with the skill of a general, or ride a horse that is known to be a man-killer, or—or do any of a million other things that prove him to be a man. Your colonial reverences that man, whatever his birth—but that doesn't make him take off his hat to him."

Lane looked over at Hantock. There was not one in Southland did

41

not reverence that Special Constable after this manner. "There's something of the heathen about us yet," he added. "The Greeks worshipped men."

"Good heavens! so do we," said the Man from England. "But we worship other things too."

"Well," said Lane, "I think the colonial doesn't—generally. But ask Hantock."

Hantock flung himself back in the hollow of his chair, and blew smoke at the ceiling.

"You haven't got the thing straight from the outset," he said. "Colonial is nearly as loose a term as European. Don't you tell a Sydney chap (fellow is technically correct over there) that you took him for a New Zealander, or ask a man from the Gulf how they pack Tasmanian apples. You'd get branded as an outcast, you know. And probably they'd call you their own special kind of a fool too."

The Man from England had been a public-school boy, and he knew something of internal splits.

"But they are all one for the honour of the Colonies."

"Are they? Don't you believe it! Each colony for itself, and "the devil take the hindmost"—that's all the others. They can't be all one. They're made on entirely different lasts. And yet there are some idiots who imagine that a colonial is merely a transplanted Englishman. He isn't. Nothing like it."

The Man from England was one of these idiots, and he was not afraid to say so.

"The colonial comes of an English stock, not three generations back."

"I grant you that. But he's grafted on to something that England doesn't know anything about. My dear chap, you'll never understand your Imperial obligations unless you consider for a little minute all the things he is grafted on to, and their results."

"Can I do it in a minute? For—"

Lane grinned.

"Let Hantock burble. He really does know a little of what he's talking about."

"See here, then." Hantock sat forward, and waved his pipe emphatically. "The Englishman is—speaking generally—the product of centuries of civilisation. For all practical purposes you can take him in the block. The colonial is—always speaking generally—the product of the land that cradles him; and he can't be taken in the block. That's the wall that so many wise men run their heads against. Well?"

"An Englishman is an Englishman, no matter what part of the world he is born in. Why is a colonial born in Sydney unlike one born in New Zealand?"

Hantock groaned, and Lane explained with a chuckle.

"You've made that exact point that Hantock has been hammering at you all the time, my dear fellow. A colonial is not a product of civilisation; he is a product of the soil. If the rest of the world saw this, it would go to the country that produced him, and not to his forebears."

"You've seen something of our land?" asked Hantock.

The Man from England had been touring New Zealand for the last two months.

"A little bit," he said.

"There you get the keynote, then—in the land. You'll see the New Zealander in the rivers. They tear out a way for themselves slap ahead, and ride down to the sea with a strength and a reckless you-be-damnedness that is entirely their own. They go their own lonely ways through the country, and if you interfere with 'em, they'll undermine your supports and leave you in a muddle of shingle. You can't sail a boat on many of our rivers; they are too untamed. We dam them occasionally—but we do it in fear."

"Might get your head knocked off," murmured the Man from England.

"Exactly. There's a lot of the New Zealand river in her men; and there's a lot of the plains too. The great wide spaces, and the miles of blowing tussock, and the flax-swamps—my word, they're dandy places for duck-shooting! And the glorious clean air that makes you fit to jump a house when it comes out of the hills where no man has breathed it yet. That is all on its own, as it were."

"You've forgotten the nor'-westers," suggested Lane.

"I haven't. I take particular interest in the nor'-wester, because I think that that's where the New Zealander gets most of his characteristics. Oh, you may jeer. I speak truth. The nor'-wester is a grand thing. Look at the plain-country. The rain-soakage would breed all the world's fevers in the rich soil if it wasn't for the winds. They'd kill any other country. They make Central New Zealand. You can't do anything but get out of the way of a nor'-wester when it's on the ramp. It will have its own pernicious way, and it does fiendish things for the pure joy of it. But it serves its country all the same. There's a lot of the nor'-wester in our men. It helps them to do things that no sane man would do. But we get there all the same. Harry Morel—eh, Lane?"

"I was thinking of him. Yes. But there's too much of the tropical temperament in Harry. He's a northerner."

"He's got the nor'-wester in his blood, all the same. You can't tame him. And there are the mountains. I've heard fellows say that we can knock spots out of Switzerland for scenery. I don't know anything about that, but, mind you, there's a power and a kind of stern reticence about our back-country that leaves its mark on our men. You won't find a New Zealander babbling of his feelings much. And that's not entirely his British breed. The everlasting hills that make the backbone of our islands make the backbone of our people too. And the knowledge that this is a new land, and theirs to handle and to shape, gives 'em that grasp of Imperialism—"

"It's grasp of the soil he means, really," said Lane; "only he's fond of big words. Perhaps you've noticed?"

"—Grasp of Imperialism that's going to carry us on to mighty issues—when we're old enough."

"You'll need to learn the outward forms of spiritual grace," suggested the Man from England.

"I believe you. A New Zealander hasn't much spiritual grace. He's a Vandal, I think. He burns the bush, and plants *Pinus insignus*; and he hasn't a decent picture-gallery in the two islands. Likewise, it is very true that he has a large lack of respect for anything—except himself."

"That," said the Man from England, "is—"

"The beginning. Of course. When he has a few hundred years to his back, and all his own full-fledged customs to respect, in place of the cut-down second-hand ones of over-seas, he'll respect 'em all right. But I don't think he will ever be an Englishman."

"But—he'll become the product of civilisation."

"Yes. But colonial civilisation is a thing that's not on the roster yet. We hardly know what the world will have to reckon with when it is. It's going to be a big thing. But the Australian and the New Zealander will eternally be Sons of the Empire, although they will eternally object to being taken in the lump."

"Do Sons of the Empire include the women?"

"Distinctly. Though, mind you, the New Zealand woman—"

"Now, you stop it," said Lane, getting up. "Don't let him tell you anything about the women, old chap. He understands the colonial man pretty artificially correctly, but he doesn't know a thing about women."

"Do any of us?" asked the Man from England ruminating.

Hantock laughed.

"She thinks we don't, anyway," he said.

Katherine Mansfield

THE WIND BLOWS

Suddenly—dreadfully—she wakes up. What has happened? Something dreadful has happened. No—nothing has happened. It is only the wind shaking the house, rattling the windows, banging a piece of iron on the roof and making her bed tremble. Leaves flutter past the window, up and away; down in the avenue a whole newspaper wags in the air like a lost kite and falls, spiked on a pine tree. It is cold. Summer is over—it is autumn—everything is ugly. The carts rattle by, swinging from side to side; two Chinamen lollop along under their wooden yokes with the straining vegetable baskets—their pigtails and blue blouses fly out in the wind. A white dog on three legs yelps past the gate. It is all over! What is? Oh, everything! And she begins to plait her hair with shaking fingers, not daring to look in the glass. Mother is talking to grandmother in the hall.

'A perfect idiot! Imagine leaving anything out on the line in weather like this. . . . Now my best little Teneriffe-work teacloth is simply in ribbons. *What* is that extraordinary smell? It's the porridge burning. Oh, heavens—this wind!'

She has a music lesson at ten o'clock. At the thought the minor movement of the Beethoven begins to play in her head, the trills long and terrible like little rolling drums. . . . Marie Swainson runs into the garden next door to pick the 'chrysanths' before they are ruined. Her skirt flies up above her waist; she tries to beat it down, to tuck it between her legs while she stoops, but it is no use—up it flies. All the trees and bushes beat about her. She picks as quickly as she can, but she is quite distracted. She doesn't mind what she does—she pulls the plants up by the roots and bends and twists them, stamping her foot and swearing.

'For heaven's sake keep the front door shut! Go round to the back,' shouts someone. And then she hears Bogey:

'Mother, you're wanted on the telephone. Telephone, Mother. It's the butcher.'

How hideous life is—revolting, simply revolting. . . . And now her hat-elastic's snapped. Of course it would. She'll wear her old tam and slip out the back way. But Mother has seen.

'Matilda. Matilda. Come back im-me-diately! What on earth have you got on your head? It looks like a tea cosy. And why have you got that mane of hair on your forehead.'

'I can't come back, Mother. I'll be late for my lesson.'

'Come back immediately!'

She won't. She won't. She hates Mother. 'Go to hell,' she shouts, running down the road.

In waves, in clouds, in big round whirls the dust comes stinging, and with it little bits of straw and chaff and manure. There is a loud roaring sound from the trees in the gardens, and standing at the bottom of the road outside Mr Bullen's gate she can hear the sea sob: 'Ah!. . . . Ah. . . . Ah-h!' But Mr Bullen's drawing-room is as quiet as a cave. The windows are closed, the blinds half pulled, and she is not late. The-girl-before-her has just started playing MacDowell's 'To an Iceberg'. Mr Bullen looks over at her and half smiles.

'Sit down,' he says. 'Sit over there in the sofa corner, little lady.'

How funny he is. He doesn't exactly laugh at you . . . but there is just something. . . . Oh, how peaceful it is here. She likes this room. It smells of art serge and stale smoke and chrysanthemums . . . there is a big vase of them on the mantelpiece behind the pale photograph of Rubin-stein . . . *à mon ami Robert Bullen*. . . . Over the black glittering piano hangs 'Solitude'—a dark tragic woman draped in white, sitting on a rock, her knees crossed, her chin on her hands.

'No, no!' says Mr Bullen, and he leans over the other girl, puts his arms over her shoulders and plays the passage for her. The stupid—she's blushing! How ridiculous!

Now the-girl-before-her has gone; the front door slams. Mr Bullen comes back and walks up and down, very softly, waiting for her. What an extraordinary thing. Her fingers tremble so that she can't undo the knot in the music satchel. It's the wind. . . . And her heart beats so hard she feels it must lift her blouse up and down. Mr Bullen does not say a word. The shabby red piano seat is long enough for two people to sit side by side. Mr Bullen sits down by her.

'Shall I begin with scales,' she asks, squeezing her hands together. 'I had some arpeggios, too.'

But he does not answer. She doesn't believe he even hears . . . and then suddenly his fresh hand with the ring on it reaches over and opens Beethoven.

'Let's have a little of the old master,' he says.

But why does he speak so kindly—so awfully kindly—and as though they had known each other for years and years and knew everything about each other.

He turns the page slowly. She watches his hand—it is a very nice hand and always looks as though it had just been washed.

'Here we are,' says Mr Bullen.

Oh, that kind voice—Oh, that minor movement. Here come the little drums. . . .

'Shall I take the repeat?'

'Yes, dear child.'

His voice is far, far too kind. The crotchets and quavers are dancing up and down the stave like little black boys on a fence. Why is he so . . . She will not cry—she has nothing to cry about. . . .

'What is it, dear child?'

Mr Bullen takes her hands. His shoulder is there—just by her head. She leans on it ever so little, her cheek against the springy tweed.

'Life is so dreadful,' she murmurs, but she does not feel it's dreadful at all. He says something about 'waiting' and 'marking time' and 'that rare thing, a woman', but she does not hear. It is so comfortable . . . for ever. . . .

Suddenly the door opens and in pops Marie Swainson, hours before her time.

'Take the allegretto a little faster,' says Mr Bullen, and gets up and begins to walk up and down again.

'Sit in the sofa corner, little lady,' he says to Marie.

The wind, the wind. It's frightening to be here in her room by herself. The bed, the mirror, the white jug and basin gleam like the sky outside. It's the bed that is frightening. There it lies, sound asleep. . . . Does Mother imagine for one moment that she is going to darn all those stockings knotted up on the quilt like a coil of snakes? She's not. No, Mother. I do not see why I should. . . . The wind—the wind! There's a funny smell of soot blowing down the chimney. Hasn't anyone written poems to the wind? . . . 'I bring fresh flowers to the leaves and showers.' . . . What nonsense.'

'Is that you, Bogey?'

'Come for a walk round the esplanade, Matilda. I can't stand this any longer.'

'Right-o. I'll put on my ulster. Isn't it an awful day!' Bogey's ulster is just like hers. Hooking the collar she looks at herself in the glass. Her face is white, they have the same excited eyes and hot lips. Ah, they know those two in the glass. Good-bye, dears; we shall be back soon.

'This is better, isn't it?'

'Hook on,' says Bogey.

They cannot walk fast enough. Their heads bent, their legs just touching, they stride like one eager person through the town, down the asphalt zigzag where the fennel grows wild and on to the esplanade. It is dusky—just getting dusky. The wind is so strong that they have to fight their way through it, rocking like two old drunkards. All the poor little pahutukawas on the esplanade are bent to the ground.

'Come on! Come on! Let's get near.'

Over by the breakwater the sea is very high. They pull off their hats and her hair blows across her mouth, tasting of salt. The sea is so high that the waves do not break at all; they thump against the rough stone wall and suck up the weedy, dripping steps. A fine spray skims from the water right across the esplanade. They are covered with drops; the inside of her mouth tastes wet and cold.

Bogey's voice is breaking. When he speaks he rushes up and down the scale. It's funny—it makes you laugh—and yet it just suits the day. The wind carries their voices—away fly the sentences like the narrow ribbons.

'Quicker! Quicker!'

It is getting very dark. In the harbour the coal hulks show two lights—one high on a mast, and one from the stern.

'Look, Bogey. Look over there.'

A big black steamer with a long loop of smoke streaming, with the portholes lighted, with lights everywhere, is putting out to sea. The wind does not stop her; she cuts through the waves, making for the open gate between the pointed rocks that leads to. . . . It's the light that makes her look so awfully beautiful and mysterious. . . . *They* are on board leaning over the rail arm in arm.

' . . . Who are they?'

' . . . Brother and sister.'

'Look, Bogey, there's the town. Doesn't it look small? There's the post office clock chiming for the last time. There's the esplanade where we walked that windy day. Do you remember? I cried at my music lesson that day—how many years ago! Good-bye, little island, good-bye. . . .'

Now the dark stretches a wing over the tumbling water. They can't see those two any more. Good-bye, good-bye. Don't forget. . . . But the ship is gone, now.

The wind—the wind.

Katherine Mansfield

AN INDISCREET JOURNEY

She is like St Anne. Yes, the concierge is the image of St Anne, with that black cloth over her head, the wisps of grey hair hanging, and the tiny smoking lamp in her hand. Really very beautiful, I thought, smiling at St Anne, who said severely: 'Six o'clock. You have only just got time. There is a bowl of milk on the writing table.' I jumped out of my pyjamas and into a basin of cold water like any English lady in any French novel. The concierge, persuaded that I was on my way to prison cells and death by bayonets, opened the shutters and the cold clear light came through. A little steamer hooted on the river; a cart with two horses at a gallop flung past. The rapid swirling water; the tall black trees on the far side, grouped together like negroes conversing. Sinister, very, I thought, as I buttoned on my age-old Burberry. (That Burberry was very significant. It did not belong to me. I had borrowed it from a friend. My eye lighted upon it hanging in her little dark hall. The very thing! The perfect and adequate disguise—an old Burberry. Lions have been faced in a Burberry. Ladies have been rescued from open boats in mountainous seas wrapped in nothing else. An old Burberry seems to me the sign and the token of the undisputed venerable traveller, I decided, leaving my purple peg-top with the real seal collar and cuffs in exchange.)

'You will never get there,' said the concierge, watching me turn up the collar. 'Never! Never!' I ran down the echoing stairs—strange they sounded, like a piano flicked by a sleepy housemaid—and on to the Quai. 'Why so fast, *ma mignonne?*' said a lovely little boy in coloured socks, dancing in front of the electric lotus buds that curve over the entrance to the Métro. Alas! there was not even time to blow him a kiss. When I arrived at the big station I had only four minutes to spare, and the platform entrance was crowded and packed with soldiers, their yellow papers in one hand and big untidy bundles. The Commissaire of Police stood on one side, a Nameless Official on the other. Will he let me pass? Will he? He was an old man with a fat swollen face covered with big warts. Horn-rimmed spectacles squatted on his nose. Trembling, I made an effort. I conjured up my sweetest early-morning smile and handed it with the papers. But the delicate thing fluttered against the horn spectacles and fell. Nevertheless, he let me pass, and I ran, ran in and out among the soldiers and up the high steps into the yellow-painted carriage.

'Does one go direct to X?' I asked the collector who dug at my ticket with a pair of forceps and handed it back again. 'No, Mademoiselle, you must change at X.Y.Z.'

'At—?'

'X.Y.Z.'

Again I had not heard. 'At what time do we arrive there if you please?'

'One o'clock.' But that was no good to me. I hadn't a watch. Oh, well —later.

Ah! the train had begun to move. The train was on my side. It swung out of the station, and soon we were passing the vegetable gardens, passing the tall blind houses to let, passing the servants beating carpets. Up already and walking in the fields, rosy from the rivers and the red-fringed pools, the sun lighted upon the swinging train and stroked my muff and told me to take off that Burberry. I was not alone in the carriage. An old woman sat opposite, her skirt turned back over her knees, a bonnet of black lace on her head. In her fat hands, adorned with a wedding and two mourning rings, she held a letter. Slowly, slowly she sipped a sentence, and then looked up and out of the window, her lips trembling a little, and then another sentence, and again the old face turned to the light, tasting it. . . . Two soldiers leaned out of the window, their heads nearly touching—one of them was whistling, the other had his coat fastened with some rusty safety-pins. And now there were soldiers everywhere working on the railway line, leaning against trucks or standing hands on hips, eyes fixed on the train as though they expected at least one camera at every window. And now we were passing big wooden sheds like rigged-up dancing halls or seaside pavilions, each flying a flag. In and out of them walked the Red Cross men; the wounded sat against the walls sunning themselves. At all the bridges, the crossings, the stations, a *petit soldat*, all boots and bayonet. Forlorn and desolate he looked,—like a little comic picture waiting for the joke to be written underneath. Is there really such a thing as war? Are all these laughing voices really going to the war? These dark woods lighted so mysteriously by the white stems of the birch and the ash—these watery fields with the big birds flying over—these rivers green and blue in the light—have battles been fought in places like these?

What beautiful cemeteries we are passing! They flash gay in the sun. They seem to be full of cornflowers and poppies and daisies. How can there be so many flowers at this time of the year? But they are not flowers at all. They are bunches of ribbons tied on to the soldiers' graves.

I glanced up and caught the old woman's eye. She smiled and folded the letter. 'It is from my son—the first we have had since October. I am taking it to my daughter-in-law.'

'. . . . . ?'

'Yes, very good,' said the old woman, shaking down her skirt and putting her arm through the handle of her basket. 'He wants me to send him some handkerchieves and a piece of stout string.'

What is the name of the station where I have to change? Perhaps I shall never know. I got up and leaned my arms across the window rail, my feet crossed. One cheek burned as in infancy on the way to the seaside. When the war is over I shall have a barge and drift along these rivers with a white cat and a pot of mignonette to bear me company.

Down the side of the hill filed the troops, winking red and blue in the light. Far away, but plainly to be seen, some more flew by on bicycles. But really, *ma France adorée*, this uniform is ridiculous. Your soldiers are stamped upon your bosom like bright irreverent transfers.

The train slowed down, stopped. . . . Everybody was getting out except me. A big boy, his sabots tied to his back with a piece of string, the inside of his tin wine cup stained a lovely impossible pink, looked very friendly. Does one change here perhaps for X? Another whose képi had come out of a wet paper cracker swung my suit-case to earth. What darlings soldiers are! 'Merci bien, Monsieur, vous êtes tout à fait aimable . . . .' 'Not this way,' said a bayonet. 'Nor this,' said another. So I followed the crowd. 'Your passport, Mademoiselle. . . .' '*We, Sir Edward Grey*. . . .' I ran through the muddy square and into the buffet.

A green room with a stove jutting out and tables on each side. On the counter, beautiful with coloured bottles, a woman leans, her breasts in her folded arms. Through an open door I can see a kitchen, and the cook in a white coat breaking eggs into a bowl and tossing the shells into a corner. The blue and red coats of the men who are eating hang upon the walls. Their short swords and belts are piled upon chairs. Heavens! what a noise. The sunny air seemed all broken up and trembling with it. A little boy, very pale, swung from table to table, taking the orders, and poured me out a glass of purple coffee. *Ssssh*, came from the eggs. They were in a pan. The woman rushed from behind the counter and began to help the boy. *Toute de suite, tout' suite!* she chirruped to the loud impatient voices. There came a clatter of plates and the pop–pop of corks being drawn.

Suddenly in the doorway I saw someone with a pail of fish—brown speckled fish, like the fish one sees in a glass case, swimming through forests of beautiful pressed sea-weed. He was an old man in a tattered jacket, standing humbly, waiting for someone to attend to him. A thin beard fell over his chest, his eyes under the tufted eyebrows were bent on the pail he carried. He looked as though he had escaped from some holy picture, and was entreating the soldiers' pardon for being there at all. . . .

But what could I have done? I could not arrive at X with two fishes hanging on a straw; and I am sure it is a penal offence in France to throw fish out of railway-carriage windows, I thought, miserably climbing into a smaller, shabbier train. Perhaps I might have taken them to—*ah, mon Dieu*—I had forgotten the name of my uncle and aunt again! Buffard, Buffon—what was it? Again I read the unfamiliar letter in the familiar handwriting.

'My dear niece,

'Now that the weather is more settled, your uncle and I would be charmed if you would pay us a little visit. Telegraph me when you are coming. I shall meet you outside the station if I am free. Otherwise our good friend, Madame Grinçon, who lives in the little toll-house by the bridge, *juste en face de la gare*, will conduct you to our home. *Je vous embrasse bien tendrement*, JULIE BOIFFARD.'

A visiting card was enclosed: *M. Paul Boiffard*.

Boiffard—of course that was the name. *Ma tante Julie et mon oncle Paul*—suddenly they were there with me, more real, more solid than any relations I had ever known. I saw *tante Julie* bridling, with the soup-tureen in her hands, and *oncle Paul* sitting at the table, with a red and white napkin tied round his neck. Boiffard—Boiffard—I must remember the name. Supposing the Commissaire Militaire should ask me who the relations were I was going to and I muddled the name—Oh, how fatal! Buffard—no, Boiffard. And then for the first time, folding Aunt Julie's letter, I saw scrawled in a corner of the empty back page: *Venez vite, vite*. Strange impulsive woman! My heart began to beat. . . .

'Ah, we are not far off now,' said the lady opposite. 'You are going to X, Mademoiselle?'

'Oui, Madame.'

'I also. . . . You have been there before?'

'No, Madame. This is the first time.'

'Really, it is a strange time for a visit.'

I smiled faintly, and tried to keep my eyes off her hat. She was quite an ordinary little woman, but she wore a black velvet toque, with an incredibly surprised looking sea-gull camped on the very top of it. Its round eyes, fixed on me so inquiringly, were almost too much to bear. I had a dreadful impulse to shoo it away, or to lean forward and inform her of its presence. . . .

'*Excusez-moi, madame*, but perhaps you have not remarked there is an *espèce de* sea-gull *couché sur votre chapeau.*'

Could the bird be there on purpose? I must not laugh. . . . I must not laugh. Had she ever looked at herself in a glass with that bird on her head?

'It is very difficult to get into X at present, to pass the station,' she said, and she shook her head with the sea-gull at me. 'Ah, such an affair. One must sign one's name and state one's business.'

'Really, is it as bad as all that?'

'But naturally. You see the whole place is in the hands of the military, and'—she shrugged—'they have to be strict. Many people do not get beyond the station at all. They arrive. They are put in the waiting-room, and there they remain.'

Did I or did I not detect in her voice a strange, insulting relish?

'I suppose such strictness is absolutely necessary,' I said coldly, stroking my muff.

'Necessary,' she cried. 'I should think so. Why, *mademoiselle*, you cannot imagine what it would be like otherwise! You know what women are like about soldiers'—she raised a final hand—'mad, completely mad. But—' and she gave a little laugh of triumph—'they could not get into X. *Mon Dieu*, no! There is no question about that.'

'I don't suppose they even try,' said I.

'Don't you?' said the sea-gull.

Madame said nothing for a moment. 'Of course the authorities are very hard on the men. It means instant imprisonment, and then—off to the firing-line without a word.'

'What are *you* going to X for?' said the sea-gull. 'What on earth are *you* doing here?'

'Are you making a long stay in X, *mademoiselle*?'

She had won, she had won. I was terrified. A lamp-post swam past the train with the fatal name upon it. I could hardly breathe—the train had stopped. I smiled gaily at Madame and danced down the steps to the platform. . . .

It was a hot little room completely furnished with two colonels seated at two tables. They were large grey-whiskered men with a touch of burnt red on their cheeks. Sumptuous and onmipotent they looked. One smoked what ladies love to call a heavy Egyptian cigarette, with a long creamy ash, the other toyed with a gilded pen. Their heads rolled on their tight collars, like big over-ripe fruits. I had a terrible feeling, as I handed my passport and ticket, that a soldier would step forward and tell me to kneel. I would have knelt without question.

'What's this?' said God I., querulously. He did not like my passport at all. The very sight of it seemed to annoy him. He waved a dissenting hand at it, with a '*Non, je ne peux pas manger ça*' air.

'But it won't do. It won't do at all, you know. Look,—read for yourself,' and he glanced with extreme distaste at my photograph, and then with even greater distaste his pebble eyes looked at me.

'Of course the photograph is deplorable,' I said, scarcely breathing with terror, 'but it has been viséd and viséd.'

He raised his big bulk and went over to God II.

'Courage!' I said to my muff and held it firmly, 'Courage!'

God II. held up a finger to me, and I produced Aunt Julie's letter and her card. But he did not seem to feel the slightest interest in her. He stamped my passport idly, scribbled a word on my ticket, and I was on the platform again.

'That way—you pass out that way.'

Terribly pale, with a faint smile on his lips, his hand at salute, stood the little corporal. I gave no sign, I am sure I gave no sign. He stepped behind me.

'And then follow me as though you do not see me,' I heard him half whisper, half sing.

How fast he went, through the slippery mud towards a bridge. He had a postman's bag on his back, a paper parcel and the *Matin* in his hand. We seemed to dodge through a maze of policemen, and I could not keep up at all with the little corporal who began to whistle. From the toll-house 'our good friend, Madame Grinçon', her hands wrapped in a shawl, watched our coming, and against the toll-house there leaned a tiny faded cab. *Montez vite, vite*! said the little corporal, hurling my suit-case, the postman's bag, the paper parcel and the *Matin* on to the floor.

'A-ie! A-ie! Do not be so mad. Do not ride yourself. You will be seen,' wailed 'our good friend, Madame Grinçon'.

'Ah, je m'en f. . . .' said the little corporal.

The driver jerked into activity. He lashed the bony horse and away we flew, both doors, which were the complete sides of the cab, flapping and banging.

'Bon jour, mon amie.'

'Bon jour, mon ami.'

And then he swooped down and clutched at the banging doors. They would not keep shut. They were fools of doors.

'Lean back, let me do it!' I cried. 'Policemen are as thick as violets everywhere.'

At the barracks the horse reared up and stopped. A crowd of laughing faces blotted the window.

'Prends ça, mon vieux,' said the little corporal, handing the paper parcel.

'It's all right,' called someone.

We waved, we were off again. By a river, down a strange white street, with little houses on either side, gay in the late sunlight.

'Jump out as soon as he stops again. The door will be open. Run straight inside. I will follow. The man is already paid. I know you will like the house. It is quite white, and the room is white, too, and the people are—'

'White as snow.'

We looked at each other. We began to laugh. 'Now,' said the little corporal.

Out I flew and in at the door. There stood, presumably, my aunt Julie. There in the background hovered, I supposed, my uncle Paul.

'Bon jour, madame!' 'Bon jour, monsieur!'

'It is all right, you are safe,' said my aunt Julie. Heavens, how I loved her! And she opened the door of the white room and shut it upon us. Down went the suit-case, the postman's bag, the *Matin*. I threw my passport up into the air, and the little corporal caught it.

* * *

What an extraordinary thing. We had been there to lunch and to dinner each day; but now in the dusk and alone I could not find it. I clop-clopped in my borrowed *sabots* through the greasy mud, right to the end of the village, and there was not a sign of it. I could not even remember what it looked like, or if there was a name painted on the outside, or any bottles or tables showing at the window. Already the village houses were sealed for the night behind big wooden shutters. Strange and mysterious they looked in the ragged drifting light and thin rain, like a company of beggars perched on the hill-side, their bosoms full of rich unlawful gold. There was nobody about but the soldiers. A group of wounded stood under a lamp-post, petting a mangy, shivering dog. Up the street came four big boys singing:

Dodo, mon homme, fais vit' dodo . . .

and swung off down the hill to their sheds behind the railway station. They seemed to take the last breath of the day with them. I began to walk slowly back.

'It must have been one of these houses. I remember it stood far back from the road—and there were no steps, not even a porch—one seemed to walk right through the window.' And then quite suddenly the waiting-boy came out of just such a place. He saw me and grinned cheerfully, and began to whistle through his teeth.

'Bon soir, mon petit.'

'Bon soir, madame.' And he followed me up the café to our special table, right at the far end by the window, and marked by a bunch of violets that I had left in a glass there yesterday.

'You are two?' asked the waiting-boy, flicking the table with a red and white cloth. His long swinging steps echoed over the bare floor. He disappeared into the kitchen and came back to light the lamp that hung from the ceiling under a spreading shade, like a haymaker's hat. Warm light shone on the empty place that was really a barn, set out with dilapidated tables and chairs. Into the middle of the room a black stove jutted. At one side of it there was a table with a row of bottles on it, behind which Madame sat and took the money and made entries in a red book. Opposite her desk a door led into the kitchen. The walls were covered with a creamy paper patterned all over with green and swollen trees— hundreds and hundreds of trees reared their mushroom heads to the ceiling. I began to wonder who had chosen the paper and why. Did Madame think it was beautiful, or that it was a gay and lovely thing to eat one's dinner at all seasons in the middle of a forest. . . . On either side of the clock there hung a picture: one, a young gentleman in black tights wooing a pear-shaped lady in yellow over the back of a garden seat, *Premier Rencontre*; two, the black and yellow in amorous confusion. *Triomphe d'Amour*.

The clock ticked to a soothing lilt, *C'est ça, C'est ça*. In the kitchen the waiting-boy was washing up. I heard the ghostly chatter of the dishes.

And years passed. Perhaps the war is long since over—there is no village outside at all—the streets are quiet under the grass. I have an idea this is the sort of thing one will do on the very last day of all—sit in an empty café and listen to a clock ticking until—.

Madame came through the kitchen door, nodded to me and took her seat behind the table, her plump hands folded on the red book. *Ping* went the door. A handful of soldiers came in, took off their coats and began to play cards, chaffing and poking fun at the pretty waiting-boy, who threw up his little round head, rubbed his thick fringe out of his eyes and cheeked them back in his broken voice. Sometimes his voice boomed up from his throat, deep and harsh, and then in the middle of a sentence it broke and scattered in a funny squeaking. He seemed to enjoy it himself. You would not have been surprised if he had walked into the kitchen on his hands and brought back your dinner turning a catherine-wheel.

Ping went the door again. Two more men came in. They sat at the table nearest Madame, and she leaned to them with a birdlike movement, her head on one side. Oh, they had a grievance! The Lieutenant was a fool—nosing about— springing out at them—and they'd only been sewing on buttons. Yes, that was all—sewing on buttons, and up comes this young spark. 'Now then, what are you up to?' They mimicked the idiotic voice. Madame drew down her mouth, nodding sympathy. The waiting-boy served them with glasses. He took a bottle of some orange-coloured stuff and put it on the table-edge. A shout from the card-players made him turn sharply, and crash! over went the bottle, spilling on the table, the floor—smash! to tinkling atoms. An amazed silence. Through it the drip-drip of the wine from the table on to the floor. It looked very strange dropping so slowly, as though the table were crying. Then there came a roar from the card-players. 'You'll catch it, my lad! That's the style! Now you've done it! . . . Sept, huit, neuf.' They started playing again. The waiting-boy never said a word. He stood, his head bent, his hands spread out, and then he knelt and gathered up the glass, piece by piece, and soaked the wine up with a cloth. Only when Madame cried cheerfully, 'You wait until *he* finds out,' did he raise his head.

'He can't say anything, if I pay for it,' he muttered, his face jerking, and he marched off into the kitchen with the soaking cloth.

'*Il pleure de colère*,' said Madame delightedly, patting her hair with her plump hands.

The café slowly filled. It grew very warm. Blue smoke mounted from the tables and hung about the haymaker's hat in misty wreath. There was a suffocating smell of onion soup and boots and damp cloth. In the din the door sounded again. It opened to let in a weed of a fellow, who stood with his back against it, one hand shading his eyes.

'Hullo! you've got the bandage off?'

'How does it feel, *mon vieux*?'

'Let's have a look at them.'

But he made no reply. He shrugged and walked unsteadily to a table, sat down and leant against the wall. Slowly his hand fell. In his white face his eyes showed, pink as a rabbit's. They brimmed and spilled, brimmed and spilled. He dragged a white cloth out of his pocket and wiped them.

'It's the smoke,' said someone. 'It's the smoke tickles them up for you.'

His comrades watched him a bit, watched his eyes fill again, again brim over. The water ran down his face, off his chin on to the table. He rubbed the place with his coat-sleeve, and then, as though forgetful, went on rubbing, rubbing with his hand across the table, staring in front of him. And then he started shaking his head to the movement of his hand. He gave a loud strange groan and dragged out the cloth again.

'*Huit, neuf, dix,*' said the card-players.

'*P'tit,* some more bread.'

'Two coffees.'

'*Un Picon!*'

The waiting-boy, quite recovered, but with scarlet cheeks, ran to and fro. A tremendous quarrel flared up among the card-players, raged for two minutes, and died in flickering laughter. 'Ooof!' groaned the man with the eyes, rocking and mopping. But nobody paid any attention to him except Madame. She made a little grimace at her two soldiers.

'*Mais vous savez, c'est un peu dégoûtant, ça,*' she said severely.

'*Ah, oui, Madame,*' answered the soldiers, watching her bent head and pretty hands, as she arranged for the hundredth time a frill of lace on her lifted bosom.

'*V'là monsieur!*' cawed the waiting-boy over his shoulder to me. For some silly reason I pretended not to hear, and I leaned over the table smelling the violets, until the little corporal's hand closed over mine.

'Shall we have *un peu de charcuterie* to begin with?' he asked tenderly.

*   *   *

'In England,' said the blue-eyed soldier, 'you drink whiskey with your meals. *N'est-ce pas, mademoiselle?* A little glass of whiskey neat before eating. Whiskey and soda with your *bifteks,* and after, more whiskey with hot water and lemon.'

'Is it true, that?' asked his great friend who sat opposite, a big red-faced chap with a black beard and large moist eyes and hair that looked as though it had been cut with a sewing-machine.

'Well, not quite true,' said I.

'*Si, si,*' cried the blue-eyed soldier. 'I ought to know. I'm in business. English travellers come to my place, and it's always the same thing.'

'Bah, I can't stand whiskey,' said the little corporal. 'It's too disgusting the morning after. Do you remember, *ma fille*, the whiskey in that little bar at Montmartre?'

'*Souvenir tendre,*' sighed Blackbeard, putting two fingers in the breast of his coat and letting his head fall. He was very drunk.

'But I know something that you've never tasted,' said the blue-eyed soldier pointing a finger at me; 'something really good.' *Cluck* he went with his tongue. '*É-pa-tant!* And the curious thing is that you'd hardly know it from whiskey except that it's'—he felt with his hand for the word—'finer, sweeter perhaps, not so sharp, and it leaves you feeling gay as a rabbit next morning.'

'What is it called?'

'Mirabelle!' He rolled the word round his mouth, under his tongue. 'Ah-ha, that's the stuff.'

'I could eat another mushroom,' said Blackbeard. 'I would like another mushroom very much. I am sure I could eat another mushroom if Mademoiselle gave it to me out of her hand.'

'You ought to try it,' said the blue-eyed soldier, leaning both hands on the table and speaking so seriously that I began to wonder how much more sober he was than Blackbeard. 'You ought to try it, and to-night. I would like you to tell me if you don't think it's like whiskey.'

'Perhaps they've got it here,' said the little corporal, and he called the waiting-boy. '*P'tit!*'

'*Non, monsieur,*' said the boy, who never stopped smiling. He served us with dessert plates painted with blue parrots and horned beetles.

'What is the name for this in English?' said Blackbeard, pointing. I told him 'Parrot'.

'Ah, *mon Dieu!* . . . Pair-rot.' He put his arms round his plate. 'I love you, *ma petite* pair-rot. You are sweet, you are blonde, you are English. You do not know the difference between whiskey and mirabelle.'

The little corporal and I looked at each other, laughing. He squeezed up his eyes when he laughed, so that you saw nothing but the long curly lashes.

'Well, I know a place where they do keep it,' said the blue-eyed soldier. '*Café des Amis.* We'll go there—I'll pay—I'll pay for the whole lot of us.' His gesture embraced thousands of pounds.

But with a loud whirring noise the clock on the wall struck half-past eight; and no soldier is allowed in a café after eight o'clock at night.

'It is fast,' said the blue-eyed soldier. The little corporal's watch said the same. So did the immense turnip that Blackbeard produced, and carefully deposited on the head of one of the horned beetles.

'Ah, well, we'll take the risk,' said the blue-eyed soldier, and he thrust his arms into his immense cardboard coat. 'It's worth it,' he said. 'It's worth it. You just wait.'

Outside, stars shone between wispy clouds, and the moon fluttered like a candle flame over a pointed spire. The shadows of the dark plume-like trees waved on the white houses. Not a soul to be seen. No sound to be heard but the *Hsh! Hsh!* of a far-away train, like a big beast shuffling in its sleep.

'You are cold,' whispered the little corporal. 'You are cold, *ma fille.*'

'No, really not.'

'But you are trembling.'

Yes, but I'm not cold.'

'What are the women like in England?' asked Blackbeard. 'After the war is over I shall go to England. I shall find a little English woman and marry her—and her pair-rot.' He gave a loud choking laugh.

'Fool!' said the blue-eyed soldier, shaking him; and he leant over to me. 'It is only after the second glass that you really taste it,' he whispered. 'The second little glass and then—ah!—then you know.'

Café des Amis gleamed in the moonlight. We glanced quickly up and down the road. We ran up the four wooden steps, and opened the ringing glass door into a low room lighted with a hanging lamp, where about ten people were dining. They were seated on two benches at a narrow table.

'Soldiers!' screamed a woman, leaping up from behind a white soup-tureen—a scrag of a woman in a black shawl. 'Soldiers! At this hour! Look at that clock, look at it.' And she pointed to the clock with the dripping ladle.

'It's fast,' said the blue-eyed soldier. 'It's fast, madame. And don't make so much noise, I beg of you. We will drink and we will go.'

'Will you?' she cried, running round the table and planting herself in front of us. 'That's just what you won't do. Coming into an honest woman's house this hour of the night—making a scene—getting the police after you. Ah, no! Ah, no! It's a disgrace, that's what it is.'

'Sh!' said the little corporal, holding up his hand. Dead silence. In the silence we heard steps passing.

'The police,' whispered Blackbeard, winking at a pretty girl with rings in her ears, who smiled back at him, saucy. 'Sh!'

The faces lifted, listening. 'How beautiful they are!' I thought. 'They are like a family party having supper in the New Testament. . . .' The steps died away.

'Serve you very well right if you had been caught,' scolded the angry woman. 'I'm sorry on your account that the police didn't come. You deserve it—you deserve it.'

'A little glass of mirabelle and we will go,' persisted the blue-eyed soldier.

Still scolding and muttering she took four glasses from the cupboard and a big bottle. 'But you're not going to drink in here. Don't you believe it.' The little corporal ran into the kitchen. 'Not there! Not there! Idiot!' she cried. 'Can't you see there's a window there, and a wall opposite where the police come every evening to. . . .'

'Sh!' Another scare.

'You are mad and you will end in prison,—all four of you,' said the woman. She flounced out of the room. We tiptoed after her into a dark smelling scullery, full of pans of greasy water, of salad leaves and meat-bones.

'There now,' she said, putting down the glasses. 'Drink and go!'

'Ah, at last!' The blue-eyed soldier's happy voice trickled through the dark. 'What do you think? Isn't it just as I said? Hasn't it got a taste of excellent—*ex-cellent* whiskey?'

Jean Devanny

THE PERFECT MOTHER

Mrs Macdonald and Mrs Leitrim were friends. But Mrs Leitrim was a thorn in the side of Mrs Macdonald because of her exceeding righteousness.

Mrs Macdonald was an easy-going soul, buxom, not too big, not too tidy, either, but full of rosy goodnature. Everybody loved her.

Mrs Leitrim was a commanding woman. Strikingly handsome in a blonde way, meticulous of speech and not sparing of it; a managing woman, superior. Everybody admired her.

The two women were close neighbours in the mining town of Millerton, West Coast. Mrs Macdonald's husband was a miner; Mrs Leitrim's the company's head clerk. An 'accountant', Mrs Leitrim styled him. This vocational distinction gave the latter woman an advantage over Mrs Macdonald to start with. Not that Leitrim made more money than Macdonald. He did not make as much. Mike Macdonald was a 'pillar' man, one of the 'royals', who knew just about all there was to know about scientific mining. But clerking was clean, refined and a one-shifted job. Mrs Leitrim was not 'messed about' with changing mealtimes, disturbed nights and the other incidentals to weekly changes of shift, as Mrs Macdonald was. She found it easy to be tidy and methodical. She had only two children, too, to Mrs Macdonald's four.

Mrs Leitrim was not aware that she was a thorn in her friend's capacious side. She would have been hurt had she known it. For she was fond of Mrs Macdonald; had no intention of making comparisons and no wish to do so. She could not help her own orderly existence and was very broad-minded and tolerant (except in one direction) besides. She was an intellectual. Before her marriage she had participated in the political agitations of New Zealand. Without attaching herself to any definite party aspect, she had been known as a sincere and implacable agitator for reforms, chiefly in regard to woman and child welfare. Her single life from childhood onward to the time of her marriage had been crowded with incident, riotous with colour, flaming with the fires of a daring and courageous self-expression. A 'career' had been open to her. She had been considered the coming woman, and yet—for love of a man and desire for a child she had pushed aside ambition and settled down.

At this time she had two baby boys, two beautiful baby boys.

She had told Mrs Macdonald of her pre-marital ambitions; of what they had meant to her—everything in the world worth living for—till love had come and with it visions of and cravings for motherhood.

'Yes,' she would say. She talked such a lot she was bound to repeat herself a good deal. 'I loved the public life. I lived for it. I felt that I was fitted—without boasting, Mrs Macdonald, really, without boasting, I felt that I was fitted to do great things in politics.'

'Of course you were,' Mrs Macdonald would put in obligingly and admiringly. 'Of course you were. Everyone knows how wonderful you were. You can do great things yet if you want to. You didn't die when you married—'

'No, no!' Mrs Leitrim would interrupt. Like all great talkers and doers, she thought other people's opinions quite irrelevant to a discussion. 'No, no. I don't want you to misunderstand me.' (There was no use at all in Mrs Macdonald trying to interpose to the effect that she did not misunderstand.) 'I've quite given it up. I made my decision. It was a public life or private life and I chose private life.'

'But, my dear, you didn't die when . . .'

'No, no, Mrs Macdonald! I have no intention of ever going back to it; at least, not till the children are grown up. A mother's duty lies with her children.' Mrs Leitrim would whisk off her pince-nez, flourish them, wipe them and plant them firmly on her classic nose again. 'Now, you mustn't misunderstand me, Mrs Macdonald. I don't regret it in the least and never will. I adore my children—' Here Mrs Macdonald would insist on pushing in:

'Of course you do, my dear. All mothers love their children.'

'But what I mean, Mrs Macdonald, is that I don't take my motherhood lightly. I realize the responsibilities of the parent; especially of the mother. Those responsibilities quite preclude the possibility of politics for me until the babies are grown up. But I don't regret it! Oh, no! I adore them!' And Mrs Leitrim would quite shame poor Mrs Macdonald with her correct speech and manner in regard to the children. Her:

'Do you want attention darling?' and the child's: 'Yes, please, Mummy dear,' made Mrs Macdonald blush for her own:

'You little devil, messing round the place. I've half a mind to rub your nose in it.'

But she liked her admirable neighbour very much. She was not at all jealous of the perfection which was the thorn in her side because of her husband's attitude towards it.

The Macdonalds had been comfortable enough before the Leitrims settled next door a year before this time. Mrs Macdonald had muddled along in her happy-go-lucky way; letting the children go a tiny bit dirty if she felt disinclined to clean them; running up bills at the grocer's while she wasted the money on pretty clothes of which she took no care; playing tennis, going to the pictures, and dances; having a good time, in fact, as she considered it. She still had her 'good time'. But after the Leitrim's perfect household had been established next door Mike Macdonald's complacent, amiable forbearance of his wife's frivolous, easy-going ways had gradually changed. He was a quiet, home-loving sort himself, very fond of the children.

Leitrim had set him carping at his wife. Leitrim was not too clever, not commanding; not superior in any way and he realized it and could never be grateful enough to his wife for marrying him. He sounded her praises to all and sundry; descanted on her housewifely virtues, her economy, her cleanliness and orderliness, but most of all on her Perfect Motherhood. And all his praises were deserved, as everyone about could see. Macdonald was always about. Leitrim and he were as friendly as the two women and most of their spare time was spent gossiping. Result, that Mike began to poke his nose into his wife's business, as she expressed it; began to make unpleasant remarks about women that could not stay in their homes, that thought more of dancing and gadding about than of their children. But Mrs Macdonald never got nasty. She would laugh in her soft, chuckling way and say something like:

'Oh, well, Mike, I know I'm not perfect. You'll have to put up with me as I am.' Even when he got to making straight-out comparisons between her and Mrs Leitrim, Mrs Macdonald felt no animus against her neighbour and little against him. A little fitful exasperation was the extent of her reaction to his criticisms.

'Mrs Leitrim is a big woman,' she would usually say at these times, not being very versatile in her ideas. 'She's big. I'm only an ordinary woman. She's clever and intellectual. I'm not.'

'You can learn,' he would argue. 'And you don't need to be intellectual or clever to clean up a house and wash the kids. Or to stay home from dances either. Mrs Leitrim won't go out dancing and leave her kids till three o'clock in the morning like you do. It's not right.' Once she asked Mike, apropos of Mrs Leitrim's perfect motherhood:

'Do her children love her any more than mine do me, Mike?' He had to answer: 'No,' to that but made it as sulky as he could. For Mrs

Macdonald's children adored their mother, who let them play in the dirt with other children as dirty as themselves, was reasonable about naughtiness and always generous in regard to lollies. Mike added after a pause, during which his wife had hummed a tune pleasantly as though his admission had settled everything:

'But her children love her, too, don't they?'

'Yes, they love her. Anyone would love her,' she put in in a burst of generosity, 'I love her. She's lovely. But you can't make me over into a Mrs Leitrim, Mike. I'm all right. I enjoy my life.'

'So does she. She's happy in her home and children and husband.' Baffled, his wife went on undressing the children, slapping one here, swearing mildly at another there, at the same time as she dressed herself for a dance.

'Get cleaned, Mike, and come with me,' she urged. 'Come and have a bit of fun. What's the use of digging your own grave? The kids will be all right. You're getting Mrs Leitrim on the brain. You'll be in love with her next.' He smiled shamefacedly at that and muttered:

'Don't talk rot. You know very well I only want my wife to be as good as another's.' She stood in the door and regarded him quizzically.

'Your wife's all right, Mike. She's happy. Are you coming?'

'No!' he snapped petulantly. So she went to the dance alone, had a jolly time and tumbled into bed at two in the morning. Mike brought her in a cup of tea when he got his own breakfast at seven, after which she got up, drowsily. The children had long been out on the road in their night-clothes, shouting, quarrelling and playing. When Mike passed Leitrims' on his way to work it soured him to see their two little boys washed and dressed and their mother out sweeping the rocky yard floor.

'Good morning, Mr Macdonald,' Mrs Leitrim called out briskly. (Mike's wife would have said: 'Hallo, there!')

'Good morning. You're up early as usual.'

'Well, it is not that I dislike my bed. The children drag me out.' Mike went on his way thinking how handsome she was. Leitrim ought to be proud.

The one subject on which Mrs Leitrim was not broadminded and tolerant was that of sex. She had married at thirty. Being splendid looking she had been much sought by men, but, as she often told Mrs Macdonald, though she had liked men very much and was really quite passionate—yes, she would freely admit she was really a passionate woman—she had preserved her moral character; she had kept men in their place.

'Of course, Mrs Macdonald, I don't presume to criticize others. I don't want you to misunderstand me. I realize that human nature is human nature and that some poor things are weak. We can't all be cut of a pattern. I don't take up a hard attitude on the matter, Mrs Macdonald. Oh, no! But there must be a limit to toleration in the interests of the race. Laxity must not be allowed to degenerate into licence. If you had only seen what I've seen around the jazz halls in Wellington and Auckland you would realize the necessity for limitations. This filthy jazz!'

Mrs Macdonald, who had seen quite a thing or two around the tin huts of the miners, who had let Mike get her 'into trouble' in the first place and had more than one innocent skeleton in her cupboard in regard to sex since, always felt particularly at a disadvantage on this subject. Not embarrassed. Oh no. She was too naturally philosophical for her conscience to be pricked by the other's preachments and predications. Everything was all right so long as it was all right, was her motto, and she was all right. Only she could never find anything satisfactory to say about the matter. And this was the only subject that Mrs Leitrim ever invited her to give an opinion on, strange to say. She thought at times it was rather funny how Mrs Leitrim harped so much on certain aspects of sex; for instance, marital infidelity; denouncing it, expansively, and yet there seemed always a question in her tone and words. Her extremist animadversions—she got passionate on the subject at times—would be accompanied by a sort of straining demand by her eyes for confirmation by Mrs Macdonald. The latter felt this but could not understand it. She would murmur:

'Yes, yes, I suppose you are right, my dear. You're always right. But what I say is: live and let live. We've only got one life.' Which kind of remark seemed to rouse impatience in Mrs Leitrim. One day she became almost bullying in her efforts to make her friend agree with her.

'Live and let live, yes, Mrs Macdonald, but you must admit that the mother who doesn't put her children first, before all things, is the lowest kind of person?'

'I don't see how it affects the children,' Mrs Macdonald answered mildly.

'Oh, it must! You can't hide these things, Mrs Macdonald. Look at my two darlings, my two beautiful boys.' Mrs Leitrim had one on her knee and the other standing beside her in Mrs Macdonald's kitchen. 'Suppose I took a lover? Could I be the same mother to them? To my beauties?'

'Well, I don't know much about these things,' the other said uncomfortably. 'You are too—too real. You make so much of everything.'

'Oh, if a thing has to be done it ought to be done properly.' Was there a feverish note in Mrs Leitrim's voice? Mrs Macdonald looked at her. She looked nervous, a condition which was altogether ridiculous in her. 'No, Mrs Macdonald. A mother can't love her children and man too. The two things act one against the other. The good mother must be wrapped up in her children. When I think of these two wonderful bodies that I have created, that I gave up my life for. — Now don't misunderstand me! I gave it up willingly; I deliberately made my choice, and I don't regret it. No, not for an instant. I don't regret it.' There was more than nervousness in her voice now; — hysteria. She pressed her boy to her breast and showered kisses on his upturned face.

Mrs Macdonald was positively startled.

'But children are a tie, aren't they, Mrs Macdonald? A great tie. I see why nature made the mother-love so strong.'

Now it is irrefutable that the intuitions of the simple ordinary woman are the strongest kind of intuitions. Mrs Macdonald's timid mind here made a leap to an astounding conclusion, though she had never heard of psychology, never heard of complexes, of inhibitions. And on the strength of her impulsive understanding she asserted herself.

'Now look here, my dear,' she said firmly. 'You're making a hash of your life with your fool ideas. Look at me. Ain't I happy. Aren't my children happy and healthy? I'm not a passionate woman; I could go along for ever without seeing a man; Mike's mostly a nuisance to me. But more than once I've had another man. It just came my way and I took it. And I'm no worse for it either. No one's any worse. Now you just put that in your pipe and smoke it.'

Mrs Leitrim stared with wide-open eyes. Then she burst into tears, rose hurriedly, took one child by the hand and the other under her arm, cried hysterically:

'You've done a bad thing to-day, Mrs Macdonald; I depended on you; I trusted you and now you've done a bad thing;' and almost ran out of the house.

Mrs Macdonald cried too. 'Oh the poor soul! The poor soul!'

Thereafter, when Mike carped and sulked and made comparisons she smiled indulgently. She even tidied up a bit, to oblige him. Until his nagging got so intense and constant as to seriously threaten her domestic life. Mike had Mrs Leitrim on the brain, it seemed, though he mentioned her name less and less. Mrs Macdonald began to cry a little and she went out more than ever. She discovered a temper in herself and kept it no secret from Mike. She had the back-blocks woman's habit of talking to herself and now as she went about her housework she muttered disjointedly.

'Yes, he's in love with her and doesn't know it. — He's bothered and worried because he doesn't know what's the matter with him. — Thinks he wants me to clean and tidy and stay home when what he really wants is her. — He hardly ever comes to me now, at night. — He's got her in his mind all the time and the best he can do is to try to make me act like her—' And so on.

But she never allowed the other woman to suspect, nor did she enlighten Mike as to her conclusions. She had her pride.

Mrs Leitrim had been different to her friend ever since that day of disclosures. Not less friendly, but different. A little more superior in her manner, perhaps; obviously an unconscious attitude, and less discursive. She tabooed the subject of sex completely. More assiduously than ever she devoted herself to her children.

They had a friend, the Leitrims, a gentleman from Christchurch, who often stayed with them for a day or two. Mrs Leitrim had informed Mrs Macdonald that 'Jarvis' was an old companion of hers before her marriage. In fact, he had greatly desired her for his wife but had behaved like a brick when she chose Leitrim. And Leitrim was awfully decent about things. He quite understood that a friend was a friend and heartily welcomed Jarvis to their home. Jarvis would have been a better match, she agreed with Mrs Macdonald. He had a good business. In fact it was his business that really brought him over the Island to the Coast. But then, she had been awfully keen on Leitrim. And she did not regret it. Oh, no!

After this friend's visit she had been in the habit of running across and chatting intimately to Mrs Macdonald of the talks she had had with Jarvis. His visits meant so much to her. He had been a part of the old busy life; part of the turmoil; the chase, the fight. Mrs Leitrim's fine eyes would flash and her nostrils quiver at the sound of the very word 'fight.' Sometimes she would close those eyes and seem to listen like a huntsman awaiting the horn.

But when Jarvis came again, stayed two days and went, she kept away from her friend; pointedly avoided her eyes when she had to come outside. Mrs Macdonald was usually at the back door or not far from it. And for some intuitive reason the latter did not go over to Leitrim's. She did not know why. Usually the two ran back and forth haphazard, in the homely manner of the hospitable West Coast. And Mrs Macdonald was puzzled to catch a glimpse now and again of Mrs Leitrim at her window, staring across at her friend with a white straining face. Even from a distance Mrs Macdonald could feel the question in her look.

As the only topics of interest in the New Zealand mining towns are the doings of one's neighbours, Mrs Macdonald began to think seriously about Mrs Leitrim; to worry a bit; even to wish that she would leave the place. She felt a bit sorry for Mike too, now, and ceased to cry in secret.

'The big boob,' she thought with contemptuous good-nature, having Mike's tousled red head and ugly thick features in mind. 'To fall for a woman like her. She hardly knows he exists. She's not in our class.'

But Mrs Leitrim came back in a day or two her old charming self.

'I see you've had your friend to visit you again,' said Mrs Macdonald.

'Yes, Jarvis was over on business. But I don't think I shall have him to stay any more, Mrs Macdonald. After all, it is hardly the thing for a married woman to have a man staying in the house when she is alone. And Harry could not stay away from work, of course. I don't want you to misunderstand me or think me straitlaced. I'm not. It would be inexcusable for a woman of my advanced trend of thought to be prudish or intolerant, but—really, the children must be considered. It is my duty as their mother not to risk my good name. I can't run the risk of having the neighbours talking. And in these places—. You know what these places are for scandal, Mrs Macdonald.'

'Why, good God, yes! Of course they scandalize! Why shouldn't they? What else is there to do? But they don't mean anything by it. There's nothing in it. But as for you! Having a gentleman friend come to stay with you for a day or two! Why, nobody even dreamt of saying a word! Nobody even thought a thing about it! Bless my soul! What ever put that into your head? Making too much of everything again! If it were me, now, or any of the others like me, but you can do as you like, my dear. And anyhow, you didn't die when you—'

'No, no!' There was a distinctly tired note in Mrs Leitrim's voice. 'I didn't die when I married. But I am one of those people who must do things thoroughly, Mrs Macdonald, if they do them at all. I won't risk the merest suspicion falling on my children's mother. I told Jarvis not to return. Surely you think I did right, Mrs Macdonald?' The questioning note was urgent, the straining demand for agreement.

'I think you're a damn fool,' said Mrs Macdonald shortly. 'Children indeed! What your children want is a human being for a mother, not a blooming iceberg or an autom—autom—what the devil is the word? How long do you think you'll last out in a place like this? If you ask me, you're a nervous wreck now. And you that big and fine and strong. You're a fighter, you are. You want fight, and when you can't get fight you want man.'

Mrs Leitrim jumped, positively jumped.

'Oh! How dare you, Mrs Macdonald? I've—I've done with you! I'll—I'll never speak to you again! You're a bad woman!' She picked up her children, her two beautiful boys, one in each arm and made for the door. Her voice was high-pitched; tears rained down her face. 'I trusted you! I—I depended on you, Mrs Macdonald, and you've talked like a wicked woman! I'm done with you!' She flew across the yard and slammed her own kitchen door behind her. Mrs Macdonald sat very still for a long time. She was upset too. Then:

'I wonder what she depended on me for,' she muttered.

The next day came out brilliantly fine. The sun, which was always close to the mining camp struck onto the yellowish-white clay of a mountain top, seemed bent on giving its inhabitants a foretaste of hell. The clay cracked with the heat and scorched the eyeballs with its ferocious glare. The tennis court, cut out of a clay bank, was unthinkable. Yet Mrs Macdonald felt that she would rather not stay close to her neighbour. She did not know what attitude to adopt towards Mrs Leitrim should they both be outside at one time. There was no rancour in her for the harsh words spoken. She suspected hidden fires and suffering of a sort she could not understand. She would have ignored the previous day and gone on as before but she was at sea in regard to the other woman's temper. Impossible to stay inside all day. Indoors beneath the corrugated iron roof would be torture in the heat. She hated to think of her two oldest children in school. Eventually she decided to take the two little ones a mile down the hill to the manuka clumps which grew there in the better soil and sit in their shade and read while the children played about. It would be a heavy climb back with the drag of the children upon her and Mike would have to put up with an improvised tea, which he hated. However, neither drawback weighed much with her so away she went immediately after lunch. Mrs Leitrim had not showed herself.

The afternoon wilted away slowly and Mrs Macdonald drowsed in the shade of the manuka. Not altogether comfortably, for her mind would return to the friend who must be broiling up above. She kept tangling the heat of the sun with Mrs Leitrim's nature, somehow. The whitish glare of the earth with her glimpses of Mrs Leitrim's staring, pallid face at her window in the days after Jarvis had left. The broken-backed clay of the mountain with the rents in Mrs Leitrim's commanding calm wrought by her astounding hysteria. Heat! The mountain seemed to wobble, to totter with it, emasculated to the point of exhaustion. And in Mrs Macdonald's fancy Mrs Leitrim tottered too. Once she dozed off, but awakened sharply with the feeling real as life upon her that Mrs Leitrim's hand had clutched at her; her voice had wailed for help; her eyes had strained for answer to a question. She got up and shook herself and wished it were time to go home.

About four o'clock her buxom, soft body panted back to her door. She was tired out. The heat was still intense, though it had lost the sweltering quality. The sky was further away and faintly blue, presaging the cool of the night. Mrs Macdonald hated that camp just then. Her amiable spirit was tired as her body. She was not used to mental stress. She was red in the face; the children cried, tired out, too, and her stomach recoiled at thought of the tough steak she had to fry for tea. But nevertheless her eyes swept her neighbour's house for sign of Mrs Leitrim. She would go over after tea and put her foot down on this nonsense. Wicked, indeed! There would be no living in the place if neighbours took to quarrelling. She was glad to see the two little boys playing about in the yard. Shut in, of course. A young girl friend was sitting on the front doorstep, too. Mrs Leitrim was not visible.

At sight of her the girl jumped up and went inside. Mrs Macdonald clumped wearily into her kitchen and dropped into a chair. She must hurry and light the fire. Mike would be home in a minute. Her oldest boy ran in.

'Hallo, Mum! I say, Mrs Leitrim's gone down the hill by herself. Went a couple of hours ago on the trucks.'

'What!' For Mrs Leitrim to go anywhere without her children was astounding. Even the child thought so. 'What! By herself?' But here the girl came to the door. She had an envelope in her hand which she held out to Mrs Macdonald.

'Here. Mrs Leitrim told me to give this to you.' She watched Mrs Macdonald curiously as she took the letter and opened it. The easy-going woman began to read with wonder in her face but she had hardly time to read a line before she dropped it as though it had stung and cried out a sharp. 'Oh!'

The girl leaped to pick it up and inquisitively spread out the sheet but the woman snatched at it and said sharply:

'Run outside, you two. I've got to get my tea on.' The girl went slowly, plainly manifesting her itch to get her nose into that letter. At the door she turned and said craftily:

'Mrs Leitrim was crying when she went away.' Her tone invited questions. But Mrs Macdonald shut the door in her face.

That letter!

When she had read it she quietly laid it down upon the table and went out and brought in some sticks. She set the fire and lit it. But when she reached to lift down the steak from the nail on which it hung in the porch she missed it, blinded by the gush of tears which ran down her face. The meat smelled. That mattered nothing; it always did in the summer; some vinegar water would fix that. But Mrs Macdonald brushed her tears aside so as not to miss any of the maggots in the creases; Mike had a peculiar and ridiculous antipathy to meat which had been blown. She hurried to get them all off before he came. She did not want to be crying when he came, either. A little flare of malicious satisfaction, the tiniest flare possible, shot up in her when she thought of Mike, but was gone almost before she realized it. She had a wish, somehow,—it must have been her pride—not even to appear to crow over Mike. She wanted to act as though Mike had never mentioned Mrs Leitrim to her, nor given a thought to her perfections.

Men! A lot they knew about women! And the less they knew the better. She had sense enough not to poke her nose into Mike's jaunts into Westport. As long as things were all right they were all right. But that poor soul! Despite herself Mrs Macdonald was crying when Mike came in. The two oldest children were with him, crowding him, chattering volubly.

'Here,' he said at once to his wife. 'What's this the kids are saying about Mrs Leitrim? That she's gone down the hill and left a letter for you?' He stared at his wife's hot, wet face.

'Send them out, Mike,' she said.

'Why?' But he told them to 'shunt,' nevertheless, and when they disappeared took the letter from his wife with a half-ashamed, bullying eagerness. His face as he read that letter was a study. If his wife had been a malicious woman she would have felt amply recompensed for the botherment he had caused her. Mike was too naive to hide his emotions; his blank dismay and consternation. And his—yes, and his jealousy too. He read it and stood there grimacing, thinking his funny faces a grin, and the paper fluttered to the floor.

Mrs Macdonald gave him one glance and then busied herself round her frying-pan, but her tears flowed faster than ever and she knew that she was crying for Mike, for her poor old Mike.

He grunted, coughed and tried to speak, becoming aware of his wife.

To give him respite she said casually:

'You'd better get the coal in, Mike. Tea won't be long.' He took up the butter box they used for a scuttle and went outside. When he returned he was mad; plain mad. His jealousy had come uppermost and he vented it in the form of virtuous denunciations. The only form possible to him. His wife knew that he was still quite unconscious of his real condition. He was sincere enough.

'So she's gone, ay?' He dropped the coal-box with a thud. 'Gone to her precious Jarvis, who'll take her away to America. America!' He seemed to be struck to the heart with realization of the distance between him and America. He stood beside his wife with hanging, limp arms and dropped jaw, his eyes peering from under his bushy red brows, following Mrs Leitrim to America. He looked like a child in pain.

'Oh, Mike!' Mrs Macdonald said. Then threw the apron she had donned over her head and cried loudly.

'Now don't you cry for her!' He almost bawled. 'I won't have my wife crying for her! A mother! A fine mother! A perfect mother! By God! And she's gone to a man and left them!'

'No, No! Mike! It isn't the man she's gone for. It's the politics, the life. I always told her she wanted light.'

'Well, isn't it the same thing? Hasn't she left them?' He marched around the room with hunched shoulders and pugnacious jaw, trying to rid himself of his mortification by shouting it at his wife. His panegyrics of Mrs Leitrim's perfect motherhood and housewifery had been eloquent and intense, but had never touched the oratorical altitudes reached by the floods of abuse and invective her perfidy now provoked from him. He picked the letter off the floor and flourished it, picking out phrases here and there.

'And she calls my wife—my wife, mind you, Rosie—her best and dearest friend. I don't want her sort calling my wife her dearest friend. She can get her friends in America, where she's going with Jarvis. My wife's a decent woman.'

A dangerous light began to creep into Mrs Macdonald's eye. Her tears were properly dry now, swallowed up in the flood of Mike's rhetoric. She watched him and thought of lots of things, but mostly of Mrs Leitrim's strained, questioning look and of her:

'I depended on you, Mrs Macdonald.' Mike smote the letter with his hand. A good hard-working hand, never meant to pull the ropes of domestic finesse, and continued:

'She couldn't stand it any longer, couldn't she? My wife can stand it and so can other women. And she knows "you'll take care of my babies, Mrs Macdonald, you are so good and true and so perfect a mother." My God! My wife to take her kids and keep them! I'm to keep her kids! while she gallivants to America with Jarvis! Politics!' Mike metaphorically spat. 'Well, her kids can go to hell where she's gone.—' But here Mike stopped. He was compelled to stop by the flat of Mrs Macdonald's hand across his mouth. She was no longer the amiable, easy-going soul; no longer the soft tolerant looker-on; but a woman inflamed to do battle for her sex; the faithful and understanding fighting for her friend. She faced him like a splendid virago, and Mike's bitterness and broken love was smitten out of his simple soul by her greatness in this, the supreme moment of her life.

For it is to each according to his station. Heroines of history may garb their thoughts in heroic words, and high-flown ladies in times of stress find a language befitting the dignity of their place. Mike and his wife belonged to the mines, and their talk furnished all that they needed. It was ugly at times and usually coarse, but—.

Mike lost nothing of the loveliness that lay in the core of his wife's strident, passionate outburst.

'You shut your mouth! Shut your mouth! You're always yapping, yapping, yapping, about something you know nothing about! You shut your mouth and get over to Leitrim's and get those kids! Do you hear? Get over and get them and then wait for him!'

(Leitrim worked till five o'clock.)

And when Mike had gone Mrs Macdonald heaved a great sigh and trembled a little. Then she turned to the stove and took the tough steak off it. It still smelt a little, the meat, but she thought it would not be so bad if she put plenty of tomato sauce in the gravy. And as she dealt out each one's portion, six pieces in all, she subsided back into her old soft, lollopy sweetness and murmured:

'Oh, well, two kids won't make much difference.'

Greville Texidor

HOME FRONT

The small sharp hills over-lapping like green waves converged on the train. The sun flashed out and the dead trees littering the hillside shone like white bones. Then it was raining again. The train stopped at a station and the carriages were suddenly empty. The passengers surged into the cafe, then hurried back with moist white sandwiches and tea. The station where Rex got down was only a long shed with an iron roof, standing alone in the middle of the green.

It was raining again, and there was no one about to tell him the way to Isaiah Chapman's place. He hailed a car that was passing along the road and the man driving said he would take him to Chapman's.

Old Chap as we call him is a cousin of mine, he told Rex. We're pretty near all related around here.

Rex asked about the farm.

Well, it's a pretty place, said the man. The park we call it. He has this hobby of growing fruit and other trees. It was clear the other dairy farmers thought it a crazy hobby. It's behind the hills over there, he said. There's a shorter way through the paddocks.

The mountains in the distance that looked wild and grand under the rain were only hills when they got up to them. Little green calvaries topped with tall dead trees.

I suppose it doesn't pay, said Rex.

It doesn't. But Isaiah's an old man. You can't tell him anything. He's really more of an idealist than a farmer.

Then, remembering he was talking to Rex he looked a bit awkward and said, You'll be the new man, I suppose? Oh well, I hope you'll like it here. Old Chap's a great Bible reader and all that, but a real good sort when you get to know him.

Rex was put down at the gate and waded through mud the half mile to the house. Mrs Chapman welcomed him at the back door and made him take off his shoes in the kitchen. She asked him if he had had a pleasant journey from Auckland and he said, Yes, very pleasant.

I expect you will find it very wet and muddy, she said, it's our normal winter state. But the spring flowers are coming on apace. Are you a flower lover too?

Mr Chapman would be in soon, she said, and Rex would like a wash in the bathroom after his journey. That means they don't wash there themselves, thought Rex. It was cold in the bathroom. The solitary towel hanging beside the coffin-shaped bath was hard and thin. Round the walls stood bottles of petrified plums and jam, all neatly labelled with the name of the fruit and the date. There were several years of fruit and jam on the shelves.

Mrs Chapman was waiting outside in the passage to show him the way to his room. The room held the cold of a whole winter. The lino was shiny as ice. A framed printed card, hung near the dressing table, looked like the rules they have up in hotel bedrooms. Rex read, To A Pound Of Love Add A Liberal Measure Of Understanding And Mix. On the dressing table was a doily, and a shell with a ship painted on it that no one could ever mistake for an ashtray.

Facing the walnut double bed with its blue-white cover, two dreadfully enlarged Chapman ancestors in thick dark oval frames possessed the room. They had dark flaws in their faces like craters on the moon. Behind the glass a cheek-bone, a button on the man's coat, and a highlight on his hair stared blankly.

Rex began to unpack, looking for dry shoes. His brush and comb looked so uncomfortable beside the shell with the painted ship that he began to feel, not homesick for any particular place, but lonely and stranded. He reminded himself of other rooms he had slept in. This one would be no worse when it had been lived in. Someone must have slept in the bed once, and sat at the dressing table doing their hair, and looked through the window over the fields when it wasn't raining like this.

Rex opened a door which he thought was a cupboard, but it opened into a small sitting room which had the same clean but stale smell. This end of the house was a blind alley. There was a fluted fireplace and a firescreen with birds on it, an upright piano, upholstered chairs and a round walnut table. Rex smiled over the things laid out on the table. The velvet album, the stereoscope, the Family Bible. These objects looked familiar, he had met them so often in books. They were always amusing. He tried to think of a funny formula for the room, but nothing crossed his mind but the Spanish slang-word, *fatal*.

Thinking of Spain Rex saw the sun on the white wall of a house. Big black ants were busy about the cracks in the plaster. Pots of carnations basked by the wall. A fat red flower burst its sheath with a silent explosion.

The shadow under the fig tree is round like a pool. Dipping your hand in the shadow you feel its edge like water. Jim is sitting waiting under the fig tree where the plates and salads are set in the shade. The midday silence is full of life, and an exuberant smell of flowers and frying.

An old peasant sits down at the table, and cocking his head at Jim hands him a wine skin. Jim takes off his shirt, is standing up and throwing his head right back to catch the crimson trickle that floods his teeth. He raises the wine skin higher and higher. The wine falls in a thin bright arc.

Rex was lucky. He had had two years of living up to the hilt, then slipped out when the game was up. He hadn't said goodbye to his Spanish friends. Jim had been killed at Huesca.

Perhaps, Rex thought, his excitements over committees, his travels, his political work which had led in the end to Spain, were only forms of escape from what he was feeling now in the Sunday smell of the sitting room.

He was young when it first got him. It was after dinner. The rain seemed to have set in and he had settled down with a book, when suddenly the sun came out in the watery way and he was told to go and play in the garden.

There was nothing in the garden but the long watery afternoon with Monday on its horizon. He walked down the path till he came to a jungle of trees and a high brick wall at the end. This was called 'down the garden.' Under the dripping wall was the puppy's grave, and an over-turned flowerpot which Rex sat on when he cried about something. He didn't cry now. This wasn't something that had happened. It was there.

You're just a lump of misery, Master Rex, his nurse would say when he had the Sunday feeling. He grew out of it. It only came back in waiting rooms, and long dull dreams. But when it did he knew it was there all the time, and his interesting life was only painted over it.

The door of the sitting room creaked and a child came in. A plain little thing in a gym tunic.

Dinner is nearly ready, Mr Rex.

So you are Lila, said Rex, and the child came over to him.

Were you looking at the pictures? That's St Peter's at Rome on top.

I've seen that one, said Rex. It has a great wide space in front dotted with frozen fountains.

Oh Mr Rex, could you play the piano then? Can you play a hymn? Our Lord Is Ever Present has a pretty tune.

I might have a try sometime.

Oh do have a pop at it, Mr Rex.

But not now. I think they're calling you to lay the table.

Mr Chapman was small and bald, and wore a neat white beard. He shook hands with Rex and they all sat down to the meal. After piling the plates with pumpkin and potato, the old lady abruptly laid her hand on her forehead as a signal. They bent their heads in an attitude of prayer. During the next few minutes' silence Rex looked through his fingers at Lila, searching her dull face for a clue that would lead back to Jim.

Rex sat facing the clear blue eyes of the old man. He talked in a slow, high, gentle voice about the government and the weather. He seemed to be looking at Rex from a long way off. He said something about Spain. That it was through lack of faith that the Republicans had perished. But when Rex began to argue the point he was not listening. Rex thought at first that he was deaf, but he was not deaf. He was only out of focus.

Mrs Chapman kept urging Rex to have some more.

I hope our simple fare agrees with your taste, she said. Our neighbours don't bother to grow veges, but Isaiah has been on a sort of diet for years. You forget to eat while you're talking, she said to her husband.

I have sufficient for my needs, said Mr Chapman. Then turning to Rex, he began to denounce the forces of evil which he said were undermining the churches. Rex didn't know what the forces were.

Whether it was the brewers or the Catholics or the Anglicans who were doing all the harm. When he appeared to have finished Rex tried to say a word about Jim. But the old chap had withdrawn again, and was absorbed in scraping the burnt edge off the pudding dish.

In the afternoon they went round the farm. The mud was so deep it oozed over the tops of the good boots Rex had been given in Spain. Rex had to see everything, Mr Chapman pointed out the places where he should have sown lupins to keep down the weeds, and telling him where things were, and where they used to be, and what might have to be done sometime.

Half his words were lost in the sudden gusts of wind that passed with a rattle of rain on the iron roofs like the sound of machine guns, leaving a dead stillness behind, and the rain quietly falling. Then the sun burst out with a startling feverish glare between the black clouds and the shivering green of the pastures.

Rex spoke of a plan that Jim had made for the farm. The old man stood very close to him while he was talking, as though he was waiting for something. Like a child who has run up with a treasure in his hand, and well-trained, waits quiet and expectant, until the people have finished their talk and will look at it. The old man waited, then with a meek insistent smile, he brought out what he had hoarded up to say.

They walked and walked through wet grass. Mr Chapman was amazingly active, and rosy as a child, but from time to time a wave of milky pallor flooded his face, like the first waves of death lapping over him, and receding so gently that he was unaware.

You see yon trees, he said happily. I have seen them all grow.

He started little gardens all over the place. Stopping at one of these forgotten gardens he said, That was Jim's garden. It's Lila now, but she doesn't take care of it much.

The afternoon seemed endless. When they got back Mrs Chapman and Lila had changed into different dresses and they had tea, stewed apples and scones and home-baked bread. Mr Chapman was quiet now, he had talked himself out. Mrs Chapman was worried because she had made too much tea, and Rex had to have a third cup. The child would go to bed soon, and then they would want to hear about Jim's death.

But when supper was over Mr Chapman began to turn the knob of the radio. There are several services on the air he said. Managing the radio the old man was pathetic. He got first a waltz, then someone talking fast in a frightening voice, but at last the organ burst bitterly through. The Presbyterians I believe, he said. He smiled like a conjurer. I hope that will be agreeable to you.

Rex longed to smoke to take the edge off it, but it was no good upsetting these left-behind old things the first night.

After the service ended Mr Chapman drew his chair to the table and began to write very slowly in a large book. Rex, passing behind him to get nearer the fire read, 'August 28. Burnt bullock in three days.'

Mr Chapman read over what he had written and shut the book. Mrs Chapman counted stitches.

Shall I bring in a log or two? asked Mr Chapman.

I hardly think it's worth it, said Mrs Chapman, looking at Rex for assent.

I suppose you heard that Jim died very bravely. I sent back the few things he always carried with him. You got them all right?

Mrs Chapman nodded. Yes thank you, we got the parcel. And then we got your letter saying you would be coming out to New Zealand just the same.

I didn't give the details of his death in my letter. Rex seemed to be saying a lesson to the old things who happened to be Jim's parents. What was left of Jim seemed now to be lost between the three of them.

He had only been ten days up at the front. The front was changing all the time and we never knew where we were, but Jim and I were always together. On this day they asked for volunteers to go to some comrades with a machine gun a bit further up the road that went to Huesca. The road was impassable, but there was some cover beside it. We thought someone could get round with a mule load of stuff. They were out of munitions, you see. Jim passed an open vineyard, but when he was under the trees a stray bullet got him.

Rex got through the story he had told again and again. It was stale even before he had begun to tell it, because so many people had been killed that way.

The old man frowned, seemed to be groping for something. Mrs Chapman flushed and swallowed. Rex thought, They still don't really believe it.

Do I understand you to say that my son met his death as a soldier, a combatant?

Why certainly, said Rex. He was a good soldier. He died like a hero.

They sat in silence while a death ripple passed over the face of the old man.

It must have been a terrible shock to you, Rex said.

It is a terrible shock, said Mr Chapman.

You see we didn't know, said his wife. He went over to do relief work for the Quakers.

Of course. Anyone could have known it. Jim had even told him once about some sect his father belonged to. Why couldn't he have remembered? How easy it would have been to say their son was killed bringing in a wounded comrade. He might have been killed any day bringing children away from Madrid. The idiocy of implying that Jim was a fighter. Even his death of a hero had been an accident. Other people had been over there to the machine gun post and nothing had happened, till in the end it seemed pretty safe to go.

Done now. Couldn't be helped now. He would leave in a day or two and find a job in Auckland, perhaps get back to Europe before the next war started. Thank God he'd hedged when he'd replied to the old man's letter offering him a job on the farm.

Well I suppose it's time to turn in, he said.

You know the way to your room, said Mrs Chapman. There's an extra blanket under the mattress if you should need it.

She said goodnight and went out to the kitchen, where Rex could hear her fussing about preparing for breakfast.

Now that Rex had said goodnight and was standing up he wanted

Mr Chapman to understand. It was easy now. The same as when you leave a house and have a last word over the fence, or when you go to bed and come back for something and stay for hours talking to the person you've supposed to have left.

If you had been there yourself I know you would understand, he said. At the front you were spiritually safe, but when you went on leave you'd find you couldn't sit in certain cafés because the 'others' were there. Jim thought it was mostly the fault of the foreigners who were coming and going, raising money and sympathy for Spain, and raising hell too. Political parties couldn't agree about what their adherents were dying for. Jim couldn't have stood any more without losing his faith.

I thought he had stuck to the Quakers because they did the least harm. They were too busy saving children's lives. But as the war went on there was too much relief and advice. Jim said he wouldn't consider the children saved if the war was lost. One day he'd been to the centre with posters they'd asked him to get. Pictures of children playing and studying with underneath, Revolution In Education. They blacked out the R before they would use them. So Jim walked out and joined the Brigade.

If only Mr Chapman would sit still. He was busy again searching methodically among the papers on top of the bookshelf. He brought down a brown paper parcel, and coming quietly round the table while Rex talked laid it in front of him.

Some of Jim's books.

Perhaps some weeks before he had thought about the books and placed the parcel there where he could easily find it, to show Jim's friend. Though he seemed so vague the little plan, independent of anything that might intervene, had firmly stuck in his mind. So now Rex had to sit down at the table again and open the parcel, and turn the leaves of the books. The first page of an exercise book had written on it in curly writing:—

September 4th 1915.   *Padded*
                Purr
                whisker curley
                claws paws
                hungry rosy

Poetry
This is the weather the cuckoo loves
And so do I
Be careful always look first to right and then to left
People generally travel on camels when crossing

Dead said the frost
Buried and lost
The leaf buds are covered with tough leather flaps called scales
We must not bring razor blades to school because they are dangerous
Do unto others (I know the rest) This is called the Golden Rule . . .

Well, I think I'll turn in now, Rex said. I'll take the books with me if you don't mind.

Certainly, said Mr Chapman. We rise at six-thirty in winter. I hope you will find your room comfortable. We call it the guest room now. I thought you might find it more convenient later to sleep in a smaller room that opens onto the back verandah. It's very handy for the sheds and you wouldn't bring dirt into the house. That's a great consideration with Mrs Chapman you know. But there is time enough to make the change after you have started work and become familiar with our way of life. Mrs Chapman was insistent that you should have Jim's room at first. I suppose you saw his picture over the bed?

Frank Sargeson

A GREAT DAY

It was beginning to get light when Ken knocked on the door of Fred's bach.

Are you up? he said.

Fred called out that he was, and in a moment he opened the door.

Just finished my breakfast, he said. We'd better get moving.

It didn't take long. The bach was right on the edge of the beach, and they got the dinghy on to Ken's back and he carried it down the beach, and Fred followed with the gear. Ken was big enough to make light work of the dinghy but it was all Fred could do to manage the gear. There wasn't much of him and he goddamned the gear every few yards he went.

The tide was well over half-way out, and the sea was absolutely flat without even a ripple breaking on the sand. Except for some seagulls that walked on the sand and made broad-arrow marks where they walked there wasn't a single thing moving. It was so still it wasn't natural. Except for the seagulls you'd have thought the world had died in the night.

Ken eased the dinghy off his shoulders and turned it the right way up, and Fred dropped the anchor and the oars on the sand, and heaved the sugar bag of fishing gear into the dinghy.

I wouldn't mind if I was a big hefty bloke like you, he said.

Well, Ken didn't say anything to that. He sat on the stern of the dinghy and rolled himself a cigarette, and Fred got busy and fixed the oars and rowlocks and tied on the anchor.

Come on, he said, we'll shove off. And with his trousers rolled up he went and tugged at the bow, and with Ken shoving at the stern the dinghy began to float, so Fred hopped in and took the oars, and then Ken hopped in and they were off.

It's going to be a great day, Fred said.

It certainly looked like it. The sun was coming up behind the island they were heading for, and there wasn't a cloud in the sky.

We'll make for the same place as last time, Fred said. You tell me if I don't keep straight. And for a time he rowed hard without sending the dinghy along very fast. The trouble was his short legs, he couldn't get them properly braced against the stern seat. And Ken, busy rolling a supply of cigarettes, didn't watch out where he was going, so when Fred took a look ahead he was heading for the wrong end of the island.

Hey, he said, you take a turn and I'll tell you where to head for.

So they changed places and Ken pulled wonderfully well. For a time it was more a mental shock you got with each jerk of the dinghy. You realised how strong he was. He had only a shirt and a pair of shorts on, and his big body, hard with muscle, must have been over six feet long.

Gee, I wish I had your body, Fred said. It's no wonder the girls chase you. But look at the sort of joker I am.

Well, he wasn't much to look at. There was so little of him. And the old clothes he wore had belonged to someone considerably bigger than he was. And he had on an old hat that came down too far, and would have come down further if it hadn't bent his ears over and sat on them as if they were brackets.

How about a smoke? Fred said.

Sure. Sorry.

And to save him from leaving off rowing Fred reached over and took the tin out of his shirt pocket.

That's the curse of this sustenance, Fred said. A man's liable to be out of smokes before pay-day.

Yes, I suppose he is, Ken said.

It's rotten being out of work, Fred said. Thank the Lord I've got this dinghy. D'you know last year I made over thirty pounds out of fishing?

And how've you done this year?

Not so good. You're the first bloke I've had go out with me this year that hasn't wanted me to go shares. Gee, you're lucky to be able to go fishing for fun.

It's about time I landed a position, Ken said. I've had over a month's holiday.

Yes I know. But you've got money saved up, and it doesn't cost you anything to live when you can live with your auntie. How'd you like to live in that damn bach of mine and pay five bob a week rent? And another thing, you've got education.

It doesn't count for much these days. A man has to take any position he can get.

Yes, but if a man's been to one of those High Schools it makes him different. Not any better, mind you. I'm all for the working class because I'm a worker myself, but an educated bloke has the advantage over a bloke like me. The girls chase him just to mention one thing, specially if he happens to be a big he-man as well.

Ken didn't say anything to that. He just went on pulling, and he got Fred to stick a cigarette in his mouth and light it at the same time as he lit his own. And then Fred lolled back in his seat and watched him, and you could tell that about the only thing they had in common was that they both had cigarettes dangling out of their mouths.

Pull her round a bit with your left, Fred said. And there's no need to bust your boiler.

It's O.K. Ken said.

You've got the strength, Fred said.

I'm certainly no infant.

What good's a man's strength anyway? Say he goes and works in an office?

I hadn't thought of that.

Another thing, he gets old. Fancy you getting old and losing your strength. Wouldn't it be a shame?

Sure, Ken said. Why talk about it?

It sort of fascinates me. You'll die someday, and where'll that big frame of yours be then?

That's an easy one. Pushing up the daisies.

It might as well be now as anytime, mightn't it?

Good Lord, I don't see that.

A man'd forget for good. It'd be just the same as it is out here on a day like this. Only better.

Ken stopped rowing to throw away his cigarette.

My God, he said, you're a queer customer. Am I heading right?

Pull with your left, Fred said. But I'll give you a spell.

It's O.K. Ken said.

And he went on rowing and after a bit Fred emptied the lines out of the sugar bag and began cutting up the bait. And after a bit longer when they were about half-way over to the island he said they'd gone far enough, so Ken shipped his oars and threw the anchor overboard, and they got their lines ready and began to fish.

And by that time it was certainly turning out a great day. The sun was getting hot but there still wasn't any wind, and as the tide had just about stopped running out down the Gulf the dinghy hardly knew which way to pull on the anchor rope. They'd pulled out less than two miles from the shore, but with the sea as it was it might have been anything from none at all up to an infinite number. You couldn't hear a sound or see anything moving. It was another world. The houses on the shore didn't belong. Nor the people either.

Wouldn't you like to stay out here for good? Fred said.

Ring off, Ken said. I got a bite.

So did I, but it was only a nibble. Anyhow it's not a good day for fish. It wants to be cloudy.

So I've heard.

I've been thinking, Fred said, it's funny you never learnt to swim.

Oh I don't know. Up to now I've always lived in country towns.

Doesn't it make you feel a bit windy?

On a day like this! Anyhow, you couldn't swim that distance yourself.

Oh couldn't I! You'd be surprised . . . get a bite?

Yes I did.

Same here . . . you'll be settling down here, won't you, Ken?

It depends if I can get a position.

I suppose you'll go on living with your auntie.

That depends too. If I got a good position I might be thinking of getting married.

Gee, that'd be great, wouldn't it?

I got another bite, Ken said.

Same here. I reckon our lines are crossed.

So they pulled in their lines and they were crossed sure enough, but Ken had hooked the smallest snapper you ever saw.

He's no good, Fred said. And he worked the fish off the hook and held it in his hand. They're pretty little chaps, aren't they? he said. Look at his colours.

Let him go, Ken said.

Poor little beggar, Fred said. I bet he wonders what's struck him. He's trying to get his breath. Funny isn't it, when there's plenty of air about? It's like Douglas Credit.

Oh for God's sake, Ken said.

I bet in less than five minutes he forgets about how he was nearly suffocated, Fred said, and he threw the fish back. And it lay bewildered for a second on the surface, then it flipped its tail and was gone. It was comical in its way and they both laughed.

They always do that, Fred said. But don't you wish you could swim like him?

Ken didn't say anything to that and they put fresh bait on their hooks and tried again, but there were only nibbles. They could bring nothing to the surface.

I'll tell you what, Fred said, those nibbles might be old men snapper only they won't take a decent bite at bait like this.

And he explained that off the end of the island there was a reef where they could get plenty of big mussels. It would be just nice with the tide out as it was. The reef wouldn't be uncovered, it never was, but you could stand on it in water up to your knees and pull up the mussels. And if you cut the inside out of a big mussel you only had to hang it on your hook for an old man snapper to go for it with one big bite.

It's a fair way, Ken said.

It doesn't matter, Fred said. We've got oceans of time. And he climbed past Ken to pull up the anchor, and Ken pulled in the lines, and then Fred insisted on rowing and they started for the end of the island.

And by that time the tide had begun to run in up the Gulf and there was a light wind blowing up against the tide, so that the sea, almost without your noticing it, was showing signs of coming up a bit rough. And the queer thing was that with the movement the effect of another world was destroyed. You seemed a part of the real world of houses and people once more. Yet with the sea beginning to get choppy the land looked a long way off.

Going back, Ken said, we'll be pulling against the wind.

Yes, Fred said, but the tide'll be a help. Anyhow, what's it matter when a man's out with a big hefty bloke like you?

Nor did he seem to be in too much of a hurry to get to his reef. He kept resting on his oars to roll cigarettes, and when Ken said something about it he said they had oceans of time.

You're in no hurry to get back, he said, Mary'll keep.

Well, Ken didn't say anything to that.

Mary's a great kid, Fred said.

Sure, Ken said. Mary's one of the best.

I've known Mary for years, Fred said.

Yes, Ken said. So I've gathered.

I suppose you have. Up to a while ago Mary and I used to be great cobbers.

I'll give you a spell, Ken said.

But Fred said it was O.K.

Mary's got a bit of education too, he said. Only when her old man died the family was hard up so she had to go into service. It was lucky she got a good place at your auntie's. Gee, I've been round there and had tea sometimes when your auntie's been out, and oh boy is the tucker any good!

Look here, Ken said, at this rate we'll never get to that reef.

Oh yes we will, Fred said, and he pulled a bit harder. If only a man hadn't lost his job, he said.

I admit it must be tough, Ken said.

And then Fred stood up and took a look back at the shore.

I thought there might be somebody else coming out, he said, but there isn't. So thank God for that. And he said that he couldn't stand anybody hanging around when he was fishing. By the way, he said, I forgot to do this before. And he stuffed pieces of cotton-wool into his ears. If the spray gets in my ears it gives me the earache, he said.

Then he really did settle down to his rowing, and with the sea more or less following them it wasn't long before they were off the end of the island.

Nobody lived on the island. There were a few holiday baches but they were empty now that it was well on into the autumn. Nor from this end could you see any landing places, and with the wind blowing up more and more it wasn't too pleasant to watch the sea running up the rocks. And Fred had to spend a bit of time manoeuvring around before he found his reef.

It was several hundred yards out with deep water all round, and it seemed to be quite flat. If the sea had been calm it might have been covered to a depth of about a foot with the tide as it was. But with the sea chopping across it wasn't exactly an easy matter to stand there. At one moment the water was down past your knees, and the next moment you had to steady yourself while it came up round your thighs. And it was uncanny to stand there, because with the deep water all round you seemed to have discovered a way of standing up out in the sea.

Anyhow, Fred took off his coat and rolled up his sleeves and his trousers as far as they'd go, and then he hopped out and got Ken to do the same and keep hold of the dinghy. Then he steadied himself and began dipping his hands down and pulling up mussels and throwing them back into the dinghy, and he worked at a mad pace as though he hadn't a moment to lose. It seemed only a minute or so before he was quite out of breath.

It's tough work, he said. You can see what a weak joker I am.

I'll give you a spell, Ken said, only keep hold of the boat.

Well, Fred held the dinghy, and by the way he was breathing and the look of his face you'd have thought he was going to die. But Ken had other matters to think about, he was steadying himself and dipping his hands down more than a yard away, and Fred managed to pull himself together and shove off the dinghy and hop in. And if you'd been sitting in the stern as he pulled away you'd have seen that he had his eyes shut.

Nor did he open them except when he took a look ahead to see where he was going, and with the cotton-wool in his ears it was difficult for him to hear.

So for a long time he rowed like that against seas that were getting bigger and bigger, but about half-way back to the shore he took a spell. He changed over to the other side of the seat, so he didn't have to sit facing the island, and he just sat there keeping the dinghy straight on. Then when he felt that he had collected all his strength he stood up and capsized the dinghy. It took a bit of doing but he did it.

And after that, taking it easy, he started on his long swim for the shore.

Frank Sargeson

OLD MAN'S STORY

He was sitting there on the waterfront, and off and on I watched him while he read the newspaper. He looked a frail old man, I don't mean feeble, just frail. Delicate. You see such old men about and you wonder how it is they've lived so long, how it is that some sickness hasn't carried them off long ago. You think perhaps life has always been easy for them, you look at their hands and feel sure about it. Though hands will sometimes deceive you just as much as faces.

It was good to be sitting there on the waterfront. Besides the old man there were ships alongside the wharves to look at, and the sea, and seagulls. The seagulls were making their horrid squabbling noises. It was because of a slice of buttered bread lying close to our seat, the butter gone soft and yellow in the sun. The seagulls wanted it, but didn't dare to come so close to us, and I watched them, wanting to see if they'd have the courage. Then the old man frightened the birds away by saying the word, Terrible! I looked at him and his cheeks had turned red, and I understood it was because of something he'd read in the newspaper.

Have you seen this? he said, and I leaned over to see the column he was pointing to.

Yes, I said. It was about a man, an adult man and a young girl. A Court case.

Terrible! the old man said.

Yes? I said. Maybe you're right. Anyhow, I said, five years in gaol is terrible.

Yes, the old man said, five years in gaol. Terrible!

Oh, I said, I get you. I don't go much on putting people away, I said.

No, the old man said, it's terrible.

But people say, I said, what can you do?

I don't know, the old man said. But I knew of a case once. It didn't get into the newspapers.

Well, the old man told me, and it was quite a story. It had all happened when he was a boy, fourteen years old perhaps, or thereabouts. He'd just finished school and for a time he went and worked on his uncle's farm.

It was a nice place, he said, an old place in a part of the country that had been settled very early. The farms round about were all old places, most of them were run by the families that had been the first to settle there. There were old orchards everywhere, and plenty of trees, English trees that had been planted right at the beginning. Some people went in for crops and some ran cows, but besides they'd have poultry and bees, and everybody had an orchard. Life was pretty quiet there, the old man said, there wasn't any hurry and bustle, it was just real old-fashioned country life. Now and then there'd be a picnic in the school grounds, where the trees were very thick and shady, or perhaps they'd hold a dance in the school itself, but that was about all. You couldn't have found a nicer place, the old man said. His uncle's house was an old place just about buried in a tangle of honeysuckle and rambler roses, not the sort of farmhouse it's so easy to find nowadays. The railway ran alongside but it was a branch line, there weren't many trains and they'd run at any old times. Why, the old man said, he could remember one time when the driver stopped the train to get off and buy a watermelon from his uncle. But nobody worried, because people took life differently in those days.

As a boy the old man used to spend his school holidays there, and he'd enjoy himself no end, so when he finished school his people sent him to help his uncle. They thought perhaps he might turn out a farmer. Anyhow it suited him fine. There were just his uncle and his aunt (they'd never had any children), both easy-going, good-natured sorts, and a man they'd had working on the place for years. This man was a little wiry fellow with a mop of curly hair that he never brushed, and a wrinkled face that was always grinning at you. It was a wicked grin, the old man said, one eye'd close up a lot more than the other. Anyhow he was quite a character. He'd turned up one day with a swag on his back, been given a job, and never moved on for years. He was no chicken, in his fifties perhaps; and they used to call him Bandy; though one leg was a lot bandier than the other. He'd had that one broken more times than he could remember was the yarn he told. When he was a boy he'd gone to sea, he said, and several times he'd fallen from aloft. But he told so many yarns about his life in different parts of the world it was hard to say whether they were all true. He was Irish, the old man said, and had the real Irishman's way of telling you far-fetched yarns. Anyhow he milked the cows and was generally useful about the place. He taught the boy to milk and the two of them were in each other's company the most part of each day. Once you got to know him, the old man said, he was a regular hard case to talk to, his aunt would have had a blue-fit if she'd found out.

But of course it was only natural for a boy that age to listen to Bandy and never let on. He was curious about life, he had to find things out sooner or later, and thinking it over later on he reckoned he'd learned more from Bandy than he ever had out of his Sunday school books. It was pretty strong stuff, granted, it had a real tang to it, but it was honest stuff all the same. Nor did it ever get him excited so far as he could remember, not in a physical way anyhow. When Bandy'd tell him he'd been with white black brown and yellow and was still clean, he never had any other feeling except a sort of hero-worship for him. It was the same as if Bandy had said he'd had fights with all colours and had always knocked the other fellow out without ever getting a scratch himself. People forget when they grow up, the old man said. Maybe they've learned to play safe by shying away from the strong stuff, but they forget it would never have appealed to them as children in anything like the same way. Children live in a different world, the old man said.

Anyhow, that was the position when the old man was a boy of about fourteen working on his uncle's farm. He was enjoying the life in that old-fashioned neighbourhood, and he was great cobbers with this Bandy, this hard old case; and besides teaching him to milk cows Bandy was every day telling him what was what. Neither his uncle nor his aunt had any idea, he said, they never seemed to worry about his always being with Bandy, and he never told them a thing.

But it turned out things didn't stay like that for very long. One day the boy's aunt went up to town for a holiday, and when she came back she brought home a girl with her. She was quite a young thing, thirteen or fourteen years old perhaps, and small for her age. It seemed she was an orphan and someone had persuaded the old man's aunt to be a good soul and give her a home, to try her out anyhow. Well, her name was Myrtle and she was nothing much to look at. She wore glasses and had curls that hung over her forehead. They made her look a bit silly, the old man said, you felt you'd like to get the scissors and clip them off. She'd annoy you too by always asking, Why? She didn't seem to know much about anything, and you could hardly do a thing without her asking, Why? Still, she seemed to be quite harmless, she helped with the house-work and did everything she was told without making any fuss about it. Nobody took much notice of her but she didn't seem to mind.

Later on, though, the boy noticed that a change had come over Bandy. To begin with he'd been like every one else and hardly taken any notice of Myrtle. Then the boy noticed he'd become interested. Up in the cowshed he'd ask, How's Myrtle this morning? Or picking fruit in the orchard he'd say, We'll keep that one for Myrtle. And the curious thing was, the old man said, Myrtle showed signs of being interested the same way. If Bandy was working in the garden anywhere near the house Myrtle would be sure to start banging about on the verandah with a broom. Bandy'd grin at her (that wicked grin, the old man said), and they wouldn't say much, but you could tell there was a sort of situation between them. One day when Myrtle was out on the verandah Bandy suddenly left off digging and picked a bunch of roses (which he wasn't supposed to do) and gave them to the girl. And instead of saying anything she just dropped the broom and ran inside, and Bandy was sort of overcome as well and went away down the garden leaving the boy to dig on his own. It was the kind of thing a boy notices, the old man said, even though he mightn't be able to make head nor tail of it. Another thing was that Bandy wasn't the company he'd been before. He'd be a bit short with the boy for no reason at all, nor would he talk in the old way. If the boy tried to get him to talk on the old subject he wouldn't bite, or else he'd tell him he'd better behave himself or he'd grow up with a dirty mind. He couldn't make it out, the old man said. The idea he'd got of Bandy right from the beginning made it just impossible for him to make it out. And you only had to look at him and look at Myrtle. So far as they were concerned, one and one didn't make two at all.

Then it happened his uncle began to get an idea of the way the wind was blowing. Perhaps he'd been told about the bunch of roses, the boy didn't know. Bandy began to spend his spare time making a garden seat (one of those rustic contraptions, the old man said). It was on the edge of the orchard, but right up against a hedge where you couldn't see it from the house. And one day when it was about finished the boy tried it out by taking a seat. Well, Bandy told him off properly. He hadn't made it for him to sit on, he said. No, he'd made it for Myrtle. But the boy's uncle just happened to be coming up on the other side of the hedge at the time, and he came round and Bandy got told off properly. The boy only heard half of it because his uncle sent him away, but after that nobody could help seeing the difference in Bandy. He went about looking black, the old man said, he'd be always muttering to himself and he'd make a mess of his work, spilling buckets of milk, putting the cows in the wrong paddock and that sort of thing. And by the way Myrtle looked she must have got a talking to as well. She looked scared, the old man said, and often enough she'd look as if she'd been crying. Nor were the pair of them the only ones you could see the difference in. Everybody in the house was affected. The boy couldn't sleep at night for thinking it all

over, and he'd hear his uncle and aunt talking in bed in the next room.
And he was pretty certain he knew what they were talking about. Why
Myrtle wasn't packed off back where she'd come from he couldn't make
out, but that didn't happen and for some weeks things just drifted along
as they were. He felt very unhappy, the old man said, he was all the time
thinking of writing his people to say he was sick of farming and wanted
to come back home.

All the same things couldn't last as they were. Myrtle wouldn't eat
her meals and Bandy did his work worse and worse. You felt something
was going to happen, the old man said, things were absolutely ripe so to
speak.

Then one evening the boy saw something. It was one evening when
he'd been across to a neighbouring farm for a game of draughts. His aunt
didn't like him being out at night on his own, but he'd begged to go, he
wanted to get away from what was going on in the house. He couldn't
stand it, the old man said. Every night Myrtle'd be sent off to bed
immediately she'd done the dishes, and you'd hear Bandy muttering to
himself in his room which was a lean-to up against the kitchen wall.
Anyhow, coming home this night the boy took a short cut through the
orchard, and looking along a row of trees he saw that somebody was
sitting on the seat Bandy had made. There was a bit of a moon and he
could see something white. He thought of Bandy and Myrtle, of course,
and for a time he waited, not knowing whether it would be safe to go
closer or not. He thought his heart was beating loud enough to give the
show away on its own, and in the dark he felt his cheeks begin to burn.
He was thinking of what he might see. But he couldn't help himself, the
old man said, he had to go closer. And Bandy and Myrtle were sitting on
the seat. Bandy was in his working clothes but Myrtle seemed to be in
her nightgown, at any rate the boy could tell she had bare feet. And they
were sitting there without saying a word, the old man said, sitting a little
apart but holding each other's hands. Every now and then the girl would
turn her face to Bandy and he'd lean over to kiss her; or Bandy would
turn his face and she'd lean over to kiss him. That was all there was to
see, the old man said. Nothing more than that. It amounted to this, that
bad old Bandy had got the girl, this young Myrtle, with her silly curls,
out on the seat with him, and there was nothing doing except those kisses.
And the whole time the boy stood there watching he never heard them
say a thing.

It was a tremendous experience for a boy, the old man said, too big for
him to be at all clear about until later on in life. All he understood at the

time was that he had somehow managed to get life all wrong. Like all boys he thought he'd got to know what was what, but as he stood there in the dark and watched Bandy and Myrtle he understood that he had a lot to learn. He'd been taken in, he thought. It wasn't a pleasant thought, the old man said.

Well, the old man told me the story sitting there on the waterfront. It had all happened a long time ago, and he didn't tell it exactly as I've written it down, but I felt there was something in the story that he wanted to make me see. And I felt it was mainly connected with the part about Bandy and Myrtle sitting on the garden seat, because when he'd told me that part the old man seemed to think his story was finished. He stopped talking and began to fold up his newspaper. But I couldn't leave it at that.

What happened? I said.

Oh, the old man said, my uncle caught the pair of them in Bandy's room one night, and the girl got packed off back where she'd come from.

I see, I said, and the old man got up to go.

And what about Bandy? I said, and I got up to kick the piece of buttered bread over to the seagulls.

Oh, the old man said, one morning when he was supposed to be milking the cows Bandy hanged himself in the cowshed.

Roderick Finlayson

ANOTHER KIND OF LIFE

Let me tell you about going down to the old people's place at Waiari to look up some of the family, especially uncle Tu. You remember, he was one of old Hone Tawa's grandsons who was living there at Waiari just before Hemi died in that motor accident. When he was up in Auckland for the Queen's Birthday races he talked a lot to me about his young days. 'Charlie,' he said, 'you should come down where you people belong. You young fellers don't keep in touch with the old folk.' But you know how it is with a job like driving the buses, you don't get anywhere.

This stopwork in the city give me the chance, so I think now's the time to go and visit uncle and auntie at Waiari. But it was all wrong from the kick-off. I say to the wife, 'The long distance buses are still running and one takes off down the coast early. Grab the baby and let's go.' Well you know, she says there's the two school kids she can't leave and she promised help with the school lunches this week and so on and so on. She's half a Pakeha in more ways than one, if you see what I mean.

In the end I'm so mad I go alone. That's not the Maori way where you take the family too. But that the way it goes now. I got down to Waiari pretty early in the day. Nice sunny morning and the sea looked good and I began wondering about the chance of a load of pipis and mussels, it was a great place for those. But when I tried to get my bearing, golly, it all looked somehow different. I nearly forget where the people live because last time I was down there was grandpa's tangi, old Hone Tawa's youngest son, and I was only a bit of a kid then. Lots of places seemed to have gone and there were a lot of new places like Pakehas live there. Looked like someone was trying to turn it into a holiday place. All used to be Maori land round the old marae.

At last I see on the little hill above the beach the old place I remember where uncle lived. Only now when I look at it it's somehow different too, newer looking, and I see that it's a newer place with a bit of a garden around it. Anyway, up I go and there's a two or three year old playing on the door step and he says hullo, and then he calls out, 'Mummy, there's a man to see you.' And this young woman comes to the door.

Now as for me I can't speak Maori, can't even understand what they say, the old people. But there was me in the old home kainga, in the middle of Maori country, and there was this young woman that looked real Maori, so the words just came naturally. 'Tenaa koe, e hine,' I said to her. I do know that greeting and a few of the old words, you see, not that I'd ever come at old Maori greetings to anyone anywhere in Auckland. But there at Waiari, my people's kainga, it just came natural. And what do you think that young woman said, eh?

She looked puzzled. 'Pardon, what did you say?' she asked, a real Kiwi accent too, not a trace of Maori. But she looked more Maori than me, and I think she don't know one word of Maori. There was me, I look near enough Maori allowing for one or two Pakeha ancestors, and I know how to say tenaa koe and so on. She surely must have heard those Maori words sometime. It got me wondering. Anyhow, I quickly kept to good old plain English from that on.

She turns out to be the girl young nephew Henare married. She wouldn't know me of course. But where was uncle Tu, I asked. Didn't he live there anymore? Oh yes, she says except when he was away at his cousins' place in Rotorua. But today he was away at work. 'Not the work on the farm here, eh?' 'No,' she says, 'the bus comes every morning at six-thirty and take the men to the Metal Industries factory in Pinewood.' He wouldn't be home till late—overtime.

I looked around and think well, well, well! 'Tu must be getting on in years now,' I say. 'Getting a bit old for hard work, eh?' 'He'll get the pension next year,' she tells me, 'but now he's got no land or anything— well, he does what he can.' I remember when I was a kid, uncle talking about his farm, I could think of him happy on the land, his own boss, eh. It's turned out a bit tough for him.

Was I staying? Well, things weren't the same with uncle not there, and one thing and another. 'I better get back to Auckland tonight,' I said. 'The stopwork's over tomorrow and I might lose my job.'

'Oh yes,' she said, 'the job. What do you do in Auckland?'

'Oh, I drive the city bus.'

'Oh,' she says, 'lots of Islanders, aren't there, driving the buses in Auckland? Lots of Islanders. The Islanders might grab your job.'

'Yes, the stopwork ends tomorrow, I better get back.'

'It's last year since Tu had a stopwork. He might have been here to meet you if only he had a stopwork now. But he goes to work every day.'

So I just had a few more words before I go, about how things changed.

'The Pakehas want to get the seaside places,' she tells me, as I noticed. 'And the government people took Tu's land for the big tourist hotels sometime. It isn't the same here anymore.'

Ae, it isn't the same anymore.

So at last I said so long, maybe see you some more. And the kid shouted goodbye as I go out the yard.

Maybe you should never go back. I felt sort of sad and lonely. Down in the settlement by the beach I wondered where the old people were. Not a soul! Surely not all at factory work, or shut up in the house like Pakehas. But I see a big sprawling new motor camp where the old-timers used to sit in the sun and yarn. A cool breeze sprang up, south-east right off the sea and the sun disappeared behind clouds. There was the meeting-house where I remembered being taken at the time of grandpa's tangi, but of course it was shut up now, and it looked a bit more dilapidated. I felt quite cold. There was time before the bus back to Auckland so I think I'll have a drink or two to warm me and cheer me up.

The old wooden pub's gone and there's this new fancy brick place for the tourist. Anyway, I go in the public bar and get me a beer. There was two middle-age Maori men at the far end of the bar and I hear them talking in Maori, but I don't try that trick and make me feel the fool again. And there's one or two Pakehas together. But anyway, I don't feel much like talking to anyone. And the beer don't cheer me or warm me. I knock back a whisky or two. But I still feel chilled and sickly. Not sick, mind you, just sickly, like I might have got on the wrong side of tapu or something like that. But cut that out, I say to myself, don't you go getting like the old people. And anyway, bloody lot you know about tapu.

I listen to the Maori voices of the two men at the other end of the bar and try to make out what they say. But it's no use, I understand only one or two words here and there. What it is, the sad beer or something, I don't know, but it makes me mad when I cannot understand. In Auckland, in the big city, I never get mad when a few times I hear some man speak Maori, but here in my own home kainga, in this Maori place, in all this Maori country I am shamed that I cannot speak my people's language, that I cannot even understand, and it makes me mad. It is because of what the Pakeha did to my father, and to all the other kids' fathers, when they were youngsters. My father told me the teacher strapped him when he was a little boy going to school the first time, and how could he know better. The teacher strapped him, a little Maori boy, for speaking Maori, and then he made him wash out his mouth with soap and water, wash the dirty Maori off his tongue. So my father stopped speaking the Maori. And I never learn.

Golly, that cold pub give me the shivers. I stretch my nerves to understand the words of the two Maori men at the other end of the bar. What the heck! Their words flowed around and about them with a big warm friendly sound. The men look into each other's eyes, and they laugh a bit and they put an arm around the other's shoulder. You can tell they're never alone and cold there in that place where the words warm the heart. Then I think of the bus load of young Maoris I drive up to a marae way up north to talk about the treaty of Waitangi—was it for good or the saddest day ever. And I begin to see what they mean. One time I never had much patience with such people, but I begin to see. They're mad because of what they've lost, everyone pushing them around to turn them Pakeha, and they wake up to find what they've lost. And they get mad. Some things you lose, you can find them again, but other things you lose you know it's for ever, and you mourn, you tangi. And for them that's Waitangi. And for me, the day of uncle Tu and the things dear to his heart, all lost. What the use me coming back to my people that I cannot speak to? And the young woman and her husband and kids lead another kind of life in that old place, something I don't know of. But their talk is what I hope I'd left behind—the stopwork, factory shift, the overtime, the sack.

I wished the Auckland bus comes soon. It was all wrong the way I came down to see uncle. It was because of the stopwork, a Pakeha thing. When a man goes back to his people's old kainga it ought to be because of a Maori thing, he mea Maori, if those the right words—you see, somewhere in the back of my head or my heart the old words kind of whisper, they keep coming up trying to get out, and give me no peace. Anyway, coming back should be because of a Maori happening—such as a tangi. Ae, a tangi for one of us departed, like grandpa when I was a little kid. Maybe it's only death that can bring us city horis back to the heart of our people now.

Then the bus comes. I know I never see my uncle Tu again.

Dan Davin

COMING AND GOING

By the time I'd got myself marched into Base Camp at Maadi and fixed up with a bed I could see it was too late that night for the spree I'd been counting on having in Cairo. Too late to bludge a lift in and rouse up a few old pals. They'd all be out taking their snakes for a walk before I could get there. Still, there was bound to be someone I knew at the Mess. If the worst came to the worst there was always the duty officer.

'Where's everyone, Jack?' I said after I'd scoured the ante-room and the bar.

'They've all gone off to the show at Shafto's, sir. I expect you could do with some scran if you've only just got in?'

'It's a bit late for that, isn't it?'

'Well, the bar's not busy, you can see that. If you'll just sit on that drink for a bit, I'll soon jack you up something. Where'd you like to have it? In the dining-hut?'

'Here'll do just as well if that's OK with you.'

'Right. It'll have to have a bully beef base, though.'

So Jack scratched round in the kitchen and before long I had my entrenching tools into a fine binder of bully fritters and fried tinned potatoes, with any amount of marge and that fig jam we used to get that's all right if you're hungry enough. I was, what with the long trip up from the rest camp and only the unexpended portion of the day's ration for company.

And then Jack fetched over a big pot of tea and two cups and we settled down to a good natter about old times. He used to cook for A Company in the early days. But then he stopped one, I forget where it was, one of the Sidi Rizegh battles I think, and they found out about his age—he'd joined up to keep an eye on his grandsons, some of the blokes used to say. So they dumped him in this job at the depot until his turn came to go back home.

'Who's all here now, Jack?' I asked him when we'd chewed the rag for a bit about the end of the war and all that.

'No one much you'd know, sir. There aren't many left out of the old crowd now. Jimmy Larsen's here on his way back to the unit, he's a captain now. He got a bad one at Ruweisat. Tiger Smith's been on leave and he's going back, too. And there's Ted Tarrant just out of OCTU, you'll remember him, he used to be QM in the November '41 show. And there's Colonel Maitland, he's OC. And Bill Adair.'

'Yes, I saw him on duty when I clocked in.'

'Well, that's about all you'd know. The rest are reinforcements. It's a here today and gone tomorrow sort of place, this. Nothing much for the officers to do except take a parade or two for the look of the thing and censor a few letters.'

'Thank Christ I'll be out of it tomorrow. It sounds worse than death.'

'I suppose that's the idea. I used to think it was Christmas, having a good bludger's job, when I first got here. Now if I hear a Bren go off on the range I get homesick for the unit. And Rommel would be a relief after the sergeant-major.'

There was a banging against the wooden slide in the bar.

'Someone wants a drink,' I said.

'Always some bastard wanting something.' He was out quite a while.

'Anyone I know?' I asked when he was back in the kitchen.

'You'll know him all right.'

'Who, then?'

'Major Reading.'

'What's he doing here? I thought he had A Company.'

'So he did.' Jack got up and began to put the gear away.

I didn't take much notice, beyond spotting he didn't seem to have much time for Reading. But then none of us, men or officers, ever did and I thought it was just this that had made him dry up on me. Anyway, it was a long time since I'd seen Reading. In a long spell on your back you usually see only the chaps in the same ward with you and any of your cobbers who happen to be back from the sharp end. And I was too glad of a bit of company over a few drinks to remember that the last time I'd seen him was when we had the run-in over company boundaries the night before I got knocked at El Mreir.

'I think I'll go round and have a yarn with him.'

Jack said nothing but just gave me a sort of look.

'Thanks very much for the feed, Jack,' I added.

'That's all right, sir. It was nice seeing one of the old faces and talking about old times.'

'I liked it, too, Jack.'

Then I went out through the bar to the ante-room.

Reading didn't look up from the old *Free Lance* he was turning over. But he must have heard me and I fancy he could see me out of the corner of his eye anyhow. He was sitting on the other side of the room from the Mess piano. The wireless was on low and someone was drivelling away in Arabic.

'You don't want to listen to that, do you?' I said and I turned it off. 'Just someone telling the poor wogs about democracy.'

'Oh, it's you, Andy.' He gave me a quick look. I grinned back at him. We were from the same battalion, after all. 'Where've you sprung from?'

'Just back from sick leave. Guaranteed a new man. I've been eating so much white fish and milk pudding it was a waste not having an ulcer. What about a drink?'

He emptied his glass. 'Gin and lemon.'

I went back and knocked on the slide.

'Might as well keep the hatch open now, Jack,' I said. 'One gin and lemon, one whisky and water. Make them doubles. Have one yourself?'

'No, thanks all the same, sir,' he said.

I brought them over to Reading's table and pulled up a chair.

'Here's looking at you,' I said.

'Cheers.'

I was just going to ask him what he was doing. But he got in first.

'Seen any of the others?'

'No, I've only just got in.'

He took his glass in his hand and sat back. The cane chair gave a creak as he relaxed.

'Any of the boys back from the battle in Number One General when you were there?' he asked.

'One or two I didn't know came in just as I was leaving for rest camp. There were a few from our lot in Number Two, they said. These chaps looked pretty bashed about. A bit of an MFU, I gather. But I ought to be asking you. When did you leave them?'

'Oh, I left after the first night on Miteiriya. Have another?'

I watched him go up to the bar. He could have been back on leave, of course. But it seemed queer. After all, you didn't usually swop company commanders on the first night of a battle. Unless you had to.

There were still two wet rings where the last glasses had been. Reading fitted the two new ones in as carefully as if he was playing some kind of game, fiddling with them this way and that until he'd got them exactly right.

'You'd miss the main part of the scrap, then? There was some pretty heavy going, after that.'

'Yes,' he said.

Neither of us spoke for a while. It wasn't a comfortable sort of silence. I ransacked my mind for something to say but I couldn't think of anything. Not my usual trouble.

'Good luck,' I said, picking up my glass. It was the best I could do.

'Good luck,' he said and picked up his.

Then we said nothing again. And I caught myself planting the glass exactly in the ring, the way he had done. This wasn't my idea of an evening. It wasn't even my idea of Reading. In the old days he'd have been shooting some line about what he did in peacetime—he used to be a stock agent I think it was and he'd got mixed up with some of the big station families.

I began to wonder when the others were coming back. It must be getting on towards the end of the film at Shafto's. Reading was breaking a little thread off the left sleeve of his battledress jacket. Well, he hadn't changed that way. He was always very fussy about his togs. It used to annoy the jokers, I remembered. And he was a terrible man to fuss before ceremonial parades and all that kind of thing. Used to do his scone completely if everything wasn't just so. 'A very smart officer,' our first CO used to say before we left him behind in Trentham. The new CO wasn't so quick to make up his mind.

'I'm off back tomorrow,' he said suddenly.

'So am I.'

'No, not back to the battalion. Back to New Zealand.'

'The hell you are? Jesus, that's a bit of luck, isn't it?'

'Luck? Yes, I suppose it is, in a way.'

'Give my best to anyone I know.'

Not that it was likely he knew anyone I knew outside the army. He came from Christchurch and was the sort of chap who, when he wasn't spending week-ends up on some sheepstation, would take an interest in the territorials and all that. Chaps like him had got off to a flying start when the war broke out. Still, you had to be fair, there were some quite good blokes among them, though I'd never have believed it in peace time and took a bit of convincing when the war came too.

He didn't seem as cheerful as you'd expect, though. After all, we'd been away three years then. And if a man had a piece of luck like this thrown at him, there was more than an even chance the war would be over before he heard shots fired in anger again. What more did he want?

Still, I thought, I suppose even old Reading feels it a bit, clearing out

and leaving the boys to it like this. It'd be better to be going home when
everyone else did, with the feeling that you'd taken your chance right up
to the last like the rest of them. Provided you weren't being left behind
for good, like so many who'd had it already; Buck Travers, for instance,
who got his the night I was hit.

'I expect you take it a bit hard, though,' I said, 'leaving the old
battalion.'

'Yes,' he said. And bugger me if I didn't suddenly get a horrible feeling
he was going to let go and bloody well cry. Why not, anyway? Just because
they didn't like him much it didn't mean he mightn't like them.

'I'll fill them up again,' I said.

It's probably the gin, I said to myself as Jack poured them out. They
always say it does that to you. It never did to me, though, and I've had a
power of it in my time.

Where the hell were all the blokes? I could have done with someone
knocking out a tune on the old piano and a bit of a sing-song with plenty
of drinks on the table and the boys letting themselves go with Samuel
Hall or The Harlot of Jerusalem or, when they'd got sentimental, 'To
you, sweetheart, Aloah'.

Reading seemed to have pulled himself together a bit by the time I
brought the drinks back.

'You work the racket all right,' I said, the way we used to talk in those
days half-thinking we meant it, 'and you should be jake sitting out the
rest of the war in some bludger's job in Trentham.'

He didn't seem to like this much. We never really talked the same
language, anyhow.

'I don't know,' he said and his accent seemed to have gone a bit pom-
mier than usual, or what he thought was pommy, only that was another
thing that meeting a lot of pommies had made some of us wise to.

'I might ask for my discharge,' he said.

I was a bit surprised, even a bit shocked. Everyone says these things
from time to time. But he sounded as if he meant it.

Just then, though, you could hear the trucks pulling up outside.

'Here they come,' I said, 'the dirty stop outs.'

'It's time I was off to bed. An early start in the morning.'

'Come off it,' I said, 'you might as well stay till you finish your drink,
at any rate.'

'Yes, why not?' But when he said it he set his jaw the way you'd think
he was sitting on one end of a tug-of-war.

Well, the door opened and a lot of the blokes came in. I didn't know any of this first lot and so I didn't take much notice when, after one look at us, they went straight to the bar without saying anything to either of us. I did think it a bit funny, though, the way they all quietened down suddenly when they'd been talking their heads off outside.

Then in came Jimmy Larsen, Ted Tarrant, Tiger Smith and several others I more or less knew. They glanced over our way. Tiger called out 'Hello, Andy,' and the others waved. They joined the rest at the bar.

This struck me as a pretty queer way of going on. And, of course, dumb as I was, it wasn't hard to guess there was something the matter and the something was Reading. I looked at him. He'd gone white in the face and as I watched him he slowly went red again, red all over.

Now I'm not a joker to kick another bloke when he's down but I'd sooner have been back in hospital, back in El Mreir for that matter, than where I was then. I couldn't think of anything to say to Reading and I don't think he was even trying to think of anything to say to me. He was just staring into his glass where there were a few little husks of lemon floating about on a thin wash of drink.

How the bloody hell was I going to get out of this one? Say what you like nobody much wants to be with someone everyone else seemed to think lower than a snake's testicles. If it was a cobber that might be a different thing. But Reading was a bloke I wouldn't have given you two knobs of goatshit for, even in ordinary times. Not my kind of chap at all. Yet I couldn't very well clear out and leave him flat, all on his lonesome like that.

'Good night, Andy,' he suddenly said.

I was relieved, I've got to admit. But at the same time I felt ashamed at feeling relieved. So I asked him to have another drink, though I must say I was pretty sure he wouldn't.

He didn't seem to hear but just got to his feet and walked straight out of the room. The other blokes didn't look at him and he didn't look at them.

I didn't like to get up and join them even then. Too much like a rat leaving a sunk ship. I felt in a way as if Reading was still there. Besides, I was damned if I was going to start explaining myself to all these jokers, a lot of them I'd never even seen before, just new chums and red-arses.

'You know I don't like to see my little Andy boy in bad company.'

It was Tiger Smith and by God I was glad to see him standing there and grinning down at me. He was the sort of joker everybody likes and if a thing or a chap's all right with him then it's got to be all right with everyone or he'll know the reason why.

'What's he done?' I said.

'What I always thought he'd do some day. Cleared out. Ratted. Buggered off. Said he had to report back to battalion. There was a counter-attack coming in. You know, just when the light was right for them. With tanks, too. Luckily the sergeant-major, old Dick Coster, was on the job. But it's mafish for Reading. The high jump. Of course, no one could prove anything. But Dick got killed and later on when Larry took over he got killed too.'

'Court martial?'

'No, no court martial. As I say, you couldn't prove anything. I don't suppose anybody'd want to. Nothing like that ever happened before in the battalion.'

'No,' I said. 'Not in the battalion. The bastard.'

Jim Larsen and Ted Tarrant had come over by this time. 'Come on, Tiger,' Jim said. 'We're all going back tomorrow. Let's make a night of it before the flies wake up and get us. Get cracking on the old piano, Andy.'

It was late when we broke up. I was still clear in the head but pretty shaky on my pins when I left the others and cut across the parade ground for my hut. You know what those huts were like, all the same size and all alike.

Anyhow, I found mine at last. I thought I was the only joker there but as I passed the end room I noticed a light coming under the door. Naturally, I thought it was one of the boys, so I knocked and went in.

'Hello, Andy,' Reading said.

He was sitting on the edge of the bed. All his kit except what he'd need in the morning was packed up. On top of his tin trunk there was a hurricane lamp and a bottle of gin and a mug.

'Sorry,' I said, 'I thought you were Bill Adair.'

'Sorry to disappoint you. Sorry to disappoint everybody. Have a drink.'

I didn't see how I could get out of it. And anyhow I felt sorry for him sitting there drinking with the flies when all the rest of us had been over in the Mess singing and wrestling and slapping one another on the back, the way we used to in those days.

I sat down. He fished out another mug from his kit, rinsed it with some water out of the seir, and poured me a stiffish gin.

'No, I'm not Bill Adair,' he said. 'I'm not Tiger Smith, either, or Ted Tarrant. And I'm not sorry I'm not. I'm damned glad.'

'You're glad you're not Dick Coster, too?' I couldn't help saying.

'They've told you all about it, of course.'

'Yes.'

'Self-satisfied bastards. Anyone'd think they'd never thought of doing the same. A hundred times, every one of them.'

'They never did it, though.' And I remembered all the times I'd had that feeling in my own guts as we went forward under the barrage, or waited shivering in the half-light for the counter-attack to come in.

'No, they never did it. Brutes, clods, that's all they are. You think it's guts. But it isn't, I tell you. It's only that they're afraid of what people'll say.'

I said nothing. But I was remembering how on mornings before a big parade he'd be nagging at his batman because his trousers weren't properly pressed and giving his platoon commanders hell if the men's gaiters weren't blancoed and every other bloody thing just exactly so.

'And anyhow I wasn't well, I tell you. I hadn't slept for nights before that.'

I still didn't say anything but that didn't worry him. He just went on and on, in a mixed up kind of way, sometimes saying he hadn't done anything and other times saying he couldn't help doing it, anyone else would have done the same and anyhow he was sick. I felt very embarrassed. At the same time I'd sobered up and I was tired and sleepy. I remembered the batman was to give me a call at first light.

From time to time he'd pour himself another but after the first one or two he forgot to offer me any—it wasn't really me he was talking to but himself. And I didn't tell him I could do with another because I knew I was too tired for any amount of gin to jack me up and besides I was looking for an excuse to get away. In fact I was so busy trying to find one that I almost missed it at first when he started off on a new track.

'I suppose they think that the only thing for a chap in my position to do is bump himself off. I suppose that's what you think too. You think I won't be able to go back to my old job because the blokes'll be back sooner or later and they'll tell the story round and people'll begin to pretend they don't see me there either. You all think that's what I ought to do, don't you?'

He wasn't shouting at all, but the way he was staring at me I could see he was looking for some kind of an answer. I felt all dopey with a hangover coming on and being in need of a bit of sleep and I didn't know what to say. And as a matter of fact I couldn't help feeling he could do worse. But I didn't say anything. Only I thought it really was time I cleared out. So I got up.

'Yes, that's what you think, the whole bloody lot of you,' he said, sitting there with the mug in one hand and the other hanging down the way you could see he was up to the eyes in booze.

'But you're bloody well mistaken,' he suddenly shouted at me and his hand came up so hard that the gin splashed out of the mug. 'You needn't think I'm going to do anything of the kind.'

'I don't,' I said. 'But look here, I've got to get to bed. I'm off back in the morning, remember.'

'That's right,' he said. 'And I'm off back, too.'

He said this so quietly I thought this was my chance.

'Good night,' I said.

He said nothing, didn't even look at me. I felt bad somehow, so I said, 'I'll look in before I go.'

'You needn't bother.'

So I left him sitting there, staring at the floor.

After I'd put my light out and was just getting off to sleep I heard someone trip over my shoes.

'It's only me, Andy,' Reading said. 'I just came to say good night. And good luck.'

'Thanks, Cliff, and good luck to you.' It was a bit of an effort but I managed to call him by his first name.

I heard him stumble back in the dark towards the door.

But I must have slept very heavily after that because I didn't hear the shot and it wasn't till the batman rushed in and told me at first light that I knew anything about it. And the Adj insisted on me staying for the court of inquiry though what the hell there was to inquire into I don't know. It all seemed plain enough to me. Anyhow by the time I got back the Div was getting ready for the left hook round Agheila and before we had time to stop and think again no one felt much interest in what had happened to Reading.

A. P. Gaskell

SCHOOL PICNIC

Miss Brown dismounted at the school gate. She hoped the bicycle saddle was not making the seat of her tweed skirt shiny. It was damn good tweed and black-market prices were terribly high. She pushed her bike into the wood-shed and took her case off the carrier. Oh hell . . . Joggling across those blasted sleepers had shaken open the powder-compact in her handbag. She shook it out and glanced at her watch. A quarter past and those damned Maoris had said they would be here at ten. Now after all her bustle she had to wait. As she lit a cigarette she noticed that she had chipped the varnish off one nail. Talk about roughing it.

She went round the front into the sunshine, unlocked the school door and entered. The sunlight was flooding the room through the windows and doorway, showing up the roughness of the match-lined walls and low ceiling. Little heaps of borer-dust lay on the desks, and as she entered a tiny stream of it filtered delicately down from the ceiling, through the slab of sunlight. The place some 30 years ago had been built as a cook-house for the old sawmill, and no quantity of desks and blackboards, of 'Rules for Writing' or lists of 'Joining Words' could make it look like the city schools she was used to. It wasn't even painted inside.

She dusted her chair and sat down, pulling impatiently at the now pink-tipped cigarette. Me of all people, she thought, stuck away out here in this god-forsaken hole, and two weeks to go yet. I'm just halfway.

She had been sent to relieve for a month at this small King Country school, four miles 'by cycle track' from a station she had never even heard of. She had to board with the railway porter and bike it each day. The cycle track was simply a mark in the pumice that wound through the tea-tree and led to a crazy swing-bridge over the river. If she watched the boards as she bounced across, the water sliding beneath them made her feel dizzy as though she were falling sideways. The other half of the track was along the sleepers of an old bush tramway which wound through the scrub and blackberry above the river until it finally reached the clearing where the charred wreckage of the sawmill stood near the school. Beyond that, another swing-bridge led across the river to a flat wilderness of grey scaly tea-tree, fire-blackened in places. Somewhere in that mess of second growth the pupils lived. She often saw wisps of smoke rising against the bush on the hills at the back. Somewhere in there too the men were working. Sometimes she heard a lokey puffing, but where it was or what it was doing she neither knew nor cared. It was quite enough being expected to teach their snotty-nosed little Maori brats. She couldn't bear to touch them. One of them smelled smoky, just like an old roll of bacon. Jabbering at her in their excited pidgin English.

And to crown it all the damned School Committee had to pick on this Saturday for their school picnic. The first time she had seen old Araroa and big fat Terari was the day she arrived. She had thought they were rather cute then. The two of them met her at the gate. Old Araroa was still very erect, white-haired, his face wrinkled like a dried apple, blue markings on his chin, his eyes looking so very old and brown and tired. He spoke softly to her in Maori, leaning on his stick and gesturing with his free hand. The skin was very dry and shiny and stretched tight over the bones. After the old man finished, Fatty rolled his eyes at her and said, 'Hello, Miss Brown. The old man he say you be very happy here while the mahita away.' Fatty wore an old hat, disgraceful pants that folded back under his belly, showing a filthy lining, and a thick black woollen jersey with short sleeves. His arms were bigger than her legs. He had long yellow teeth like a horse. He was so much like the comic Maori of the illustrated papers that she felt safe and reassured at once. But she wasn't so pleased when they visited her again to tell her about the picnic. Fatty was rather excited himself at the idea. 'We give the kids the jolly good picnic eh?' he said. 'The old man here he say pretty near time we give the kids the picnic. Have the feed eh, and the races. You don't worry Miss Brown, we fix him all up. These jolly good worker these committee. We have him on Saturday.'

'On Saturday?' Of all days. Her voice was shrill.

'Saturday,' the old man whispered, and apparently satisfied, turned and walked off. Fatty stayed to reassure her. 'You don't worry Miss Brown. These committee fix him. You be here ten o'clock.'

And of course Saturday was the worst possible day. She had intended to have the day in Taumarunui, to go to the matinee and see Joan Crawford who always wore such stunning dresses and really did look wizard when she sat round sipping cocktails. She had really been looking forward to that. It was a pity Taumarunui was dry. She could do with a few spots herself to take away the taste of these last two weeks. Besides, she needed to have her hair set again, some of the rolls were coming out of place. At any rate she would feel a bit civilized again for a day at least.

She threw her butt in the empty fireplace. One of the schoolgirls usually cleaned the place. The sunlight outside was just pouring down and glinting off the pumice bank. She had to squint to see properly. Damn it, she should have brought her sunglasses. George didn't like wrinkles.

How the gang at home would laugh if they could see me now, she thought, awaiting the pleasure of a tribe of Maoris. I wonder if George has thought of me at all. Lucky devils, I suppose they'll all be going out on George's launch again. They'll probably have a few in by this time too, and boy, would I like to be the same. If it's fine George will be taking them up to his crib. George was a nice job, beautifully muscled. He had dark wavy hair, white teeth, and he oiled his body before he lay in the sun. Sometimes he would let her do it for him. His swimming shorts were always tight around his small hips and flat stomach. He knew what he wanted and had a lot of fun. She was trying to do a line with George but the competition was so keen. Still, just before she left she had thrown a spanner in Vonnie's works. She told George there was a rumour that Vonnie had a dose. George would keep well clear of her. Anything like that, even people with skin trouble, made him feel sick.

A shadow darkened the doorway. 'Hello, Miss Brown,' cried Terari, his big belly bulging out above his pants. 'You the first one here? Look nobody else here. You pretty keen on these picnic eh?'

'You said ten o'clock, and look at it, nearly eleven.' Her eyes focussed, hardened.

'Crikey, that late? By golly I ring the bell. Wake them up. Those lazy Maori must sleep in eh? You can't trust those Maori. Always late.' A dark smell of sweat preceded him into the room. 'You didn't light the fire?'

'I certainly didn't light the fire.'

'Nemind. We put him outside. If those fellow come you tell him off eh? They shouldn't be late.' He lumbered out and began striking the length of iron railing that hung from a tree near the door. The strong sound dinned and vibrated around her and rolled back off the hills. He was grinning in at her again. 'Just like school eh? You give them the strap for late.'

She heard the sound of his axe at the back.

A small head was thrust round the doorpost. 'Please Miss Brown.'

'Hello Lena. Are you the first one? Have you got a clean nose this morning?'

Lena sniffed and licked her upper lip. She came shyly into the room, barefoot but clean, with her hair drawn back and plaited tightly. Two even smaller children stayed at the door looking in at the teacher.

'Please Miss Brown, we gotta hundred pies.'

'My word that's a lot. You'll all have the bellyache. It's a pity they don't get you some decent food.' The poor kid had hardly a sound tooth in her head.

'Fizz,' said a small voice at the doorway.

'And please Miss Brown we gotta hundred fizz.'

'Fizz?'

'And straws,' cried the child at the door.

'Who are these, Lena?'

'Please, Miss Brown, these my cousin. This Gwendoline and that one Harris. They Mrs Patutai baby. They coming to school maybe next year.'

'Mrs Patutai? I haven't heard of her.'

'Please Miss Brown, she live over at Tokaanu. Our last baby die so these one come and live with us. She got too many.'

I don't blame her, she thought, for giving them away. If this is populate or perish, I'll take perish. There were more voices outside. She went out to look. The children at the door stared at her as she passed. They both had running noses. 'Wah. Red hands too,' she heard one of them say. 'That's varnish,' came Lena's voice. 'I done mine with blackberry. Look. I done my mouth too but I lick him off. Sour.' Miss Brown decided to ignore it. After all you could hardly blame them, they were so out of touch with civilization away back here.

At the end of the building, where the sunlight made the white-washed wall hard to look at, three middle-aged women in dark cotton dresses were squatting. One was Terari's wife, a big fat wahine, barefooted, with a rug around her and a sleeping baby's head on her shoulder. The others she didn't know. They were talking softly, making guttural noises to one another in Maori, and smoking. They smiled up at her. 'Tenakoe.'

'A lovely day Miss Brown,' said Mrs Terari. 'We come early to do some work but they never brought the stuff yet. Get things ready for the picnic.'

'Picnic,' the others smiled and nodded.

'My husband here?'

'Yes. That's him chopping round at the back.' She was wondering what to say. These old dames were hard to talk to. She stood uncomfortably before them. One of them looked up and caught her eye. 'Picnic.' She smiled and nodded again.

Some children were running about in the paddock, the boys looking very clean in white shirts and with their hair plastered down. They were, as usual, being aeroplanes, dive-bombing and making zooming noises. One of the women called out sharply to them. Mrs Terari pointed to her. 'This lady's son was killed in Crete. He go to this school before.'

'Aie, Crete.' The mother covered her face with her hands, then broke into rapid Maori. Fatty came round the corner. 'Wah. You here? Where all those other fellow? Those damn lazy Maori, they no good for nothing.' He went and struck the rail again. Just then there were shouts at the gate, and men and women came in carrying parcels and boxes. 'Hey, you fellow,' he called. 'Miss Brown give you the strap for late.' Mrs Terari shrieked with laughter. The place was suddenly crowded with voices and movement. The children all gathered round, guessing what was in the boxes.

After that everything happened quickly. The women all went inside to arrange the food. The men grouped round the fire, talking and laughing. They were a cut-throat looking crew. Miss Brown wished she could understand what they were laughing so much about. Telling dirty yarns probably.

Fatty went out in the middle of the paddock and started the races. The boys ran fiercely, showing their teeth and straining hard especially when the men cheered. Fatty gave her an old notebook and asked her to take down the results. 'For prizes. This afternoon.' She stood there for ages, watching the children run and writing their names down. The men got excited, the children were hot, and when they grouped round her she could hardly breathe. She always deodorized herself so carefully too.

An elderly woman, tall, very thin, with blue markings on her nose and chin and a dark shawl over her hair came towards the group, shrilling angrily at them. They fell silent. She seemed to be picking on Fatty. He began to expostulate but she brushed past him and inclined her head very graciously to Miss Brown, 'Haeremai, haeremai,' and smiled showing empty gums. She took Miss Brown's arm and led her over to the school. I hope her hand's clean, thought Miss Brown. I'll have to wash this sweater now. 'My son-in-law got no manners,' said the old lady. 'He shouldn't left you out there with all those men. My name Mrs Te Ahuru. You come in and see all our baby. Nice for the girls to have the lady teacher.'

The schoolroom seemed crowded with women of all shades of brown and all ages. Sunken-cheeked old crones squatted against the wall in the sunlight under the windows, rolling cigarettes. Flash young things with lipstick, long-legged in high-heeled shoes, stood silkily, smoking tailor-mades. The desks were covered with food, buns and cakes on plates, and sandwiches in boxes and on newspapers. Boxes of pies stood near the fireplace and rows of red and yellow fizz bottles along the wall. Old Mrs Te Ahuru led her in and said something in Maori lingo, ending up with 'Miss Brown.' They all looked up and smiled and nodded. She didn't know what to say. 'How do you do?' she said. 'Isn't it a lovely day.' Everyone seemed pleased. Smiles in all directions.

She was taken round to admire the babies. It was agony. She wasn't interested in babies. All she could see of most of them was a small brown head lolling out of a blanket on the mother's back, or staring big-eyed over the mother's shoulder. She tried to say something nice. And there was Micky, her smallest primer, a little wizened creature with sad eyes like a monkey. 'Hello Micky. Why aren't you out running races?'

Micky grinned, crossing his legs with embarrassment but his eye was on the fizz. A youngish woman beside him answered; she was rather nice-looking but had very bad teeth. She spoke so pleasantly that Miss Brown decided she must have been somewhere to a Maori High School and then come back to the mat. Another baby hung on to her skirt and a third stared over her shoulder.

'I don't want Micky to run round,' said the young woman. 'He must keep quiet. He going to die soon.'

'To die!' Good Lord. And so matter-of-fact about it too. In school Micky was always full of beans.

'Yes.' The young woman fixed serious eyes on her. 'You know that Chinese doctor who come around with all the medicine?'

Miss Brown nodded. Some peddling herbalist had been around just before she came, she had heard the kids talking about him.

'I took Micky to see him. Micky not well, he so thin.'

'And what did he say?'

'When I go in the room he just look at me. He don't speak, he just look for long time. He got sharp eyes too. Then he say "You Mrs Pine?" I say "Yes." He say "Your husband name Joe?" I say "Yes." He say "I can tell all about you. Your husband fall off his horse and break his shoulder. He can't chop the trees now." He say "Your second baby die and this one Micky not Joe's baby. This Micky very sick." He keep looking at me all the time and I get frightened and think I go out but he say "Don't go out. I tell you about Micky." So he say Micky all twisted up inside and pretty soon he die. He give me some medicine in the little bottle.' She showed the size with her finger and thumb. 'Seven and six. But I don't get many bottle. Too dear. So I suppose Micky going to die.' She rubbed Micky's head gently with her hand. 'That doctor right about those other things. You think he right about Micky too?'

'Good Heavens no,' said Miss Brown. 'That's terrible. Why don't you tell the police?'

'He make me frightened. Those sharp eyes they go right in me.'

'But, but really you mustn't take any notice of all that nonsense. You get the nurse to look at Micky next time she's round. I don't think there's much the matter with him.' Poor thing, how terrible. She must have believed it all too, the way she was looking. They were all so damnably ignorant of civilized procedure. 'I'll tell the nurse about it.'

The clang of the iron railing was reverberating through the room. 'Come and get it,' yelled Mrs Terari. 'Heigh-oh Silver,' called one of the men, and they all came trooping in. The smell got stronger. They moved about, pushing, laughing, calling, helping themselves. Each child was sucking fizz through a straw, even the tiny ones. Miss Brown worked her way through them to the table, and from her case took her small lunch wrapped in a clean white serviette.

'Here Miss Brown, you sit down.' Fatty was offering her a chair. 'Wah, the poetry eh? By golly I say the poetry. Here Miss Brown, you sit down. Here Miss Brown, you sit down.' He roared with laughter. Fragments of half-chewed food lay on his tongue. She shuddered and looked away.

'Miss Brown, you have this nice pie.' Old Mrs Te Ahuru held out a clean plate with a pie on it. 'I keep him for you. And these sandwich.'

'But I have my own lunch here.'

'That leetle bit. You eat more, that's why you so thin eh? You have this nice pie.'

'Oh no really I. . . . '

'Oh but you must. You shouldn't brought your dinner. You come to our picnic you eat our dinner.' She turned to her son-in-law. 'You get Miss Brown the nice cup of tea. In the clean cup.'

Somehow she got them down. There were so many things she couldn't bear to watch—the old women mumbling soft sandwiches, Fatty eating pies enormously, the children with the wet under their noses mingling with the sticky wet round their mouths and chins from the fizz. Somehow the lunch ended and they went outside. Half-way, she thought. I've got the worst half over.

The sky was clouding, and a cool breeze came rustling across the tops of the tea-tree.

'By golly we better hurry before the rain,' shouted Fatty, and they ran the races in a frenzy of haste and shouting. The cheering was deafening for the grown-ups' races. Some of the men were going out into the bushes just outside the gate and coming back wiping their mouths. When the unmarried women ran with their skirts tucked up above their knees the men whistled and cat-called.

Miss Brown sneaked away to the girls' lavatory but when she tried to open the door there was a whiff of cigarette smoke and a guttural voice muttered something. She paused in indecision and an old crone came out and held the door for her, smiling gummily. She went in but could not bear to sit on that seat. After a decent interval she went back to the sports. Large isolated drops of rain were falling and rolling, still globular, in the dust. There was a sighing in the tea-tree as a grey curtain of rain moved towards them.

Soon they were all inside again. It's beer they've got out there, thought Miss Brown, sniffing. Fatty lit the fire inside and carried in kerosene tins of water for another cup of tea. The tins looked small when he held them. Old Araroa had arrived and was standing there leaning firmly on his stick, white-haired, full of gentleness and dignity, handing out the cheap toys for prizes. The children were rather in awe of him. He spoke softly, knowing most of the names. When all the prizes were gone and Micky was left standing beside his mother, the old man beckoned him over and gave him some money out of his pocket. The other kids crowded round. 'How much you got, Micky?' but he wouldn't show them. He couldn't count it.

No one knew what to do next. The rain was rattling on the roof and splashing against the windows. One young woman opened her blouse and began feeding her baby.

Fatty was approaching. 'The old man like to hear the kids sing.' Even he spoke quietly. 'You make them sing something?' Miss Brown finally had them in their desks, all self-conscious, pushing and showing off a little, looking to the sides to see who was watching.

The singing started, school songs for a while with Miss Brown beating time, then requests for popular songs and Maori tunes. Some of the men and women joined in. They began to warm up. The girls went in front and sang an action song. Even Lena went with them. The small girls moved stiffly, but the bigger ones were relaxed, their hands fluttered delicately, moving easily and clapping exactly in time. They finished and blushed at the applause. Some young women came out. More familiar cheering and whistling followed their number. Then the men lined up and started a vigorous song. The old ladies round the walls were nodding and smiling and moving their hands. Fatty was out in front leading the men with actions. Miss Brown was feeling out of things, when she noticed Fatty's eye upon her. Oh hell, here he was, coming over, showing the whites of his eyes, his tongue, jerking and posturing about, wobbling his big belly, quivering his hands. She shrank back against the wall while he performed in front of her. She could smell beer. The crowd was shrieking with laughter. She felt her throat and cheeks burning. The big fat bastard, making a laughing-stock of her. Suddenly and savagely she smacked his face. There was a sudden silence, then a scream of laughter. His face was hanging there before her, utterly astonished, his mouth hung open, his hands slowly sank. She was amazed at what she had done and very frightened, but he turned and saw the mirth, then clowning, clapped his hand over one eye and staggered back shouting with laughter. Old Mrs Te Ahuru was beside her. 'You serve him right,' she was shouting. 'You serve him damn well right.' She shooed some children out of a desk. 'We sit here.'

The show went on, there was no stopping them now. A new man was out in front leading a haka. The men shouted, smacked, jumped, stamped, the beat thundered round the room. The veins stood out on their throats and foreheads. The old women around the walls were mouthing, twitching, jerking their hands, grimacing. First one then another got up and moved jerkily across the floor, keeping in time with the beat, to join the line. Everybody was doing it, the kids too. The din was immense, the building shook, borer dust showered down, dust rose from the floor. Crash! The climax. Sweaty faces smiling, all coughing in the dust.

'Tea, tea,' called old Mrs Te Ahuru beside her. 'Water boiling. We make tea.'

Miss Brown felt overpowered, helpless. These people were of another kind altogether. She was utterly alone among them. She felt suffocated. She couldn't stand it. She got her case and made for the door. A hand on her arm. Old Mrs Te Ahuru. And Fatty too.

'You can't go. Look. It's still raining.'

'I must. I've got to be back early.'

'But raining. You get wet through.'

'I can't help it. I can't stay any longer.'

'You got no coat?'

'No.'

'You take my rug.' Old Mrs Te Ahuru was unwrapping it. 'Look, I show you how to wear it.'

'No, no, please.'

'You want some coat?' Fatty turned and called to the crowd. A girl came forward with a raincoat. 'Here. You bring him back on Monday eh?'

They helped her into the coat. 'You come and see us some more,' said Mrs Te Ahuru. Old Araroa was approaching but she picked up her bag, got her bike. The rain was cold on her face and neck but oh, the air was clean and sweet, and she was away from them. Oh Christ, she thought, I must get out of it. I must get George somehow, get him drunk, have a baby even. Anything.

After all, she thought, they're nothing but a pack of savages. Not even civilized.

The rain was very steady, and by the time she reached the porter's house she was wet through. All the rolls were washed out of her hair and her make-up was streaky.

All this for a pack of bloody savages, she thought.

Amelia Batistich

A DALMATIAN WOMAN

When the boat came into Auckland she was at the ship rail with the other proxy brides, all of them waiting to see their husbands for the first time, all looking down anxiously at the crowd of faces on the wharf, trying to pick the one face out. She looked at the unfamiliar scene, listened to the noise of the people chattering in the strange English tongue all around them, and wondered suddenly what madness had possessed her to marry a man she had never seen, knew only from his photograph and the letters he had written, all for the chance to come to New Zealand. It felt like the end of a life, not the beginning. The others were younger. They chattered like starlings, pointing to people down on the wharf. 'What is wrong, Lucia?' they said. 'Don't you feel excited? You are going to see your husband!'

They had not long to wait. The ship's officer who had looked after them so kindly on the way out came towards them with another man, a fussy little man with a ginger moustache and yellow teeth. He was holding a handful of papers. A little behind him were the husbands. She decided that was who they must be. They looked so shy and clumsy and eager. She scanned their faces, looking for hers, and found him easily enough. He was older than he looked in the photograph, big and awkward.

The little man took charge. He called out their names, fussed over the papers. She felt like a bought thing. One after another the husbands came forward to be introduced to the wives. She waited for hers. He came forward, put out his hand, changed his mind and kissed her clumsily. She felt his mouth, wet and awkward on her face. She put up her hand to brush the kiss away, then remembered it was her husband who had kissed her.

They went to a Dalmatian boarding-house for dinner. There had been one in Sydney where they had stayed a day and talked with their fellow countrymen. It was good to hear your own speech around you. It made New Zealand seem not so frightening. It even seemed like home. But it was not home. That afternoon she said goodbye to the others, all of them going, like her, to face a life as strange. Her trunk and her cane hamper were put on the train and with Toma she went out to find her new home.

Toma was not a man to speak easily. Words came slowly as if he had to think hard for them. He looked at her and smiled and put out a hand hardened from work on her own. She felt a revulsion to this stranger, and would have pulled her hand away but something in his eyes made her keep it there. Perhaps it was because she had always thought herself a little above the other girls in the village at home that she felt like this. But this rough stranger, with his shy eyes, and his groping hands, how would she ever get to know him?

She did not know that he was awkward because he did not feel like himself in the new suit he was wearing. The collar was tight and the coat held him like a strait-jacket. He was not used to sitting and doing nothing, unused to having a woman by his side. Later, when he had time, he would tell her of the great loneliness of life without a woman of your own, not even a mother or a sister. Later, but now he had no words.

As they sped through the country she marvelled at the greenness of this land. The vastness of the fields. The fat cattle. It was nothing like home. 'It will be good here,' he said. 'A few years and we will be rich. Wait and see.' But when they came to Waiotira, and he told her to carry the hamper while he took the trunk, all she could see was emptiness. He hoisted the box on to his shoulders and they set off, leaving the little station to its desolation. The road was dusty and the dust covered the vegetation on the side of it. She couldn't see a house anywhere.

'Where is our home?' she asked.

'There!' he said, pointing to something that looked like a matchbox.

She was too tired to walk, too tired to think even. All she wanted was to get to the matchbox, to sit down and take off her shoes and to cry her heart out. But he trudged stolidly on, never complaining about the heavy trunk, shifting it patiently from one shoulder to the other and back again.

'There!' he said, when they had walked a million miles, and she looked to where his finger pointed and there was a hut no bigger than the place they had for the goats at home. Only it wasn't made of stone, but of rough, unpainted wood, with a tin chimney on the outside wall. They went inside. The door hung drunkenly on one hinge. There was a smell of smoke. The rough wooden walls were hung with cobwebs. The one window had a sack for a curtain. She looked for a place to sit down. He pulled a box from under the table. She sat down and kicked off her shoes. Her hat fell off when she bent down and the red flowers on it made a splash of brightness on the floor.

'It will be better when we light the fire,' he said. She looked round for the stove. He lit the fire in a well of stones on an open hearth. A heavy black iron pot swung from a chain over it. It was her first sight of a camp-oven. She put her hands to her aching head. 'I would like some coffee,' she said.

'Coffee!' He shook his head. There was none.

No coffee! What did they drink in this New Zealand?

He took down a tin and showed her what was in it. 'Tea,' he said. 'That is what you drink in New Zealand.' Already she was beginning to think that New Zealand was a place where the world stood on its head. But she drank the tea when he made it and it wasn't too bad, smoke and all. She drank it from a mug made of a condensed milk tin with the edges beaten down. She was too numbed by now even to question it. If everything else was as it was, then you had to accept the tin cup.

Revived a little by the tea, she looked with dull curiosity about her again. Boxes for chairs, a table made of boxes, a stove that was a pot hanging over an open fire. Floor of caked earth, a window with no glass in it, the bed—where was the bed? And then she saw that one end of the room was curtained off with sacking. She got up and went to look behind it. There was the bed. Four posts dug into the floor. Sacking nailed across it. One black woollen blanket. Two pillows, one old, one new. The bridal bed. She thought of the finely embroidered linen in her trunk. Then she wept.

The man looked at her dumbly. He wanted to say things to her. How lonely the years had been. How hard he had worked to buy this first piece of land. Now at least the loneliness would be gone. She would be there to warm his days and nights.

'Wait,' he said, 'a year, two, three like this, then we will be on our feet. The land needs money, all the money I can get working outside. If I feed it the money now, it will return to us later on.' But all she could say was that she had not thought New Zealand would be like this. When he had written why did he not tell her. Why did everyone believe it was so different. 'And I am from a good house,' she said. 'It is harder for me.' But when she looked down at her hands there was the wedding ring, solid and gold and binding.

They went to sleep in the marriage bed. Long after he had drowsed off she lay awake. It was cold and the one blanket hardly warmed the two. She got up and dressed in her clothes and lay down beside her sleeping man.

Before he went off to his work the next day he showed her the paddock he had prepared for potato planting. He showed her the seed. It was already cut and ready. 'You plant them like this,' he said, beginning the first row. 'But I have never worked in the fields!' she wanted to cry out, but she didn't. Instead she watched what he was doing and followed the row to its end. Another and another. Her back ached, but there was something in the feel of earth in her hands. Generations of peasant blood warmed to it. Earth! And it belonged to her and her husband. Her hands stung, the skin broke and she sucked the blood from it, but she worked on.

That night she was too tired to complain about the bed. The man wanted to talk, to keep her awake, but she only wanted sleep. He wanted to tell her all about his dreams for the farm, the shed he would build, the fences he would put up, the ditches he would dig . . . 'You and your farm,' she said, and shut her eyes and the sound of him out.

And the funny thing was that she was soon used to it all. The rough kindness of the man, his clumsy lovemaking. The hard days and harder nights on the sack bed. The old country faded from her thoughts. She began to feel herself part of something in the making. The acres of land became an obsession with her as with him, and when their first child was born and she brought it home from the hospital, she held it up to the land and said—

'See what we are making for you!'

G. R. Gilbert

A GIRL WITH AMBITION

Round about 1933 things in New Zealand were not so good. You didn't notice them so much if your father owned a newspaper, it was having no money that made the difference. You noticed things more then, you felt that possibly capitalism was not operating as the *Dominion* and the *Evening Post* intended it to. In fact you felt hungry.

I didn't have a job either. But I was working on a relief scheme; three days a week I was filling in and digging up again a piece of ground in Hataitai. It was supposed to be a playing-field. The worst times New Zealand had struck, and all they could think of was to make playing-fields. They took great care to get the surface microscopically level and true—it took them and us months. Then they would decide to lower the whole thing six inches or so. It gave us work of course. If the slump had only lasted we'd have made all Wellington into playing-fields. We dug them out of the sides of hills, filled in valleys, diverted creeks and reclaimed swamps. All for playing-fields.

You got almost enough money to live on doing this. It wasn't bad digging until the murder, either. It was a great murder. I was extremely interested until it was decided that the girl's body was hidden under the spoil in our playing-field. I lost interest suddenly then. We were supposed to dig round for the remains, but I didn't feel like it—I didn't mind drowning kittens or cutting the head off a fowl if there was no one else, but digging round for a body was not my choice; why your spade might have gone into her and lifted her out in pieces. I hadn't been educated up to that sort of thing.

Leave her where she is, I said, forget about it. Why does one little body matter so much? It's quite unimportant and small; people die every day from more or less unnatural causes, particularly hunger. They die every day and it's all right. What does one little killing matter? Maybe she deserved to die, maybe he got mad at her for having the baby— wouldn't you? The silly kid having the baby and you no money and no likelihood. Two starve quicker than one you thought, and three a damsight quicker. She shouldn't have had him on. What would you do? and her buried so nicely beneath tons of spoil. Leave her there, damn it,

I said, and forget about her.

But they ignored me and even got an excavator to work, so I quit and went up north. I got a job on a farm which lasted until the cocky decided to pay me less and less and practically no food, so I quit again and went further north. But that's by the way. What the story is about is this:

I was on the dole, on relief at about eighteen shillings a week in 1933, and things were worse than they had ever been. I had a small room in Cuba Street and some nights given the chance and the money I had dinner at Tony's. He was a Greek. They are all Greeks in Cuba Street, the restaurants have tins of spaghetti, parsley, bottles of soda-water and oysters-in-season in the window—they are very Greek. Inside you get boiled cabbage etc., and in some places the crockery was more cracked than others. The Greeks all wore black alpaca coats and shaven hair. They mostly spent their time standing behind the till collecting the shillings.

Eating at the same restaurant for long periods you get to know a bit about the waitresses. In this particular place, in Tony's, there were three, May, Sadie and Hettie. They were slightly different in detail as are all other people, but they all had the same intense way of calling out your order behind the screen.

At irregular intervals during the week and every Friday a fourth waitress appeared. And now the story is beginning because it is only about Lena, this waitress.

She was a lonely sort of dame. She had no great beauty, she was not the sort you longed to touch, she didn't walk very well and her hands were like the advertisement before taking Marvell Lotion for white hands. Yes, her hands were red.

But Lena and I got on pretty well after a while. I'd ask her about her boy-friend and was she going out tonight, and I bet she had a good time with the boys, and Lena would giggle and look pleased as though she had Prince Charming waiting in a V8 outside the kitchen door. It was Lena who kept me posted about the goings-on of Alexiouple the Greek, how he had married for the third time and his wife dead only two months, and how all the other children of his two previous marriages were indignant but they couldn't do anything about it, they all hanging round and smarming up to the old man, and his marrying again in spite of them. So they kept standing round in groups like stop-work meetings, all simmering with Greek hatred.

Lena was half Polish, at least half. Her father had come from somewhere near Tschenstochau; he had come out to New Zealand and died. It was peasant blood that Lena had from her father, you almost could see it running in her veins, snappy and sluggish; but it was good honest blood that made Lena like the earth and the growing things upon it. She had a window box to her room and used to grow daffodils. It made me feel good knowing that Lena grew flowers, it was something that she did—I felt proud of her. Once she brought me a daffodil from her garden. I put it in my button-hole and wore it proudly all that day although it looked rather peculiar. I'd have liked to be able to buy Lena a little farm with some pigs and a cow and a garden, she deserved it.

Lena looked after me well whenever she happened to be there. She saw I had the best, no scraggy endpieces for me, or messy left-overs for sweet.

What'll you have? she would say.

If I were you, she would say, I'd have mutton. The mutton's good but the beef—and she would screw her face up and shake her head—don't have the beef, have the mutton.

So I would have mutton.

Who's taking you out tonight? I would ask, and Lena would giggle; I bet you've got the boys on a string.

All this before we began digging for the body when I was still interested in the murder. Coming in from all that digging, and lifting the playing-field up and down so many inches, it was pretty good having a placid one like Lena, even though only once a week, to talk to. She was like a cow really, like a clean tame cow.

Lena, I said, would you like to live on a farm? A nice little farm with pigs?

Me on a farm, cried Lena, why me on a farm? I like my job where I am, I get great chances in my job, I get on. All the week I only wash dishes and sweep round in the back and the kitchen, I do work anyone could do. But on Fridays and when one of the girls is off I do work, skilled work. You got to be built that way to be a good waitress. Mr Alexiouple gives me my chance. All the week I only wash dishes but Fridays I am a waitress. Maybe sometimes I'll be a full time waitress. What would I do with a farm or pigs—I like it here, I got chances here—what would I do with a farm?

It was crazy that, and so wonderful. It was so damfool mad not to want pigs if you were a peasant. Having great ambition like that, you wanted to tell everyone about it, how great it was. If only a few had ambition like that how good things would be.

And all you with the assured positions and the cars, riding round in the cars, having homes on the hills with gardens and a view of the harbour, you laugh, you think of a poor polack being a waitress and having red hands. Only being a waitress once a week and thinking she's great. And you laugh. Well, you can laugh, but your laughter can't get us—we know how crazy beauty is, you only know soft things.

* * *

That was in 1933 and a few days after I went north because of the dead girl's body and digging for it.

Maurice Duggan

ALONG RIDEOUT ROAD THAT SUMMER

I'd walked the length of Rideout Road the night before, following the noise of the river in the darkness, tumbling over ruts and stones, my progress, if you'd call it that, challenged by farmers' dogs and observed by the faintly luminous eyes of wandering stock, steers, cows, stud-bulls or milk-white unicorns or, better, a full quartet of apocalyptic horses browsing the marge. In time and darkness I found Puti Hohepa's farmhouse and lugged my fibre suitcase up to the verandah, after nearly breaking my leg in a cattlestop. A journey fruitful of one decision—to flog a torch from somewhere. And of course I didn't. And now my feet hurt; but it was daylight and, from memory, I'd say I was almost happy. Almost. Fortunately I am endowed both by nature and later conditioning with a highly developed sense of the absurd; knowing that you can imagine the pleasure I took in this abrupt translation from shop-counter to tractor seat, from town pavements to back-country farm; with all those miles of river-bottom darkness to mark the transition. In fact, and unfortunately there have to be some facts, even fictional ones, I'd removed myself a mere dozen miles from the parental home. In darkness, as I've said, and with a certain stealth. I didn't consult dad about it, and, needless to say, I didn't tell mum. The moment wasn't propitious; dad was asleep with the *Financial Gazette* threatening to suffocate him and mum was off somewhere moving, as she so often did, that this meeting make public its whole-hearted support for the introduction of flogging and public castration for all sex offenders and hanging, drawing and quartering, for almost everyone else, and as for delinquents (my boy!) . . . Well, put yourself in my shoes, there's no need to go on. Yes, almost happy, though my feet were so tender I winced every time I tripped the clutch.

Almost happy, shouting Kubla Khan, a bookish lad, from the seat of the clattering old Ferguson tractor, doing a steady five miles an hour in a cloud of seagulls, getting to the bit about the damsel with the dulcimer and looking up to see the reputedly wild Hohepa girl perched on the gate, feet hooked in the bars, ribbons fluttering from her ukulele. A perfect moment of recognition, daring rider, in spite of the belch of carbon monoxide from the tin-can exhaust up front on the bonnet. Don't, however, misunderstand me: I'd not have you think we are here embarked on the trashy clamour of boy meeting girl. No, the problem, you are to understand, was one of connection. How connect the dulcimer with the ukulele, if you follow. For a boy of my bents this problem of how to cope with the shock of the recognition of a certain discrepancy between the real and the written was rather like watching mum with a shoehorn wedging nines into sevens and suffering merry hell. I'm not blaming old STC for everything, of course. After all, some other imports went wild too, and I've spent too long at the handle of a mattock, a critical function, not to know that. The stench of the exhaust, that's to say, held no redolence of that old hophead's pipe. Let us then be clear and don't for a moment, gentlemen, imagine that I venture the gross unfairness, the patent absurdity, the rank injustice (your turn) of blaming him for spoiling the pasture or fouling the native air. It's just that there was this problem in my mind, this profound, cultural problem affecting dramatic-ally the very nature of my inheritance, nines into sevens in this lovely smiling land. His was the genius as his was the expression which the vast educational brouhaha invited me to praise and emulate, tranquillizers ingested in maturity, the voice of the ring-dove, look up though your feet be in the clay. And read on.

Of course I understood immediately that these were not matters I was destined to debate with Fanny Hohepa. Frankly, I could see that she didn't give a damn; it was part of her attraction. She thought I was singing. She smiled and waved, I waved and smiled, turned, ploughed back through gull-white and coffee loam and fell into a train of thought not entirely free of Fanny and her instrument, pausing to wonder, now and then, what might be the symptoms, the early symptoms, of carbon monoxide poisoning. Drowsiness? Check. Dilation of the pupils? Can't check. Extra cutaneous sensation? My feet. Trembling hands? Vibrato. Down and back, down and back, turning again, Dick and his Ferguson, Fanny from her perch seeming to gather about her the background of green paternal acres, fold on fold. I bore down upon her in all the eager erubescence of youth, with my hair slicked back. She trembled, wavered, fragmented and re-formed in the pungent vapour through which I viewed her. (Oh for an open-air job, eh mate?) She plucked, very picture in jeans and summer shirt of youth and suspicion, and seemed to sing. I couldn't of course hear a note. Behind me the dog-leg furrows and the bright ploughshares. Certainly she looked at her ease and, even through the gassed-up atmosphere between us, too deliciously substantial to be creature down on a visit from Mount Abora. I was glad I'd combed my hair. Back, down and back. Considering the size of the paddock this could have gone on for a week. I promptly admitted to myself that her present position, disposition or posture, involving as it did some provocative tautness of cloth, suited me right down to the ground. I mean to hell with the idea of having her stand knee-deep in the thistle thwanging her dulcimer and plaintively chirruping about a pipedream mountain. In fact she was natively engaged in expressing the most profound distillations of her local experience, the gleanings of a life lived in rich contact with a richly understood and native environment: A Slow Boat To China, if memory serves. While I, racked and shaken, composed words for the plaque which would one day stand here to commemorate our deep rapport: *Here played the black lady her dulcimer. Here wept she full miseries. Here rode the knight Fergus' son to her deliverance. Here put he about her ebon and naked shoulders his courtly garment of leather, black, full curiously emblazoned—Hell's Angel.*

When she looked as though my looking were about to make her leave I stopped the machine and pulled out the old tobacco and rolled a smoke, holding the steering wheel in my teeth, though on a good day I could roll with one hand, twist and lick, draw, shoot the head off a pin at a mile and a half, spin, blow down the barrel before you could say:

Gooday. How are yuh?

All right.

I'm Buster O'Leary.

I'm Fanny Hohepa.

Yair, I know.

It's hot.

It's hot right enough.

You can have a swim when you're through.

Mightn't be a bad idea at that.

Over there by the trees.

Yair, I see it. Like, why don't you join me, eh?

I might.

Go on, you'd love it.

I might.

Goodoh then, see yuh.

A genuine crumpy conversation if ever I heard one, darkly reflective of the Socratic method, rich with echoes of the Kantian imperative, its universal mate, summoning sharply to the minds of each the history of the first trystings of all immortal lovers, the tragic and tangled tale, indeed, of all star-crossed moonings, mum and dad, mister and missus unotoo and all. Enough? I should bloody well hope so.

Of course nothing came of it. Romantic love was surely the invention of a wedded onanist with seven kids. And I don't mean dad. Nothing? Really and truly nothing? Well, I treasure the under-statement; though why I should take such pleasure in maligning the ploughing summer white on loam, river flats, the frivolous ribbons and all the strumming, why I don't know. Xanadu and the jazzy furrows, the wall-eyed bitch packing the cows through the yardgate, the smell of river water. . . . Why go on? So few variations to an old, old story. No. But on the jolting tractor I received that extra jolt I mentioned and am actually now making rather too much of, gentlemen: relate Fanny Hohepa and her uke to that mountain thrush singing her black mountain blues.

But of course now, in our decent years, we know such clay questions long broken open or we wouldn't be here, old and somewhat sour, wading up to our battered thighs (forgive me, madam) at the confluence of the great waters, paddling in perfect confidence in the double debouchment of universal river and regional stream, the shallow fast fan of water spreading over the delta, Abyssinia come to Egypt in the rain . . . ah, my country! I speak of cultural problems, in riddles and literary puddles, perform this act of divination with my own entrails: Fanny's dark delta; the nubile and Nubian sheila with her portable piano anticipating the transistor-set; all gathered into single demesne, O'Leary's orchard. Even this wooden bowl, plucked from the flood, lost from the hand of some anonymous herdsman as he stopped to cup a drink at the river's source. Ah, Buster. Ah, Buster. Buster. Ah, darling. Darling! Love. You recognize it? Could you strum to that? Suppose you gag a little at the sugar coating, it's the same old fundamental toffee, underneath.

No mere cheap cyn . . . sm intended. She took me down to her darkling avid as any college girl for the fruits and sweets of my flowering talents, taking me as I wasn't but might hope one day to be, honest, simple and broke to the wide. The half-baked verbosity and the conceit she must have ignored, or how else could she have borne me? It pains me, gentlemen, to confess that she was too good for me by far. Far. Anything so spontaneous and natural could be guaranteed to be beyond me: granted, I mean, my impeccable upbringing under the white hot lash of respectability, take that, security, take that, hypocrisy, take that, cant, take that where, does it seem curious?, mum did all the beating flushed pink in ecstasy and righteousness, and that and that and THAT Darling! How then could I deem Fanny's conduct proper when I carried such weals and scars, top-marks in the lesson on the wickedness of following the heart. Fortunately such a question would not have occurred to Fanny: she was remarkably free from queries of any kind. She would walk past the Home Furnishing Emporium without a glance.

She is too good for you.

It was said clearly enough, offered without threat and as just comment, while I was bent double stripping old Daisy or Pride of the Plains or Rose of Sharon after the cups came off. I stopped what I was doing, looked sideways until I could see the tops of his gumboots, gazed on Marathon, and then turned back, dried off all four tits and let the cow out into the race where, taking the legrope with her, she squittered off wild in the eyes.

She is too good for you.

So I looked at him and he looked back. I lost that game of stare-you-down, too. He walked off. Not a warning, not even a reproach, just something it was as well I should know if I was to have the responsibility of acting in full knowledge—and who the hell wants that? And two stalls down Fanny spanked a cow out through the flaps and looked at me, and giggled. The summer thickened and blazed.

The first response on the part of my parents was silence; which can only be thought of as response in a very general sense. I could say, indeed I will say, stony silence; after all they were my parents. But I knew the silence wouldn't last long. I was an only child (darling, you never guessed?) and that load of woodchopping, lawnmowing, hedgeclipping, dishwashing, carwashing, errandrunning, gardenchoring and the rest of it was going to hit them like a folding mortgage pretty soon. I'd like to have been there, to have seen the lank grass grown beyond window height and the uncut hedges shutting out the sun: perpetual night and perpetual mould on Rose Street West. After a few weeks the notes and letters began. The whole gamut, gentlemen, from sweet and sickly to downright abusive. Mostly in mum's masculine hand. A unique set of documents reeking of blood and tripes. I treasured every word, reading between the lines the record of an undying, all-sacrificing love, weeping tears for the idyllic childhood they could not in grief venture to touch upon, the care lavished, the love squandered upon me. The darlings. Of course I didn't reply.

I didn't even wave when they drove past Fanny and me as we were breasting out of the scrub back on to the main road, dishevelled and, yes, almost happy in the daze of summer and Sunday afternoon. I didn't wave. I grinned as brazenly as I could manage with a jaw full of hard boiled egg and took Fanny's arm, brazen, her shirt only casually resumed, while they went by like burnished doom.

Fanny's reaction to all this? An expression of indifference, a down-curving of that bright and wilful mouth, a flirt of her head. So much fuss over so many fossilized ideas, if I may so translate her expression which was, in fact, gentlemen, somewhat more direct and not in any sense exhibiting what mum would have called a due respect for elders and betters. Pouf! Not contempt, no; not disagreement; simply an impatience with what she, Fanny, deemed the irrelevance of so many many words for so light and tumbling a matter. And, for the season at least, I shared the mood, her demon lover in glossy brilliantine.

But as the days ran down the showdown came nearer and finally the stage was set. Low-keyed and sombre notes in the sunlight, the four of us variously disposed on the unpainted Hohepa verandah, Hohepa and O'Leary, the male seniors, and Hohepa and O'Leary, junior repre-sentatives, male seventeen, female ready to swear, you understand, that she was sixteen, turning.

Upon the statement that Fanny was too good for me my pappy didn't comment. No one asked him to: no one faced him with the opinion. Wise reticence, mere oversight or a sense of the shrieking irrelevance of such a statement, I don't know. Maori girls, Maori farms, Maori housing: you'd only to hear my father put tongue to any or all of that to know where he stood, solid for intolerance, mac, but solid. Of course, gentle-men, it was phrased differently on his lips, gradual absorption, hmm, perhaps, after, say, a phase of disinfecting. A pillar of our decent, law-abiding community, masonic in his methodism, brother, total abstainer, rotarian and non-smoker, addicted to long volleys of handball, I mean pocket billiards cue and all. Mere nervousness, of course, a subconscious habit. Mum would cough and glance down and dad would spring to attention hands behind his back. Such moments of tender rapport are sweet to return to, memories any child might treasure. Then he'd forget again. Straight mate, there were days, especially Sundays, when mum would be hacking away like an advanced case of t.b. Well, you can picture it, there on the verandah. With the finely turned Fanny under his morose eye, you know how it is, hemline hiked and this and that visible from odd angles, he made a straight break of two hundred without one miscue, Daddy! I came in for a couple of remand home stares myself, bread and water and solitary and take that writ on his eyeballs in backhand black while his mouth served out its lying old hohums and there's no reason why matters shouldn't be resolved amicably, etc, black hanging-cap snug over his tonsure and tongue moistening his droopy lip, ready, set, drop. And Puti Hohepa leaving him to it. A dignified dark prince on his ruined acres, old man Hohepa, gravely attending to dad's mumbled slush, winning hands down just by being there and saying nothing, nothing, while Fanny with her fatal incapacity for standing upright unsupported for more than fifteen seconds, we all had a disease of the spine that year, pouted at me as though it were all my fault over the back of the chair (sic). All my fault being just the pater's monologue, the remarkably imprecise grip of his subject with consequent proliferation of the bromides so typical of all his ilk of elk, all the diversely identical representatives of decency, caution and the colour bar. Of course daddy didn't there and then refer to race, colour creed or uno who. Indeed he firmly believed he believed, if I may recapitulate, gentlemen, that this blessed land was free from such taint, a unique social experiment, two races living happily side by side, respecting each other's etc and etc. As a banker he knew the value of discretion, though what was home if not a place to hang up your reticence along with your hat and get stuck into all the hate that was inside you, in the name of justice? Daddy Hohepa said nothing, expressed nothing, may even have been unconscious of the great destinies being played out on his sunlit verandah, or of what fundamental principles of democracy and the freedom of the individual were being here so brilliantly exercised; may have been, in fact, indifferent to daddy's free granting tautologies now, of the need for circumspection in all matters of national moment, all such questions as what shall be done for our dark brothers and sister, outside the jails? I hope so. After a few minutes Hohepa rangatira trod the boards thoughtfully and with the slowness of a winter bather lowered himself into a pool of sunlight on the wide steps, there to lift his face broad and grave in full dominion of his inheritance and even, perhaps, so little did his expression reveal of his inward reflection, full consciousness of his dispossessions.

What, you may ask, was my daddy saying? Somewhere among the circumlocutions, these habits are catching among the words and sentiments designed to express his grave ponderings on the state of the nation and so elicit from his auditors (not me, I wasn't listening) admission, tacit though it may be, of his tutored opinion, there was centred the suggestion that old man Hohepa and daughter were holding me against my will, ensnaring me with flesh and farm. He had difficulty in getting it out in plain words; some lingering cowardice, perhaps. Which was why daddy Hohepa missed it, perhaps. Or did the view command all his attention?

Rideout Mountain far and purple in the afternoon sun; the jersey cows beginning to move, intermittent and indirect, towards the shed; the dog jangling its chain as it scratched; Fanny falling in slow movement across the end of the old cane lounge chair to lie, an interesting composition of curves and angles, with the air of a junior and rural odalisque. Me? I stood straight, of course, rigid, thumbs along the seams of my jeans, hair at the regulation distance two inches above the right eye, heels together and bare feet at ten to two, or ten past ten, belly flat and chest inflated, chin in, heart out. I mean, can you see me, mac? Dad's grave-suit so richly absorbed the sun that he was forced to retreat into the shadows where his crafty jailer's look was decently camouflaged, blending white with purple blotched with silver wall. Not a bad heart, surely?

As his audience we each displayed differing emotions. Fanny, boredom that visibly bordered on sleep: Puti Hohepa, an inattention expressed in his long examination of the natural scene: Buster O'Leary, a sense of complete bewilderment over what it was the old man thought he could achieve by his harangue and, further, a failure to grasp the relevance of it all for the Hohepas. My reaction, let me say, was mixed with irritation at certain of father's habits. (Described.) With his pockets filled with small change he sounded like the original gypsy orchestra, cymbals and all. I actually tried mum's old trick of the glance and the cough. No luck. And he went on talking, at me now, going so wide of the mark, for example, as to mention some inconceivable, undocumented and undemonstrated condition, some truly monstrous condition, called your-mother's-love. Plain evidence of his distress, I took it to be, this obscenity uttered in mixed company. I turned my head the better to hear, when it came, the squelchy explosion of his heart. And I rolled a smoke and threw Fanny the packet. It landed neatly on her stomach. She sat up and made herself a smoke then crossed to her old man and, perching beside him in the brilliant pool of light, fire of skin and gleam of hair bronze and blue-black, neatly extracted from his pocket his battered flint lighter. She snorted smoke and passed the leaf to her old man.

Some things, gentlemen, still amaze. To my dying day I have treasured that scene and all its rich implications. In a situation so pregnant of difficulties, in the midst of a debate so fraught with undertones, an exchange (quiet there, at the back) so bitterly fulsome on the one hand and so reserved on the other. I ask you to take special note of this observance of the ritual of the makings, remembering, for the fullest savouring of the nuance, my father's abstention. As those brown fingers moved on the white cylinder, or cone, I was moved almost, to tears, almost, by this companionable and wordless recognition of our common human frailty, father and dark child in silent communion and I too, in some manner not to be explained because inexplicable, sharing their hearts. I mean the insanity, pal. Puti Hohepa and his lass in sunlight on the steps, smoking together, untroubled, natural and patient; and me and daddy glaring at each other in the shades like a couple of evangelists at cross pitch. Love, thy silver coatings and castings. And thy neighbours! So I went and sat by Fanny and put an arm through hers.

The sun gathered me up, warmed and consoled; the bitter view assumed deeper purples and darker rose; a long way off a shield flashed, the sun striking silver from a water trough. At that moment I didn't care what mad armies marched in my father's voice nor what the clarion was he was trying so strenuously to sound. I didn't care that the fire in his heart was fed by such rank fuel, skeezing envy, malice, revenge, hate and parental power. I sat and smoked and was warm; and the girl's calm flank was against me, her arm through mine. Nothing was so natural as to turn through the little distance between us and kiss her smoky mouth. Ah yes, I could feel, I confess, through my shoulder blades as it were and the back of my head, the crazed rapacity and outrage of my daddy's Irish stare, the blackness and the cold glitter of knives. (Father!) While Puti Hohepa sat on as though turned to glowing stone by the golden light, faced outward to the violet mystery of the natural hour, monumentally content and still.

You will have seen it, known it, guessed that there was between this wild, loamy daughter and me, sunburnt scion of an ignorant, insensitive, puritan and therefore prurient, Irishman (I can't stop) no more than a summer's dalliance, a season's thoughtless sweetness, a boy and a girl and the makings.

In your wisdom, gentlemen, you will doubtless have sensed that something is lacking in this lullaby, some element missing for the articulation of this ranting tale. Right. The key to daddy's impassioned outburst, no less. Not lost in this verbose review, but so far unstated. Point is he'd come to seek his little son (someone must have been dying because he'd never have come for the opposite reason) and, not being one to baulk at closed doors and drawn shades, wait for it, he'd walked straight in on what he'd always somewhat feverishly imagined and hoped he feared.

Fanny took it calmly: I was, naturally, more agitated. Both of us ballocky in the umber light, of course. Still, even though he stayed only long enough to let his eyes adjust and his straining mind take in this historic disposition of flesh, those mantis angles in which for all our horror we must posit our conceivings, it wasn't the greeting he'd expected. It wasn't quite the same, either, between Fanny and me, after he'd backed out, somewhat huffily, on to the verandah. Ah, filthy beasts! He must have been roaring some such expression as that inside his head because his eyeballs were rattling, the very picture of a broken doll, and his face was liver-coloured. I felt sorry for him, for a second, easing backward from the love-starred couch and the moving lovers with his heel hooked through the loop of Fanny's bra, kicking it free like a football hero punting for touch, his dream of reconciliation in ruins.

It wasn't the same. Some rhythms are slow to re-form. And once the old man actually made the sanctuary of the verandah he just had to bawl his loudest for old man Hohepa, Mr Ho-he-pa, Mr Ho-he-pa. It got us into our clothes anyway, Fanny giggling and getting a sneezing fit at the same time, bending forward into the hoof-marked brassiere and blasting off every ten seconds like a burst air hose until I quite lost count on the one-for-sorrow two-for-joy scale and crammed myself sulkily into my jocks.

Meantime dad's labouring to explain certain natural facts and common occurrences to Puti Hohepa, just as though he'd made an original discovery; as perhaps he had considering what he probably thought of as natural. Puti Hohepa listened, I thought that ominous, then silently deprecated, in a single slow movement of his hand, the wholly inappropriate expression of shock and rage, all the sizzle of my daddy's oratory.

Thus the tableau. We did the only possible thing, ignored him and let him run down, get it off his chest, come to his five battered senses, if he had so many, and get his breath. Brother, how he spilled darkness and sin upon that floor, wilting collar and boiling eyes, the sweat running from his face and, Fanny, shameless, languorous and drowsy, provoking him to further flights. She was young, gentlemen: I have not concealed it. She was too young to have had time to accumulate the history he ascribed to her. She was too tender to endure for long the muscular lash of his tongue and the rake of his eyes. She went over to her dad, as heretofore described, and when my sweet sire, orator general to the dying afternoon, had made his pitch about matters observed and inferences drawn, I went to join her. I sat with my back to him. All our backs were to him, including his own. He emptied himself of wrath and for a moment, a wild and wonderful moment, I thought he was going to join us, bathers in the pool of sun. But no.

Silence. Light lovely and fannygold over the pasture; shreds of mist by the river deepening to rose. My father's hard leather soles rattled harshly on the bare boards like rim-shots. The mad figure of him went black as bug out over the lawn, out over the loamy furrows where the tongue of ploughed field invaded the home paddock, all my doing, spurning in his violence anything less than this direct and abrupt charge towards the waiting car. Fanny's hand touched my arm again and for a moment I was caught in a passion of sympathy for him, something as solid as grief and love, an impossible pairing of devotion and despair. The landscape flooded with sadness as I watched the scuttling, black, ignominious figure hurdling the fresh earth, the waving arms, seemingly scattering broadcast the white and shying gulls, his head bobbing on his shoulders, as he narrowed into distance.

I wished, gentlemen, with a fervour foreign to my young life, that it had been in company other than that of Puti Hohepa and his brat that we had made our necessary parting. I wished we had been alone. I did not want to see him diminished, made ridiculous and pathetic among strangers, while I so brashly joined the mockers. (Were they mocking?) Impossible notions; for what was there to offer and how could he receive? Nothing. I stroked Fanny's arm. Old man Hohepa got up and unchained the dog and went off to get the cows in. He didn't speak; maybe the chocolate old bastard was dumb, eh? In a minute I would have to go down and start the engine and put the separator together. I stayed to stare at Fanny, thinking of undone things in a naughty world. She giggled, thinking, for all I know, of the same, or of nothing. Love, thy sunny trystings and nocturnal daggers. For the first time I admitted my irritation at that girlish, hiccoughing, tenor giggle. But we touched, held, got up and with our arms linked went down the long paddock through the infestation of buttercup, our feet bruising stalk and flower. Suddenly all I wanted and at whatever price was to be able, sometime, somewhere, to make it up to my primitive, violent, ignorant and crazy old man. And I knew I never would. Ah, what a bloody fool. And then the next thing I wanted, a thing far more feasible, was to be back in that room with its shade and smell of hay-dust and warm flesh, taking up the classic story just where we'd been so rudely forced to discontinue it. Old man Hohepa was bellowing at the dog; the cows rocked up through the paddock gate and into the yard: the air smelled of night. I stopped; and holding Fanny's arm suggested we might run back. Her eyes went wide: she giggled and broke away and I stood there and watched her flying down the paddock, bare feet and a flouncing skirt, her hair shaken loose.

Next afternoon I finished ploughing the river paddock, the nature of Puti Hohepa's husbandry as much a mystery as ever, and ran the old Ferguson into the lean-to shelter behind the cow shed. It was far too late for ploughing: the upper paddocks were hard and dry. But Puti hoped to get a crop of late lettuce off the river flat; just in time, no doubt, for a glutted market, brown rot, wilt and total failure of the heart. He'd have to harrow it first, too; and on his own. Anyway, none of my worry. I walked into the shed. Fanny and her daddy were deep in conversation. She was leaning against the flank of a cow, a picture of rustic grace, a rural study of charmed solemnity. Christ knows what they were saying to each other. For one thing they were speaking in their own language: for another I couldn't hear anything, even that, above the blather and splatter of the bloody cows and the racket of the single cylinder diesel, brand-name Onan out of Edinburgh so help me. They looked up. I grabbed at stool and got on with it, head down to the bore of it all. I'd have preferred to be up on the tractor, poisoning myself straight out, bellowing this and that and the other looney thing to the cynical gulls. Ah, my mountain princess of the golden chords, something was changing. I stripped on, sullenly: I hoped it was me.

We were silent through dinner: we were always silent, through all meals. It made a change from home where all hell lay between soup and sweet, everyone taking advantage of the twenty minutes of enforced attendance to shoot the bile, bicker and accuse, rant and wrangle through the grey disgusting mutton and the two veg. Fanny never chattered much and less than ever in the presence of her pappy: giggled maybe but never said much. Then out of the blue father Hohepa opened up. Buster, you should make peace with your father. I considered it. I tried to touch Fanny's foot under the table and I considered it. A boy shouldn't hate his father: a boy should respect his father. I thought about that too. Then I asked should fathers hate their sons; but I knew the answer. Puti Hohepa didn't say anything, just sat blowing into his tea, looking at his reputedly wild daughter who might have been a beauty for all I could tell, content to be delivered of the truth and so fulfilled. You should do this: a boy shouldn't do that—tune into that, mac. And me thinking proscription and pre-scription differently ordered in this farm world of crummy acres. I mean I thought I'd left all that crap behind the night I stumbled along Rideout

Road following, maybe, the river Alph. I thought old man Hohepa, having been silent for so long, would know better than to pull, of a sudden, all those generalizations with which for seventeen years I'd been beaten dizzy—but not so dizzy as not to be able to look back of the billboards and see the stack of rotting bibles. Gentlemen, I was, even noticeably, subdued. Puti Hohepa clearly didn't intend to add anything more just then. I was too tired to make him an answer. I think I was too tired even for hate; and what better indication of the extent of my exhaustion than that? It had been a long summer; how long I was only beginning to discover. It was cold in the kitchen. Puti Hohepa got up. From the doorway, huge and merging into the night, he spoke again: You must make up your own mind. He went away, leaving behind him the vibration of a gentle sagacity, tolerance, a sense of duty (mine, as usual) pondered over and pronounced upon. The bastard. You must make up your own mind. And for the first time you did that mum had hysterics and dad popped his gut. About what? Made up my mind about what? My black daddy? Fanny? Myself? Life? A country career and agricultural hell? Death? Money? Fornication? (I'd always liked that.) What the hell was he trying to say? What doing but abdicating the soiled throne at the first challenge? Did he think fathers shouldn't hate their sons, or could help it, or would if they could? Am I clear? No matter. He didn't have one of the four he'd sired at home so what the hell sort of story was he trying to peddle? Father with the soft centre. You should, you shouldn't, make up you own mind. Mac, my head was going round. But it was brilliant, I conceded, when I'd given it a bit of thought. My livid daddy himself would have applauded the perfect ambiguity. What a bunch: they keep a dog on a chain for years and years and then let it free on some purely personal impulse and when it goes wild and chases its tail round and round, pissing here and sniffing there in an ecstasy of liberty, a freedom for which it has been denied all training, they shoot it down because it won't come running when they hold up the leash and whistle. (I didn't think you'd go that way, son.) Well, my own green liberty didn't look like so much at that moment; for the first time I got an inkling that life was going to be simply a matter of out of one jail and into another. Oh, they had a lot in common, her dad and mine. I sat there, mildly stupefied, drinking my tea. Then I looked up at Fanny; or, rather, down on Fanny. I've never known such a collapsible sheila in my life. She was stretched on the kitchen couch, every vertebra having turned to juice in the last minute and a half. I thought maybe she'd have the answer, some comment to offer on the state of disunion. Hell. I was the very last person to let my brew go cold while I pondered the nuance of the incomprehensible, picked at the dubious unsubtlety of thought of a man thirty years my senior who had never, until then, said more than ten words to me. She is too good for you: only six words after all and soon forgotten. Better, yes, if he'd stayed mum, leaving me to deduce from his silence whatever I could, Abora Mountain and the milk of paradise, consent in things natural and a willingness to let simple matters take their simple course.

I was wrong: Fanny offered no interpretation of her father's thought. Exegesis to his cryptic utterance was the one thing she couldn't supply. She lay with her feet up on the end of the couch, brown thighs charmingly bared, mouth open and eyes closed in balmy sleep, displaying in this posture various things but mainly her large unconcern not only for this tragedy of filial responsibility and the parental role but, too, for the diurnal problem of the numerous kitchen articles, pots, pans, plates, the lot. I gazed on her, frowning on her bloom of sleep, the slow inhalation and exhalation accompanied by a gentle flare of nostril, and considered the strength and weakness of our attachment. Helpmeet she was not, thus to leave her lover to his dark ponderings and the chores.

Puti Hohepa sat on the verandah in the dark, hacking over his bowl of shag. One by one, over my second cup of tea, I assessed my feelings, balanced all my futures in the palm of my hand. I crossed to Fanny, crouched beside her, kissed her. I felt embarrassed and, gentlemen, foolish. Her eyes opened wide; then they shut and she turned over.

The dishes engaged my attention not at all, except to remind me, here we go, of my father in apron and rubber gloves at the sink, pearl-diving while mum was off somewhere at a lynching. Poor bastard. Mum had the natural squeeze for the world; they should have changed places. (It's for your own good! Ah, the joyous peal of that as the razor strop came whistling down like tartar's blade.) I joined daddy Hohepa on the verandah. For a moment we shared the crescent moon and the smell of earth damp under dew, Rideout Mountain massed to the west.

I've finished the river paddock.

Yes.

The tractor's going to need a de-coke before long.

Yes.

I guess that about cuts it out.

Yes.

I may as well shoot through.

Buster, is Fanny pregnant?

I don't know. She hasn't said anything to me so I suppose she can't be.

You are going home?

No. Not home. There's work down south. I'd like to have a look down there.

There's work going here if you want it. But you have made up your mind?

I suppose I may as well shoot through.

Yes.

After milking tomorrow if that's okay with you.

Yes.

He hacked on over his pipe. Yes, yes, yes, yes, yes is Fanny pregnant? What if I'd said yes? I didn't know one way or the other. I only hoped, and left the rest to her. Maybe he'd ask her; and what if she said yes? What then, eh Buster? Maybe I should have said why don't you ask her. A demonstrative, volatile, loquacious old person: a tangible symbol of impartiality, reason unclouded by emotion, his eyes frank in the murk of night and his pipe going bright, dim, bright as he calmly considered the lovely flank of the moon. I was hoping she wasn't, after all. Hoping; it gets to be a habit, a bad habit that does you no good, stunts your growth, sends you insane and makes you, demonstrably, blind. Hope, for Fanny Hohepa.

Later, along the riverbank, Fanny and I groped, gentlemen, for the lost rapport and the parking sign. We were separated by just a little more than an arm's reach. I made note then of the natural scene. Dark water, certainly; dark lush grass underfoot; dark girl, the drifting smell of loam in the night: grant me again as much. Then, by one of those fortuitous accidents not infrequent in our national prosings, our hands met, held, fell away. Darkness. My feet stumbling by the river and my heart going like a tango. Blood pulsed upon blood, undenied and unyoked, as we busied ourselves tenderly at our ancient greetings and farewells. And in the end, beginning my sentence with a happy conjunction, I held her indistinct, dark head. We stayed so for a minute, together and parting as always, with me tumbling down upon her the mute dilemma my mind then pretended to resolve and she offering no restraint, no argument better than the dark oblivion of her face.

Unrecorded the words between us: there can't have been more than six, anyway, it was our fated number. None referred to my departure or to the future or to maculate conceptions. Yet her last touch spoke volumes. (Unsubsidized, gentlemen, without dedication or preamble.) River-damp softened her hair: her skin smelled of soap: Pan pricking forward to drink at the stream, crushing fennel, exquisitely stooping, bending. . . .

And, later again, silent, groping, we ascended in sequence to the paternal porch.

Buster?

Yair?

Goodnight, Buster.

'Night, Fanny. Be seein' yuh.

. . . .

Fourteen minute specks of radioactive phosphorus brightened by weak starlight pricked out the hour: one.

In the end I left old STC in the tractor tool box along with the spanner that wouldn't fit any nut I'd ever tried it on and the grease gun without grease and the last letter from mum, hot as radium. I didn't wait for milking. I was packed and gone at the first trembling of light. It was cold along the river-bottom, cold and still. Eels rose to feed: the water was like pewter; old pewter. I felt sick, abandoned, full of self-pity. Everything washed through me, the light, the cold, a sense of what lay behind me and might not lie before, a feeling of exhaustion when I thought of home, a feeling of despair when I thought of Fanny still curled in sleep. Dark. She hadn't giggled: so what? I changed my fibre suitcase to the other hand and trudged along Rideout Road. The light increased; quail with tufted crests crossed the road: I began to feel better. I sat on the suitcase and rolled a smoke. Then the sun caught a high scarp of Rideout Mountain and began to finger down slow and gold. I was so full of relief, suddenly, that I grabbed my bag and ran. Impetuous. I was lucky not to break my ankle. White gulls, loam flesh, dark water, damsel and dome; where would it take you? Where was there to go, anyway? It just didn't matter; that was the point. I stopped worrying that minute and sat by the cream stand out on the main road. After a while a truck stopped to my thumb and I got in. If I'd waited for the cream truck I'd have had to face old brownstone Hohepa and I wasn't very eager for that. I'd had a fill of piety, of various brands. And I was paid up to date.

I looked back. Rideout Mountain and the peak of ochre red roof, Maori red. That's all it was. I wondered what Fanny and her pappy might be saying at this moment, across the clothes-hanger rumps of cows. The rush of relief went through me again. I looked at the gloomy bastard driving: he had a cigarette stuck to his lip like a growth. I felt almost happy. Almost. I might have hugged him as he drove his hearse through the tail-end of summer.

Ronald Hugh Morrieson

CROSS MY HEART AND CUT MY THROAT

Wilma told me of a talk she had with her mother one day. 'I'm sick of learning the violin off Mr Henderson. I want to learn the guitar off Mr Wood. He played the guitar for Josephine last night at the school social. It was beauty.'

From what I gathered, her mother answered, 'I didn't know Mr Wood played the guitar. I knew he played the piano and he drinks.'

Then Wilma said, 'He can play the guitar all right. Josephine said she never sang better. She reckoned it was Mr Wood that made her sing like she did. Gee, he can play all right. All the kids clapped like mad.'

Her mother rang my mother up and made an appointment. In the murky gloom of an October dusk Wilma kept her appointment.

The night before the band had played until five a.m. (so it might be better to say the morning before); one of the biggest sessions of spanking chords on the most beat-up piano I want to forget. I could light a lot of fires with that piano.

When the bell rang there was Wilma holding a guitar case. I was on the phone booking in another job for the band when she rang. I was half asleep and I was dressed in a pair of crumpled slacks, a pyjama jacket and I remember I was wearing carpet slippers with a great big hole in the toe of one of them. I had had a bath the day before so at least I was clean but I had forgotten to cut my toenails.

There was no-one else in our big old house at the time so I had to go to the door myself. I rolled up my pyjama sleeves and put on an overcoat. The bell rang again but I still took time out to light a cigarette before I went to the door.

And there was Wilma. I was too tired to see what a cute-looking kid she was, but I remembered the moment I saw she was carrying a guitar case that my mother had booked in my first pupil. She saved me the trouble of trying to remember her name. She said, 'I'm Wilma so and so.'

'Come on in, Wilma.'

Wilma followed me down a long passage and I took her into a room with the oldest grand piano in the world in it. She was so interested in the big flat piano that she put her guitar case on the floor and she leaned over to look under the raised rosewood lid. I bent down and unsnapped the clips of the guitar case.

It was winter and in the Antipodes this can be the beginning of spring or it can be the heart of winter. It depended on the schools what sort of uniforms the girls wore. It was so cold this October that the pupils were in winter clothing and I guess the only thing I noticed were Wilma's worn and badly laddered black stockings and about an inch of flesh above them.

A hangover raises your blood pressure, your temperature, and makes you as sexy as a pedigree ram. While I was undoing the second clip on the case I tipped the whole damned case over because I was so busy looking up Wilma's legs.

My pyjama sleeves had become unrolled and were now showing around my wrists. My cigarette had fallen on to the top of the overturned guitar case. It was only half-smoked so I picked it up and had a drag. Wilma said, 'I've never seen a big piano like this before.'

I told her there were bigger pianos. I told her about table grands and concert grands. By this time she had stood up straight again so there wasn't any point in trying to see any further up her legs. Standing up must have taken a bit of the blood away from my head but I was still shaking a bit with a mixture of passion, self-control and alcoholic withdrawal.

'Look here, Wilma, how's about you hook out this cigar box of yours while I get myself a handkerchief.' I could tell she was looking at my pyjama sleeves.

I went down another long passage which led to the dining-room. The decanter on the sideboard was three-quarters full of whisky. I grabbed a seven ounce tumbler and poured myself a jolt that would have knocked a horse over; but all it did to me was make me drop my cigarette again with the first gulp. When I had drained the glass my stomach was hot and I counted up to ten to hold the booze down. I could feel my don't-give-a-damn attitude coming back. I picked up the cigarette which hadn't even scorched the Wilton. I pushed up my pyjama sleeves. Then I went back to Wilma.

Wilma said, 'I think it's out of tune. Mr Henderson was for ever telling me my violin was out of tune.'

That was when she told me about the conversation she had with her mother about leaving Mr Henderson. She gave it to me pretty nearly verbatim including the coda about me drinking. She grinned and I began to like her.

'Wilma,' I said, 'I'm sorry it's so cold in here. I'll put the heater on.'

To put the heater on in this music room was a fairly complicated business. It involved finding a long lead for one thing and a second jolt of whisky for another. After this I felt fine.

Just then someone started playing major scales in the next room so I knew my mother was home teaching one of her pupils. Although my mother loved me to distraction I had enough intuition to know she had a dreadful fear of me becoming an out-and-out waster. I was making good money in the band but no-one knew better than she or myself that the bulk of it was going on booze. It hit me right in the guts when I remembered how happy she looked when she told me that I had my first guitar pupil. Mum's pupil was playing the scale of D major now so I decided I could have another jolt before it got played contrary motion. Back I went to Wilma.

The first thing I did was tune her guitar. If her violin was anything like her guitar it would have made Stradivarius turn cartwheels.

Then I made a tremendous effort. I tore some pages out of the back of an exercise book and taught Wilma the diagram system, four chords and a simple practice routine. I explained it all very carefully and she seemed to dig. She had good hands. While I was doing this my mother looked in and smiled at us both.

I said, 'Practise that, Wilma.' And then, Lord save us, I fell asleep. Wilma woke me up about half an hour later and said she would have to go. I told her I had been playing the piano all night in a dance band.

'Wilma, I'm awfully sorry about this. I really am. Now, have you got your chords? Next week, Wilma, I'll be as fresh as a daisy.'

'That's all right, Mr Wood,' she said. She looked a bit cheesed off.

'I really am awfully sorry about dozing off, Wilma,' I said. 'You better not tell your folks about me dozing off like that. Crumbs, they'll think I'm a great teacher if you tell them that.'

And then Wilma did something I shall never ever forget. She crossed herself and made that age-old pretence of cutting her throat with a finger. I was so relieved that I made the first big blue of the day. I reached over and tried to kiss her but she ducked underneath my arm and walked out the door. I followed her down the hall and said, or rather croaked, 'Wilma,' but she didn't answer me so all I could do was let her out.

I felt ghastly. I was twenty-three years old and she was thirteen. Jail-bait and I was hooked. Nothing desperate had happened but she only had to blow it up a little to get me in real hot water. There was only one thing to do. I went back to the sideboard and poured myself a massive slug. Mum was still teaching in the front studio and I could have cut my throat.

Then the bell rang and I went down the long hall and opened the front door. There were two girls there. One was my blonde girlfriend who had been chasing me for eighteen months and the other was Wilma. I had no intention of marrying Dulcie because her family was downright common and she could swear like a bullock driver. I put on a big act. 'Come on in, girls. Dulcie, Wilma, come on in.'

Dulcie said, 'My God, do you have to wear an overcoat *inside* the house?' Neither of them had stepped inside yet. Maybe my breath was like a barbed wire fence.

Wilma said, 'Can I have my guitar please?'

'Shucks, Wilma, fancy forgetting your guitar. Come on, we'll get it now.'

So, keeping as steady as I could, I set off back along the long hall. I went into the room where the grand piano was and there was the guitar propped against the keyboard. The case was on the floor beside the chair I had fallen asleep on.

Wilma walked so softly that I didn't even know she was behind me. It wasn't until I turned around with the guitar and stooped down to put it back in its case that I saw her black stockinged legs about two feet in front of my glazed eyes.

The lid of the case was open towards me which meant I was doing everything back to front. I put the guitar down on the floor while I turned the case around. Wilma crouched down and her gym frock rode up. Now I could see five or more inches of bare leg above the black stockings and the tightest little pair of pants you ever saw in your life. They were like a snow-white handkerchief pulled into her crutch.

'Jesus,' I said huskily. 'You got nice legs, Wilma.'

'Thank you,' said Wilma primly.

I reached out and ran my hand up the inside of her left leg. She stood up quickly. I shut up the case and fastened the clips, just numb fumbling. She took the handle of the guitar case and picked it up and I lurched upright.

My blonde twenty-year-old girl friend, Dulcie, was standing in the doorway. She said, 'I get the picture.'

Wilma couldn't get past Dulcie and she said, 'Can I leave, please? I'm late for tea.' It was quite dark outside now.

Dulcie was so mad she didn't budge. Wilma did the nicest thing since she crossed her heart and cut her throat. She squeezed past Dulcie, belting her to one side with the guitar case. Dulcie took a smack at her but she missed by nearly as much as I had done when I tried to kiss her.

'I'm going to put you up for carnal knowledge,' said Dulcie viciously. 'You dirty, lecherous, rotten bastard.'

The front door slammed. Wilma had found her way out.

'In your pyjamas and overcoat,' Dulcie said. 'You're nothing but a ratbag.'

Deep inside me I felt I was doomed, but the Scotch reasserted itself to give me enough bravado to say, 'What's wrong with this overcoat? You liked it well enough when you had your bare bum on it beside my car the other night.'

I fished out my packet of cigarettes and there was only one left. I went over to the heater to light it. I had one eye on Dulcie in case she belted me over the skull. Just as I had my smoke going nicely she made a threatening twitch in my direction but I stood up fast and she knew how well I could fight, so she spun around and walked away. As she went down the hall she called out. 'Ratbag.'

Poor old Mum came out of the front studio without knowing all the trouble there had been. Dulcie must have looked pretty grim but at least she had the good grace to say (or snarl), 'Good night, Mrs Wood.'

I didn't have to play for a dance that night so I went and got a new pack of smokes and headed for the sideboard.

I said I was off my tucker, which was nothing but the truth, and all I wanted to do was go to bed. Instead of undressing I just slumped down on the side of the bed and chain smoked.

Mum came into my bedroom and kissed me goodnight and said, 'Well you had your first little pupil today.' It would be an insult to the reader's intelligence to describe what went through my mind when she said that.

'Of course she'll tell,' I brooded and muttered. 'A kid like that. She won't be able to help it. I'll just have to deny everything. The police'll be here tomorrow. Even tonight. This'll kill Mum.'

My mind went over the same track so often I thought I was going nuts. When the front doorbell did ring, although my heart missed a couple of beats, it was a relief.

There was the outline of a big guy in the front porch.

'Mr Wood?'

'Too late to hush it up now,' the Scotch in me said, and I attempted a friendly smile.

'I'm Wilma's father.'

'C'mon in.' I opened the door wide and stood back. He came in. He was big sure enough; tall, broad and he had bushy eyebrows.

'You know what Wilma tells me?' he said. No smile.

I shook my head. It nearly fell off.

'She left her guitar behind after her lesson.'

'Holy smoke,' I said. 'I'll have a look.'

Sure enough the guitar was lying on the floor by the grand.

When I took it back to him, he said, 'Can you imagine a girl being so dumb she didn't know the difference between an empty case and a full one?'

I frowned, tucked my chin in on my Adam's apple and made a clicking noise with my tongue. 'Beats me.'

After we had said good night I did what those heroines in the old movies used to do. As soon as I had closed the door I put my back against it and leaned there with my eyes closed.

It was my big day for doing crazy things. Later on, in the dark, my bedroom, pyjamas, on my marrowbones, I offered up thanks to the mysterious Creator who, on reflection, by imbuing me with passion (and all of us, for that matter) and making us what we are, was the true culprit of the episode.

Janet Frame

THE RESERVOIR

It was said to be four or five miles along the gully, past orchards and farms, paddocks filled with cattle, sheep, wheat, gorse, and the squatters of the land who were the rabbits eating like modern sculpture into the hills, though how could we know anything of modern sculpture, we knew nothing but the Warrior in the main street with his wreaths of poppies on Anzac Day, the gnomes weeping in the Gardens because the seagulls perched on their green caps and showed no respect, and how important it was for birds, animals and people, especially children, to show respect!

And that is why for so long we obeyed the command of the grownups and never walked as far as the forbidden Reservoir, but were content to return 'tired but happy' (as we wrote in our school compositions), answering the question, Where did you walk today? with a suspicion of blackmail, 'Oh, nearly, nearly to the Reservoir!'

The Reservoir was the end of the world; beyond it, you fell; beyond it were paddocks of thorns, strange cattle, strange farms, legendary people whom we would never know or recognize even if they walked among us on a Friday night downtown when we went to follow the boys and listen to the Salvation Army Band and buy a milk shake in the milk bar and then return home to find that everything was all right and safe, that our mother had not run away and caught the night train to the North Island, that our father had not shot himself with worrying over the bills, but had in fact been downtown himself and had bought the usual Friday night treat, a bag of licorice allsorts and a bag of chocolate roughs, from Woolworth's.

The Reservoir haunted our lives. We never knew one until we came to this town; we had used pump water. But here, in our new house, the water ran from the taps as soon as we turned them on, and if we were careless and left them on, our father would shout, as if the affair were his personal concern, 'Do you want the Reservoir to run dry?'

That frightened us. What should we do if the Reservoir ran dry? Would we die of thirst like Burke and Wills in the desert?

'The Reservoir,' our mother said, 'gives pure water, water safe to drink without boiling it.'

149

The water was in a different class, then, from the creek which flowed through the gully; yet the creek had its source in the Reservoir. Why had it not received the pampering attention of officialdom which strained weed and earth, cockabullies and trout and eels, from our tap water? Surely the Reservoir was not entirely pure?

'Oh no,' they said, when we inquired. We learned that the water from the Reservoir had been 'treated'. We supposed this to mean that during the night men in light-blue uniforms with sacks over their shoulders crept beyond the circle of pine trees which enclosed the Reservoir, and emptied the contents of the sacks into the water, to dissolve dead bodies and prevent the decay of teeth.

Then, at times, there would be news in the paper, discussed by my mother with the neighbours over the back fence. Children had been drowned in the Reservoir.

'No child,' the neighbour would say, 'ought to be allowed near the Reservoir.'

'I tell mine to keep strictly away,' my mother would reply.

And for so long we obeyed our mother's command, on our favourite walks along the gully simply following the untreated cast-off creek which we loved and which flowed day and night in our heads in all its detail— the wild sweet peas, boiled-lolly pink, and the mint growing along the banks; the exact spot in the water where the latest dead sheep could be found, and the stink of its bloated flesh and floating wool, an allowable earthy stink which we accepted with pleasant revulsion and which did not prompt the 'inky-pinky I smell Stinkie' rhyme which referred to offensive human beings only. We knew where the water was shallow and could be paddled in, where forts could be made from the rocks; we knew the frightening deep places where the eels lurked and the weeds were tangled in gruesome shapes; we knew the jumping places, the mossy stones with their dangers, limitations, and advantages; the sparkling places where the sun trickled beside the water, upon the stones; the bogs made by roaming cattle, trapping some of them to death; their gaunt telltale bones; the little valleys with their new growth of lush grass where the creek had 'changed its course', and no longer flowed.

'The creek has changed its course,' our mother would say, in a tone which implied terror and a sense of strangeness, as if a tragedy had been enacted.

We knew the moods of the creek, its levels of low-flow, half-high-flow, high-flow which all seemed to relate to interference at its source—the Reservoir. If one morning the water turned the colour of clay and crowds of bubbles were passengers on every suddenly swift wave hurrying by, we would look at one another and remark with the fatality and reverence which attends a visitation or prophecy,

'The creek's going on high-flow. They must be doing something at the Reservoir.'

By afternoon the creek would be on high-flow, turbulent, muddy, unable to be jumped across or paddled in or fished in, concealing beneath a swelling fluid darkness whatever evil which 'they', the authorities, had decided to purge so swiftly and secretly from the Reservoir.

For so long, then, we obeyed our parents, and never walked as far as the Reservoir. Other things concerned us, other curiosities, fears, challenges. The school year ended. I got a prize, a large yellow book the colour of cat's mess. Inside it were editions of newspapers, *The Worms' Weekly*, supposedly written by worms, snails, spiders. For the first part of the holidays we spent the time sitting in the long grass of our front lawn nibbling the stalks of shamrock and reading insect newspapers and relating their items to the lives of those living on our front lawn down among the summer-dry roots of the couch, tinkertailor, daisy, dandelion, shamrock, clover, and ordinary 'grass'. High summer came. The blowsy old red roses shed their petals to the regretful refrain uttered by our mother year after year at the same time, 'I should have made potpourri, I have a wonderful recipe for potpourri in Dr Chase's Book.'

Our mother never made the potpourri. She merely quarrelled with our father over how to pronounce it.

The days became unbearably long and hot. Our Christmas presents were broken or too boring to care about. Celluloid dolls had loose arms and legs and rifts in their bright pink bodies; the invisible ink had poured itself out in secret messages; diaries frustrating in their smallness (two lines to a day) had been filled in for the whole of the coming year. . . . Days at the beach were tedious, with no room in the bathing sheds so that we were forced to undress in the common room downstairs with its floor patched with wet and trailed with footmarks and sand and its tiny barred window (which made me believe that I was living in the French Revolution).

Rumours circled the burning world. The sea was drying up, soon you could paddle or walk to Australia. Sharks had been seen swimming inside the breakwater; one shark attacked a little boy and bit off his you-know-what.

We swam. We wore bathing togs all day. We gave up cowboys and ranches; and baseball and sledding; and 'those games' where we mimicked grown-up life, loving and divorcing each other, kissing and slapping, taking secret paramours when our husband was working out of town. Everything exhausted us. Cracks appeared in the earth; the grass was bled yellow; the ground was littered with beetle shells and snail shells; flies came in from the unofficial rubbish-dump at the back of the house; the twisting flypapers hung from the ceiling; a frantic buzzing filled the room as the flypapers became crowded. Even the cat put out her tiny tongue, panting in the heat.

We realized, and were glad, that school would soon reopen. What was school like? It seemed so long ago, it seemed as if we had never been to school, surely we had forgotten everything we had learned, how frightening, thrilling and strange it would all seem! Where would we go on the first day, who would teach us, what were the names of the new books?

Who would sit beside us, who would be our best friend?

The earth crackled in early-autumn haze and still the February sun dried the world; even at night the rusty sheet of roofing-iron outside by the cellar stayed warm, but with rows of sweat-marks on it; the days were still long, with night face to face with morning and almost nothing in-between but a snatch of turning sleep with the blankets on the floor and the windows wide open to moths with their bulging lamplit eyes moving through the dark and their grandfather bodies knocking, knocking upon the walls.

Day after day the sun still waited to pounce. We were tired, our skin itched, our sunburn had peeled and peeled again, the skin on our feet was hard, there was dust in our hair, our bodies clung with the salt of sea-bathing and sweat, the towels were harsh with salt.

School soon, we said again, and were glad; for lessons gave shade to rooms and corridors; cloakrooms were cold and sunless. Then, swiftly, suddenly, disease came to the town. Infantile Paralysis. Black headlines in the paper, listing the number of cases, the number of deaths. Children everywhere, out in the country, up north, down south, two streets away.

The schools did not reopen. Our lessons came by post, in smudged print on rough white paper; they seemed makeshift and false, they inspired distrust, they could not compete with the lure of the sun still shining, swelling, the world would go up in cinders, the days were too long, there was nothing to do, there was nothing to do; the lessons were dull; in the front room with the navy-blue blind half down the window and the tiny splits of light showing through, and the lesson papers sometimes covered with unexplained blots of ink as if the machine which had printed them had broken down or rebelled, the lessons were even more dull.

Ancient Egypt and the flooding of the Nile!

The Nile, when we possessed a creek of our own with individual flooding!

'Well let's go along the gully, along by the creek,' we would say, tired with all these.

Then one day when our restlessness was at its height, when the flies buzzed like bees in the flypapers, and the warped wood of the house cracked its knuckles out of boredom, the need for something to do in the heat, we found once again the only solution to our unrest.

Someone said, 'What's the creek on?'

'Half-high flow.'

'Good.'

So we set out, in our bathing suits, and carrying switches of willow.

'Keep your sun hats on!' our mother called.

All right. We knew. Sunstroke when the sun clipped you over the back of the head, striking you flat on the ground. Sunstroke. Lightning. Even tidal waves were threatening us on this southern coast. The world was full of alarm.

'And don't go as far as the Reservoir!'

We dismissed the warning. There was enough to occupy us along the gully without our visiting the Reservoir. First, the couples. We liked to find a courting couple and follow them and when, as we knew they must do because they were tired or for other reasons, they found a place in the grass and lay down together, we liked to make jokes about them, amongst ourselves. 'Just wait for him to kiss her,' we would say. 'Watch. There. A beaut. Smack.'

Often we giggled and lingered even after the couple had observed us. We were waiting for them to do it. Every man and woman did it, we knew that for a fact. We speculated about technical details. Would he wear a frenchie? If he didn't wear a frenchie then she would start having a baby and be forced to get rid of it by drinking gin. Frenchies, by the way, were for sale in Woolworth's. Some said they were fingerstalls, but we knew they were frenchies and sometimes we would go downtown and into Woolworth's just to look at the frenchies for sale. We hung around the counter, sniggering. Sometimes we nearly died laughing, it was so funny.

After we tired of spying on the couples we would shout after them as we went our way.

> Pound, shillings and pence,
> a man fell over the fence,

he fell on a lady,
and squashed out a baby,
pound, shillings and pence!

Sometimes a slight fear struck us—what if a man fell on us like that and squashed out a chain of babies?

Our other pastime along the gully was robbing the orchards, but this summer day the apples were small green hard and hidden by leaves. There were no couples either. We had the gully to ourselves. We followed the creek, whacking our sticks, gossiping and singing, but we stopped, immediately silent, when someone—sister or brother—said, 'Let's go to the Reservoir!'

A feeling of dread seized us. We knew, as surely as we knew our names and our address Thirty-three Stour Street Ohau Otago South Island New Zealand Southern Hemisphere The World, that we would some day visit the Reservoir, but the time seemed almost as far away as leaving school, getting a job, marrying.

And then there was the agony of deciding the right time—how did one decide these things?

'We've been told not to, you know,' one of us said timidly.

That was me. Eating bread and syrup for tea had made my hair red, my skin too, so that I blushed easily, and the grownups guessed if I told a lie.

'It's a long way,' said my little sister.

'Coward!'

But it *was* a long way, and perhaps it would take all day and night, perhaps we would have to sleep there among the pine trees with the owls hooting and the old needle-filled warrens which now reached to the centre of the earth where pools of molten lead bubbled, waiting to seize us if we tripped, and then there was the crying sound made by the trees, a sound of speech at its loneliest level where the meaning is felt but never explained, and it goes on and on in a kind of despair, trying to reach a point of understanding.

We knew that pine trees spoke in this way. We were lonely listening to them because we knew we could never help them to say it, whatever they were trying to say, for if the wind who was so close to them could not help them, how could we?

Oh no, we could not spend the night at the Reservoir among the pine trees.

'Billy Whittaker and his gang have been to the Reservoir, Billy Whittaker and the Green Feather gang, one afternoon.'

'Did he say what it was like?'

'No, he never said.'

'He's been in an iron lung.'

That was true. Only a day or two ago our mother had been reminding us in an ominous voice of the fact which roused our envy just as much as our dread, 'Billy Whittaker was in an iron lung two years ago. Infantile paralysis.'

Some people were lucky. None of us dared to hope that we would ever be surrounded by the glamour of an iron lung; we would have to be content all our lives with paltry flesh lungs.

'Well are we going to the Reservoir or not?'

That was someone trying to sound bossy like our father,—'Well am I to have salmon sandwiches or not, am I to have lunch at all today or not?'

We struck our sticks in the air. They made a whistling sound. They were supple and young. We had tried to make musical instruments out of them, time after time we hacked at the willow and the elder to make pipes to blow our music, but no sound came but our own voices. And why did two sticks rubbed together not make fire? Why couldn't we ever *make* anything out of the bits of the world lying about us?

An aeroplane passed in the sky. We craned our necks to read the writing on the underwing, for we collected aeroplane numbers.

The plane was gone, in a glint of sun.

'Are we?' someone said.

'If there's an eclipse you can't see at all. The birds stop singing and go to bed.'

'Well are we?'

Certainly we were. We had not quelled all our misgiving, but we set out to follow the creek to the Reservoir.

What is it? I wondered. They said it was a lake. I thought it was a bundle of darkness and great wheels which peeled and sliced you like an apple and drew you toward them with demonic force, in the same way that you were drawn beneath the wheels of a train if you stood too near the edge of the platform. That was the terrible danger when the Limited came rushing in and you had to approach to kiss arriving aunts.

We walked on and on, past wild sweet peas, clumps of cutty grass, horse mushrooms, ragwort, gorse, cabbage trees; and then, at the end of the gully, we came to strange territory, fences we did not know, with the barbed wire tearing at our skin and at our skirts put on over our bathing suits because we felt cold though the sun stayed in the sky.

We passed huge trees that lived with their heads in the sky, with their great arms and joints creaking with age and the burden of being trees, and their mazed and linked roots rubbed bare of earth, like bones with the flesh cleaned from them. There were strange gates to be opened or climber over, new directions to be argued and plotted, notices which said TRESPASSERS WILL BE PROSECUTED BY ORDER. And there was the remote immovable sun shedding without gentleness its influence of burning upon us and upon the town, looking down from its heavens and considering our infantile-paralysis epidemic, and the children tired of holidays and wanting to go back to school with the new stiff books with their crackling pages, the scrubbed ruler with the sun rising on one side amidst the twelfths, tenths, millimetres, the new pencils to be sharpened with the pencil shavings flying in long pickets and light-brown curls scalloped with red or blue; the brown school, the bare floors, the clump clump in the corridors on wet days!

We came to a strange paddock, a bull-paddock with its occupant planted deep in the long grass, near the gate, a jersey bull polished like a wardrobe, burnished like copper, heavy beams creaking in the wave and flow of the grass.

'Has it got a ring through its nose? Is it a real bull or a steer?'

Its nose was ringed which meant that its savagery was tamed, or so we thought; it could be tethered and led; even so, it had once been savage and it kept its pride, unlike the steers who pranced and huddled together and ran like water through the paddocks, made no impression, quarried no massive shape against the sky.

The bull stood alone.

Had not Mr Bennet been gored by a bull, his own tame bull, and been rushed to Glenham Hospital for thirty-three stitches? Remembering Mr Bennet we crept cautiously close to the paddock fence, ready to escape.

Someone said, 'Look, it's pawing the ground!'

A bull which pawed the ground was preparing for a charge. We escaped quickly through the fence. Then, plucking courage, we skirted the bushes on the far side of the paddock, climbed through the fence, and continued our walk to the Reservoir.

We had lost the creek between deep banks. We saw it now before us, and hailed it with more relief than we felt, for in its hidden course through the bull-paddock it had undergone change, it had adopted the shape, depth, mood of foreign water, foaming in a way we did not recognize as belonging to our special creek, giving no hint of its depth. It seemed to flow close to its concealed bed, not wishing any more to communicate with us. We realized with dismay that we had suddenly lost possession of our creek. Who had taken it? Why did it not belong to us any more? We hit our sticks in the air and forgot our dismay. We grew cheerful.

Till someone said that it was getting late, and we reminded one another that during the day the sun doesn't seem to move, it just remains pinned with a drawing pin against the sky, and then, while you are not looking, it suddenly slides down quick as the chopped-off head of a golden eel, into the sea, making everything in the world go dark.

'That's only in the tropics!'

We were not in the tropics. The divisions of the world in the atlas, the different coloured cubicles of latitude and longitude fascinated us.

'The sand freezes in the desert at night. Ladies wear bits of sand. . . .'

'grains . . . '

'grains or bits of sand as necklaces, and the camels . . . '

'with necks like snails . . . '

'with horns, do they have horns?'

'Minnie Stocks goes with boys. . . .'

'I know who your boy is, I know who your boy is. . . . '

> Waiting by the garden gate,
> Waiting by the garden gate . . .

'We'll never get to the Reservoir!'

'Whose idea was it?'

'I've strained my ankle!'

Someone began to cry. We stopped walking.

"I've strained my ankle."

There was an argument.

'It's not strained, it's sprained.'

'strained.'

'sprained.'

'All right sprained then. I'll have to wear a bandage, I'll have to walk on crutches. . . . '

'I had crutches once. Look. I've got a scar where I fell off my stilts. It's a white scar, like a centipede. It's on my shins.'

'Shins! Isn't it a funny word? Shins. Have you ever been kicked in the shins?'

'shins, funnybone . . . '

'It's humerus. . . . '

'knuckles . . . '

'a sprained ankle . . . '

'a strained ankle . . . '

'a whitlow, an ingrown toenail the roots of my hair warts spinal meningitis infantile paralysis . . . '

'Infantile paralysis, Infantile paralysis you have to be wheeled in a chair and wear irons on your legs and your knees knock together. . . . '

'Once you're in an iron lung you can't get out, they lock it, like a cage. . . . '

'You go in the amberlance . . . '

'*ambulance* . . . '

'amberlance . . . '

'ambulance to the hostible. . . . '

'the *hospital*, an *amberlance to the hospital* . . . '

'Infantile Paralysis . . . '

'Friar's Balsam! Friar's Balsam!'

'Baxter's Lung Preserver, Baxter's Lung Preserver!'

'Syrup of Figs, California Syrup of Figs!'

'The creek's going on high-flow!'

Yes, there were bubbles on the surface, and the water was turning muddy. Our doubts were dispelled. It was the same old creek, and there, suddenly, just ahead, was a plantation of pine trees, and already the sighing sound of it reached our ears and troubled us. We approached it, staying close to the banks of our newly claimed creek, until once again the creek deserted us, flowing its own private course where we could not follow, and we found ourselves among the pine trees, a narrow strip of them, and beyond lay a vast surface of sparkling water, dazzling our eyes, its centre chopped by tiny grey waves. Not a lake, nor a river, nor a sea.

'The Reservoir!'

The damp smell of the pine needles caught in our breath. There were no birds, only the constant sighing of the trees. We could see the water clearly now; it lay, except for the waves beyond the shore, in an almost perfect calm which we knew to be deceptive—else why were people so afraid of the Reservoir? The fringe of young pines on the edge, like toy trees, subjected to the wind, sighed and told us their sad secrets. In the Reservoir there was an appearance of neatness which concealed a disarray too frightening to be acknowledged except, without any defence, in moments of deep sleep and dreaming. The little sparkling innocent waves shone now green, now grey, petticoats, lettuce leaves; the trees sighed, and told us to be quiet, hush-sh, as if something were sleeping and should not be disturbed—perhaps that was what the trees were always telling us, to hush-sh in case we disturbed something which must never ever be awakened?

What was it? Was it sleeping in the Reservoir? Was that why people were afraid of the Reservoir?

Well we were not afraid of it, oh no, it was only the Reservoir, it was nothing to be afraid of, it was just a flat Reservoir with a fence around it, and trees, and on the far side a little house (with wheels inside?), and nothing to be afraid of.

'The Reservoir, The Reservoir!'

A noticeboard said DANGER, RESERVOIR.

Overcome with sudden glee we climbed through the fence and swung on the lower branches of the trees, shouting at intervals, gazing possessively and delightedly at the sheet of water with its wonderful calm and menace,

'The Reservoir! The Reservoir! The Reservoir!'

We quarrelled again about how to pronounce and spell the word.

Then it seemed to be getting dark—or was it that the trees were stealing the sunlight and keeping it above their heads? One of us began to run. We all ran, suddenly, wildly, not caring about our strained or sprained ankles, through the trees out into the sun where the creek, but it was our creek no longer, waited for us. We wished it were our creek, how we wished it were our creek! We had lost all account of time. Was it nearly night? Would darkness overtake us, would we have to sleep on the banks of the creek that did not belong to us any more, among the wild sweet peas and the tussocks and the dead sheep? And would the eels come up out of the creek, as people said they did, and on their travels through the paddocks would they change into people who would threaten us and bar our way, TRESPASSERS WILL BE PROSECUTED, standing arm in arm in their black glossy coats, swaying, their mouths open, ready to swallow us? Would they ever let us go home, past the orchards, along the gully? Perhaps they would give us Infantile Paralysis, perhaps we would never be able to walk home, and no one would know where we were, to bring us an iron lung with its own special key!

We arrived home, panting and scratched. How strange! The sun was still in the same place in the sky!

The question troubled us, 'Should we tell?'

The answer was decided for us. Our mother greeted us as we went in the door with, 'You haven't been long away, kiddies. Where have you been? I hope you didn't go anywhere near the Reservoir.'

Our father looked up from reading his newspapers.

'Don't let me catch you going near the Reservoir!'

We said nothing. How out-of-date they were! They were actually afraid!

Janet Frame

THE BATH

On Friday afternoon she bought cut flowers—daffodils, anemones, a few twigs of a red-leaved shrub, wrapped in mauve waxed paper, for Saturday was the seventeenth anniversary of her husband's death and she planned to visit his grave, as she did each year, to weed it and put fresh flowers in the two jam jars standing one on each side of the tombstone. Her visit this year occupied her thoughts more than usual. She had bought the flowers to force herself to make the journey that each year became more hazardous, from the walk to the bus stop, the change of buses at the Octagon, to the bitterness of the winds blowing from the open sea across almost unsheltered rows of tombstones; and the tiredness that overcame her when it was time to return home when she longed to find a place beside the graves, in the soft grass, and fall asleep.

That evening she filled the coal bucket, stoked the fire. Her move ments were slow and arduous, her back and shoulder gave her so much pain. She cooked her tea—liver and bacon—set her knife and fork on the teatowel she used as a tablecloth, turned up the volume of the polished red radio to listen to the Weather Report and the News, ate her tea, washed her dishes, then sat drowsing in the rocking chair by the fire, waiting for the water to get hot enough for a bath. Visits to the cemetery, the doctor, and to relatives, to stay, always demanded a bath. When she was sure that the water was hot enough (and her tea had been digested) she ventured from the kitchen through the cold passageway to the colder bathroom. She paused in the doorway to get used to the chill of the air then she walked slowly, feeling with each step the pain in her back, across to the bath, and though she knew that she was gradually losing the power in her hands she managed to wrench on the stiff cold and hot taps and half-fill the bath with warm water. How wasteful, she thought, that with the kitchen fire always burning during the past month of frost, and the water almost always hot, getting in and out of a bath had become such an effort that it was not possible to bath every night nor even every week!

She found a big towel, laid it ready over a chair, arranged the chair so that should difficulty arise as it had last time she bathed she would have some way of rescuing herself; then with her nightclothes warming on a page of newspaper inside the coal oven and her dressing-gown across the chair to be put on the instant she stepped from the bath, she undressed and pausing first to get her breath and clinging tightly to the slippery yellow-stained rim that now seemed more like the edge of a cliff with a deep drop below into the sea, slowly and painfully she climbed into the bath.

—I'll put on my nightie the instant I get out, she thought. The instant she got out indeed! She knew it would be more than a matter of instants yet she tried to think of it calmly, without dread, telling herself that when the time came she would be very careful, taking the process step by step, surprising her bad back and shoulder and her powerless wrists into performing feats they might usually rebel against, but the key to controlling them would be the surprise, the slow stealing up on them. With care, with thought. . . .

Sitting upright, not daring to lean back or lie down, she soaped herself, washing away the dirt of the past fortnight, seeing with satisfaction how it drifted about on the water as a sign that she was clean again. Then when her washing was completed she found herself looking for excuses not to try yet to climb out. Those old woman's finger nails, cracked and dry, where germs could lodge, would need to be scrubbed again; the skin of her heels, too, growing so hard that her feet might have been turning to stone; behind her ears where a thread of dirt lay in the rim; after all, she did not often have the luxury of a bath, did she? How warm it was! She drowsed a moment. If only she could fall asleep then wake to find herself in her nightdress in bed for the night! Slowly she rewashed her body, and when she knew she could no longer deceive herself into thinking she was not clean she reluctantly replaced the soap, brush and flannel in the groove at the side of the bath, feeling as she loosened her grip on them that all strength and support were ebbing from her. Quickly she seized the nail-brush again, but its magic had been used and was gone; it would not adopt the role she tried to urge upon it. The flannel too, and the soap, were frail flotsam to cling to in the hope of being borne to safety.

She was alone now. For a few moments she sat swilling the water against her skin, perhaps as a means of buoying up her courage. Then resolutely she pulled out the plug, sat feeling the tide swirl and scrape at her skin and flesh, trying to draw her down, down into the earth; then the bathwater was gone in a soapy gurgle and she was naked and shivering and had not yet made the attempt to get out of the bath.

How slippery the surface had become! In future she would not clean it with kerosene, she would use the paste cleaner that, left on overnight, gave the enamel rough patches that could be gripped with the skin.

She leaned forward, feeling the pain in her back and shoulder. She grasped the rim of the bath but her fingers slithered from it almost at once. She would not panic, she told herself; she would try gradually, carefully, to get out. Again she leaned forward; again her grip loosened as if iron hands had deliberately uncurled her stiffened blue fingers from their trembling hold. Her heart began to beat faster, her breath came more quickly, her mouth was dry. She moistened her lips. If I shout for help, she thought, no-one will hear me. No-one in the world will hear me. No-one will know I'm in the bath and can't get out.

She listened. She could hear only the drip-drip of the cold water tap of the wash-basin, and a corresponding whisper and gurgle of her heart, as if it were beating under water. All else was silent. Where were the people, the traffic? Then she had a strange feeling of being under the earth, of a throbbing in her head like wheels going over the earth above her.

Then she told herself sternly that she must have no nonsense, that she had really not tried to get out of the bath. She had forgotten the strong solid chair and the grip she could get on it. If she made the effort quickly she could first take hold of both sides of the bath, pull herself up, then transfer her hold to the chair and thus pull herself out.

She tried to do this; she just failed to make the final effort. Pale now, gasping for breath, she sank back into the bath. She began to call out but as she had predicted there was no answer. No-one had heard her, no-one in the houses or the street or Dunedin or the world knew that she was imprisoned. Loneliness welled in her. If John were here, she thought, if we were sharing our old age, helping each other, this would never have happened. She made another effort to get out. Again she failed. Faintness overcoming her she closed her eyes, trying to rest, then recovering and trying again and failing, she panicked and began to cry and strike the sides of the bath; it made a hollow sound like a wild drum-beat.

Then she stopped striking with her fists; she struggled again to get out; and for over half an hour she stayed alternately struggling and resting until at last she did succeed in climbing out and making her escape into the kitchen. She thought, I'll never take another bath in this house or anywhere. I never want to see that bath again. This is the end or the beginning of it. In future a district nurse will have to come to attend me. Submitting to that will be the first humiliation. There will be others, and others.

In bed at last she lay exhausted and lonely thinking that perhaps it might be better for her to die at once. The slow progression of difficulties was a kind of torture. There were her shoes that had to be made specially in a special shape or she could not walk. There were the times she had to call in a neighbour to fetch a pot of jam from the top shelf of her cupboard when it had been only a year ago that she herself had made the jam and put it on the shelf. Sometimes a niece came to fill the coal-bucket or mow the lawn. Every week there was the washing to be hung on the line—this required a special technique for she could not raise her arms without at the same time finding some support in the dizziness that overcame her. She remembered with a sense of the world narrowing and growing darker, like a tunnel, the incredulous almost despising look on the face of her niece when in answer to the comment

—How beautiful the clouds are in Dunedin! These big billowing white and grey clouds—don't you think, Auntie?

She had said, her disappointment at the misery of things putting a sharpness in her voice,

—I never look at the clouds!

She wondered how long ago it was since she had been able to look up at the sky without reeling with dizziness. Now she did not dare look up. There was enough to attend to down and around—the cracks and hollows in the footpath, the patches of frost and ice and the potholes in the roads; the approaching cars and motorcycles; and now, after all the outside menaces, the inner menace of her own body. She had to be guardian now over her arms and legs, force them to do as she wanted when how easily and dutifully they had walked, moved and grasped, in the old days! They were the enemy now. It had been her body that showed treachery when she tried to get out of the bath. If she ever wanted to bath again—how strange it seemed!—she would have to ask another human being to help her to guard and control her own body. Was this so fearful? she wondered. Even if it were not, it seemed so.

She thought of the frost slowly hardening outside on the fences, roofs, windows and streets. She thought again of the terror of not being able to escape from the bath. She remembered her dead husband and the flowers she had bought to put on his grave. Then thinking again of the frost, its whiteness, white like a new bath, of the anemones and daffodils and the twigs of the red-leaved shrub, of John dead seventeen years, she fell asleep while outside, within two hours, the frost began to melt with the warmth of a sudden wind blowing from the north, and the night grew warm, like a spring night, and in the morning the light came early, the sky was pale blue, the same warm wind as gentle as a mere breath, was blowing, and a narcissus had burst its bud in the front garden.

In all her years of visiting the cemetery she had never known the wind so mild. On an arm of the peninsula exposed to the winds from two stretches of sea, the cemetery had always been a place to crouch shivering in overcoat and scarf while the flowers were set on the grave and the narrow garden cleared of weeds. Today, everything was different. After all the frosts of the past month there was not trace of chill in the air. The mildness and warmth were scarcely to be believed. The sea lay, violet-coloured, hush-hushing, turning and heaving, not breaking into foamy waves; it was one sinuous ripple from shore to horizon and its sound was the muted sound of distant forests of peace.

Picking up the rusted garden fork that she knew lay always in the grass of the next grave, long neglected, she set to work to clear away the twitch and other weeds, exposing the first bunch of dark blue primroses with yellow centres, a clump of autumn lilies, and the shoots, six inches high, of daffodils. Then removing the green-slimed jam jars from their grooves on each side of the tombstone she walked slowly, stiff from her crouching, to the ever-dripping tap at the end of the lawn path where, filling the jars with pebbles and water she rattled them up and down to try to clean them of slime. Then she ran the sparkling ice-cold water into the jars and balancing them carefully one in each hand she walked back to the grave where she shook the daffodils, anemones, red leaves from their waxed paper and dividing them put half in one jar, half in the other. The dark blue of the anemones swelled with a sea-colour as their heads rested against the red leaves. The daffodils were short-stemmed with big ragged rather than delicate trumpets—the type for blowing; and their scent was strong.

Finally, remembering the winds that raged from the sea she stuffed small pieces of the screwed-up waxed paper into the top of each jar so the flowers would not be carried away by the wind. Then with a feeling of satisfaction—I look after my husband's grave after seventeen years. The tombstone is not cracked or blown over, the garden has not sunk into a pool of clay. I look after my husband's grave—she began to walk away, between the rows of graves, noting which were and were not cared for. Her father and mother had been buried here. She stood now before their grave. It was a roomy grave made in the days when there was space for the dead and for the dead with money, like her parents, extra space should they need it. Their tombstone was elaborate though the writing was now faded; in death they kept the elaborate station of their life. There were no flowers on the grave, only the feathery sea-grass soft to the touch, lit with gold in the sun. There was no sound but the sound of the sea and the one row of fir trees on the brow of the hill. She felt the peace inside her; the nightmare of the evening before seemed far away, seemed not to have happened; the senseless terrifying struggle to get out of a bath!

She sat on the concrete edge of her parents' grave. She did not want to go home. She felt content to sit here quietly with the warm soft wind flowing around her and the sigh of the sea rising to mingle with the sighing of the firs and the whisper of the thin gold grass. She was grateful for the money, the time and the forethought that had made her parents' grave so much bigger than the others near by. Her husband, cremated, had been allowed only a narrow eighteen inches by two feet, room only for the flecked grey tombstone In Memory of My Husband John Edward Harraway died August 6th 1948, and the narrow garden of spring flowers, whereas her parents' grave was so wide, and its concrete wall was a foot high; it was, in death, the equivalent of a quarter-acre section before there were too many people in the world. Why when the world was wider and wider was there no space left?

Or was the world narrower?

She did not know; she could not think; she knew only that she did not want to go home, she wanted to sit here on the edge of the grave, never catching any more buses, crossing streets, walking on icy footpaths, turning mattresses, trying to reach jam from the top shelf of the cupboard, filling coal buckets, getting in and out of the bath. Only to get in somewhere and stay in; to get out and stay out; to stay now, always, in one place.

Ten minutes later she was waiting at the bus stop; anxiously studying the destination of each bus as it passed, clutching her money since concession tickets were not allowed in the weekend, thinking of the cup of tea she would make when she got home, of her evening meal—the remainder of the liver and bacon—, of her nephew in Christchurch who was coming with his wife and children for the school holidays, of her niece in the home expecting her third baby. Cars and buses surged by, horns tooted, a plane droned, near and far, near and far, children cried out, dogs barked; the sea, in competition, made a harsher sound as if its waves were now breaking in foam.

For a moment, confused after the peace of the cemetery, she shut her eyes, trying to recapture the image of her husband's grave, now bright with spring flowers, and her parents' grave, wide, spacious, with room should the dead desire it to turn and sigh and move in dreams as if the two slept together in a big soft grass double-bed.

She waited, trying to capture the image of peace. She saw only her husband's grave, made narrower, the spring garden whittled to a thin strip; then it vanished and she was left with the image of the bathroom, of the narrow confining bath grass-yellow as old baths are, not frost-white, waiting, waiting, for one moment of inattention, weakness, pain, to claim her for ever.

Barbara Anderson

UP THE RIVER WITH MRS GALLANT

Mr Levis invited them to call him Des. And this is Arnold he said.

Mr Kent said Hi Arnold.

Mrs Kent said that she was pleased to meet him.

Mrs Gallant said Hullo, Arnold.

Mr Gallant said Good morning.

Mr Borges said nothing.

Des said that if they just liked to walk down to the landing stage Arnold would bring the boat down with the tractor.

Mrs Gallant said wasn't Mr Gallant going to leave the car in the shade.

Mr Gallant said that if Mrs Gallant was able to tell him where the shade from one tree was going to be for the next six hours he would be happy to.

Mr Kent said that he was going to give it a burl anyway and reparked the Falcon beneath the puriri.

Mrs Kent told Mrs Gallant that she and Stan were from Hamilton.

Mrs Gallant told Mrs Kent that she and Eric were from Rotorua.

Mrs Kent said that she had a second cousin in Rotorua. Esme. Esme. She would be forgetting her own head next. And that she supposed she should wait for Stan but what the hell.

Mrs Gallant smiled at Mr Borges.

Mr Borges nodded.

At the landing stage Des said that he would like them to take turns sitting in the front and perhaps the ladies?

Mrs Kent remarked that the landing stage looked a bit ass over tip.

Arnold said that the landing stage was safe as houses and would the lady get into the boat.

Mrs Kent said Where was Stan.

Mr Kent said Here.

Mrs Kent asked Mr Kent where he had got to. She hopped across the landing stage, climbed onto the boat and into one of the front seats. She said that it wasn't too lady like but that she would be right.

Mrs Gallant followed.

Mr Kent and Mr Gallant climbed into the next row.

Des said that Arnold was on the Access Training Scheme and doing very well but it was difficult to fit in the hundred hours river time in a business like this and that he hoped that the customers would have no objection if Arnold came with them and drove the boat back because of the hundred hours.

Mrs Kent said that she would be delighted anytime.

Mr Kent said Well.

Mr Gallant asked how many passengers the boat was licensed for.

Des said that it was licensed for seven passengers.

Mrs Gallant smiled.

Mr Borges said nothing.

Arnold said Good on them, climbed into the boat and sat in the back row with Mr Borges. Mr Borges smiled.

Des started the motor and picked up the microphone. He said that the river was approximately ninety miles long and had been called the Rhine Of New Zealand. It had been used as a waterway since the time of the first Maoris. Perhaps the busiest time on the river, he said, was the end of the nineteenth century and the beginning of the twentieth until the Main Trunk was completed. River boats plied, freight and passengers were transported in thousands and in all that time there were only two deaths which must be something of a record.

Mr Gallant said that he hoped that it would stay that way.

Des invited him to come again.

Mrs Kent said that Mr Gallant was only kidding.

Mr Gallant said No he wasn't.

Mrs Gallant said Eric.

Des said that he was born and brought up on the river. He had lived on the river all his life and he knew the river like the back of his hand and his aim was for every one of his passengers to learn more about this beautiful river which was steeped in history.

Mr Kent said that Des would do him.

Mrs Kent said Hear Hear.

Mr Borges, Mr Gallant and Arnold said nothing.

Mrs Gallant said that it was a lovely day.

Des said that she wasn't running as sweet as usual, probably a few stones up the grille.

Mrs Gallant asked What did that mean.

Des said Stones you know up the grille.

Mrs Gallant said that she realised that.

Mr Gallant smiled.

Mrs Kent said that they had a lovely day for it anyhow.

Des said they certainly had and to take a look at the flying fox across the river. He explained that the alignment of the posts was very important indeed.

Mr Gallant said that it would be.

Des said that otherwise she could come across but she wouldn't go back. On the other hand if it was wrong the other way she would go back but she wouldn't come across.

Mr Gallant said Exactly.

Mr Kent said it was all Dutch to him Ooh Pardon.

Mrs Kent said that the young man wasn't Dutch and that Stan needn't worry.

Mr Kent said Then what was he?

Mrs Kent said that yes the day certainly was a cracker.

Mrs Gallant smiled.

Des said that the cooling system wasn't operating as per usual either. Usually she stayed at twenty. That was what he liked her at. Twenty.

Mrs Gallant said that it was at seventy now was it not.

Des said Yes it was.

Mrs Gallant said Oh.

Mr Gallant laughed.

Des said that they certainly would like Pipiriki.

Mrs Kent said That was for sure.

Des moored the boat at the Pipiriki landing stage. Everyone climbed out. Des put a large carton on an outdoor table and said they could help themselves to tea or coffee.

Mrs Gallant said that she and Eric would only need one teabag between them as they both took tea very weak without milk.

Des said that Mrs Gallant needn't worry as he had provided two tea bags each per person as usual.

Mr Gallant said that she was only trying to help.

Mrs Kent asked if there was a toilet.

Arnold pointed up the path.

Des said that after lunch they should go up and look at Pipiriki. Pipiriki House had once been a world famous hotel. It had burned down in 1959. He said to have a good look at the shelter and to go around the back as there were some flush toilets.

Mrs Kent said that now Des told her and they both laughed.

Mrs Gallant said What shelter.

Des said A shelter for tourists you know trampers, that sort of thing.

Everyone liked Pipiriki very much. After an hour they climbed back into the boat.

Mr Kent said that he wished some of those activists could see all those kids happy and swimming.

Mr Gallant said Why?

Mr Kent said to look at that one jumping there. That he hadn't a care in the world.

Mr Gallant said that that was hardly the point.

Mrs Gallant said Eric.

Mr Gallant said Hell's delight woman.

Mr Borges smiled.

Mrs Kent said that they used to live near Cambridge but that they had moved in to Hamilton when the boy took over.

Mrs Gallant said Was that right, and that she wished they had been able to land at Jerusalem.

Arnold said that he could go a swim.

Des said that he had been going to have a good look at her yesterday but that he hadn't had a break for so long and that he just hadn't felt like it.

No one said anything.

Des said that anyway he had had another booking in the end as things had turned out.

The boat leapt and bucked high in the air.

Mrs Kent said Ooops.

Des said that that showed you what happened if you let your concentration slip even for a second with a jettie. She had hit a stump.

Mr Gallant laughed.

Arnold asked if the Boss would like him to take over.

Des and Arnold laughed.

Mrs Gallant said to look at that kingfisher.

Mrs Kent said Where.

Mrs Gallant said There. That Mrs Kent was too late. That it had gone.

Des pointed out many points of interest and said that no she certainly wasn't going too good.

Mrs Gallant said that hadn't the temperature gauge gone up to eighty or was she wrong.

Des said that no she was not wrong and that he had better give her a breather and stopped the boat. He said it was probably the temperature of the water, it being a hot day.

Nobody said anything. The boat rocked, silent on the trough of its own waves. The sun shone.

Des said that that should have cooled her down a bit and started the boat.

The temperature gauge climbed to seventy.

Des said that that was more like it and that there had been a Maori battle on that island between the Hau Hau supporters and the non-supporters.

Mr Gallant wondered why they had chosen an island.

Des said that Mr Gallant had him there and swung the boat into a shallow tributary of the river. He told Arnold that they had better check the grille and how would Arnold like a swim.

Arnold said that that would be no problem. He climbed around onto the bow of the boat and said that they would now see his beautiful body. He removed his shirt and told Mrs Gallant and Mrs Kent to control themselves.

Mrs Kent yelped.

Arnold faced the vertical cliff of the bank, presented his shorts clad buttocks and shook them.

Everyone laughed except Mr Gallant and Mr Borges.

Mr Borges stood up quickly, took a photograph of Arnold's back view, and sat down again.

Arnold jumped into the water and swam to the back of the boat. Des fumbled beneath his feet and handed the passengers various pieces of equipment for Arnold to poke up the grille. The male passengers handed the things on to Arnold with stern efficiency.

After some time Arnold said that he had found three stones up the grille.

Des said that that was good.

Arnold said that they were not big buggers though.

Des said Never mind.

Arnold handed the equipment back into the boat and did a honeypot jump from the shallow water into a deep pool.

Mr Kent said See?

Arnold swam to the bow of the boat and heaved himself into the boat.

Mr Borges took a photograph of Arnold's front view.

Mrs Gallant said that they were lucky that Arnold had come with them.

Mrs Kent said that Mrs Gallant could say that again and would the boat go better now that Arnold had removed the stones.

Des said that he hoped so.

Mr Gallant laughed.

They stopped several times on the return trip for the boat to cool down and as she was not going too well Des sometimes had to make several sweeps before she could pick up enough speed for her to lift up over the rapids. Des said that normally at this stage, when she was less than half full of gas he could fling her about all over the place no sweat.

Mr Gallant said that they must be thankful for small mercies.

Des swung the boat in a wide spraying circle and pulled into the jetty at the old flour mill. They climbed the hill, Des carrying the afternoon tea carton. After tea Des said that he would tell them about the old flour mill and the river in general. Everyone expressed interest. They trooped into the warm shadowy old building and Des began.

After half an hour Mrs Kent asked whether Des would mind if she sat down.

Des said that although perhaps it was technically more correct to call them river boats he still thought of them as steamers though strictly speaking they weren't steamers for long.

Mrs Kent sat down.

Mrs Gallant sat down.

Mr Kent looked as though he was going to cry.

Mr Gallant closed his eyes.

Arnold sat outside in the shade.

Mr Borges joined him.

After three quarters of an hour Des said that he hoped they had all learned something of the river.

They climbed down to the river in silence.

Des said that as she wasn't the best perhaps if Mrs Gallant and Mr Kent would like to sit in front.

Mr Gallant muttered something about sensible arrangement of ballast.

Mrs Kent asked Des why.

Arnold said it was because he liked the good-looking girls in the back with him.

Mrs Kent told Arnold to get away and climbed nimbly into the back seat.

Mrs Gallant said nothing.

They set off with Des at the wheel. The temperature gauge rose above eighty. Des asked the passengers to look around their feet for a tool which would enable Arnold to take another poke up the grille without getting out of the boat.

Mrs Gallant said that there was a pipe thing here if that was any help.

Mrs Kent gave a startled cry and said What was that smoke.

Mr Gallant said that that was steam.

Mrs Kent said that it was red hot that pipe thing there.

Mr Gallant said that he was not at all surprised.

Arnold said that she would be right.

Des said that she had better have another cool off and stopped the boat.

The boat limped to the original landing jetty two hours later than planned. The passengers collected their belongings without comment and trailed up the hill.

Des told Arnold that he could bring the boat up.

Arnold said that Des was the Boss.

Mrs Gallant remarked that it had been a very interesting day and that wasn't the river beautiful.

Mrs Kent said that yes it was but that she had felt so sorry for the poor chap.

Mr Gallant said God in Heaven.

Mrs Gallant remarked that she saw that Mr Kent's car was in the shade.

Mr Gallant said that it probably had not been for the first six hours.

Mrs Gallant said that that remark was typical absolutely typical.

Mrs Kent said that they used to have Jerseys but the boy had switched to Friesians.

Mr Kent said that he had been happy enough in Jerseys but that there you were.

Mrs Kent said that they just want to be different and that it was quite understandable.

Mr Kent said that he had never said it wasn't.

Mr Borges said nothing.

Arnold appeared on the tractor, pulling the boat on its trailer. He parked it in the shed and appeared with a Visitors' Book. He invited the passengers to make their crosses.

Everyone laughed except Mr Gallant and Mr Borges.

Des said that he would give her an overhaul tomorrow that was for sure.

Mrs Kent signed the book and wrote Lovely day under Comments.

Mr Kent signed and wrote Ditto.

Mr Gallant signed his name only.

Mr Borges signed and wrote Sweden.

Mrs Gallant missed the signing. She stumped across the bleached grass and stood gazing at the river.

It said nothing.

Renato Amato

ONE OF THE TITANS

He was tired. There was an abandoned slackness in his arms and legs as he stood in front of the concrete-mixer, continuing to wash it even when he did not need to any longer. The bowl was clean. But just now he liked playing with the water; he liked the noise the water made when the solidity of what seemed to be a shaft of glass broke and twirled. It was easy; he did not have to move. He could be still and just flick his wrist one way and the other.

There was concrete, as solid as rock, hardened all round the rim but he would not try to scrape it off. It was not his fault that it had been allowed to settle. He could hardly believe that anybody might be so careless with their equipment, but nobody really cared. Why should he worry? The only thing that mattered was the big money. As big as their mouths could make it. That was all that counted: the big money earned with a constant grudge at being forced to work long hours, and away from the city. But then, to people like him, to all the ditch-diggers and concrete-shovellers and timber-carriers and steel-benders and nail-pushers he knew, money was all they could have. . . .

Once he had seen an old, tall, somehow masculine woman in the bank where he worked before he came away; and now she kept hammering at him, coming back to him, with one sentence that, when he had first heard it, had had no meaning at all.

The woman had been as if iron-bound; she had looked metallic and hard in her antiquated dress—a country woman come to town from the other end of the world— while she stood in front of his teller's window to change her traveller's cheques. She had come from Australia which, then, to him, was only a series of glowing reports from the pages of some propaganda booklet.

He had asked one question of this woman, because he had decided to go somewhere near there, some sort of Paradise on earth, or Garden of Eden, just like Australia: two islands called New Zealand, another colony of Great Britain.

'What's Australia like?'

Of all the things she might have said, or might have kept to herself, he only remembered a sort of cowed, sorrowful, inward look in her eyes and one short cryptic sentence. 'Yes, the money is good.'

It had not been clear then, but he understood it now. She had said it in Italian, in what she thought was the right way of saying it in Italian, but all she had done was to use Italian words that resembled the English ones but did not render the ideas behind them.

'Si,' she had said. 'La moneta e' buona,' which, to an Italian, meant only 'Yes. The coin is good-hearted.' And that woman, tall, old, faceless, soured by he now knew what, kept saying to him, silently and maddeningly, 'Yes, the money is good; yes, the money is good; yes. . . .'

Of all the tinselled brilliance that this part of the world had been in the pamphlets and statistics and papers he had read before coming, only that remained, that 'Si. La moneta e' buona', which no Italian could understand unless he first understood what 'Yes, the money is good' could mean.

He was tired. Guiliano Martine, the only Eye-tie on the job, the only Eye-tie earning the coin that was good-hearted, was glad that work was over for the day.

It was not that he was physically tired. His tiredness seemed to come from inside, it was all in his mind. It was a sort of numbness that paralysed his brains and for which he had confusedly and conveniently found a name that, in reality, did not apply.

It was more like the continued effect of an unexpected shock. The way that 'La moneta e' buona' had meant to him 'The coin is good-hearted', everything, before he came, seemed to have had a meaning which, here, did not apply. From 'freedom', which now encompassed a peculiar licence to booze-up and brawl and curse to hell everybody and everything within a limited mental reach, to 'Christian love' and 'standards of living' and 'the best in the world'.

He could not say what he might have understood at one time by the words 'building a city' and 'turning the wilderness into a land of milk and honey'. But whatever it might have been, he knew what they meant now—BIG MONEY.

He was helping with the building of a city. The foolish thing had been that nothing had forced him to get a job up country, to go into the middle of nowhere, except perhaps another distorted concept, that of 'man pushing back yet another frontier', or of 'man marching ahead in the name of progress'. Concepts which, as usual, had turned out to be something else.

But . . . 'Oh yes, the money is good.'

There had been nothing when he had first arrived: just a store and the company office and two big huts for the men and a stretch of yellow pumice land where the township was going to be. Now, with the help of God, the houses had been built and the camp with single huts for the men was ready, and he couldn't care less. The way he couldn't care less for the big money that kept growing in his bank account.

Chris, the leading hand in charge of the work on the group of ten houses where they were now working, shouted at him from the door of the toolshed.

'What the hell are you doing? Come on, get moving. Want to sleep here tonight?'

Guiliano started.

'Coming!' he shouted back. He turned the tap off and stored a few tools that were still scattered on the ground. Chris stood aside and watched as Guiliano went into the shed. He made a slight gesture of annoyance at what he thought was the Wop's unwarranted and unnecessary slowness. He liked using 'Wop' better than 'Eye-tie', although 'Wop' was an American term, because it was quicker, sharper. The word in itself was good, he thought, although he wouldn't use it to his face. He could not say why, but Guiliano annoyed him more than all the other Eye-ties he had met or knew of. It was the first time he had actually worked with one, and at times he wished the Wop was working under someone else. He was a funny bird, refusing to tell him what the Italian words were for this, that and the other thing, and never talking of women and never laughing and never singing a song. What the hell had he been lingering for tonight? His annoyance grew.

'Come on,' he said, 'don't forget your gloves. . . . ' The Eye-tie with the gloves, the Wop who doesn't want to get his hands dirty. 'Those gloves must cost you a lot of money,' he said again. 'Found the ones you lost?' It was a joke. The boys kept throwing his gloves away, and the Wop kept buying a new pair without saying a word.

'No.'

'What do you wear them for? Nobody else does.'

'I like wearing them,' Guiliano said.

Chris locked the door impatiently and then went towards his car, parked on the road a short distance away.

'No point in giving you a lift,' he said, 'because it'll be quicker for you to walk. You're a fast one, aren't you?' Just a dig that—he hoped Guiliano would know what he meant.

'I'd rather walk myself. Thank you for the thought,' Guiliano said.

Just a dig back—he hoped that Chris would know that he meant he didn't want his company. He could have cursed at Chris, following a pattern he knew by heart by now; he could have said, 'Who f——' wants to f——' go in that f——' bomb of yours?' but, somehow, it would have been like putting a mere facade on an empty lot and calling it a complete building. The words would have been there, but the spirit behind them—that sort of automatic conviction that was in the voices of the Johnnies and Chrises and Tommies around him—to give them meaning and a reason to be, would have been missing. 'I'd rather walk myself,' was not what he wanted to say either, but that did not need much spirit behind it.

Chris started his car and drove off, raising clouds of pumice dust along the road. He felt that, in the circumstances, he had done the only possible thing. Confusedly, it seemed unfair to leave a man behind. Still, apart from everything else, if he had asked that joe into his car, the boys might have come to think that he was taking his side. And if they thought that, he would have trouble on the job. What did the Wop think he was doing? he asked himself. Five minutes' travelling time! Only a bloody fool could be so damn stupid.

Guiliano went down to the road and started shuffling slowly towards the camp where his hut was, and the new cookhouse and the shower-block.

He had wanted to be late tonight, to be the last one to leave the job, because he wanted to check again how long it took to walk from the houses on which they were working to the camp where they slept. He knew it took only six minutes, but he just wanted to make sure once again. Then he would go and tell them, then he would show them that they had no reason to make such a fuss about it. Why should he have said a quarter of an hour? It did not take six minutes.

The pumice crunched under his feet. He kept his eyes on the ground. The soil had a dry, gritty quality which did not seem to hold any promise of growth and yield. A ground for digging a hole in and lying down and cursing and crying and shutting your eyes forever. They had had to add cobalt salts to make that artificial forest grow. It was like an ovum in a test-tube, a chick in an incubator. It was like translating a country and its people on to a piece of paper in neat lines of small print. Everything was lies.

Or perhaps it was like translating a country and its people into a theoretical concept in his own imagination. That, too, was lies.

Guiliano kept walking, dragging his feet in the dust, all the time conscious of a dormant desire to run away. Up into those wooded hills on the left—nowhere, that is. Away from nowhere to get nowhere else. Which, he thought, would maybe make him something like the other fellows on the job. They, too, came and went, like shuttlecocks being struck endlessly from here to there, scurrying around like wood-lice when you upturn the stone under which they are hiding. He would then be one of them: not with them, but *like* them. One of the 'builders of a country', an outstanding specimen, drunken and broke, run-down and grumpy, hating everything and fighting everybody.

And then, his loneliness would end.

One of the pioneers, one of the titans, talking and moving and shouting and sweating and swearing, without knowing what or whom he was doing it for. For the country, or himself, or maybe the free world.

Or, maybe, for Archie Mell who ran the taxi business, the cinema, the rental car agency and sold beer and spirits wholesale, or for that fellow Mosom who ran the store and was a J.P. and looked at you with hard pig's eyes as if he thought you were just a bit of dirt, a no-good louse.

Who else could he, and all the others, do it for? Or what else? The legend? Of course, the legend of men who are giants and roam the countryside and master nature; the legend of lands that flow with milk and honey.

And it was good to feel that he himself, by doing that, by swearing and sweating and smelling and going, might just make it and get into the legend.

Noel Hilliard

CORRECTIVE TRAINING

After thinking it over for a week Marcia wrote a note:

Dear Henny,
I want to be frends with you. I am so lonely. All the girls in here will
not be frends with me. They think I must be someone else frend and
they do not want a fight. But I am nobodys I have not been here long
enough. And I do not care for that what they do. I have had boyfrends
and that is what I like. My boyfrend said he will meet me when I come
out. But I need somebody to talk to. Somebody I can trust. I like you
Henny you got a kind face. I want to talk about things to you will you
let me?

                                    Your frend if you will have me
                                    Marcia

Henny sat in her room. She was a tall good-looking girl of nineteen with
large hands. On the first knuckles of her left-hand fingers were the letters
E S U K in amateur tattoo and on the right fingers L T F C. She wrote:

Dear Marcia,
I got your illegle note and I have hid it. I liked it when you said you
like me. But I did not get that other bit you said about not liking what
the girls do. Thats your problem kiddo. You got to sort that one out
for yourself. And you never told me how long you are in for. That has
a lot to do with it. I have been here on what they call indeteminit
sentence but I been a good girl (ha ha) and they letting me out soon.
Want to get rid of me I spose. So you dont have long to make up your
mind.

                                    Yours in the meantime
                                    Henny
                                    0 4 1 0 E

Dearest Henny,

This is your kiddo again. I have thought over what you said about *that* and if we can meet you can tell me what you want. Or show me. But take it easy because I am new at this. It is raining now and cold and the wind blows leaves on to my window and the rain water makes them stick to the glass. Then a splash of rain hits the window and the leaves wash away. I always feel sad when its raining and I am inside and nowhere to go and nothing to do. And what is worst is, is nobody to talk to. When we meet we will talk and tell each other about ourselves and make frends before we do that. But I will let you. Thats a promise. You are so sweet I like to look at you. Your a bit like my Aunty Sara in Morrinsville.

> Your
> Marcia
> 0 4 1 0 E 2

Dear Kiddo,

Your got a cheek to tell me what I can do and I cant do. I dont need you really because I got all the darls I need just now. Your not the only one that wants to be frends with Sweetsie. I will tell you who my darls are and that will make you jelous. They are Cuddles Sister Blanket Noddie Podge Cobra. Hows that now. But I will not tell you who my Special Darl is. That is my secret and I hope you get even more jelous. But I like you and hope you can get some sense into that sweet sixteen head of yours. You got a lot to learn girl.

> So long
> Sweetsie
> (you can call me that so
> you are at first base)

PS Fuck your Aunty Sara.

My dearest Sweetsie Darling,

It was so nice how that happened we never planned it and yet there we were together and nobody else around and at last I had somebody nice and frendly and tender and loving in my arms and nothing else mattered. Nothing else in the world. All the best things seem to happen like that. There was me and this boy once I never even new his name but never mind that. Was worried before but now I no its you I truly love. I am so glad I have met you properly now. This place can never get too bad so long as you are here for me to think about all day long. The sun is shining through the window on to my bed and its nice. It will warm the blankets and that is good this is such a cold place. After I was with you I felt all sort of loose and good and cheerful. Then I got all tight again and grumpy and all I can think about is you and me and when we can meet again. It cant be soon enough for me. With you close and wanting me I no who I am and I can like myself for a while. Not much but a bit when you want me. I love you Sweetsie and what you said about us that made me feel real good. And that is for the first time since I been in this dump. But it must be all right if a lovely sweet kind darling like you is in here too. I am encloseing some pictures of flowers I tore from a magazine. Thought you might like them for your wall. So this note is a fat one and I hope it gets to you safely.

Your ever loving

XXX OOO XXX   Kiddo

Dear Kiddo,
Dont get too smart now. I seen you talking to Porkchop yesterday. She is not one of my darls but you are. I do not like my darls to talk to any girls that are not my darls. You just remember that or your out. But I do not want to be rough on you. Your such a sweet kid. I am sorry I said that just now. I was in a bad mood and I get jelous. If people are going to like me they have to like ME and not anybody else. That is just the way I am. So glad you like me Kiddo darling. When you was talking to Porkchop you never had a coat on. You should of else you might have catch cold. That is no good for my sweet Kiddo. Did I tell you I like your new shoes there nice did your parents send them? I wish I had folks would send me things. I am going to see if I can steal a present for you.

So long for now
Sweetsie

Dearest Sweetsie,
I love you so much I do not want to share you with your other darls. I hate them. Sweetsie my treasure I want to be your Special Darl. I never asked you who your Special is I never want to no else I might kill her. I would too. You no you like me a lot and we have such fun together and I like you telling me all the mad things you done in your life and we laugh together I never laugh with anyone except you

Sweetsie my pet. You make me feel good all over and warm and laughing and kind and loving. You have to *ditch* your Special who ever she is and I am going to be your Special Darl from now on. Take me in those cuddly arms of yours and tell me not to worry and that you love me and I am your own Special Darling. I will believe you. I can believe anything you say when you hold me in your warm arms. Gosh you had your hair done nice at chapel today. Real neat and I never took my eyes off you.

Yours for ever
Kiddo
(Special Darling please?)
X X X X X X O O O O O O

My dearly beloved Kiddo,
I ditched Bonkers but not because you told me to. She was only a fucken shop lifter anyway she got no style and she never had any class. She pisses me off and I will be glad when she gets out of here. But you do not get to be my Special as easy as that. When I see you I will tell you what I mean. I do not want to write it down else someone find this note. I do not want them to know about us. You make me happy Kiddo and I want to make you happy to. But you got to let me. Next time I see you I will give you some lollies I pinched from Charmaine's room. She is a dead loss any way just like her fucken mate Bonkers.

Love

Sweetsie

PS I thought yesterday you was looking a bit thin are you sure your eating properly? Its not much what they give us here but you should eat it.

My closest darling lovely Sweetsie,
I just had a letter from Mummy and my Aunty Sara died. Yes she died in our old house where we use to live before and my uncle Bob (that is Saras husband) he moved there family in there after. I feel so sad and lonely and awful. I got a brooch my Aunty Sara gave me I use to wear it on my hat when I wore a hat. She was the one to make pikelets. We use to pick lemons from our tree and cut them in four long ways and sqweeze them on her pikelets. Gee they were nice. I thought I would hate it in here and I did at the start but now I dont because it brought us together you and me Sweetsie and I feel safe

with you and I would stay in here for ever if it meant being with you. Now without my Aunty Sara nothing is settled for me up there. Sweetsie my darling we will try the other one tonight. I promise. That one you told me about for me to be your Special. The one I would not do. I want to now. But only for you. So please come. I will do it but only with you. Come tonight. I cant stand to be alone. Your been here much longer and will no how to work it. Or see if you can meet. Please Sweetsie. My empty arms are longing to hold you.

from your Kiddo
who tonight becomes your
SPECIAL DARL (please)
come here for X and O and?

Dear Kiddo,

No I do not show your notes to any one else. I might do that with my darls but not with my Special Darl. Thats what special means and you have ernt it. You dont want to get so suspishus. Or jelous because I am nice to all my darls not just you. I am alowd to make other girls happy arnt I? They think a lot of me to you know. And when I was talking with Blanket no we were not talking about you so there. Anyone who hurts any of my darls hurts me to so just you remember that. Or is against them. You better watch out I don't see you talking to girls who are not my darls. Other girls want to be my darls now and other darls want to be my Special. I will not tell you there names. I trust you but dont get smart. You say when I talk to my other darls I hurt you. Sweetheart I know what it is to be hurt. That is why I never go all one way. That is how to get real bad hurt. You trust me and stick to me and I will look after you and protect you. I told you I love you and when I say that I mean it. Of course I am not forgetting you. So stop your fucken moaning. There I go getting wild again. I get these moods. What it is sweetest is that I am scared you might stop loving me. Just a bit. That would be awful. I need your love so much. There is nothing else in here just only our love for each other. That is the most precious thing in all the world. I feel good now I have told you that because I know you will believe me. We should make up a special tattoo for you and me and put it on ourselves where nobody can see it only us when we are going to be special. But it might be to sore. I have been worried about you since I heard you coughing in the bathroom you sure your all right? Think of a night together just us. Wonder what we would be like in the morning a sight I bet. Put your hand down there and swear you will always be true to me. I am doing that now to you and its good it always is with you and that is why you are my Special Darling. Must lie down and think about you. Do the same for me when you get this.

> Must rush
> Sweetsie

PS Later—I have not sent this yet because I lost my best messenger today she is gone outside where we all want to be.

> I FLY

My dearest darling Sweetsie pet,
Your going today and I will give this note to Miriam to give you at the door. I feel like killing myself and it is only your promise that is stopping me. You said you will write and that is what will keep me going. The thought of a letter from you. Am deeply hurt to no we are to part. I saw the new girls today that has just come in and I was wishing it was you and me. That is a mad thing to say I no but if it was us we could start all over again. I do not no what I am going to do without you. Sweetsie my Special and Only Darling your the only one who talks to me and tells me jokes and makes me laugh and loves me for *real*. I owe every thing to you. The only nice things that happened to me in this dump was when I was with you. After I seen you I always lie awake in bed and think over all the things we said to each other. The ways you have of loving me they make me feel real close to you. I can not have any secrets from you after we been doing that. Only just a while. Now your going away from me. Have nothing left but dreams. I will be a good girl (true) and try to get out soon with remishun and you will be waiting for me. I will be true to you and you no I will because I never liked any these other girls here much you no that. Never like I love you. So I will not fall for any one else and will do any thing you want when I am out there with you. Promise. Sweetsie my darling that Special Darl one you got me to do to you the one on my knees it took some getting use to. I have been thinking we might try that one together you and me. But not any one standing or kneeling you figer it out. And take our time. I will keep out of trouble and if they want me at home after all this I will go but you must come too. You told me you had no where. I can easy be faithful when I think of our times together. And the times that are to be. I never seen any one in the new girls as nice as you. Now I am lonely again and now I am crying. Gosh it is hard and cruel them letting you

out and not me and yet it is what we all long for and in a way I am glad for you. I have your photo for my treasure. The half with Bonkers in it I tore that half off and put it down the toilet. Good job. You must promise me you will not start going with Bonkers again now you are going out and she is out too. She must think she is smart. She is out there and me in here. I wish you the best of luck and love you more than ever. I am still crying and I cried before when I went past and saw your things gone and new you was in the office and soon you would be gone for ever. And another girl in your room and to sleep in your bed and put her things where all your dear things use to be on the dressing table and the shelf and put up new pictures. It will hurt me every time I look there to no you have gone. God I am feeling awful. Wish I could stop being me and be some body else for a while. That is until this goes away. But I do not think it will ever go away so long as I am in here and you gone. My heart is yours and my body and soul and I can not see the paper any more. I hope you will be very happy. Keep your promise.

> For ever and ever YOURS
> Marcia (Kiddo S D No. 1)
> X X X X X X   O O O O O O
> xxxx (for you no where)
> WAIT FOR ME

Marcia got off the train in Wellington. She walked up the platform and stood in the concourse, her suitcase in her hand, looking for Henny. The masses of people were bewildering. She looked at the women's clothes and particularly the girls'. She put the suitcase at her feet.

Henny came out of the women's rest room. She wore a shirt and jeans and no shoes. They smiled, and put their arms about each other, and kissed. Henny was a head taller. She nearly lifted Marcia off her feet. They kissed again. People at the bookstall turned to look at them.

They went to a seat. Henny put an arm around Marcia's shoulders and Marcia put one around Henny's waist and they gripped hands on their knees. They kissed again.

'Kiddo.'

'Sweetsie.'

Henny gripped Marcia's hand and placed it on her thigh.

'You cold?'

'Not now.'

'You should of borrowed a coat though. You look cold.'

'Not any more.'

'Glad to be here?'

'Glad to be away. Out. At last. With you.'

'Counting the days.'

'Only till I see you again.'

They kissed. Henny licked Marcia's lips.

'I've missed you Kiddo.'

'Me too. You.'

Henny pressed her hand harder. 'You know what I like about you Kiddo? You're so affectionate.'

'I feel frightened here. All these people.'

'You're with Sweetsie now Kiddo.'

'Where we stay tonight?'

'I don't know.'

'Where you last night?'

'Never mind. Dead loss anyway.'

'Where's your things.'

'Got none.'

Henny went to the bookstall and bought the evening paper.

'Let's see what's all it say here.'

They searched the classified advertisements for the accommodation section. 'You read it,' Henny said.

'I can't read too good. You.'

Henny squinted at the page.

'Nothing here,' she said. 'Nothing here for *us*.'

'You sure?'

Henny screwed up the paper and pushed it under the seat.

'How about Tawa then?' Marcia asked.

'You know anyone in Tawa?'

'One or two.'

'But it's a cold dump, Tawa. Cold and wet and too long to get to.'

'What about Newtown?'

'It's changed a lot. You wouldn't know it now. It's not cheap up there any more. Same at Aro Street.'

'Where we go then?'

'I don't know.'

'So long as it's just you and me Sweetsie.'

'It will be.'

'Promise?'

'Course.'

'Even if it's just only tonight. Please?'

'Sure.'

'Promise?'

'I said so, Kiddo.'

'Where we go then?'

'We'll find somewhere.'

'Anywhere. Just you and me.'

'That's all there'll be. Nobody else. Promise.'

'Come on then.'

Hand in hand, Henny carrying Marcia's suitcase, they walked out into the street.

Yvonne du Fresne

THE MORNING TALK

The weeks marched up to Midwinter Day. It never stopped raining. Brown rain, brown paddocks.

'Daneweather!' exulted the Bedstemoder, squinting out of the streaming windows like a Vikingwife. 'But of course, not the *ice*!'

Astrid had to admit the beauty of the Lillebaelt, the pink ice in the sunset, after hearing so much about it.

'Lit candles we pushed into the snowbanks in the garden,' intoned the Bedstemoder. 'The flames and the black birch-trunks. . . .'

Astrid could see that picture, but she was concentrating on the creek. Each day it rose a little higher and threatened Mr Semple's beautiful new road. Soon it would be covered, they would be cut off from school. Out of the ground-fog on an impossible morning she would see with eyes that gleamed with welcome the first Daneship steal over the flood. A neat Daneship, accommodated to small-sized floods, it would be manned by her six-foot cousins standing motionless and golden-haired, broad-swords at the salute, ready to take their cousin Astrid on board and show their flag, the Dannebrog, to the Wainui District Primary School.

It was dark in the mornings and dark in the late afternoons. Gleams of watery sun at midday glanced over the sodden grass in the muddy playground at school.

'Aak! Aak!' screamed the children, like ravens, swooping over the mud, under the brown sky. Doing her solitary reconnaissance before school, Astrid roamed the school hall, spying on the British Empire, looking at the English heroes in the pictures on the walls. They were all dying very gently, held up in comrades' arms on bloodied ships' decks, or on trampled battle-fields. Two were active dying heroes, waving swords and leaping elegantly toward distant clumps of the enemy, who wore striped turbans too low for fashion over their brows, and drooping pantaloons. Everywhere, *Ragnarok*, the world's last battle, was being fought, but nobody was laughing.

Inside the classroom, the Englanders struggled with overflowing inkwells and light upstrokes and dark down-strokes. And Morning Talks.

The dark classroom ceiling beams were pointed like an ark, the rain drummed on the roof, and the Headmaster gave his regular morning commentary on the war-news. Astrid felt keenly the empty space at her waist that should have held the comforting shape of her Danegirl's knife, freshly whetted that morning. Just a little flash of blade in weak sun would have sufficed as a warning in Harald Bluetooth's time, but like Prince Amleth, this was a game of wits. No weapons but one's brain. In the bleak reality of the present, the Second World War, Denmark had fallen in a matter of hours. A fight had raged around the King's Palace for six hours, waged by the traffic police, among others. Rumour had it that the King had waved a handkerchief as a sign of surrender. Holger the Dane, fast at his marble table at Kronborg, had failed to rise up and bring lightning down from the skies on Denmark's foes. The situation needed Astrid's smiling, golden cousins, sitting at the tip-up desks in a solid circle around her to maintain a show of solidity and calm. But they were twenty miles away, no doubt fighting their battles of wits in their own schools. She remained, the sole representative of the over-confident, treacherous, fallen European nations in the district, and accepted the responsibility proudly.

'Over-excitable, over-emotional, unreliable, unprepared. . . . ' The well-trodden words rolled over Astrid's head as she sat wearing a new neutral smile to avert a little of the flood-tide. She dwelt on the pictures in her mind that became richer day by day, of the long-ships bearing down on the English coast, and fires starting here and there.

She apologised inwardly for her over-blonde hair and wolf's eyes. The Headmaster seemed confused in his knowledge of the ethnic groupings of Northern Europe. She suspected that he lumped the Danes in with the Northern Germanic tribes, which had also muddled the Romans in their reluctant forays into her homelands. And if *they* had been confused, what chance had he to clear his mind?

'Foreigners,' he stated on this morning of the flood, 'have the gift of the gab. Can you give us a little talk tomorrow? A *brief* talk, if that is at all remotely possible, Westingad.'

'Westergaard!' snapped an irritable voice in Astrid's mind. She must check her temper; Prince Amleth would have stumbled in his contest if he had been led astray by rage. She was a master of the English Public School language, knowing *Tom Brown's Schooldays* nearly off by heart.

'I can only try, Sir!' she essayed. Right on the nail.

'Try Denmark then. Entertain us. *Dazzle* us!' A wintry smile. 'If there's anything left there to talk about.'

A neutral chuckle. Incautious. Nobody laughed in this class.

Astrid sat stolidly on. In her mind, more long-ships beached. The Golden Warriors leapt into the surf. The Headmaster and his family made a clumsy attempt to run up a hill, but were losing ground. . . .

After school, at the gate the car waited. Fader leaned out.

'The flood's come. Hurry!' he shouted, and laughed. The rain fell like Thor's hammers. The Golden Warriors raced up the crown of the main road, beating the quivering line of speeding water rising on each side.

'Alley-oop!' roared Fader, hitting the side of the car with clenched fist. Spray flew in their bow-wave. They landed. On the veranda the women shouted exultantly. Brown water stretched over the land, up to the house.

'You are *home*!' they called. Bedstemoder waved a dressmaking ruler.

'Three feet!' she screamed, a Warrior Queen, 'and still rising!'

'Ah!' gasped Fader, and swooped her over the flood to safety.

The wind blew, the rain fell and the flood hissed past the house. Inside the fire blazed, the soup bubbled in its pot on the stove, and the talk swung between floods defeated and the Morning Talk.

'A little talk about our Denmark. An honour!'

Astrid dug into her good soup, working out chillier tactics. It would have to be, she decided, a war of wits, she being weaponless and but ten years old. Wits—and magic. She prayed for Prince Amleth's cunning.

After dinner they went out on to the veranda. In the night before Midwinter's Day the flood roared over the paddocks, a boiling current ran past the veranda steps, but the wall Fader had cleverly built by the creek was slowing it down. The house rode the waters like a Viking ship. *Ragnarok* was at hand, when the warriors rode the sky, the battle-maidens sang and the arrows fell hissing in the hail.

'Not through the floorboards yet!' said Fader and went restlessly inside to put the *Karelia* on the gramophone to give them heart to design the Morning Talk. Astrid chanted to his prompting—

'Reaching out into the sea in the north of Europe lies the small, but brave Kingdom of Denmark. . . . ' Butterfat yields, the draining of the marshes, the Silver Kings buried in the peat at their house door in Jutland, universal education, agrarian reform. . . .

'You tell them—*everything*!' instructed Fader, stabbing his pen at Astrid's chest. 'And our families fighting in the Underground. You tell them that!'

The women took up the needle work and by the bright eye of the fire showed Astrid how to make a running stitch trace a magic bird, a marsh flower, a ship and a crown. They beamed at her while Fader's pen drove over the paper and the rain thundered on the roof.

'Tell them the stories, Astrid!' commanded the Bedstemoder, cheeks red with excitement. Then she paused and looked keenly at her, taking in the situation with her fingertips, as usual.

'Storytellers,' she said softly, 'hold all men. Stories win all hearts. The voice, well used, ends wars.'

Astrid looked up sharply.

'Tell them the stories, Astrid,' said Bedstemoder, 'of love and death and brave men. *Lille Fortaeller* Astrid.'

Astrid went to sleep muttering statistics of butterfat returns and the Silver Kings in the marshes. In the dawn she cried out in her sleep, and woke herself. By the edge of her bed, where she had rolled in her dream of ice and war, lay two little signs, put there by the Norne, the reader of signs, Bedstemoder. A little Dannebrog, its cross of white on scarlet bright in the dim light, and a picture of her example, the fourteenth-century Queen Margrethe, with the motto 'God's Help, the People's Love, Denmark's Strength' printed underneath.

Next morning, even though the flood crouched and drew in breath for a fresh onslaught that day, Fader got the car through for the honour of the Morning Talk. She sat perched on the hard draughty seat beside him and held the Dannebrog furled in both hands. As the true warriors of old had gone into battle chanting the sacred runes, she chanted the Talk inside her head, and the words, 'God's Help, the People's Love, Denmark's Strength', for the sake of Dronning Margrethe.

She still held it as she reluctantly climbed on to the bar of the black-board easel to try and find Denmark in a welter of black names on the old yellow varnished school map of Europe. The Headmaster watched in mocking silence as she regrettably stabbed the Dannebrog on to Holland.

'Lost at sea?' he inquired.

'*Nej!*' she answered curtly, searching for the maddeningly small patch that said 'Jutland'.

'Here lies Jutland!' she cried, unmanned with delight, giving it the full glottal stop. The class lifted heads in alarm.

'Reaching out into the sea in the north of Europe lies the small, but brave Kingdom of Denmark—' she began, and rolled on through the butterfat returns, the agrarian reforms and so on. Squinting sideways at the Headmaster, she saw him lean against the fireplace and yawn.

'Vikings,' she said abruptly, 'had their training camps at the back of our farm at Trelleborg.' The class lifted its drowsy head.

'From the marshes the Golden Warriors have been raised and we have seen their faces,' she announced. The silence she had heard people speak of when the *skalds* struck their first silver chord was in the class-room. She obeyed it. She climbed carefully off the wobbly easel and advanced towards the class, pointing the Dannebrog at them.

'I will tell you the old story,' she said. 'Today is Midwinter's Day. Today Jarnvid strikes his harp. The wolf-children of Fenris break forth to hunt the sun and moon, and Garn, the hound of Hel, leaps over the earth.'

The Headmaster straightened his tie as if summoned to a meeting of Inspectors. Astrid, the mouthpiece, recited the Fortaelling of her people.

'Nidhaggr gnaws through the last root of Yggdrasil, and Jormungan, the serpent that circles the world, turns itself so that a wave sweeps over the earth. Sleipner bears Odin to his last battle. The sky is split by a flaming sword. *Ragnarok* is upon us. The Gods die. Darkness falls over the earth. *Ragnarok* is upon us now.'

The class looked apprehensively at the rain outside and back again. 'But I will tell you of the end,' said Astrid. 'For thousands of years there is darkness, and then a small star, no bigger than a little spark, appears. Thousands of years pass, and it slowly grows. Until at last the first faint dawn appears. First we will have the flaming sword rending the sky in two, and then our dawn. But the darkness will be always on the edge of the world, because of that sword in the sky.'

The pattern of that old *Fortaelling* had been changed when she had been its mouthpiece. The Gods are here, she thought humbly.

'The years,' she said clumsily, 'we can read as meaning "days". Then Denmark rises again. And England!' she added hastily, careful not to offend.

'Kind of you,' said the Headmaster. But the silence still held. Astrid folded up the Dannebrog and started the drained-out tramp back to her desk. The Gods departed in a breath. The class rustled and several people turned and looked at her. *Skalds* had awkward lives—to *foretael* one moment and do the spelling tests the next.

'Well,' said the Headmaster, 'if we survive *Ragnarok* you could give us another sample next Monday, Westingad.'

'Westergaard, said Astrid. '*Astrid* Westergaard.'

'Astrid,' repeated the Headmaster with a shocking accent. 'Any other bits you have straight from the horse's mouth would be welcome. It quite takes one's mind off the rain.'

'I'll do my best, Sir!' answered Astrid, Denmark's Strength, in vintage Tom Brown language.

Maurice Gee

A GLORIOUS MORNING, COMRADE

Mercy tied her father's scarf in a mean granny knot.

'Now remember, darling, if you want the little house just bang on the wall. We don't want any wets with the girls all here.' And Barbie, gentler, but not to be outdone, knelt and zipped up his slippers. 'You'll be lovely and warm in the sun, won't you? Just bang on the wall. No little accidents please. 'Bye daddums.'

They left him in his rocking chair on the veranda and he rocked a little, pitying their innocence. He did not mean to pee in his pants today. He had other plans.

Presently the 'girls' came, driving their little cars; and they walked up the path in twos and threes, dumpy women or stringy, the lot, in Saturday clothes and coloured hair. They stopped for a little chat of course, politely, and sniffed behind their hands to see if he had behaved himself today. They were good-hearted women. Mercy and Barbie attracted such.

'Lucky you, Mr Pitt-Rimmer. Just loafing in the sun.'

He counted them. Ten. Three tables. There was Madge Ogden, a daughter of divorcees; and Pearl Edwards who taught mathematics at the Girls' High School; and Mary Rendt who had wanted to be a nun but had lost her faith and married a German Christian Scientist and lost that faith and her husband too; and the three Bailey girls, with not a husband amongst them, whose mother had broken their hearts by choosing to live in an old people's home; and Christine Hunt who had been caught shoplifting when she was a girl and lived it down and married the son of the mayor; and Jean Murray-Briggs, whose name annoyed him; and last the lesbians, though none of the others knew— Phyllis Wedderburn and Margaret Way. Charles Pitt-Rimmer, he knew. He winked at them and they blushed, but seemed a little pleased.

'Such lovely sun. We've only got old bridge.'

He gave them time to get warmed up. Mercy looked out once and wagged her finger, and Barbie once and kissed him on the cheek.

They would forget him when they were well ahead. His daughters were the top pair in the district and he wished he could feel more pleased with them for it.

When the time came he stood up and walked along the veranda. He went down the path, down the steps, along the footpath to the park, and into the trees. It was twenty-nine minutes past two. He had run away twice before. Today he would outfox them. He would keep away from roads and butcher shops, where he had been caught twice before looking at roasts of beef. They would not think of searching on the hill.

Girls, he wrote in his mind, *There are other things than meat. Your father played chess.*

At nineteen minutes to three he reached the dairy. 'Here, you children, out of my way,' he said, and they stood aside with a quickness that pleased him. He did not mind that they giggled. That was proper in children.

'A bag of Turkish delight,' he said. He had planned it all morning and it came out with an English sound. 'And a packet of cigarettes.'

The woman behind the counter had a half-witted face, a nose that seemed to snuffle for scent like a dog's. She gave a smile and said. 'It's Mr Pitt-Rimmer, isn't it?'

'My name is not your concern. Turkish delight. And a packet of cigarettes.'

'Sit down, Mr Pitt-Rimmer. There's a chair right there. As soon as I've served these kiddies I'll ring Mrs Parsloe.'

'You will not ring Mrs Parsley. I wish to be served. Am I a customer or am I not? And are you in business? Answer me that.'

He was pleased to see confusion in her eyes. 'I'll have de Reszke.'

'Whosie?'

'De Reszke. You don't seem to know your business, madam. Do you make a living? I wonder at it.'

'There's nothing here called de Reszke.'

'Cigarettes. Cigarettes. Named after a great operatic tenor. Before your time, of course. I understand. It's all Bing Crosby today.'

The woman went suddenly to the telephone. 'You kiddies wait.' She started to dial.

'Very well,' cried Charles Pitt-Rimmer. 'You may ring Mrs Parsley. Tell her I'm striking out. I have my life. Tell her I'm smoking again. De Reszke. And eating Turkish delight.' He stopped at the door. 'And if she wishes to know where I am you may say that I've gone to the butcher's for a piece of German sausage.'

'Mrs Parsloe?' the woman said. 'It's the Regal dairy. Your father's here.'

He was very pleased with himself as he turned up the hill. Capablanca would have been proud of that move.

Girls, bridge is for simple folk. You must think ahead. I've never cared for German sausage.

He looked at his watch. It was thirteen minutes to three. Already he had beaten his old record. He pictured the little cars scuttling about Hardinge, driven in a dangerous manner by women with blue and pink hair. Barbie would be crying—he was sorry about that—and Mercy with her eye like a hanging judge's.

Girls, a man's a man for a' that.

He followed a path into the trees and climbed until he stood on the edge of the cliff with the wharves below him. Three minutes past three. He would have liked some Turkish delight. He had not had any since his last day in court, which was twenty-two years ago. His secretary used to bring in a paper bag full with his lunch. The gob-stopper he'd taken from the Regal dairy's corner would be no substitute. But he found that he enjoyed it once he'd torn the paper off. It tasted of raspberry, a flavour he'd forgotten.

He went to the safety fence and looked down. A girl had jumped down there on Boxing Day because her employer, a well-known man in Hardinge, had put her in the family way. She had lived for two hours but not said a word. He had heard Mercy and Barbie discussing it, in voices hushed but full of glee and dread. The man, Barbie said, was 'a weed in the garden of life'—which she'd pinched from her mother, who had also believed that such men should be hanged. Women had a poor understanding of certain needs.

The gob-stopper made him feel bilious. He put it in his pocket. Below him ships were tied up at the wharves, all piddling water out of their sides. One of them was a phosphate tub, moored at a wharf that he remembered now was Pitt-Rimmer Wharf. There had been those years on the Harbour Board—a tedious business. Jack Hunt had picked his nose behind the agenda. The Hunts had never been up to much though they liked to believe that they were the bosses of Hardinge. He walked on and the cape came into sight, standing up like Chunuk Bair. He had no wish to be reminded of that. That had been a very great piece of nonsense.

Girls, you persist in reminding me. . . .

A woman came towards him leading a tiny black dog in a tartan jacket.

'I don't care for dogs, madam. Keep him off.'

'Mr Pitt-Rimmer. Don't you remember me?'

'I've met many people. Fifteen thousand is my calculation.'

'But I'm Maisie Transome. Maisie Jack that was. You used to give me lollies.'

'Your mother was an excellent secretary. And a kindly soul. She had extraordinary bosoms.'

'Ooh, Mr. Pitt-Rimmer, you're a rogue.'

'I don't care for animals sniffing about my feet.'

'Come here, Bruce. Where are your manners, darling? Mr Pitt-Rimmer, can I walk home with you? You shouldn't be out you know, dressed like that. Barbie told me you're being very naughty.'

'My daughter has more kindness than sense. She's a good woman but she's had a tragic life.'

'Who? Barbie?'

'She fell in love with a young man in my office. Parsley was his name. Mercy stole him away. "Mercy" was not my choice. I want that understood. My wife had a poor grip on reality. But Parsley—she married him and broke her sister's heart. Barbie never married. Parsley was not a good catch, mind you. She was well out of it. He played around as they say. There was a woman in my office called Rona Jack. Her marriage was unsatisfactory. Parsley used to visit there.'

'Oh Mr Pitt-Rimmer—'

'He died of course. They nursed him. My daughters are good girls.'

'But my parents had an ideal marriage. They were in love till the day they died.'

'Indeed. I congratulate them. You should not speak with strangers. The risks are very great. Good day to you.'

'But I'm taking you home, remember?'

'I wish to relieve myself.'

She did not follow him though her dog yapped in an impertinent way. The path led downhill and had many troublesome curves. His legs began to be sore. But a bank of nasturtiums pleased him and a smell of fennel. Fennel made him think of aniseed balls. He stopped at the memory. When sucked an aniseed ball turned white. And Turkish delight left sugar round the mouth.

Girls, when you were children I bought you sweets. Straps of licorice. Be fair. Bags of sherbert. Bags of chocolate fudge.

The path ended by the Salvation Army Eventide Home. Two old men were sitting on a bench. 'A glorious morning, comrade,' one of them said.

'Glorious,' Charles Pitt-Rimmer agreed, smiling at his better knowledge. It was twenty-nine minutes past three in the afternoon and his daughters were thoroughly bamboozled. He stopped by the reservoir and sat down on a bank. A boy was walking along a pipe, and a smaller boy rode up on a tricycle.

'Why are you wearing your dressing-gown?'

'Old men are allowed to.'

'Mummy makes me get dressed. Have you wet your pants?'

'I believe I have.'

'Couldn't you find a toilet? You could use ours.'

'The word is lavatory. You should not be frightened of calling things by their names.'

'Mummy said lavatory's not nice.'

'And you should not pay too much attention to women.'

Charles Pitt-Rimmer dozed for a moment. 'Poor Parsley. They made him eat his vegetables. Curly kale. A weed.'

'Mummy makes me eat my vegetables.'

'What do you have for pudding?'

His mind was lucid about food but cloudy about everything else. He was not quite sure where he was. 'My favourite is lemon meringue pie.' He felt in his pocket for the gob-stopper and gave it to the child who put it in his mouth at once, leaving only the stick poking out.

'You speak too much of your mother. The conspiracy starts at the cradle.'

The boy who had been walking on the pipe ran up to join them.

'Give us a lick, Tony. Come on.'

Charles Pitt-Rimmer went to sleep. He believed he was in a bath of luke-warm water that was turning cold about his legs. Soon he was wakened by a woman's voice.

'Let me see that. Give it to me at once. It's filthy. It's got a hair on it.'

She moved her arm violently and the boy on the tricycle cried. Charles did not know what was happening, but he saw that the woman was looking at him with hatred and was astonished at the ease with which people felt this emotion. Forty years of court work had not got him used to it.

'Beware, madam. It can get to be a habit.'

'You ought to be ashamed of yourself. And you'—she rounded on the older boy—'I told you to look after him. Why can't you listen for once? Get into the wash-house and wait till your father comes home.'

Now the older boy cried. They were an emotional family and seemed to be without reason, Charles decided. They vanished and he was relieved. He lay on the bank and tried to sleep, curled into a ball to defeat the cold. Where were his daughters? Where were the wretched women?

Girls, you're selfish creatures . . .

Again a woman woke him. This time it was Christine Hunt, with her hair like candy floss. He reached out for some.

'What are you doing? Oh! Mr Pitt-Rimmer. Let go.'

'Christine Perkins, you were lucky to get off with a fine. If you hadn't had me to conduct your defence you would have gone to prison.'

'Oh! Oh! My hair. You've ruined it.'

'Why did you choose such frilly things, Christine? If you remember, I told the court they were for your glory box? A clever touch. But you can tell me. I can be discreet.'

'You're a horrible man. Oh, look, you've wet your pyjamas. This is dreadful.'

'I understand, Christine. It's difficult to be poor. No nice frillies, eh? A girl likes frillies. But I always believed you married beneath you. Your father-in-law picks his nose.'

'My father-in-law has been dead for twenty years. And you've ruined our afternoon. You know that, don't you? It's a wonder to me how Mercy and Barbie keep going. They must be saints.'

'They're vegetarians. They struggle to ward off despair. I do my best.'

'Mr Pitt-Rimmer, I'm going to take you home. I am. Now come with me. Come on.'

She put out her hand and he was appalled at the size of it. It went right round his wrist, and her silver nails poked up from the underside. She was appalled too. She jerked away.

'Barbie will be the invalid when I'm dead,' said Charles Pitt-Rimmer.

Christine Hunt went away. 'I'm going to get your daughters. Don't you move.' Her little car scuttled off, and Charles lay curled up tightly.

Girls, it's time for my nap. You're selfish creatures . . .

'Oh daddums, daddums, why do you do these things?'

'Put down the rubber sheet, Barbie. No, spread it out, you ninny.'

They put him in the back seat and Barbie sat with him, rubbing his hands.

'You're so naughty, so naughty—'

'I've had enough,' Mercy cried. 'I'm going to put you in a home. You've made a fool of me for the last time. Wipe his mouth Barbie, can't you see?'

'You make it so hard for us, daddums. Oh, your hands are so cold.'

'I walked on the pipe, Mercy. If I'd fallen off you would never have been born.'

They washed him and put him to bed. He slept smiling for two hours, then rang his bell for tea. They propped him up with pillows, and Barbie sat with him while he ate.

'It's a special salad, daddums. One Mercy found. It's got avocados in it. Now drink your apple juice.'

She took away the tray and came back with his library book.

'Promise me you won't be naughty again. It makes us so sad.'

'What was the time when you caught me?'

'Four o'clock. You were gone for two hours. Oh daddums—'

'An hour and thirty-one minutes.' He grinned at her.

When she had gone he finished his book. He corrected one split infinitive and underlined two mentions of female breasts. Then he made his secret sign on page eighty-eight.

Barbie was doing the dishes and Mercy watching a television show full of American voices. On the final page, below a scene of love, Charles wrote a message:

My daughters are keeping me prisoner. Help! I have not had a piece of meat for twenty years . . .

Maurice Shadbolt

THE PEOPLE BEFORE

I

My father took on that farm not long after he came back from the first war. It was pretty well the last farm up the river. Behind our farm, and up the river, there was all kind of wild country. Scrub and jagged black stumps on the hills, bush in gullies where fire hadn't reached; hills and more hills, deep valleys with caves and twisting rivers, and mountains white with winter in the distance. We had the last piece of really flat land up the river. It wasn't the first farm my father'd taken on—and it certainly wasn't to be the last—but it was the most remote. He always said that was why he'd got the place for a song. This puzzled me as a child. For I'd heard, of course, of having to sing for your supper. I wondered what words, to what tune, he was obliged to sing for the farm; and where, and why? Had he travelled up the river, singing a strange song, charming his way into possession of the land? It always perplexed me.

And it perplexed me because there wasn't much room for singing in my father's life. I can't remember ever having heard him sing. There was room for plodding his paddocks in all weathers, milking cows and sending cream down river to the dairy factory, and cursing the bloody government; there was room in his life for all these things and more, but not for singing.

In time, of course, I understood that he only meant he'd bought the place cheaply. Cheaply meant for a song. I couldn't, even then, quite make the connexion. It remained for a long while one of those adult mysteries. And it was no use puzzling over it, no use asking my father for a more coherent explanation.

'Don't be difficult,' he'd say. 'Don't ask so many damn questions. Life's difficult enough, boy, without all your damn questions.'

He didn't mean to be unkind; it was just his way. His life was committed to winning order from wilderness. Questions were a disorderly intrusion, like gorse or weed springing up on good pasture. The best way was to hack them down, grub out the roots, before they could spread. And in the same way as he checked incipient anarchy on his land he hoped, perhaps, to check it in his son.

By that time I was old enough to understand a good many of the things that were to be understood. One of them, for example, was that we weren't the first people on that particular stretch of land. Thirty or forty years before, when white men first came into our part of the country, it was mostly forest. Those first people fired the forest, right back into the hills, and ran sheep. The sheep grazed not only the flat, but the hills which rose sharply behind our farm; the hills which, in our time, had become stubbly with manuka and fern. The flatland had been pretty much scrub too, the day my father first saw it; and the original people had been gone twenty years—they'd given up, or been ruined by the land; we never quite knew the story. The farmhouse stood derelict among the returning wilderness.

Well, my father saw right away that the land—the flat land—was a reasonable proposition for a dairy farm. There was a new launch service down to the nearest dairy factory, in the township ten miles away; only in the event of flood, or a launch breakdown, would he have to dispose of his cream by carrying it on a sledge across country, three miles, to the nearest road.

So he moved in, cleared the scrub, sowed new grass, and brought in cows. Strictly speaking, the hills at the back of the farm were his too, but he had no use for them. They made good shelter from the westerlies. Otherwise he never gave the hills a thought, since he had all the land he could safely manage; he roamed across them after wild pig, and that was about all. There were bones up there, scattered skeletons of lost sheep, in and about the scrub and burnt stumps.

Everything went well; he had the place almost paid off by the time of the depression. 'I never looked back, those years,' he said long afterwards. It was characteristic of him not to look back. He was not interested in who had the farm before him. He had never troubled to inquire. So far as he was concerned, history only began the day he first set foot on the land. It was his, by sweat and legal title: that was all that mattered. That was all that could matter.

He had two boys; I was the elder son. 'You and Jim will take this place over one day,' he often told me. 'You'll run it when I get tired.'

But he didn't look like getting tired. He wasn't a big man, but he was wiry and thin with a lean face and cool blue eyes; he was one of those people who can't keep still. When neighbours called he couldn't ever keep comfortable in a chair, just sitting and sipping tea, but had to start walking them round the farm—or at least the male neighbours—pointing out things here and there. Usually work he'd done, improvements he'd made: the new milking-shed, the new water-pump on the river. He didn't strut or boast, though; he just pointed them out quietly, these jobs well done. He wanted others to share his satisfaction. There was talk of electricity coming through to the farm, the telephone; a road up the river was scheduled. It would all put the value of the property up. The risk he'd taken on the remote and abandoned land seemed justified in every way.

He didn't ever look like getting tired. It was as if he'd been wound up years before, like something clockwork, and set going: first fighting in the war, then fighting with the land; now most of the fighting was done, he sometimes found it quite an effort to keep busy. He never took a holiday. There was talk of taking a holiday, one winter when the cows dried off; talk of us all going down to the sea, and leaving a neighbour to look after the place. But I don't think he could have trusted anyone to look after his land, not even for a week or two in winter when the cows were dried off. Perhaps, when Jim and I were grown, it would be different. But not until. He always found some reason for us not to get away. Like our schooling.

'I don't want to interfere with their schooling,' he said once. 'They only get it once in their lives. And they might as well get it while they can. I didn't get much. And, by God, I regret it now. I don't know much, and I might have got along all right, but I might have got along a damn sight better if I'd had more schooling. And I'm not going to interfere with theirs by carting them off for a holiday in the middle of the year.'

Yet even then I wondered if he meant a word of it, if he really wasn't just saying that for something to say. He was wrangling at the time with my mother, who held opinions on a dwindling number of subjects. She never surrendered any of these opinions, exactly; she just kept them more and more to herself until, presumably, they lapsed quietly and died. As she herself, much later, was to lapse quietly from life, without much complaint.

For if he'd really been concerned about our schooling, he might have been more concerned about the way we fell asleep in afternoon classes. Not that we were the only ones. Others started getting pretty ragged in the afternoons too. A lot of us had been up helping our fathers since early in the morning. Jim and I were up at half-past four most mornings to help with the milking and working the separators. My father increased his herd year after year, right up to the depression. After school we rode home just in time for the evening milking. And by the time we finished it was getting dark; in winter it was dark by the time we were half-way through the herd.

I sometimes worried about Jim looking worn in the evenings, and I often chased him off inside before milking was finished. I thought Jim needed looking after; he wasn't anywhere near as big as me. I'd hear him scamper off to the house, and then I'd set about stripping the cows he had left. Father sometimes complained.

'You'll make that brother of yours a softy,' he said. 'The boy's got to learn what work means.'

'Jim's all right,' I answered. 'He's not a softy. He's just not very big. That's all.'

He detested softies, even the accomplices of softies. My mother, in a way, was such an accomplice. She'd never been keen about first me, then Jim, helping with work on the farm. But my father said he couldn't afford to hire a man to help with the herd. And he certainly couldn't manage by himself, without Jim and me.

'Besides,' he said, 'my Dad and me used to milk two hundred cows'— sometimes, when he became heated, the number rose to three hundred— 'when I was eight years old. And thin as a rake too, I was. Eight years old and thin as a rake. It didn't do me no harm. You boys don't know what work is, let me tell you.'

So there all argument finished. My mother kept one more opinion to herself.

And I suppose that, when I chased Jim off inside, I was only taking my mother's side in the argument—and was only another accomplice of softies. Anyway, it would give me a good feeling afterwards—despite anything my father would have to say—when we tramped back to the house, through the night smelling of frost or rain, to find Jim sitting up at the table beside my mother while she ladled out soup under the warm yellow lamplight. He looked as if he belonged there, beside her; and she always looked, at those times, a little triumphant. Her look seemed to say that one child of hers, at least, was going to be saved from the muck of the cowshed. And I suppose that was the beginning of how Jim became his mother's boy.

I remained my father's. I wouldn't have exchanged him for another father. I liked seeing him with people, a man among men. This happened on winter Saturdays when we rode to the township for the football. We usually left Jim behind to look after my mother. We tethered our horses near the football field and went off to join the crowd. Football was one of the few things which interested my father outside the farm. He'd been a fine rugby forward in his day and people respected what he had to say about the game. He could out-argue most people; probably out-fight them too, if it ever came to that. He often talked about the fights he'd had when young. For he'd done a bit of boxing too, only he couldn't spare the time from his father's farm to train properly. He knocked me down once, with his bare fists, in the cowshed; and I was careful never to let it happen again. I just kept my head down for days afterwards, so that he wouldn't see the bruises on my face or the swelling round my eye.

At the football he barracked with the best of them in the thick of the crowd. Sometimes he called out when the rest of the crowd was silent and tense; he could be very sarcastic about poor players, softies who were afraid to tackle properly.

After the game he often called in, on the way home, to have a few beers with friends in the township's sly-grog shop—we didn't have a proper pub in the township—while I looked after the horses outside. Usually he'd find time, while he gossiped with friends, to bring me out a glass of lemonade. At times it could be very cold out there, holding the horses while the winter wind swept round, but it would be nice to know that I was remembered. When he finished we rode home together for a late milking. He would grow talkative, as we cantered towards dark, and even give me the impression he was glad of my company. He told me about the time he was young, what the world looked like when he was my age. His father was a sharemilker, travelling from place to place; that is, he owned no land of his own and did other people's work.

'So I made up my mind, boy,' he told me as we rode along together, 'I made up my mind I'd never be like that. I'd bend my head to no man. And you know what the secret of that is, boy? Land. Land of your own. You're independent, boy. You can say no to the world. That's if you got your own little kingdom. I reckon it was what kept me alive, down there on the beach at Gallipoli, knowing I'd have some land I could call my own.' This final declaration seemed to dismay him for some reason or other, perhaps because he feared he'd given too much of himself away. So he added half-apologetically, 'I had to think of something, you know, while all that shooting was going on. They say it's best to fix your mind on something if you don't want to be afraid. That's what I fixed my mind on, anyhow. Maybe it did keep me alive.'

In late winter or spring we sometimes arrived back, on Saturdays, to see the last trembling light of sunset fade from the hills and land. We'd canter along a straight stretch, coast up a rise, rein in the horses, and there it was—his green kingdom, his tight tamed acres beneath the hills and beside the river, a thick spread of fenced grass from the dark fringe of hillscrub down to the ragged willows above the water. And at the centre was his castle, the farmhouse, with the sheds scattered round, and the pine trees.

Reining in on that rise, I knew, gave him a good feeling. It would also be the time when he remembered all the jobs he'd neglected, all the work he should have done instead of going to the football. His conscience would keep him busy all day Sunday.

At times he wondered—it was a conversation out loud with himself— why he didn't sell up and buy another place. There were, after all, more comfortable farms, in more convenient locations nearer towns or cities. 'I've built this place up from nothing,' he said, 'I've made it pay, and pay well. I've made this land worth something. I could sell out for a packet. Why don't I?'

He never really—in my presence anyway—offered himself a convincing explanation. Why didn't he? He'd hardly have said he loved the land: love, in any case, would have been an extravagance. Part of whatever it was, I suppose, was the knowledge that he'd built where someone else had failed; part was that he'd given too much of himself there, to be really free anywhere else. It wouldn't be the same, walking on to another successful farm, a going concern, everything in order. No, this place— this land from the river back up to the hills—was his. In a sense it had only ever been his. That was why he felt so secure.

If Sunday was often the day when he worked hardest, it was also the best day for Jim and me, our free day. After morning milking, and breakfast, we did more or less what we liked. In summer we swam down under the river-willows; we also had a canoe tied there and sometimes we paddled up-river, under great limestone bluffs shaggy with toi toi, into country which grew wilder and wilder. There were huge bearded caves in the bush above the water which we explored from time to time. There were also big eels to be fished from the pools of the river.

As he grew older Jim turned more into himself, and became still quieter. You could never guess exactly what he was thinking. It wasn't that he didn't enjoy life; he just had his own way of enjoying it. He didn't like being with his father, as I did; I don't even know that he always enjoyed being with me. He just tagged along with me: we were, after all, brothers. When I was old enough, my father presented me with a ·22 rifle; Jim never showed great enthusiasm for shooting. He came along with me, all right, but he never seemed interested in the rabbits or wild goat I shot, or just missed. He wandered around the hills, way behind me, entertaining himself and collecting things. He gathered leaves, and tried to identify the plants from which the leaves came. He also collected stones, those of some interesting shape or texture; he had a big collection of stones. He tramped along, in his slow, quiet way, poking into everything, adding to his collections. He wasn't too slow and quiet at school, though; he was faster than most of us with an answer. He borrowed books from the teacher, and took them home. So in time he became even smarter with his answers. I grew to accept his difference from most people. It didn't disturb me particularly: on the farm he was still quiet, small Jim. He was never too busy with his books to come along with me on Sundays.

There was a night when Jim was going through some new stones he'd gathered. Usually, in the house, my father didn't take much notice of Jim, his reading or his hobbies. He'd fought a losing battle for Jim, through the years, and now accepted his defeat. Jim still helped us with the herd, night and morning, but in the house he was ignored. But this night my father went across to the table and picked up a couple of the new stones. They were greenish, both the same triangular shape.

'Where'd you get these?' he asked.

Jim thought for a moment; he seemed pleased by the interest taken in him. 'One was back in the hills,' he said. 'The other was in a cave up the river. I just picked them up.'

'You mean you didn't find them together?'

'No,' Jim said.

'Funny,' my father said. 'They look like greenstone. I seen some greenstone once. A joker found it, picked it up in the bush. Jade, it is; same thing. This joker sold it in the city for a packet. Maori stuff. Some people'll buy anything.'

We all crossed to the table and looked down at the greenish stone. Jim's eyes were bright with excitment.

'You mean these used to belong to the Maoris?' he said. 'These stones?'

'Must have,' my father said. 'Greenstone doesn't come natural round here. You look it up in your books and you'll see. Comes from way down south, near the mountains and glaciers. Had to come up here all the way by canoe. They used to fight about greenstone once.' He paused and looked at the stones again. 'Yes,' he added. 'I reckon that's greenstone, all right. You never know, might be some money in that stuff.'

Money was a very important subject in our house at that time. It was in a lot of households, since that time was the depression. In the cities they were marching in the streets and breaking shop windows. Here on the farm it wasn't anywhere near so dramatic. The grass looked much the same as it had always looked; so did the hills and river. All that had happened, really, was that the farm had lost its value. Prices had fallen; my father sometimes wondered if it was worth while sending cream to the factory. Some of the people on poorer land, down the river, had walked off their properties. Everything was tighter. We had to do without new clothes, and there wasn't much variety in our eating. We ran a bigger garden, and my father went out more frequently shooting wild pig for meat. He had nothing but contempt for the noisy people in the city, the idlers and wasters who preferred to go shouting in the streets rather than fetch a square meal for their families, as he did with his rifle. He thought they, in some way, were to blame for the failure of things. Even so, he became gripped by the idea that he might have failed himself, somehow; he tried to talk himself out of this idea—in my presence—but without much success. Now he had the land solid beneath his feet, owned it entirely, it wasn't much help at all. If it wasn't for our garden and the wild pig we might starve. The land didn't bring him any money; he might even have to leave it. He had failed, perhaps much as the land's former owners had failed; why? He might have answered the question for himself satisfactorily, while he grubbed away at the scrub encroaching on our pasture; but I doubt it.

'Yes,' he said. 'Might be some money in that stuff.'

But Jim didn't seem to hear, or understand. His eyes were still bright. 'That means there must have been Maoris here in the old days,' he said.

'I suppose there must have,' my father agreed. He didn't seem much interested. Maoris were Maoris. There weren't many around our part of the river; they were mostly down towards the coast. (Shortly after this, Jim did some research and told me the reason why. It turned out that the land about our part of the river had been confiscated from them after the Maori wars.) 'They were most places, weren't they?' he added.

'Yes,' Jim said. 'But I mean they must have been here. On our place.'

'Well, yes. They could of been. Like I said, they were most places.'

It didn't seem to register as particularly important. He picked up the greenstone again. 'We ought to find out about this,' he continued. 'There might be a bit of money in it.'

Later Jim took the stones to school and had them identified as Maori adzes. My father said once again that perhaps there was money in them. But the thing was, where to find a buyer? It mightn't be as easy as it used to be. So somehow it was all forgotten. Jim kept the adzes.

Jim and I did try to find again that cave in which he had picked up an adze. We found a lot of caves, but none of them seemed the right one. Anyway we didn't pick up another adze. We did wander down one long dripping cave, striking matches, and in the dark I tripped on something. I struck another match and saw some brownish-looking bones. 'A sheep,' I said. 'It must have come in here and got lost.'

Jim was silent; I wondered why. Then I saw he wasn't looking at the bones, but at a human skull propped on a ledge of the cave. It just sat there sightless, shadows dancing in its sockets.

We got out of that cave quickly. We didn't even talk about it when we reached home. On the whole I preferred going out with my ·22 after rabbits.

II

It was near the end of the depression. But we didn't know that then, of course. It might have been just the beginning, for all we knew. My father didn't have as much interest in finishing jobs as he used to have. He tired easily. He'd given his best to the land, and yet his best still wasn't good enough. There wasn't much sense in anything and his dash was done. He kept going out of habit.

I'd been pulled out of school to help with the farm. Jim still more or less went to school. I say more or less because he went irregularly. This was because of sickness. Once he was away in hospital two months. And of course it cost money; my father said we were to blame, we who allowed Jim to become soft and sickly. But the doctor thought otherwise; he thought Jim had been worked hard enough already. And when Jim returned to the farm he no longer helped with the herd. And this was why I had to leave school: if he couldn't have both of us working with him part-time, my father wanted one full-time. Jim was entirely surrendered at last, to the house and books, to school and my mother. I didn't mind working on the farm all day, with my father; it was, after all, what I'd always wanted. All the same, I would have been happier if he had been: his doubts about himself, more and more frequently expressed, disturbed me. It wasn't like my father at all. He was convinced now he'd done the wrong thing, somewhere. He went back through the years, levering each year up like a stone, to see what lay beneath; he never seemed to find anything. It was worst of all in winter, when the land looked bleak, the hills were grey with low cloud, and the rain swirled out of the sky. All life vanished from his face and I knew he detested everything: the land which had promised him independence was now only a muddy snare; he was bogged here, between hills and river, and couldn't escape. He had no pride left in him for the place. If he could have got a price for the farm he would have gone. But there was no longer any question of a price. He could walk off if he liked. Only the bush would claim it back.

It was my mother who told us there were people coming. She had taken the telephone message while we were out of the house, and Jim was at the school.

'Who are they?' my father said.

'I couldn't understand very well. It was a bad connexion. I think they said they were the people who were here before.'

'The people who were here before? What the hell do they want here?' His eyes became suspicious under his frown.

'I think they said they just wanted to have a look around.'

'What the hell do they want here?' my father, repeated baffled.

'Nothing for them to see. This farm's not like it was when they were here. Everything's different. I've made a lot of changes. They wouldn't know the place. What do they want to come back for?'

'Well,' my mother sighed, 'I'm sure I don't know.'

'Perhaps they want to buy it,' he said abruptly; the words seemed simultaneous with his thought, and he stiffened with astonishment.

'By God, yes. They might want to buy the place back again. I hadn't thought of that. Wouldn't that be a joke? I'd sell, all right—for just about as much as I paid for the place. I tell you, I'd let it go for a song, for a bloody song. They're welcome.'

'But where would we go?' she said, alarmed.

'Somewhere,' he said. 'Somewhere new. Anywhere.'

'But there's nowhere,' she protested. 'Nowhere any better. You know that.'

'And there's nowhere any worse,' he answered. 'I'd start again somewhere. Make a better go of things.'

'You're too old to start again,' my mother observed softly.

There was a silence. And in the silence I knew that what my mother said was true. We all knew it was true.

'So we just stay here,' he said. 'And rot. Is that it?' But he really wished to change the subject. 'When are these people coming?'

'Tomorrow, I think. They're staying the night down in the township. Then they're coming up by launch.'

'They didn't say why they were interested in the place?'

'No. And they certainly didn't say they wanted to buy it. You might as well get that straight now. They said they just wanted a look around.'

'I don't get it. I just don't get it. If I walked off this place I wouldn't ever want to see it again.'

'Perhaps they're different,' my mother said. 'Perhaps they've got happy memories of this place.'

'Perhaps they have. God knows.'

It was early summer, with warm lengthening days. That sunny Saturday morning I loitered about the house with Jim, waiting for the people to arrive. Eventually, as the sun climbed higher in the sky, I grew impatient and went across the paddocks to help my father. We were working together when we heard the sound of the launch coming up the river.

'That's them,' he said briefly. He dropped his slasher for a moment, and spat on his hands. Then he took up the slasher again and chopped into a new patch of unruly gorse.

I was perplexed. 'Well,' I said, 'aren't you going down to meet them?'

'I'll see them soon enough. Don't worry.' He seemed to be conducting an argument with himself as he hacked into the gorse. 'I'm in no hurry. No, I'm in no hurry to see them.'

I just kept silent beside him.

'Who are they, anyway?' he went on. 'What do they want to come traipsing round my property for? They've got a bloody cheek.'

The sound of the launch grew. It was probably travelling round the last bend in the river now, past the swamp of raupo, and banks prickly with flax and toi toi. They were almost at the farm. Still chopping jerkily, my father tried to conceal his unease.

'What do they want?' he asked for the last time. 'By God, if they've come to gloat, they've got another thing coming. I've made something decent out of this place, and I don't care who knows it.'

He had tried everything in his mind and it was no use: he was empty of explanation. Now we could see the launch white on the gleaming river. It was coasting up to the bank. We could also see people clustered on board.

'Looks like a few of them,' I observed. If I could have done so without upsetting my father, I would have run down to meet the launch, eager with curiosity. But I kept my distance until he finished arguing with himself.

'Well,' he said, as if he'd never suggested otherwise, 'we'd better go down to meet them, now they're here.' He dug his slasher into the earth and began to stalk off down to the river. I followed him. His quick strides soon took him well ahead of me; I had to run to keep up.

Then we had our surprise. My father's step faltered; I blundered up alongside him. We saw the people climbing off the launch. And we saw who they were, at last. My father stopped perfectly still and silent. They were Maoris. We were still a hundred yards or more away, but there was no mistaking their clothing and colour. They were Maoris, all right.

'There's something wrong somewhere,' he said at last. 'It doesn't make sense. No Maori ever owned this place. I'd have known. Who the hell do think they are, coming here?'

I couldn't answer him. He strode on down to the river. There were young men, and two old women with black head-scarves. And last of all there was something the young men carried. As we drew nearer we saw it was an old man in a rough litter. The whole party of them fussed over making the old man comfortable. The old women, particularly; they had tattoos on their chins and wore sharktooth necklaces. They straightened the old man's blankets and fixed the pillow behind his head. He had a sunken, withered face and he didn't look so much sick, as tired. His eyes were only half-open as every one fussed around. It looked as if it were a great effort to keep them that much open. His hair was mostly grey, and his dry flesh sagged in thin folds about his ancient neck. I reckoned that he must have been near enough to a hundred years old. The young men talked quickly among themselves as they saw my father approaching. One came forward, apparently as spokesman. He looked about the oldest of them, perhaps thirty. He had a fat, shiny face.

'Here,' said my father. 'What's all this about?' I knew his opinion of Maoris: they were lazy, drank too much, and caused trouble. They just rode on the backs of the men on the land, like the loafers in the cities. He always said we were lucky there were so few in our district. 'What do you people think you're doing here?' he demanded.

'We rang up yesterday,' the spokesman said. 'We told your missus we might be coming today.'

'I don't know about that. She said someone else was coming. The people who were here before.'

'Well,' said the young man, smiling. 'We were the people before.'

'I don't get you. You trying to tell me you owned this place?'

'That's right. We owned all the land round this end of the river. Our tribe.'

'That must have been a hell of a long time ago.'

'Yes,' agreed the stranger. 'A long time.' He was pleasantly spoken and patient. His round face, which I could imagine looking jolly, was very solemn just then.

I looked around and saw my mother and Jim coming slowly down from the house.

'I still don't get it,' my father said. 'What do you want?'

'We just want to go across your land, if that's all right. Look, we better introduce ourselves. My name is Tom Taikaka. And this—'

My father was lost in a confusion of introductions. But he still didn't shake anyone's hand. He just stood his ground, aloof and faintly hostile. Finally there was the old man. He looked as though he had gone to sleep again.

'You see he's old,' Tom explained. 'And has not so long to live. He is the last great man of our tribe, the oldest. He wishes to see again where he was born. The land over which his father was chief. He wishes to see this before his spirit departs for Rerengawairua.'

By this time my mother and Jim had joined us. They were as confused as we were.

'You mean you've come just to—' my father began.

'We've come a long way,' Tom said. 'Nearly a hundred miles, from up the coast. That's where we live now.'

'All this way. Just so—'

'Yes,' Tom said. 'That's right.'

'Well,' said my father. 'What do you know? What do you know about that?' Baffled, he looked at me, at my mother, and even finally at Jim. None of us had anything to say.

'I hope we're not troubling you,' Tom said politely. 'We don't want to be any trouble. We just want to go across your land, if that's all right. We got our own tucker and everything.'

We saw this was true. The two old women had large flax kits of food.

'No liquor?' my father said suspiciously. 'I don't want any drinking round my place.'

'No,' Tom replied. His face was still patient. 'No liquor. We don't plan on any drinking.'

The other young men shyly agreed in the background. It was not, they seemed to say, an occasion for drinking.

'Well,' said my father stiffly, 'I suppose it's all right. Where are you going to take him?' He nodded towards the old sleeping man.

'Just across your land. And up to the old *pa*.'

'I didn't know there used to be any *pa* round here.'

'Well,' said Tom. 'It used to be up there.' He pointed out the largest hill behind our farm, one that stood well apart and above the others. We called it Craggy Hill, because of limestone outcrops. Its flanks and summit were patchy with tall scrub. We seldom went near it, except perhaps when out shooting; then we circled its steep slopes rather than climbed it, 'You'd see the terraces,' Tom said, 'if it wasn't for the scrub. It's all hidden now.'

Now my father looked strangely at Tom. 'Hey,' he said, 'You sure you aren't having me on? How come you know that hill straight off? You ever been here before?'

'No,' Tom said. His face shone as he sweated with the effort of trying to explain everything. 'I never been here before. I never been in this part of the country before.'

'Then how do you know that's the hill, eh?'

'Because,' Tom said simply, 'the old men told me. They described it so well I could find the place blindfold. All the stories of our tribe are connected with that hill. That's where we lived, up there, for hundreds of years.'

'Well, I'll be damned. What do you know about that?' My father blinked, and looked up at the hill again. 'Just up there, eh? And for hundreds of years.'

'That's right.'

'And I never knew. Well, I'll be damned.'

'There's lots of stories about that hill,' Tom said. 'And a lot of battles fought round here. Over your place.'

'Right over my land?'

'That's right. Up and down here, along the river.'

My father was so astonished he forgot to be aloof. He was trying to fit everything into his mind at once—the hill where they'd lived hundreds of years, the battles fought across his land—and it was too much.

'The war canoes would come up here,' Tom went on. 'I reckon they'd drag them up somewhere here'—he indicated the grassy bank on which we were standing—'in the night, and go on up to attack the *pa* before sunrise. That's if we hadn't sprung a trap for them down here. There'd be a lot of blood soaked into this soil.' He kicked at the earth beneath our feet. 'We had to fight a long while to keep this land here, a lot of battles. Until there was a day when it was no use fighting any more. That was when we left.'

We knew, without him having to say it, what he meant. He meant the day when the European took the land. So we all stood quietly for a moment. Then my mother spoke.

'You'd better come up to the house,' she said. 'I'll make you all a cup of tea.'

A cup of tea was her solution to most problems.

We went up to the house slowly. The young men followed behind, carrying the litter. They put the old man in the shade of a tree, outside the house. Since it seemed the best thing to do, we all sat around him; there wouldn't have been room for everyone in our small kitchen anyway. We waited for my mother to bring out the tea.

Then the old man woke. He seemed to shiver, his eyes opened wide, and he said something in Maori. 'He wonders where he is,' Tom explained. He turned back to the old man and spoke in Maori.

He gestured, he pointed. Then the old man knew. We all saw it the moment the old man knew. It was as if we were all willing him towards that moment of knowledge. He quivered and tried to lift himself weakly; the old women rushed forward to help him. His eyes had a faint glitter as he looked up to the place we called Craggy Hill. He did not see us, the house, or anything else. Some more Maori words escaped him in a long, sighing rush. '*Te Wahiokoahoki*,' he said.

'It is the name,' Tom said, repeating it. 'The name of the place.'

The old man lay back against the women, but his eyes were still bright and trembling. They seemed to have a life independent of his wrinkled flesh. Then the lids came down, and they were gone again. We could all relax.

'*Te Wahiokoahoki*,' Tom said. 'It means the place of happy return. It got the name when we returned there after our victories against other tribes.'

My father nodded. 'Well, I'll be damned,' he said. 'That place there. And I never knew.' He appeared quite affable now.

My mother brought out tea. The hot cups passed from hand to hand, steaming and sweet.

'But not so happy now, eh?' Tom said. 'Not for us.'

'No. I don't suppose so.'

Tom nodded towards the old man. 'I reckon he was just about the last child born up there. Before we had to leave. Soon there'll be nobody left who lived there. That's why they wanted young men to come back. So we'd remember too.'

Jim went into the house and soon returned. I saw he carried the greenstone adzes he'd found. He approached Tom shyly.

'I think these are really yours,' he said, the words an effort.

Tom turned the adzes over in his hand. Jim had polished them until they were a vivid green. 'Where'd you get these, eh?' he asked.

Jim explained how and where'd he found them. 'I think they're really yours,' he repeated.

There was a brief silence. Jim stood with his eyes downcast, his treasure surrendered. My father watched anxiously; he plainly thought Jim a fool.

'You see,' Jim added apologetically, 'I didn't think they really belonged to anyone. That's why I kept them.'

'Well,' Tom said, embarrassed. 'That's real nice of you. Real nice of you, son. But you better keep them, eh? They're yours now. You find, you keep. We got no claims here any more. This is your father's land now.'

Then it was my father who seemed embarrassed. 'Leave me out of this,' he said sharply. 'You two settle it between you. It's none of my business.'

'I think you better keep them all the same,' Tom said to Jim.

Jim was glad to keep the greenstone, yet a little hurt by rejection of his gift. He received the adzes back silently.

'I tell you what,' Tom went on cheerfully, 'You ever find another one, you send it to me, eh? Like a present. But you keep those two.'

'All right,' Jim answered, clutching the adzes. He seemed much happier. 'I promise if I find any more, I'll send them to you.'

'Fair enough,' Tom smiled, his face jolly. Yet I could see that he too really wanted the greenstone.

After a while they got up to leave. They made the old man comfortable again and lifted him. 'We'll see you again tomorrow,' Tom said. 'The launch will be back to pick us up.'

'Tomorrow?' my father said. It hadn't occurred to him that they might be staying overnight on his land.

'We'll make ourselves a bit of a camp up there tonight,' Tom said, pointing to Craggy Hill. 'We ought to be comfortable up there. Like home, eh?' The jest fell mildly from his lips.

'Well, I suppose that's all right.' My father didn't know quite what to say. 'Nothing you want?'

'No,' Tom said. 'We got all we want, thanks. We'll be all right. We got ourselves. That's the important thing, eh?'

We watched them move away, the women followed by the young men with the litter. Tom went last, Jim trotting along beside him. They seemed, since the business of the greenstone, to have made friends quickly. Tom appeared to be telling Jim a story.

I thought for a moment that my father might call Jim back. But he didn't. He let him go.

The old women now, I noticed, carried green foliage. They beat it about them as they walked across our paddocks and up towards Craggy Hill; they were chanting or singing, and their wailing sound came back to us. Their figures grew smaller with distance. Soon they were clear of the paddocks and beginning to climb.

My father thumbed back his hat and rubbed a handkerchief across his brow. 'Well, I'll be damned,' he said.

*   *   *

We sat together on the porch that evening, as we often did in summer after milking and our meal. Yet that evening was very different from any other. The sun had set, and in the dusk we saw faint smoke rising from their campfire on Craggy Hill, the place of happy return. Sometimes I thought I heard the wailing sound of the women again, but I couldn't quite be sure.

What were they doing up there, what did they hope to find? We both wondered and puzzled, yet didn't speak to each other.

Jim had returned long before, with stories. It seemed he had learned, one way and another, just about all there was to be learned about the tribe that had once lived on Craggy Hill. At the dinner table he told the stories breathlessly. My father affected to be not much interested; and so, my father's son, did I. Yet we listened, all the same.

'Then there was the first musket,' Jim said. 'The first musket in this part of the country. Someone bought it from a trader down south and carried it back to the *pa*. Another tribe, one of their old enemies, came seeking *utu*—*utu* means revenge—for something that had been done to them the year before. And when they started climbing up the hill they were knocked off, one by one, with the musket. They'd never seen anything like it before. So the chief of the tribe on Craggy Hill made a sign of peace and called up his enemies. It wasn't a fair fight, he said, only one tribe with a musket. So he'd let his enemies have the musket for a while. They would have turns with the musket, each tribe. He taught the other tribe how to fire and point the musket. Then they separated and started the battle again. And the next man to be killed by the musket was the chief's eldest son. That was the old man's uncle—the old man who was here today.'

'Well, I don't know', said my father. 'Sounds bloody queer to me. That's no way to fight a battle.'

'That's the way they fought,' Jim maintained.

So we left Jim, still telling stories to my mother, and went out on the porch.

The evening thickened. Soon the smoke of the campfire was lost. The hills grew dark against the pale sky. And at last my father, looking up at the largest hill of all, spoke softly.

'I suppose a man's a fool,' he said. 'I should never have let that land go. Shouldn't ever have let it go back to scrub. I could of run a few sheep up there. But I just let it go. Perhaps I'll burn it off one day, run a few sheep. Sheep might pay better too, the way things are now.'

But it wasn't somehow, quite what I expected him to say. I suppose he was trying to make sense of things in his own fashion.

III

They came down off Craggy Hill the next day. The launch had been waiting for them in the river some time.

When we saw the cluster of tiny figures, moving at a fair pace down the hills, we sensed there was something wrong. Then, as they drew nearer, approaching us across the paddocks, we saw what was wrong. There was no litter, no old man. They all walked freely, separately. They were no longer burdened.

Astonished, my father strode up to Tom. 'Where is he?' he demanded.

'We left him back up there,' Tom said. He smiled sadly and I had a queer feeling that I knew exactly what he would say.

'Left him up there?'

'He died last night, or this morning. When we went to wake him he was cold. So we left him up there. That's where he wanted to be.'

'You can't do that,' my father protested. 'You can't just leave a dead man like that. Leave him anywhere. And, besides, it's my land you're leaving him on.'

'Yes,' Tom said. 'Your land.'

'Don't you understand? You can't just leave dead people around. Not like that.'

'But we didn't just leave him around. We didn't just leave him anywhere. We made him all safe and comfortable. He's all right. You needn't worry.'

'Christ, man,' my father said. 'Don't you see?'

But he might have been asking a blind man to see. Tom just smiled patiently and said not to worry. Also he said they'd better be catching the launch. They had a long way to go home, a tiring journey ahead.

And as he walked off, my father still arguing beside him, the old women clashed their dry greenery, wailing, and their shark-tooth necklaces danced under their heaving throats.

In a little while the launch went noisily off down the river. My father stood on the bank, still yelling after them. When he returned to the house, his voice was hoarse.

He had a police party out, a health officer too. They scoured the hills, and most of the caves they could find. They discovered no trace of a burial, nor did they find anything in the caves. At one stage someone foolishly suggested we might have imagined it all. So my father produced the launchman and people from the township as witnesses to the fact that an old Maori, dying, had actually been brought to our farm.

That convinced them. But it didn't take them anywhere near finding the body. They traced the remnants of the tribe, living up the coast, and found that indeed an old man of the tribe was missing. No one denied that there had been a visit to our farm. But they maintained that they knew nothing about a body. The old man, they said, had just wandered off into the bush; they hadn't found him again.

He might, they added, even still be alive. Just to be on the safe side, in case there was any truth in their story, the police put the old man on the missing persons register, for all the good that might have done.

But we knew. We knew every night we looked up at the hills that he was there, somewhere.

So he was still alive, in a way. Certainly it was a long time before he let us alone.

And by then my father had lost all taste for the farm. It seemed the land itself had heaped some final indignity upon him, made a fool of him. He never talked again, anyway, about running sheep on the hills.

When butter prices rose and land values improved, a year or two afterwards, he had no hesitation in selling out. We shifted into another part of the country entirely, for a year or two, and then into another. Finally we found ourselves milking a small herd for town supply, not far from the city. We're still on that farm, though there's talk of the place being purchased soon for a city sub-division. We think we might sell, but we'll face the issue when it arises.

Now and then Jim comes to see us, smart in a city suit, a lecturer at the university. My father always found it difficult to talk to Jim, and very often now he goes off to bed and leaves us to it. One thing I must say about Jim: he has no objection to helping with the milking. He insists that he enjoys it; perhaps he does. It's all flatland round our present farm, with one farm much like another, green grass and square farmhouses and pine shelter belts, and it's not exactly the place to sit out on a summer evening and watch shadows gathering on the hills. Because there aren't hills within sight; or shadows either, for that matter. It's all very tame and quiet, apart from cars speeding on the highway.

I get on reasonably well with Jim. We read much the same books, have much the same opinions on a great many subjects. The city hasn't made a great deal of difference to him. We're both married, with young families. We also have something else in common: we were both in the war, fighting in the desert. One evening after milking, when we stood smoking and yarning in the cool, I remembered something and decided I might put a question to Jim.

'You know,' I began, 'they say it's best, when you're under fire in the war, to fix your mind on something remote. So you won't be afraid. I remember Dad telling me that. I used to try. But it never seemed any good. I couldn't think of anything. I was still as scared as hell.'

'I was too. Who wasn't?'

'But, I mean, did you ever think of anything?'

'Funny thing,' he said. 'Now I come to think of it, I did. I thought of the old place—you know, the old place by the river. Where,' he added, and his face puckered into a grin, 'where they buried that old Maori. And where I found those greenstones. I've still got it at home, you know, up on the mantelpiece. I seem to remember trying to give it away once, to those Maoris. Now I'm glad I didn't. It's my only souvenir from there, the only thing that makes that place still live for me.' He paused. 'Well, anyway, that's what I thought about. That old place of ours.'

I had a sharp pain. I felt the dismay of a long-distance runner who, coasting confidently to victory, imagining himself well ahead of the field, finds himself overtaken and the tape snapped at the very moment he leans forward to breast it. For one black moment it seemed I had been robbed of something which was rightfully mine.

I don't think I'll ever forgive him.

C. K. Stead

A NEW ZEALAND ELEGY

We were sitting around the table at the end of the meal.

'He'll be seventeen soon,' my mother said.

'What's that got to do with it?' my father wanted to know.

'And he'll be going to university. . . .'

'If giving him a good education is going to mean I have to agree with every tinpot theory he runs up off the top of his head I'd rather stop paying now.'

'I thought the State was paying,' Ellie said.

'Milton said,' I began. The subject of our disagreement was Freedom. There was something Milton had said but as I thought of it it evaporated.

'It's all very well for poets,' my father said. 'Some of us have to live in the real world. And that means you, my boy.'

'Your father's only thinking of you,' my mother said. 'He's afraid you'll land yourself in trouble with the authorities.'

'What authorities?' Ellie wanted to know.

I preferred to think I was taking risks. 'You call yourself a socialist . . .' I began.

But my grandmother had come in from the kitchen where she was already stacking the dishes to be washed. 'Ian's here,' she said.

'Ian,' my father grumbled. 'I'm not sure he's not to blame. . . .'

'Tying yourself in "nots" again,' Ellie said.

'Come in Ian,' my mother said.

He was there now, behind my grandmother. He came in smiling, confident. I got up from the table.

'I'm ready,' I said. 'I'll get my jacket.'

Trying to bring back that face of thirty years ago I remember his long upper lip and his olive skin. I don't remember that I ever especially noticed his eyes—large, brown, bland, smiling inwardly, not giving anything away. That's how he appears in the Mt Albert First Eleven photograph I found the other day. My own expression in that photograph is eager, innocent. Ian by contrast is already a man.

I had known him at primary school but not particularly well. There I remembered him because his father died when he was seven or eight.

This seemed so terrible I watched him to see how he would be affected. He didn't appear to be affected at all. I was puzzled. I thought he should look different. One day I asked him how he felt about his father dying. He looked at me angrily.

'I don't care,' he said.

I don't think I ever asked him about it again, not even when we were older and I knew him well.

Ian had two sisters and a brother, and after the father's death they and their mother were looked after by the grandfather, a Scotsman who ran a firm called the Loch Lomond Tile & Grate Company. Grandfather owned shares in South African diamond mines, and a Rover car. He spent the summer in New Zealand and then sailed to Europe for another summer. He paid the family bills, and it was he who decided Ian should be enrolled at Mt Albert as a boarder. That was because he didn't have a father to knock him into shape. Boarders were supposed to be better disciplined than the rest of us, and tougher.

That evening as we came out the front door the sun hadn't quite gone down. It was bright behind a thick puff of pale cloud, bursting out in orange shafts through two holes on either side. The shafts suggested something eternal and hidden on the far side of the Waitakere Range.

'There it is, brother,' Ian said. 'God's at His wonderful work again.'

'Amen brother,' I replied, and we stopped between the lavender and the rosemary to sing in harmony:

Softerly tenderly Jesus is calling,
Calling to you and to me.
See by the portholes He's watching and waiting,
Waiting for you and for me.

'And now onward,' Ian said. 'Softerly sneakily.'

We skirted the path so that our iron heel- and toe-plates wouldn't clatter on the concrete. Between the lilac and the board fence we stopped to stare into the next door sitting room. It was brightly lit. Three china ducks flew up the rosy wall. In a silver frame, two horses reared up in swirling mist. The radio on the sideboard showed a Pan figure blowing a horn against the fabric over the speaker. The clock on the mantelpiece swung three silver balls back and forth inside a glass dome like an upturned test-tube.

Marion came into the room. She looked around, picked up the newspaper, headed for the door again, then stopped, looking for something among the sheets of newsprint.

'Look at that bum,' Ian whispered. 'Look at those tits.'

'I'm looking,' I said.

The truckdriver came in. She pointed to something in the newspaper and they stood together reading it.

'That's the back page,' Ian said. 'They're going to the pics.'

'So are we,' I said. 'And we haven't got a truck.'

'Look at him now,' Ian urged. 'He's rubbing her twat.'

'I'm looking,' I said—but I could hardly bear it. It made me sick with desire and frustration.

'Let's go,' I said. 'We'll be late.'

We moved away from the fence, through the gate and into the street.

'You missed your chance there boy,' Ian said.

'Don't rub it in,' I said. 'And anyway, I haven't given up hope.'

But I had really. Marion's husband was away down the country at Trentham with the regular army. She used to come in from time to time and use our phone. My mother didn't approve. I don't know what my father thought, but to me Marion was the subject of erotic fantasies. She was young, beautifully shaped with dark wavy hair and an easy laugh. I hung about when she came to use the phone and I suppose she noticed that I did. One night she had come with a friend, a young woman. I answered the door and they said they wanted to use the phone. They were giggling and leaning together and I noticed wine on their breath. I showed them into the front room. The friend used the phone and while she talked Marion swayed and smiled, standing close beside me, sometimes leaning against me. I became so excited I did something quite out of character. I put my arm around her and closed my hand over her breast. She turned towards me, opening her eyes wide, pretending to be shocked.

'Naughty boy,' she said. 'Mustn't touch . . .' and she pitched forward, off balance, catching at my shoulder with one hand to steady herself. The other hand had come to rest against the front of my trousers.

'Mmmmm.' She hummed in my ear. 'You bring that to visit me one day and I'll show you what to do with it.'

For weeks afterwards I found it hard to think of anything else. I went to sleep thinking of Marion and woke with her still on my mind. I couldn't concentrate on my schoolwork. I don't know how many times I set off, determined to knock at her door and say I'd come, I'd brought it to visit her, but each time I got cold feet. I suppose it was just ordinary shyness, though I could always think of reasons against proceeding. I worried that someone would see me and report it to my family. Or that one of the family would see me. Then there was the fear that Marion would laugh; or worse—that sober, she would deny having invited me, or forget that she had, and fly into a rage or lay a complaint. I imagined so many possibilities, from total erotic success to disaster. We were studying *Hamlet* at school and I saw myself as the Prince of Denmark, 'a sensibility so radiant,' (one of the books said) 'a mind so alive, it sustains itself upon the mere prospect of action'.

So much about Marion was imagined I sometimes felt uncertain what was real and what wasn't. Had she really put her hand against my trousers and told me to bring my cock to visit her?

I'm not sure how many days or weeks went by in this state, but I know it lost all its romantic Hamlet flavour when the truckdriver appeared on the scene. There one night was the truck, and there it continued to be night after night, parked outside, and Marion shamelessly welcoming him at the door, kissing him in the sitting room not bothering to draw the blinds, going driving with him, sitting in the cab of the truck, an arm around his thick neck. It was disgusting. Sitting around the dining table, huffing and puffing, we agreed about that. It was bad enough that they weren't married; but with Gavin—Marion's husband—away in the New Zealand Armed Forces, that made it worse.

Before the truckdriver turned up, Ian had been urging me to get on in there and find out what it was all about. There was a race on between us to see who would be first to have a fuck, and although he was keen to win, because the loser had to buy the winner six milk shakes, he was more keen that one of us—either one—should prove that it wasn't impossible. We expected it to be difficult, but we were finding it so difficult we'd begun to worry. It had to be possible—like climbing Everest, or running the four-minute mile (neither of which had been done in those days). Otherwise life was going to be one long wank and then marriage and old age.

'We could let down his tyres,' Ian said as we walked down the road past the parked truck.

I grunted, depressed, and we walked on in silence. The sun was gone now and the streetlights had come on. We were almost at the bottom of the street when the truck droned past on its way to the main road. I could just make out the outline of Marion's head. She was smoking a cigarette.

'Bitch,' I said.

'Bloody whore,' Ian agreed.

I tried to be tough about her but the truth was that since the truck-driver had come into the picture I'd begun to feel a strange sentimental longing for her. She figured in beautiful lyrical dreams, she came into my mind when Nat King Cole sang 'Mona Lisa'; desire for her—a hard precise desire to push between her legs the cock she'd put her hand on—was mixed up with daydream fantasies in which she needed me, wanted me, etc., etc. The truckdriver just faded away, grumbling, unwanted, and Marion turned to me instead.

That night when we got back from the pictures (it was a Danny Kaye movie: funny, but sentimental too, with sentimental songs, and Danny Kaye burning the toast thinking about a girl who reminded me of Marion) the truck was already parked outside her gate. Inside the house all the lights were out.

'He's humping her in there,' Ian said.

We stood by the fence listening. Sometimes we thought we could hear the bed creaking and bumping but tonight the house was quiet.

'She's got it in her mouth,' Ian said. 'They're having a bit of quiet sixty-nine.'

'Come on,' I said.

We hung our jackets on the fence, tucked our grey flannel trousers into our socks, took off our ties, and went down the slope under the lilac trees to the lawn. Ian got a wristlock on me but I slipped out of it and got a headlock on him. I forced him down slowly, tripping him at the last minute so he wouldn't break out of the hold in falling, but he flipped sideways and got his legs around me in a body scissors. He had it on from behind, with his legs locked in front of me, and I managed to lock my legs over his in a double scissors, stretching his legs against my sides. He was in pain—he was grunting with it—but so was I. It was a question of who would give in first. He seemed to release his scissors, but then he flipped sideways and it was on again from the side so I couldn't close my legs over. I forced myself up on one arm, making grabs at his head with the other, while he squeezed the scissors in jerks, moving his head back out of reach. For a moment he loosened his hold to get a better grip on me and I was out of it and up on my feet.

Now the blood was flowing, we weren't angry but full of aggression. I got him in a headlock, he countered, and we crashed down together and lay there panting, each tightening his hold, neither able to escape. It was strange how warm and comfortable and even in a way restful it could be, lying there locked together inflicting pain on one another. It used to go on for twenty minutes or half an hour until we just rolled apart and lay on our backs panting up at the stars.

As my mother predicted would happen, I turned seventeen. I was accredited a pass in the exam for University Entrance. Ian, who had done no work for it, sat and failed. That summer he and I took a job together at the freezing works, working long hours because it was the height of the killing season. We had to start at four in the morning and that meant leaving home at 3.30 to bike the miles from Mt Eden to Penrose. It was dark and the streets were empty and wet with dew and we raced along the footpaths or on either side of the road, whichever suited us, making tremendous speeds. It seemed downhill all the way. By seven when we stopped work for breakfast it was full daylight. From 7.30 there were five long hours until lunch, with only a short break for smoko. The last hours until 4.30 were dismal. All the bounce and energy of that early morning start had gone. We dragged ourselves around, no one talked much, there were only snarls. The ride home in the heat of the afternoon was the worst part of the day. Pushing pedal after pedal as if they rose out of the ground and had to be pushed back again for ever, our legs ached and didn't belong to us. We reached Ian's house first and he peeled off with only a grunt and a wave. We were bored but we had no energy for anything, not for tennis, not even for the pictures.

The work was in the fellmongery, forking pelts out of vats into trolleys and heaving the trolleys to the fleshing machines. There were four Tongans worked with us, they were brothers or cousins, the oldest called Billy, and they worked together in the off-season as a dance band that went by the name of Billy von Strum and his Hawaiians. Ian and I had heard them sometimes on the radio. One morning we were sitting around a table in the canteen eating sausages for breakfast and Billy said he couldn't fuck his missus so often when he worked overtime.

'How often you fuck your girlfriend when you working overtime fullah?' he asked.

I shrugged. I didn't want to admit I didn't fuck my girlfriend at all.

'He doesn't fuck his girlfriend,' Ian said.

'Neither do you,' I said.

'I'll fuck your girlfriend if you want me to,' Ian said.

'He's never had a fuck in his life,' I said. 'And neither have I.'

The Tongans wanted to know if that was true. I told them it was. We both had girlfriends and we wanted to fuck them but they wouldn't let us.

'That means you don't know how to do it,' Billy said. 'You got to play with her titties, see? That turn on the water downstairs.'

They all laughed, rolling around on their benches and slapping their big hands down on the table-top. I looked at Ian. I didn't know what Billy meant and I didn't think Ian knew either.

'What if she still says no?' Ian asked.

'She won't say no fullah. You play with her titties right, be real nice with the pointy bits—' He rolled the tips of his fingers gently over his thumbs. 'Out pops the pointy bit, see. Oh!' He closed his eyes and jumped up, thrusting his heavy thighs this way and that around the room. 'The big fuck, eh?'

'You do what he says,' Billy's brother told me. 'You get the real good fuck eh. She won't say no.'

Riding home I managed to forget the heat and the ache in my legs long enough to ask Ian what he thought Billy meant.

'It's got something to do with lubrication,' Ian said. 'I read about it in a medical book. It's so your cock can slide in and out.'

'I used to play with Beryl's tits,' I said. 'It didn't make any difference.'

'Maybe it's not so simple with white sheilas,' Ian said.

And we rode on in silence.

We got fifteen pounds a week, sometimes more when there was Sunday work—it was unbelievable riches. Ian was saving for a motor bike. He wanted one of those big hundred-mile-an-hour Nortons. I was saving just so I would have some money during the year when I would be back at school, hoping for a university scholarship.

After four weeks at the freezing works we'd had enough. We stopped work and went camping on the West Coast. We strapped a tent, ground sheets, sleeping bags, a primus stove, a lantern—all our camping gear— on the bikes, and on our backs we each carried a pack, mostly of food, enough to keep us eating for a week. We rode up into the Waitakeres, along the Scenic Drive and out on the Piha Road, skidding and sliding on the unsealed surface. At Karekare we padlocked our bikes and hid them in the bush by the roadside and ferried our gear in loads around the rocks at low tide, over the sand dunes and up the Pararaha Valley where we made our camp. Up there we saw an occasional tramper or group of trampers. Mostly there was just the bush, and the stream running by our tent, and the boom of the surf echoing up from beyond the dunes. We swam, fished, gathered mussels and cooked them over our fire, tramped up the valley and over the hills, or along the dunes to Whatipu and the Manukau, read cowboy yarns and murder mysteries, and at night lay looking up at the moon shining on the spikes of flax and cabbage tree and talked about Marion and Beryl and Barbara and Jean and all the others, and about the Billy von Strum method. Ian had brought a ruler and we measured our cocks for length and circumference and tried to work out which one had the greater cubic volume but neither of us was very good at maths and we couldn't be sure which of several answers was right. But the mathematical problem was less important than the other one. How were we going to get these bulky instruments, which we liked so much and wanted so much to use, into action? The four-minute mile was getting closer, and the conquest of Everest still looked more likely than the conquest of Barbara or Beryl or Jean.

At the end of the holidays I went back to school for a final year before university. Ian was apprenticed to a motor mechanic. He thought this was his grandfather's revenge on him for failing University Entrance but he didn't argue because he wanted to learn about cars and motor bikes. He didn't imagine being a motor mechanic all his life—after all there were those shares in South African diamond mines, not to mention the Loch Lomond Tile & Grate Company—and one of these days the old boy had to croak. In the meantime Ian didn't mind spending a year or two learning about engines.

Those were the years of the Cold War. The excitements of the real war had gone; so had the political idealism of the thirties. The Left was in retreat. I didn't understand it then but I felt it. The defeat of Labour after fourteen years in office was like a family tragedy. But what troubled me more was the feeling that my father had been defeated too, in himself. It was as if his manhood had been undermined at the very moment when my own was arriving. He still called himself a socialist but he didn't seem to have any courage and we quarrelled every time the talk was of politics. It had been a political household. Now my mother had to hush and smooth things over and change the subject, afraid of explosions.

At school I spent most of my time with a boy whose father was a wharfie, a real worker and a militant. Bruce and I played chess, we went to political meetings, read the *Communist Manifesto* and the *People's Voice*, and harassed our history master with questions about revolution and the class war. We wanted to believe in Russia and we were being asked to see it as the enemy. Our war, we were told, the next one, which was coming soon, would be fought on the steppes.

I still met Ian at tennis, we won the Club junior doubles together; but summer was passing, I was beginning to work for a scholarship, we didn't wrestle any more, we saw one another less often.

One evening in early autumn the family were still at the table when the phone rang. It was Ian.

'Are you free tonight?' he asked. 'I've got the Rover. The old boy's gone. He sailed on Friday. I'm supposed to look after it while he's away.'

He wasn't supposed to drive it, except once around the block on Saturday mornings to tune it up. But he had oiled the garage door so it opened quietly. He used to turn the radio up in the sitting room just as he was leaving. Then he opened the garage door and pushed the Rover out into the street that ran along one side of their section. There was a gentle slope which the car ran down and at the corner Ian jumped in and turned on the engine. By the time he came back his mother would be asleep.

'There's a dance at Valley Road,' he said. 'We can pick up some girls and take them for a drive.'

'You'd better park out of sight,' I said. 'There'll be trouble here if they know we've got the car.'

Back at the table there had to be the usual family inquest about what I was planning to do and whether it was a good idea. The collective family wits were brought to bear on it. Did I have homework? Was it right to put Bruce off when I had said I would go over a chess problem with him? What time would I be home? How would I feel in the morning?

It was still going on when Ian arrived, suspiciously soon after having phoned if anyone had thought about it, but nobody did. I got myself ready and we left. Down the path we stopped to look over the fence but Marion's blinds were down. The truck was parked out in the street. I'd almost given up hope of Marion and I felt more detached about her.

We walked up the road and around the corner. Ian had parked outside the local school where there were no lights. 'There she is,' he said.

Even in the darkness I could see the coat of polish he had given it. The black body shone, the chrome on the bumper bars and around the huge headlights gleamed. We got in and sat in the flash bucket seats admiring the wood-panelled dashboard with all its dials and even a clock.

'Cigarette,' Ian offered.

He held out a silver case. I took one and he lit it, and his own, with a chromium lighter.

'Listen,' he said, turning on the engine. 'She purrs.'

'It's like the pictures,' I said.

'It's like real life,' he corrected. And we drove away up the road.

It wasn't difficult to get two girls to come for a drive with us. We left before the dance was over and headed out to Dominion Road Extension. In those days the trams ran to Mt Roskill and stopped, but the double concrete road, with a space in the middle where the tram tracks were to run, continued for miles. The planned extension never went ahead so there was a road like a motorway before motorways had begun. You could go fast out there and never meet anything head-on coming the other way. The Rover accelerated smoothly up to sixty and beyond. The girls squealed; Ian smiled; I hid my fear. I had never been so fast in my life.

We went all the way to Blockhouse Bay. We got out and went down through trees to the beach. It was a very calm night, the water was still, there were the sounds of gulls squabbling for space under the cliffs, and occasionally the plop of a fish jumping. I had an arm around my girl, Merle, and when I looked back Ian was kissing the other one beside the changing sheds. There was a patch of soft grass and ferns under the trees and I steered Merle there and we lay down together.

She shivered. 'It's a nice night,' she said. 'But it's cold.'

I took my jacket off and draped it over her. I bent closer to kiss her. She turned her head aside but then she changed her mind. Her mouth darted at mine. It was a nice mouth.

Kissing a girl was like an electric shock. I hadn't got used to it. It made me dizzy, confused, and at the same time there was the strong feeling that kissing wasn't enough and that I didn't know how to get beyond it. One hand was already spread over her breast; but as I moved it down her body she pushed it away. It was the old story. It was what always happened.

'Don't you want to?' I asked.

She shook her head.

'Why not?'

'Don't want to have a baby.'

'But I've got a. . . . You know. A thing.' It was in my wallet. Ian had given it to me.

She didn't say anything.

'So you wouldn't have a baby.'

She was silent, staring past my shoulder at the moon. I kissed her again and although she was passive I thought she liked it. I put my hand down between her legs and she didn't push it away.

'Do you want to?' I asked.

'Mmmm,' she said.

I sat up, hunting through my jacket for the wallet, through the wallet for the sheath. I got the wrong pocket, then the wrong compartment. She shivered. I put the jacket over her again.

'It's here,' I said. I was thinking I would have to take off my shoes and then my trousers and what would she do while I did that?

She shook her head. 'I don't want to,' she said.

Then I remembered I hadn't used the Billy von Strum method. I reached under the jacket for her nipples. She flinched as if I had hurt her.

'Don't,' she said, and she sat up.

'What school do you go to?' she asked.

'I'm a student,' I said.

'You're not. I've seen you in uniform. You go to Mt Albert.'

'Well why did you ask?'

I sat beside her with the sheath in my hand, blowing it up like a balloon and then letting the air out. I felt depressed.

'What's the matter?' she asked.

'Don't girls want to?' I said.

'Yes. . . . Well. . . .' She thought about it. I could hear the gulls and the very gentle lap of the water that was moonlit now. The tide was coming in.

'Girls want to,' she explained. 'But not with anyone in particular.'

'What do you mean?'

'Not with anyone real. At least. . . .' She thought some more. 'I want to do it—because you have to sooner or later, don't you? But I can't think of anyone I want to do it with.'

'You mean you don't like me enough,' I said.

'I like you. . . .'

As she hesitated again I was thinking despite the kisses and the moonlit water it wasn't much fun. I was cold and she was a bore.

'I like you,' she said. 'And your friend.' (It flashed through my mind that she preferred Ian—they both did. He was probably humping the other one now.) 'But not enough for that.'

And then she looked at me—stared at me in the half-light. 'Do you like me?' She asked it timidly.

I hadn't thought about it. I liked her eyes, and her hair, and her skin, and the feel of her lips, and when I thought of all that it seemed as if I liked her a lot. But a moment ago I'd been thinking she was a bore. And if Ian asked me I would probably say she was a dumb bitch.

'Of course I like you,' I said.

'No you don't,' she said, suddenly flat and angry. 'All you want is a fuck.'

I was shocked she should use the word. I had never heard a girl or a woman say it. 'Let's go back to the car,' I said. 'I'm cold.'

We had to wait a long time for Ian and I felt sure he had won the six milk shakes, but he hadn't had any luck either. He had just tried harder.

'They were a pair of cock-teasers,' Ian said as he dropped me at the bottom of the street. 'Better luck next time, old boy.' And he lit a cigarette and drove smoothly away.

I remember more than one of those fast drives along Dominion Road Extension, with the needle in its wood-panelled enclosure quivering up towards seventy. There were other dances and other girls too. We took them along the waterfront, or to the top of Mt Eden to look at the lights of Auckland, or into the Domain to park among the trees. But in the end it was always the same. You could touch but you couldn't fuck, and the Billy von Strum method made no difference.

All this must have been spread over autumn, winter, and on into spring again. Grandfather returned from Europe and reclaimed his car (grandson, the useful apprentice, had adjusted the mileage)—but by now Ian had bought his Norton. It was second-hand, but huge and powerful, and now the rides I had with him were altogether different. The acceleration, the noise, the rush of air, the sight of the road tearing away just there below you like a mad conveyor belt ready to chew your feet off, the leaning into curves and the recovery from impossible angles, the sense of living violently, dangerously—one ride like that wiped out everything but itself and the real world only came back slowly. While it lasted there was no school, no politics, no French irregular verbs, no tennis or soccer, there weren't even girls. There were only the two of us, helmetless, and the big things—Speed, Power, Life and Death.

Bruce disapproved of those rides and he disapproved of Ian. He called him a leather-jacketed fascist. But Ian was no fascist. He hated all politics. 'Left, right and centre,' he said, 'it's all bullshit.'

The last time I went to a dance with him we got into a fight. I don't remember exactly how it started. It was something trivial—someone complaining he'd been jostled by Ian on the dance-floor. There was an exchange of insults and we found ourselves confronting three boys who looked strong and tough.

People were watching, waiting for the fists to fly.

'We'll be thrown out if we fight here', Ian said. 'I'll take one of you on after the dance. Wait for us outside.' And he turned away, walked across the floor, and asked a girl to dance.

I couldn't believe he meant it. I thought he must have some plan of escape. I wouldn't have taken on even the weakest looking of those three, but when I got a chance to talk to him he said if they were waiting he would fight. 'So long as I don't have to deal with more than one I'll be O.K.' he said.

After the dance they were waiting. We had all cooled down, there was a feeling of embarrassment, but honour had to be satisfied. We walked along the main road until we came to a side street lined with houses and gardens and with a grass verge along the footpath.

Ian handed me his jacket and tie and tucked his trousers into his socks. 'Let's go,' he said. 'You three wait here.'

He walked with his opponent down the street and they disappeared into the darkness between the streetlights. My stomach was tight, not so much from fear now but nervousness. I didn't know how he could do it, how he could remain so cool, walking into that dark street with someone who looked older and tougher. The other two who waited with me seemed nervous too. We lit cigarettes. There was a feeling of friendliness.

I suppose ten minutes passed—dragged by—before we saw a figure coming out of the darkness. We went towards him. It was Ian.

'Where's Jack?' the others asked.

'He's there,' Ian said. Then I noticed his shirt. It was spattered with stains that looked black in the half-light but I knew they could only be blood.

The others had hurried on into the dark.

'Are you bleeding?' I asked.

He shook his head, putting on his jacket. 'It's his.'

'What did you do to him?'

'Let's go,' Ian said. 'He'll be O.K.'

There was a note of excitement in his voice. He had been afraid, and he'd overcome his fear, but he wouldn't talk about it, and he wouldn't talk about the fight.

'I beat him,' he said. 'That's all.'

The weather began to get warmer and I was working hard now for my scholarship. In my room I had an old roll-top desk that had belonged to my grandfather and I sat at it late into the night, reading, taking notes, jotting down ideas. Sometimes I sat it seemed for hours staring at its square compartments, its dark panels, my mind heavy and blank, my back sore, not working but feeling there was more to do before I went to bed. The conjugation of French irregular verbs, the solutions to certain geometrical equations—some of these things still come back to me now as if out of the dark compartments of that desk.

One night I was working late when I heard the Norton outside. A moment later Ian was knocking at the back door, the one nearest my bedroom.

'I've got something to tell you,' he said.

He hustled me along the veranda to my room, looking over his shoulder.

'Let's shut the door,' he said. And then he stood quiet, listening to make sure no one was coming.

When he turned, his face was lit up, a broad grin spreading over it.

'I've done it,' he said. And then in case I hadn't understood: 'I've had a fuck.'

I banged him on the back and mimed three cheers silently. 'You beaut,' I said. 'What was it like?'

'Shit,' he said, falling back into a chair. 'Fuck—it was. . . . It was fucking marvellous.' He shook his head slowly, remembering. 'Well, it wasn't perfect. She didn't let me finish. But Jesus it felt good in there.'

He spread his legs, threw his head and shoulders back and sprawled, staring at the ceiling. 'When your cock's in there all of a sudden you think so that's it. That's what it's all about. That's the place it's supposed to go.' He sat up to see if I was understanding what he was trying to say. 'Cocks are made to go in cunts,' he said. 'I don't know why the whole world isn't fucking itself to death.'

'Maybe it is,' I said. I sometimes thought it was, and that Ian and I were just unlucky.

'But there are all these pricks going around saying you shouldn't do it, it's bad and dirty and wicked. . . .' He cupped his hands behind his head and smiled luxuriously. 'It's bad and dirty and bloody marvellous,' he said.

'But she didn't let you finish,' I said.

'Not inside. I finished. Like a rocket. I think it must have hit the ceiling.' He mimed a tommy gun. 'I probably drilled holes in her roof. She's probably lying there now with her fingers in her fanny thinking about my cock with the rain coming down through the holes in the roof.'

A sort of shudder passed over me at the thought of her fingers in her fanny—not a shudder of horror. It was such a marvellous thought it was almost too much for me.

'Did she like it?' I asked.

'She was scared. The usual thing. Afraid of getting pregnant—and I didn't have a french letter. It was my cousin and you don't take frenchies when you go to stay with cousins, do you? That's why I had to pull out. But she liked it. Hell yes—she liked it a lot.'

'Your cousin. . . .' I wondered about that. But then there was a cousin of mine I lusted after. Even Ellie excited me, my own sister.

'Meg,' he said. 'The one at Maramarua. I went down for the weekend. I spent the day cutting scrub with her. We got on fine—we told one another a lot of dirty jokes. But I never thought of trying anything because she's my cousin. I've never even kissed her. I'd gone to bed, I think I was just about asleep and this figure came into my room. I didn't know who it was. She got into bed and I still didn't know—I didn't think of Meg. I said who the fuck are you and she said I'm Meg, I want you to do me over.'

I laughed. We both laughed. We rolled about, stuffing handkerchiefs in our mouths to keep the noise down. 'Did she really say that? I want you to do me over?'

'That's what she said. I'm Meg. I want you to do me over. Sounds kind of formal doesn't it. My cock was so hard it was hurting. You know how it gets sometimes—like an over-inflated tyre. And then I couldn't get it in. I had to push and push and I thought I must have the wrong place but every time I moved it she moved it back with her hand. She kept groaning and rolling her head from side to side but if I stopped pushing she said Don't stop. I thought she was groaning because it hurt so much but she told me afterwards it did hurt a bit because she hadn't done it before but she was groaning mostly because it was so good. And then all of a sudden it went in. . . .' He shook his head again, as if he couldn't believe it. 'The whole bloody thing—it just slid in.'

He stopped talking and his eyes were blinking and for a moment I thought he was going to cry.

'I'll make some tea,' I said. 'The kettle's still hot.' I went out to the kitchen and made it strong—real black tea—because that was how Ian liked it.

'Wasting tea again,' Ellie said.

I couldn't think of a smart answer because I was looking at her and thinking about Ian and Meg, and Ian's cock sliding in. I shivered.

'God you look stupid,' Ellie said. 'What's wrong with you?'

'Trigonometry,' I said. 'It's bad for the brain.'

Back in the bedroom I handed Ian his cup. 'It should be milk shakes,' I said.

He grinned, taking the cup. 'It's taken a long time. How many was it supposed to be? Six. You'd better buy me two packets of Ardath. Let's have one.'

He put his cup down on the desk and took out the cigarette case. I watched him, trying to see some difference in him. This was something that always puzzled me. People got married and went away on honeymoons and when they came back you couldn't see the difference. You knew they were different. They'd *done* it. But on the outside they were mysteriously the same. And now Ian had done it. I felt such a wave of affection for him I punched him on the arm, hard.

'Shit,' I said. 'You've done it.'

He nodded, drawing on his cigarette. 'I've done it, boyo.'

'And it was good?'

'And God said let there be fucks and God saw that they were good.'

'And you're going to do it again?'

'Shit am I ever. Only next time I'll have the rubber goods.'

But there wasn't a next time. When he went back to the farm his cousin had gone to Wellington. He wrote to her but she didn't reply. He wrote again saying he was coming to Wellington and she sent back a card saying 'Stay away I'm scared. I don't want to see you.' He kept writing and threatening to go to Wellington but he never went.

All that—the disappointment and drama of it—was spread over the time when I was sitting for my scholarship, and then on into the summer. We met from time to time and we always talked about Meg, and the big fuck, and how he was going to get to her and do it again. He seemed jumpy, full of jokes but unhappy.

Bruce was going on with me to university and we had taken a summer job together on a fence-building gang at the Southdown Freezing Works. The fence was to run over volcanic land, with stony outcrops that had to be blasted before the posts could be put in. I thought the foreman disliked me because it was always my job to hold the spike while he drove it into the rock with a sledge-hammer, to make the hole for the plug of explosive. I lay there holding it absolutely still while he lifted the hammer over his head and swung it full force on to the head of the spike. Only a fraction of an inch to one side or the other and he would have smashed my hand or my wrist to pieces.

'I haven't missed one yet,' he used to say.

And I would drag a crooked grin over my face, feeling sick with fear. But it was outdoors work, less boring than most jobs, and you could see something for your efforts, the fence going across the stony paddock, looking strong and tight and shipshape.

Coming home one night I noticed the truck wasn't parked outside Marion's house. The next night it was gone too and the night after. I wondered whether it was all over with the truckdriver, and whether, it if was, I would have the courage to go and visit her. I didn't think I would.

It was my grandmother and Ellie who told me Gavin was back. They were in the kitchen one morning when I came in still half asleep.

'He's back,' Ellie said.

'Who's back?'

'Gavin, Marion's husband.'

'He's on leave,' they said together.

'With his kitbag and his golf-clubs,' my grandmother said.

'And they're arguing already.' Ellie added.

'I quite liked that truckdriver,' my grandmother admitted. 'He looked a nice young man.'

No one knew whether Gavin had been told about the truckdriver, but the rows in there were fierce enough to suggest he had some idea what had been going on. In the daytime he sat frowning in a deck-chair on the back veranda with a bottle of beer, a glass, and a revolver on a table beside him. The veranda looked over what had been a back garden enclosed by a rock wall, but in the time Gavin had been away Marion had done nothing to it—the grass had grown waist high, wattles and what we called tobacco trees had shot up, there was a tangle of fennel and honeysuckle and passionfruit and choko. And in the wall, Gavin told my father, who asked about the revolver in a nervous, joking voice one morning, there were rats—'thousands of the buggers'. We didn't know whether it was safest to humour him, or to complain that you couldn't shoot rats in a rocky suburban garden. Mostly we feared for Marion, though my mother didn't forget to point out that whatever happened, 'maid Marion', as she liked to call her, had brought it on herself. And meanwhile there were reports of the truck parked here and there in the streets at night, and of Marion hurrying out in the dark, looking furtive, not acknowledging greetings, not wanting to be seen. We weren't sure whether this was just gossip, or whether it was still going on between Marion and the truck-driver, until one weekend Ellie stayed with a friend in Mission Bay and saw them together at the pictures.

I was glad. I had changed sides. Like my grandmother I now favoured the truckdriver, but my reasons, unlike hers, were political. The Korean War had begun, New Zealand was sending a force, and the whole neigh-bourhood knew that Gavin had been commissioned and that he would be going to fight. To Bruce and me that war was a piece of American imperialism. We went to meetings at which it was condemned, and we listened to speakers who had been to China or to Russia who told us how it all looked from the other side. In our minds the truckdriver, though we didn't know him, was a worker; Gavin was a fascist. We liked Marion and so we hoped she would divorce the fascist and marry the worker.

But it was also rumoured that the worker had a wife. That made it more complicated.

February came and it was time to stop work and think about university. The foreman shook hands with me the day I was leaving. 'Still in one piece?' he said.

I was surprised he seemed so friendly. I said, 'I'm sorry I won't be here to see the fence when it's finished.'

'I'll be looking around for another spike holder,' he said.

That was the part of the job I hadn't liked. 'I don't know why I was always the one who had to hold it,' I said.

'It's got to be held steady,' he said. 'You weren't scared.'

'I was scared to death,' I said. 'My nerves are in shreds.'

'Well lad,' he said. 'In that case you've got a steady hand.'

And so I enrolled at the university and began a new life of lectures and working in the library and sitting talking in what was called in those days the Caf. On the way home sometimes if there weren't late lectures I used to get off the tram and call at the garage where Ian worked. He would be under a jacked-up car, lying on his back on a little trolley, and when I called he would come wheeling out wiping his black hands on an oily rag. We would light up cigarettes and grumble over our boredoms— his with engines, mine with French grammar. We planned a holiday together in May. Ian would be due for leave then and there would be the university vacation. We would go south on the Norton, all the way to Wellington. We would find Meg, Ian would fuck her again, and maybe there would be someone—a friend of Meg's—for me.

On Friday evenings we usually looked out for one another at the shopping centre. One Friday I came out of a shop—it must have been almost nine o'clock, just before the shops were due to shut—and I saw Ian cruising along on the Norton looking for me in the crowd. I waved but he missed me, a U-turn, and accelerated away in the other direction. I let ten minutes go by and then phoned from a call-box but his sister said he wasn't at home. I thought he must have found something else to do by now and I walked on to Bruce's place for a game of chess.

Next morning I was still in bed when the phone rang. My father answered it. After a minute or two he came out to the kitchen and spoke quietly to my mother, but I heard what he said. I leaped out of bed. For just a moment the rush of blood, the shock, the shot of adrenalin, was so sharp it felt indistinguishable from a moment of sheer joy.

Ian was dead.

Towards the end of the war, when the German death camps were one by one being over-run by the advancing Allies, our newspapers had been full of photographs of the dead and the nearly dead—piles of corpses, their stick-like arms and legs pointing in all directions, or living skeletons covered with skin crawling to the barbed wire, their eyes huge like lamps. I was twelve at the time and those photographs, together with the accounts of gas chambers, sadism, torture and mass death, were a daily horror to which was soon to be added the details of the Hiroshima and Nagasaki bombs. We had grown up, my friends, my sister and I, with the idea of death in war—in tank battles, infantry and machine gun attacks, artillery bombardments, and in air raids on cities—not heroic exactly, but exciting. Now death took on a new and horrible look—so horrible we shied away from it, buried it. And it was all happening somewhere else. At home there had been no death more real than that of a domestic pet, a neighbour, one or two distant relatives.

Later the death camps and the bombed cities, those real but in the end manageable horrors, were gathered into our politics. The piles of dead, the living corpses with their headlamp eyes, still sent shivers down the spine. But we remembered them only when we wanted to put them to use in some argument about fascism, anti-semitism, the atomic bomb, the continuing argument of Left and Right.

When I think again of the family together at the table, my grand-mother interrupting our argument about freedom to announce that Ian was at the door, I realise that all of them except Ellie are dead, and Ellie is far away in another country, unlikely ever to return. If that scattering had happened to us in a single moment, as at the blast of a bomb, it would have been the kind of thing that gets described as a tragedy. But a tragedy—even the kind you get in the theatre, like the end of *Hamlet* when the stage is littered with corpses—is only a speeding up of what time in any case brings about. Ian, my grandmother, my father, my mother—one by one they have died, and because of that I now know that what I believed then was untrue. I believed that no other death could have moved me to such grief as I was feeling at Ian's. It was a new experience and I was almost frightened at how deep into myself the pain burned. And as well as pain there was frustration. I wanted to give vent to my feeling, to let it out, to share it around, even maybe to show it off, and there was no way I could find to do it.

I remember lying at night face down on the lawn where Ian and I had wrestled, holding the grass in both hands and feeling that if I didn't hold tight I would fly off the world into the spaces between the stars. I thought of Laertes, then Hamlet, leaping into Ophelia's open grave to insist on their love, arguing and clawing at one another over her dead body, each asserting greater love and greater loss. What bad form, and how satisfying!

That Saturday morning the clouds were very white, sailing high and fast in a clear sky, and the Waitakeres were ink-blue beyond the green-grey slopes of Mt Albert. I was walking slowly to Ian's place, my eyes cast up there watching the clouds that were so white and satisfying, aloof and laundered.

Ian's sister Jan answered the door. 'Don't look like that,' she said. 'Come in.'

I felt rebuked. I had prepared a funeral face and it was false. But how could you find an appearance to match your feeling, short of throwing yourself in the dry earth of the garden and rolling in it, howling?

Jan took me into the kitchen where her boyfriend, Len, was making toast. Ian's mother was receiving adult relatives and callers in another part of the house.

'Bad business,' Len said, buttering the burned slices.

'I'll say,' I said. 'Terrible.'

We ate the toast and talked about the National Tennis Championships. I loved Jan, I wanted to kiss her, but of course I didn't. At the door when she was showing me out I half turned and reached towards her. My hand closed around the ends of her fingers in an awkward clasp.

'Sorry,' I said. And I bolted away down the steps as the tears sprang into my eyes.

That was Saturday and by the end of the day the suburb was buzzing, you could almost hear the phones ringing up and down the street. Ian had run into the back of a parked truck. Marion and her boyfriend had been parked in the shadow outside the primary school where there were no lights. Ian had come around the corner on the Norton, accelerated into the shadow and run into the tray of the truck. His smashed ribs had punctured his lungs and he had died on the road before the ambulance arrived. Now the police were enquiring. Gavin had learned the truth, so had the truckdriver's wife—it was all out in the open. So there was more to talk about than just Ian's death. There was the scandal as well, everyone agreeing it was a shocking business. Already there had been a big blow-up next door and Gavin had left in a taxi taking his kitbag and his golf-clubs.

That night I couldn't keep still. I walked to the dance at Valley Road but I felt it wouldn't be right to go in even if I had wanted to. I walked to

Mt Eden, climbed the hill and looked down on the lights of the city and the two harbours. Hours later when the dance was ending I was back in Valley Road. I saw the two girls Ian and I had taken to Blockhouse Bay leaving with their partners. I stayed out of sight. The crowd dispersed and again I was walking—along Dominion Road, through the park, through the grounds of the school, past Ian's house, through the tennis club. I went on and on until I was shuffling in a stupor of exhaustion.

The funeral was to be on Monday afternoon. I had been told Ian could be seen in his coffin that morning. I took a tram to the undertaker's. I walked past the door, turned and walked past it again, but the third time I got up the courage to walk in. I gave the receptionist Ian's name.

'You wish to view the deceased,' she said.

'Yes please.'

'Are you a relative?'

'No.'

'Come this way please.'

I followed him over carpets, through doors, over further carpets.

Ian's face and head were quite unmarked. His brow and cheeks were smooth and tranquil, artificially coloured over the pallor of death that showed through. I noticed his long dark eyelashes. His hair was parted and brushed. His lips were firmly closed. I looked for a hint of his old humour but there was none, he was sunk in so deep a stillness and silence. He was dead.

The receptionist had left me alone. I reached out, forcing myself, and put my hand over his brow. It was cold. It was not living flesh. The skin was dead under my hand.

I walked out into the street and again I had the sense of cloud high and white and travelling fast.

At the end of the service that afternoon, concertina curtains slid apart and the coffin was rolled slowly, mechanically, into the gap. No grave for a Laertes to leap into, no earth to crumble in the hand and rattle on the lid, no proximity of ancient companion bones, no breath of wind or flutter of blown leaf, just the whirr of a motor and of well-oiled rollers. What was on the far side of the eternal curtain? A team of stokers removing silverware from caskets before consigning them in batches to an oil-fired oven.

I was young and puritanical and unappeased. In the crowd, among all the murmuring, through the movement of gloves and hats and waistcoats, I caught sight of another face bitter and unsatisfied. She was a strange, wild-looking girl and I decided it must be Meg, the one who had wanted

Ian to do her over. I don't know whether it was and I never saw her again.

For what remained of the day I went walking again. It seemed to me something had to happen. It couldn't be allowed to pass so casually. At university I had been reading *Antony and Cleopatra*, and I kept thinking of Caesar hearing of Antony's death and protesting:

> The breaking of so great a thing should make
> A greater crack. The round world
> Should have shook lions into civil streets
> And citizens to their dens.

I walked through our civil streets, conjuring lions.

The thought of visiting Marion didn't come suddenly. It was forming all the time I was walking and I knew I would keep going until I had worked up the courage to do it. I kept imagining Ian's voice saying 'Get on in there, boyo. Cocks were made to go in cunts. Look at that bum, look at those tits. . . .'

I thought out pretty exactly how I thought it would go. Marion would invite me in, pretending she didn't know what I had come for. We would talk about Ian. She would recognise how sad I was and feel sorry for me. She would probably make some tea or coffee. Then she would drop a hint—she might ask why I had come and if she did I would say 'Because you invited me.' Probably she would pretend she had forgotten but I would be able to tell by the way she smiled that she remembered and that she was glad I had come. And then. . . . The rest was a blur, a hot flush of anticipation, a pressure inside the head of white skin and dark hair, and the old awkwardness of walking through the streets with your cock bulging upward against the cloth of your trousers.

It was dark when I walked up Marion's drive and knocked. When she answered the light was behind her—I couldn't see her face clearly. She just stood there, leaning slightly.

'Can I come in for a moment?' I said.

She nodded and moved aside to let me pass.

I walked down the passage and into the sitting room. I was glad the blinds were drawn. I turned to look at her. She was staring at me aggressively. She didn't look beautiful any more. There was a shadow under one eye and her lips were swollen and cracked. Behind her I saw the head was broken off one of the china ducks, and the picture of the two horses was hanging crooked. There was the stain of something spilled over the rosy wallpaper. The clock's silver balls had stopped inside their glass dome.

'I'm sorry about your friend,' she said.

She didn't sound sorry. She sounded angry. I didn't know what to say.

'Well don't just stand there staring at me, Mister Smarty-pants,' she said. 'If you've got something to say, out with it. I know what they're saying out there—all the nosy parkers. Well that's too bad, and I'm sorry about the kid. But it wasn't our fault. It's a free country and if you can't park a truck in a dark street without having some young hooligan on a bike run up your tailpipe it's a pretty poor show. Nobody cares about the kid anyway. All they care about is that it was us in the truck, and that's given them a lot to chat about hasn't it? Don't think I haven't seen you all craning your necks to see what's going on on this side of the fence. Busybody lot you are, you'd think you'd have something better to do than prying into other people's business. . . .'

She sniffed. It was almost a sob, choked back and full of resentment. I wondered whether she was drunk. I wondered how I could get out of that room, away from her.

'I didn't come about that,' I said.

'Well what did you come for?'

'What I mean is,' I said, 'I didn't come because I thought it was your fault. I didn't think about that. I just wanted to ask. . . .'

I couldn't think what I could say I had come for. But her hard face had softened a little. 'I'm sorry,' she said. 'I mean—I know how you must be feeling. He was your friend wasn't he? Poor kid, he couldn't breathe. Roger ran to phone for an ambulance but there was nothing we could do. I just held on to him. He couldn't talk. I think he tried to say something. I don't think he was conscious for more than a minute or two. . . .'

I could feel the tears pushing into my own eyes now. There was such a sense of ugliness, of defeat.

'I'm selling the house,' she said.

I pushed past her, choking, shaking my head. 'Sorry,' I said. 'Thanks Marion. Sorry.'

'Sorry,' she called after me from the doorway.

Sorry. Sorry. Sorry. Thanks. Sorry. Jesus shit wasn't there anything more to be said than that? And what was I to do with the image I carried with me now of Ian, unable to breathe, maybe trying to say something, dying on the dark road, held in Marion's arms.

I stumbled through the dark towards the school, walking fast, then jogging. On the football field I ran hard, sucking in the cool air that Ian hadn't been able to breathe. By the clump of native trees at the far side of the ground I stopped, panting, and stared up at the hulking darkness of Mt Eden brooding over the suburb. Everything was dark and ugly, there was nothing to be said or done and nowhere to go.

Alexander Guyan

AN OPINION OF THE BALLET

Finally there it was. Even while we were engaged, no, before then, perhaps from the first moment I met her, I sensed something of it. Then it was a certain look in her eyes, or a gesture. I sensed it, but was blind to it; incapable in love.

After we were married it appeared more in the open. Not directly afterwards of course; during our honeymoon, and for the first few weeks in our new home, we were blissfully happy together. Perhaps that was the reason, the fact that we were really together then, with no one else to talk to, or talk about.

Like every other newly married couple we knew, we were paying our home off. I'd managed to save a fair deposit, and we were able to keep the car, and we had managed to buy some good furniture. We even had a little in the bank. We certainly weren't rich, but then we weren't poor either. And the fact that all our friends were in much the same boat seemed to me to be a kind of security. I mentioned this to Pam one day.

'What I mean is that as it seems to be working out well enough for the others, I can't see how it won't for us.'

I knew right away that I had said the wrong thing. She started at me with that slow look she has, as if she is examining everything I have said before she gives a definite reply.

'Don't you think it would be fun', she said, 'if they came and took the 'fridge back because we couldn't keep up the payments?'

She didn't sound angry, only cold. 'Fun?' I said.

'Yes. Like what happened to the Marsdens.'

'That was two years ago', I snapped, 'and they are over all that now. They struck a sticky patch. *Practically* everyone has forgotten about it.'

'And has *practically* everyone forgiven them for it?'

'Do you have to be so quarrelsome?' I asked feeling frightened.

'No, I don't have to be. I'm not really. I was only joking. Do forget about it.'

She wasn't joking, and I didn't forget about it.

Some weeks afterwards we were invited to a party at the Browns. We have both known Jennifer and Cliff Brown for years; I went to school with Cliff—he has a pretty secure job with a petrol company—and we have always been close friends.

Pam didn't want to go.

'Well it's too late to pull out now,' I said.

'You could ring them and say that I have a headache.'

I felt a bubble of annoyance burst inside me. 'But why?'

'I just can't be bothered, and—', she paused, glaring at me, '—I detest Jennifer Brown.'

'Well, that's new to me,' I said.

'That b-bloody accent. A damned nurse, emptying bed pans, marries a clerk, and she develops an accent like that.'

'She—'

'It's all such a bloody pose.'

'There's no need to swear.'

'Oh to hell with you,' she said, and began to cry.

Pam swears quite a lot, especially when she is angry, and I don't like it. Not that I mind women swearing, a little that is. They don't do it properly anyway, and I think that is what makes it sound so, if not attractive, amusing. They are so obviously conscious that they are doing it. But in Pam's case that isn't so. She is quite unconscious that she is doing it, as if it was the most natural thing in the world.

Surprisingly enough we went to the party, because later when she had cooled down, and said she was sorry, she insisted that we go. I watched her closely during the evening and she certainly seemed to be enjoying herself, laughing and talking with everyone, and getting slightly tipsy.

But again it could not be forgotten. I was conscious now of what I sensed to be a feeling of rebellion in her. It wasn't always as obvious as it had been on the eve of the Browns' party, but it was there just the same: a gesture of irritation at something quite trivial, a completely uninterested attitude towards anything that concerned our friends, a calculated absentmindedness as if she was thinking about something that wasn't pleasant, and that I did not know anything about.

She refused to admit that there was something wrong, insisted in fact that she was perfectly happy, which merely made me more certain that she wasn't. The only consolation I had was that nothing of her queer behaviour was ever apparent in public, and even that did not remain so for long.

When a well-known ballet company came to town for a brief season Pam and I were invited to join a group of our friends who were all going together one evening. Pam seemed keen, which surprised me. I didn't especially want to go, but then neither did any of the men. The women were very excited about it.

There were four couples including Pam and me. I don't know if the ballet was any good, but during the interval the women went into raptures about it. Bill Cummings—he has a fairly good position in insurance—spoke for the rest of the men when he laughingly admitted that he wasn't much up on the ballet. Not that anyone minded that, because after all men aren't supposed to know much about it.

Pam was quiet, but I wasn't worried about that. She had seemed so keen on the evening, and the other women were so insistent that the ballet was good, that I presumed she was enjoying herself. Then suddenly, filling up one of those silences that occur inside a maze of conversation, she spoke.

'I hate the ballet,' she said.

I think it was the most painful few seconds of my life. Yet on the surface nothing very terrible happened: there was another brief silence, and then someone said something that changed the subject, and everyone joined in trying to cover up. But she had said it and that could not be covered up, nor could the way she had said it: as if she were cursing everyone for being fools.

I don't understand it. What is she trying to do? Does she have no sense of responsibility! How can I ever introduce a business acquaintance into my home when I don't know how she will behave? Even if she does hate the ballet, does she have to say so, and in that manner? What is it that she is fighting? I don't know.

Russell Haley

FOG

Simon Fesk's mother had a sense of humour. There was no denying that. She was seventy-five years old and still wrote to him when she believed the occasion significant. These times were not always personal though they often were. Once she wrote to him on Armistice Day: 'Imagine all the silent people,' she said. Another time he received a telegram on *her* birthday which simply read: 'But for me.'

Today was his birthday. He thought of it as half-way to ninety. His mother, though, felt differently. The home-made card stood on the side-table.

That is less than an exact description. The card could not stand by itself. It was not made from paper stiff enough to support an upright position. It leaned idly against a milk bottle, insolently concave—a spiv of cards with its trilby hat tipped over its eyes working out a paper deal. A breeze could set it flapping around the rented room.

Nor was the table an ideal surface. He had bought the thing, knocked-down in both senses, at an auction in Karangahape Road. The legs were shaped like the side frames of a lyre and they slotted into grooves on the underside of the top. A smaller shelf fitted near the feet and prevented the legs from splaying or collapsing inwards. The surface of the top was carved with jungle blossoms of an unknown species and of such high bas-relief and low intaglio that even the milk bottle was unstable.

Fesk bought it because he liked the colour—dark honey. He also needed a table. Simon had a streak of practicality.

Such was the form of the card. Its contents were no less pliable.

'Think only of the future,' his mother wrote. 'You have your whole young life ahead of you.' The card was quarto size, folded once across the centre. These words were written in pencil on the front. His mother's hand was still firm. Inside, however, were two printed charts.

A physical impatience welled inside Fesk. He was sitting in his old brown uncut moquette armchair. The chair was also from an auction. It rattled and chimed mysteriously whenever it was moved. No doubt it contained treasures of small change, lost pens, shopping lists. Fesk did not feel this impatience in his head. It stemmed from his legs. He raised his feet in turn from the carpet as though he were walking in a crouch and then he squeezed his thigh muscles. He wore Donegal tweed trousers. Fesk bought them in a Mission shop.

They were not charts. Inside the card were two tables. If he had been in a better mood he might have laughed. A thin card containing two printed tables slumped on his decisively carved table.

He did smile. His eyes lit up. Simon forgot his legs. His impatience ceased to exist. Like the tree in the forest which falls unseen and unheard. So large in this country that you could make a whole house from one of them. But people would have to come in and out of doors and switch on radios.

Table One described the various classes of fog signals in use on the 1st of January, 1910, in certain countries. Fesk's own adopted country was not mentioned. As far as fog was concerned this country might not have existed in 1910. Hundreds of years of Polynesian voyaging had been made in the clear sunlight of the Pacific. New Zealand was not tabulated. Fog was infrequent in Auckland though it existed in the thermal areas. Perhaps too in the Marlborough Sounds. Fesk's meteorology was sketchy. So too his geography. He had sailed here on a ship which took many weeks to arrive. Since then he had not moved. His memories of Suez and Aden were dim and blurred. He could not remember whether he saw the Bitter Lakes first or the Red Sea. There was an image of the heat-hazed coastline of North Africa.

But in this table England, Scotland, Ireland, France, the United States, and British North America were fully examined in terms of fog and signals: sirens, diaphones, horns, trumpets, whistles, explosive devices, guns, bells, gongs and submarine bells.

To lie there underwater and listen to bells—undersea Sunday—aqua-Christmas!

1910 must have been a festive year if foggy. His mother would have been six years old. He thought of her as a small girl called Lydia clutching a penny. Her maiden name was Martello. But she was born in Ravensthorpe far away from these detailed sea signals. Almost as far away from the sea as you could get in England. Unlike here where he could look out to the islands and the Gulf if he opened his curtains.

But the local blanket mill did fire a cannon at ten o'clock every evening fog or no fog. It was called the ten o'clock gun. You could set your watch or close a pub by it. And hooters signalled lunch.

Perhaps she married his father because of the gun—future nostalgia. He was a sailor—shipped out of Hull for Rotterdam and Antwerp. Maybe this card came from prodigious papers. With senility he had lost the ability to control them. Instead, he grew massive sunflowers in the narrow garden of the new bungalow.

Last Christmas his mother sent him a clipping from the local newspaper. His father, lined beyond comprehension, pouring the dregs of his tea on the earth at the foot of the sunflowers. She wrote a different message then: 'Keep us always in mind.'

Fesk kept them in his head. Where else? They were his prototypes for the future. Though he would have no children to send clippings and obscurities.

His birthday came in cold weather in this country. If he'd remained in Ravensthorpe it would occur in summer. Impossible to blow out the breath like this and make a small cloud of mist. Bigger there then at eleven and a half, winter, a plume from your lips. Adding minutely to the fog-bank which obscured the poplars on the boundary of the football field. Thicker and closer than that suggested. Run three paces and lose yourself. Or your friends. Screaming in wet wool.

'Nobody can get me!' Lighting a tab with his last match. Woodbine smoke and breath pouring from both nostrils. Perfect freedom.

His cat jumped up on the arm of his chair. It ripped at the upholstery and then forced its head against his hand. There were beads of moisture on its whiskers. Titus turned his head as though it were articulated on a ball-joint. The underside of his chin was white. Ten. Close to senility.

'Grow flowers,' Fesk said. He prodded the cat and it jumped to the floor. Titus landed awkwardly.

Half way to ninety. Two-thirds of the way to nothing. The last fog. Lying there in your cold sheets with the room dissolving.

There was an unclear patch already. In the top corner of the living-room where last winter's rain soaked through obscuring the pattern of the wallpaper. It looked like a small cloud. Miniature gun, diaphone, or bell? Some tiny warning signal: bang—hraarnm—ting!

But perfect freedom. The field like iron. They did that game with breathing. Deep. Deep—sucking in the fog. Then hold it with Wally squeezing his chest. Fooo! Falling forwards on hands and knees with the world crashing. Rehearsals.

It was bigger, that blurred patch. A slide of mucus in his eye. It moved when his gaze altered.

Fesk got up and bathed his eyes in warm water at the sink. He put the kettle on for tea then went to the table to re-read the card.

According to Sir Boverton Redwood (1904), duplex burners which gave a flame of 28 candle-power have an average oil consumption of 50 grains per candle per hour.

Grains of oil! Solidified fog. You could reverse anything with words. His mother implanting him in the past. The cat sailing up from the floor, its startled look turning to placidity. The head turning. The white chin. Striations in the moquette fading.

Steam issued from the spout of the kettle. Simon knew less about physics than the little he retained of geography. But he remembered that certain bits of water were agitated and changed their form. Slow them down and they turn to ice. Tea does not taste the same at the top of Mount Everest. Water boils quicker and colder. So the tea fails to mash, to draw.

He drank his cup in his chair. A knowing smile passed over his face.

She was a cunning old bugger. Fog itself was the warning. Not the signals. She was telling him about change, mutability: fog was the future. Everything gone out of shape. A low ceiling.

He had once caught a bus in thick fog. So dense that the conductor walked ahead, showing the driver the way. And the passengers trudged behind. Walking to keep warm and following the bus so that they did not lose their way. He'd paid full fare. Sixpence to walk!

Whatever light Sir Boverton tried to cast we were walking into darkness. Follow the bus.

It was late now but Simon did not turn on his light. A cruise ship hooted three times as it left the harbour. He had seen flying fish, an albatross, dolphins. The stern and a white trail blazed across the sea. You have been there. You leave your own wake.

After he left home he moved to London. In those days fog was green and frequent. He lived in Archway. Could walk to Hampstead Heath. The fogs drove him wild with desire. He was young. The possibility was held out of meeting a fellow-soul in the fog. Lighted windows took on a special diffuse quality. You could draw close. Who curtained against that blanket?

The city changed shape and decayed under that floor of fog. Lagan to be retrieved in discrete fragments of treasure. A girl dressed in mist— her hair like dark water.

Meetings were an astonishment—looming, distorted, and immediate. And people talked excitedly, their breath catching.

'Are you there? Are you there?'

'Where am I?'

'Haa! I thought I was nearly home.'

'Is this the kerb?'

'I've passed that corner three times.'

And were there really smudge-pots burning in the roads? One could walk naked and undetected.

There were more deaths. The old and frail gave up when their boundaries dissolved. They simply merged with whatever was to come. Their bits vibrating in a different mode. Passing out into something else. Steam or ice.

The young survived. They kept their shape because their memories were sharper. Matter is solidified memory of form. In fog a key which had been too long a key could slip its form and run as a bright trickle of amnesia down the thigh. So the old flew out from there. Officials called it pneumonia or influenza.

Fesk knew now that he loved it, fog, as some men loved danger. He should not have washed his eyes although the room was comfortingly dark now. It was a poor simulation but it would have to serve. He should be colder than he was, his skin transparent to the air.

Simon removed everything he had on and sat in his armchair, nude.

Rather than take those sounds as warnings, one could orchestrate them into a hymn in praise of fog:

Boom crack wheep bong ding blah hoooo

dong fooo crash ting boom wheee!

Repeat and vary. A fifty-grain candle burning as an offering.

Finally Simon knew what he was celebrating. He would leave this meridian of sun where fog, at the very best, came three times a year. He would seek out some industrial valley in a northern clime where factory chimneys poured out their libations to invisibility. Perhaps Ravensthorpe if it had not been ruined by the Clean Air Act.

Certainly not that bright little suburb on the outskirts of York where sunflowers grew in profusion. It would have to be a mucky place where dark bricks absorbed acid from the air. Where the skin was an osmotic device and not a dry barrier tanned and leathered by the sun.

She had made him homesick after all these years.

He would find desire again. One evening. Some dark girl in a mackintosh. Walking huddled streets glazed with rain, inundated with mist.

Fesk sang, the old song, before he retired:

> Oh I am a bachelor and I live all alone
> And I work at the weaver's trade
> And the only only thing I ever did wrong

Was to woo a fair young maid
I wooed her in the winter time
And in the summer too
And the only only thing I ever did wrong
Was to save her from the foggy foggy dew.

He straightened the card against the milk bottle. It bent again. A meniscus of hope.

Before Simon went to bed he emptied the tea-pot outside the back door. He flung the soggy leaves against the agapanthus growing there.

Somewhere or other his father smiled a blank bright unimpassioned smile. His mother prepared a congratulatory sheet.

Fog descended immediately on all points.

Joy Cowley

THE SILK

When Mr Blackie took bad again that autumn both he and Mrs Blackie knew that it was for the last time. For many weeks neither spoke of it; but the understanding was in their eyes as they watched each other through the days and nights. It was a look, not of sadness or despair, but of quiet resignation tempered with something else, an unnamed expression that is seen only in the old and the very young.

Their acceptance was apparent in other ways, too. Mrs Blackie no longer complained to the neighbours that the old lazy-bones was running her off her feet. Instead she waited on him tirelessly, stretching their pension over chicken and out-of-season fruits to tempt his appetite; and she guarded him so possessively that she even resented the twice-weekly visits from the District Nurse. Mr Blackie, on the other hand, settled into bed as gently as dust. He had never been a man to dwell in the past, but now he spoke a great deal of their earlier days and surprised Mrs Blackie by recalling things which she, who claimed the better memory, had forgotten. Seldom did he talk of the present, and never in these weeks did he mention the future.

Then, on the morning of the first frost of winter, while Mrs Blackie was filling his hot water bottle, he sat up in bed, unaided, to see out the window. The inside of the glass was streaked with tears of condensation. Outside, the frost had made an oval frame of crystals through which he could see a row of houses and lawns laid out in front of them, like white carpets.

'The ground will be hard,' he said at last. 'Hard as nails.'

Mrs Blackie looked up quickly. 'Not yet,' she said.

'Pretty soon, I think.' His smile was apologetic.

She slapped the hot water bottle into its cover and tested it against her cheek. 'Lie down or you'll get a chill,' she said.

Obediently, he dropped back against the pillow, but as she moved about him, putting the hot water bottle at his feet, straightening the quilt, he stared at the frozen patch of window.

'Amy, you'll get a double plot, won't you?' he said. 'I wouldn't rest easy thinking you were going to sleep by someone else.'

'What a thing to say!' The corner of her mouth twitched. 'As if I would.'

'It was your idea to buy single beds,' he said accusingly.

'Oh Herb—' She looked at the window, away again. 'We'll have a double plot,' she said. For a second or two she hesitated by his bed, then she sat beside his feet, her hands placed one on top of the other in her lap, in a pose that she always adopted when she had something important to say. She cleared her throat.

'You know, I've been thinking on and off about the silk.'

'The silk?' He turned his head towards her.

'I want to use it for your laying out pyjamas.'

'No Amy,' he said. 'Not the silk. That was your wedding present, the only thing I brought back with me.'

'What would I do with it now?' she said. When he didn't answer, she got up, opened the wardrobe door and took the camphorwood box from the shelf where she kept her hats. 'All these years and us not daring to take a scissors to it. We should use it sometime.'

'Not on me,' he said.

'I've been thinking about your pyjamas.' She fitted a key into the brass box. 'It'd be just right.'

'A right waste, you mean,' he said. But there was no protest in his voice. In fact, it had lifted with a childish eagerness. He watched her hands as she opened the box and folded back layers of white tissue paper. Beneath them lay the blue of the silk. There was a reverent silence as she took it out and spread it under the light.

'Makes the whole room look different, doesn't it?' he said. 'I nearly forgot it looked like this.' His hands struggled free of the sheet and moved across the quilt. Gently, she picked up the blue material and poured it over his fingers.

'Aah,' he breathed, bringing it closer to his eyes. 'All the way from China.' He smiled. 'Not once did I let it out of me sight. You know that, Amy? There were those on board as would have pinched it quick as that. I kept it pinned round me middle.'

'You told me,' she said.

He rubbed the silk against the stubble of his chin. 'It's the birds that take your eye,' he said.

'At first,' said Mrs Blackie. She ran her finger over one of the peacocks that strutted in the foreground of a continuous landscape. They were proud birds, iridescent blue, with silver threads in their tails. 'I used to like them best, but after a while you see much more, just as fine only smaller.' She pushed her glasses on to the bridge of her nose and leaned over the silk, her finger guiding her eyes over islands where waterfalls hung, eternally suspended, between pagodas and dark blue conifers, over flat lakes and tiny fishing boats, over mountains where the mists never lifted, and back again to a haughty peacock caught with one foot suspended over a rock. 'It's a work of art like you never see in this country,' she said.

Mr Blackie inhaled the scent of camphorwood. 'Don't cut it, Amy. It's too good for an old blighter like me.' He was begging her to contradict him.

'I'll get the pattern tomorrow,' she said.

The next day, while the District Nurse was giving him his injection, she went down to the store and looked through a pile of pattern books. Appropriately, she chose a mandarin style with a high collar and piped cuffs and pockets. But Mr Blackie, who had all his life worn striped flannel in the conventional design, looked with suspicion at the pyjama pattern and the young man who posed so easily and shamelessly on the front of the packet.

'It's the sort them teddy bear boys have,' he said.

'Nonsense,' said Mrs Blackie.

'That's exactly what they are,' he growled. 'You're not laying me out in a lot of new-fangled nonsense.'

Mrs Blackie put her hands on her hips. 'You'll not have any say in the matter,' she said.

'Won't I just? I'll get up and fight—see if I don't.'

The muscles at the corner of her mouth twitched uncontrollably. 'All right, Herb, if you're so set against it—'

But now, having won the argument, he was happy. 'Get away with you, Amy. I'll get used to the idea.' He threw his lips back against his gums. 'Matter of fact, I like them fine. It's that nurse that done it. Blunt needle again.' He looked at the pattern. 'When d'you start?'

'Well—'

'This afternoon?'

'I suppose I could pin the pattern out after lunch.'

'Do it in here,' he said. 'Bring in your machine and pins and things and set them up so I can watch.'

She stood taller and tucked in her chin. 'I'm not using the machine,' she said with pride. 'Every stitch is going to be done by hand. My eyes mightn't be as good as they were once, mark you, but there's not a person on this earth can say I've lost my touch with a needle.'

His eyes closed in thought. 'How long?'

'Eh?'

'Till it's finished.'

She turned the pattern over in her hands. 'Oh—about three or four weeks. That is—if I keep it up.'

'No,' he said. 'Too long.'

'Oh Herb, you'd want a good job done, wouldn't you?' she pleaded.

'Amy—' Almost imperceptibly, he shook his head on the pillow.

'I can do the main seams on the machine,' she said, lowering her voice. 'How long?'

'A week,' she whispered.

When she took down the silk that afternoon, he insisted on an extra pillow in spite of the warning he'd had from the doctor about lying flat with his legs propped higher than his head and shoulders.

She plumped up the pillow from her own bed and put it behind his neck; then she unrolled her tape measure along his body, legs, arms, around his chest.

'I'll have to take them in a bit,' she said, making inch-high black figures on a piece of cardboard. She took the tissue-paper pattern into the kitchen to iron it flat. When she came back, he was waiting, wide eyed with anticipation and brighter, she thought, than he'd been for many weeks.

As she laid the silk out on her bed and started pinning down the first of the pattern pieces, he described, with painstaking attempts at accuracy, the boat trip home, the stop at Hong Kong, and the merchant who had sold him the silk. 'Most of his stuff was rubbish,' he said. 'You wouldn't look twice at it. This was the only decent thing he had and even then he done me. You got to argue with these devils. Beat him down, they told me. But there was others as wanted that silk and if I hadn't made up me mind there and then I'd have lost it.' He squinted at her hands. 'What are you doing now? You just put that bit down.'

'It wasn't right,' she said, through lips closed on pins. 'I have to match it—like wallpaper.'

She lifted the pattern pieces many times before she was satisfied. Then it was evening and he was so tired that his breathing had become laboured. He no longer talked. His eyes were watering from hours of concentration; the drops spilled over his red lids and soaked into the pillow.

'Go to sleep,' she said. 'Enough's enough for one day.'

'I'll see you cut it out first,' he said.

'Let's leave it till the morning,' she said, and they both sensed her reluctance to put the scissors to the silk.

'Tonight,' he said.

'I'll make the tea first.'

'After,' he said.

She took the scissors from her sewing drawer and wiped them on her apron. Together they felt the pain as the blades met cleanly, almost without resistance, in that first cut. The silk would never again be the same. They were changing it, rearranging the pattern of fifty-odd years to form something new and unfamiliar. When she had cut out the first piece, she held it up, still pinned to the paper, and said, 'The back of the top.' Then she laid it on the dressing table and went on as quickly as she dared, for she knew that he would not rest until she had finished.

One by one the garment pieces left the body of silk. With each touch of the blades, threads sprang apart; mountains were divided, peacocks split from head to tail; waterfalls fell on either side of fraying edges. Eventually, there was nothing on the bed but a few shining snippets. Mrs Blackie picked them up and put them back in the camphorwood box, and covered the pyjama pieces on the dressing table with a cloth. Then she removed the extra pillow from Mr Blackie's bed and laid his head back in a comfortable position before she went into the kitchen to make the tea.

He was very tired the next morning but refused to sleep while she was working with the silk. She invented a number of excuses for putting it aside and leaving the room. He would sleep then, but never for long. No more than half an hour would pass and he would be calling her. She would find him lying awake and impatient for her to resume sewing.

In that day and the next, she did all the machine work. It was a tedious task, for first she tacked each seam by hand, matching the patterns in the weave so that the join was barely noticeable. Mr Blackie silently supervised every stitch. At times she would see him studying the silk with an expression that she still held in her memory. It was the look he'd given her in their courting days. She felt a prick of jealousy, not because she thought that he cared more for the silk than he did for her, but because he saw something in it that she didn't share. She never asked him what it was. At her age a body did not question these things or demand explanations. She would bend her head lower and concentrate her energy and attention into the narrow seam beneath the needle.

On the Friday afternoon, four days after she'd started the pyjamas, she finished the buttonholes and sewed on the buttons. She'd deliberately hurried the last of the hand sewing. In the four days, Mr Blackie had become weaker, and she knew that the sooner the pyjamas were completed and put back in the camphorwood box out of sight, the sooner he would take an interest in food and have the rest he needed.

She snipped the last thread and put the needle in its case.

'That's it, Herb,' she said, showing him her work.

He tried to raise his head. 'Bring them over here,' he said.

'Well—what do you think?' As she brought the pyjamas closer, his eyes relaxed and he smiled.

'Try them on?' he said.

She shook her head. 'I got the measurements,' she said. 'They'll be the right fit.'

'Better make sure,' he said.

She hesitated but could find no reason for her reluctance. 'All right,' she said, switching on both bars of the electric heater and drawing it closer to his bed. 'Just to make sure I've got the buttons right.'

She peeled back the bedclothes, took off his thick pyjamas and put on the silk. She stepped back to look at him.

'Well, even if I do say so myself, there's no one could have done a better job. I could move the top button over a fraction, but apart from that they're a perfect fit.'

He grinned. 'Light, aren't they?' He looked down the length of his body and wriggled his toes. 'All the way from China. Never let it out of me sight. Know that, Amy?'

'Do you like them?' she said.

He sucked his lips in over his gums to hide his pleasure. 'All right. A bit on the tight side.'

'They are not, and you know it,' Mrs Blackie snapped. 'Never give a body a bit of credit, would you? Here, put your hands down and I'll change you before you get a chill.'

He tightened his arms across his chest. 'You made a right good job, Amy. Think I'll keep them on a bit.'

'No.' She picked up his thick pyjamas.

'Why not?'

'Because you can't,' she said. 'It—it's disrespectful. And the nurse will be here soon.'

'Oh, get away with you, Amy.' He was too weak to resist further but as she changed him, he still possessed the silk with his eyes. 'Wonder who made it?'

Although she shrugged his question away, it brought to her a definite picture of a Chinese woman seated in front of a loom surrounded by blue and silver silkworms. The woman was dressed from a page in a geographic magazine, and except for the Oriental line of her eyelids, she looked like Mrs Blackie.

'D'you suppose there's places like that?' Mr Blackie asked.

She snatched up the pyjamas and put them in the box. 'You're the one that's been there,' she said briskly. 'Now settle down and rest or you'll be bad when the nurse arrives.'

The District Nurse did not come that afternoon. Nor in the evening. It was at half-past three the following morning that her footsteps, echoed by the doctor's sounded along the gravel path.

Mrs Blackie was in the kitchen, waiting. She sat straight-backed and dry-eyed, her hands placed one on top of the other in the lap of her dressing gown.

'Mrs Blackie. I'm sorry—'

She ignored the nurse and turned to the doctor. 'He didn't say goodbye,' she said with an accusing look. 'Just before I phoned. His hand was over the side of the bed. I touched it. It was cold.'

The doctor nodded.

'No sound of any kind,' she said. 'He was good as gold last night.'

Again, the doctor nodded. He put his hand, briefly, on her shoulder, then went into the bedroom. Within a minute he returned, fastening his leather bag and murmuring sympathy.

Mrs Blackie sat still, catching isolated words. Expected. Peacefully. Brave. They dropped upon her—neat, geometrical shapes that had no meaning.

'He didn't say goodbye.' She shook her head. 'Not a word.'

'But look, Mrs Blackie,' soothed the nurse. 'It was inevitable. You knew that. He couldn't have gone on—'

'I know, I know.' She turned away, irritated by their lack of understanding. 'He just might have said goodbye. That's all.'

The doctor took a white tablet from a phial and tried to persuade her to swallow it. She pushed it away; refused, too, the cup of tea that the District Nurse poured and set in front of her. When they picked up their bags and went towards the bedroom, she followed them.

'In a few minutes,' the doctor said. 'If you'll leave us—'

'I'm getting his pyjamas,' she said. 'There's a button needs changing. I can do it now.'

As soon as she entered the room, she glanced at Mr Blackie's bed and noted that the doctor had pulled up the sheet. Quickly, she lifted the camphorwood box, took a needle, cotton, scissors, her spectacle case, and went back to the kitchen. Through the half-closed door she heard the nurse's voice. 'Poor old thing,' and she knew, instinctively, that they were not talking about her.

She sat down at the table to thread the needle. Her eyes were clear but her hands were so numb that for a long time they refused to work together. At last, the thread knotted, she opened the camphorwood box. The beauty of the silk was always unexpected. As she spread the pyjamas out on the table, it warmed her, caught her up and comforted her with the first positive feeling she'd had that morning. The silk was real. It was brought to life by the electric light above the table, so that every fold of the woven landscape moved. Trees swayed towards rippling water and peacocks danced with white fire in their tails. Even the tiny bridges—

Mrs Blackie took off her glasses, wiped them, put them on again. She leaned forward and traced her thumbnail over one bridge, then another. And another. She turned over the pyjama coat and closely examined the back. It was there, on every bridge; something she hadn't noticed before. She got up, and from the drawer where she kept her tablecloths, she took out a magnifying glass.

As the bridge in the pattern of the silk grew, the figure which had been no larger than an ant, became a man.

Mrs Blackie forgot about the button and the murmur of voices in the bedroom. She brought the magnifying glass nearer her eyes.

It was a man and he was standing with one arm outstretched, on the highest span between two islands. Mrs Blackie studied him for a long time, then she straightened up and smiled. Yes, he was waving. Or perhaps, she thought, he was beckoning to her.

Patricia Grace

JOURNEY

He was an old man going on a journey. But not really so old, only they
made him old buttoning up his coat for him and giving him money.
Seventy-one that's all. Not a journey, not what you would really call a
journey—he had to go in and see those people about his land. Again.
But he liked the word Journey even though you didn't quite say it. It
wasn't a word for saying only for saving up in your head, and that way
you could enjoy it. Even an old man like him, but not what you would
call properly old.

The coat was good and warm. It was second-hand from the jumble
and it was good and warm. Could have ghosts in it but who cares, warm
that's the main thing. If some old pakeha died in it that's too bad because
he wasn't scared of the pakeha kehuas anyway. The pakeha kehuas they
couldn't do anything, it was only like having a sheet over your head and
going woo-oo at someone in the lavatory. . . .

He better go to the lavatory because he didn't trust town lavatories,
people spewed there and wrote rude words. Last time he got something
stuck on his shoe. Funny people those town people.

Taxi.

It's coming Uncle.

Taxi Uncle. They think he's deaf. And old. Putting more money in
his pocket and wishing his coat needed buttoning, telling him it's windy
and cold. Never mind, he was off. Off on his journey, he could get round
town good on his own, good as gold.

Out early today old man.

Business young fulla.

Early bird catches the early worm.

It'll be a sorry worm young fulla, a sorry worm.

Like that is it?

Like that.

You could sit back and enjoy the old taxi smells of split upholstery
and cigarette, and of something else that could have been the young
fulla's hair oil or his b.o. It was good. Good. Same old taxi same old stinks.
Same old shop over there, but he wouldn't be calling in today, no. And

264

tomorrow they'd want to know why. No, today he was going on a journey, which was a good word. Today he was going further afield, and there was a word no one knew he had. A good wind today but he had a warm coat and didn't need anyone fussing.

Same old butcher and same old fruit shop, doing all right these days not like before. Same old Post Office where you went to get your pension money, but he always sent Minnie down to get his because he couldn't stand these old-age people. These old-age people got on his nerves. Yes, same old place, same old shops and roads, and everything cracking up a bit. Same old taxi. Same old young fulla.

How's the wife?

Still growling old man.

What about the kids?

Costing me money.

Send them out to work that's the story.

I think you're right you might have something there old man. Well here we are, early. Still another half hour to wait for the train.

Best to be early. Business.

Guess you're right.

What's the sting?

Ninety-five it is.

Pull out a fistful and give the young fulla full eyes. Get himself out on to the footpath and shove the door, give it a good hard slam. Pick me up later young fulla, ten past five. Might as well make a day of it, look round town and buy a few things.

Don't forget ten past five.

Right you are old man five ten.

People had been peeing in the subway the dirty dogs. In the old days all you needed to do to get on to the station was to step over the train tracks, there weren't any piss holes like this to go through, it wasn't safe. Coming up the steps on to the platform he could feel the quick huffs of his breathing and that annoyed him, he wanted to swipe at the huffs with his hand. Steam engines went out years ago.

Good sight though seeing the big engines come bellowing through the cutting and pull in squealing, everything was covered in soot for miles those days.

New man in the ticket office, looked as though he still had his pyjamas on under his outfit. Miserable looking fulla and not all impressed by the ten-dollar note handed through to him. A man feels like a screwball yelling through that little hole in the glass and then trying to pick up the change that sourpuss has scattered all over the place. Feels like giving sourpuss the fingers, yes. Yes he knows all about those things, he's not deaf and blind yet, not by a long shot.

Ah warmth. A cold wait on the platform but the carriages had the heaters on, they were warm even though they stank. And he had the front half of the first carriage all to himself. Good idea getting away early. And right up front where you could see everything. Good idea coming on his own, he didn't want anyone fussing round looking after his ticket, seeing if he's warm and saying things twice. Doing his talking for him, made him sick. Made him sick them trying to walk slow so they could keep up with him. Yes he could see everything. Not many fishing boats gone out this morning and the sea's turning over rough and heavy—Tamatea that's why. That's something they don't know all these young people, not even those fishermen walking about on their decks over there. Tamatea a Ngana, Tamatea Aio, Tamatea Whakapau—when you get the winds— but who'd believe you these days. They'd rather stare at their weather on television and talk about a this and a that coming over because there's nothing else to believe in.

Now this strip here, it's not really land at all, it's where we used to get our pipis, any time or tide. But they pushed a hill down over it and shot the railway line across to make more room for cars. The train driver knows it's not really land and he is speeding up over this strip. So fast you wait for the nose dive over the edge into the sea, especially when you're up front like this looking. Well too bad. Not to worry, he's nearly old anyway and just about done his dash, so why to worry if they nose dive over the edge into the sea. Funny people putting their trains across the sea. Funny people making land and putting pictures and stories about it in the papers as though it's something spectacular, it's a word you can use if you get it just right and he could surprise quite a few people if he wanted to. Yet other times they go on as though land is just a nothing. Trouble is he let them do his talking for him. If he'd gone in on his own last time and left those fusspots at home he'd have got somewhere. Wouldn't need to be going in there today to tell them all what's what.

Lost the sea now and coming into a cold crowd. This is where you get swamped, but he didn't mind, it was good to see them all get in out of the wind glad to be warm. Some of his whanaungas lived here but he couldn't see any of them today. Good job too, he didn't want them hanging round wondering where he was off to on his own. Nosing into his business. Some of the old railway houses still there but apart from that everything new, houses, buildings, roads. You'd never know now where the old roads had been, and they'd filled a piece of the harbour up too to make more ground. A short row of sooty houses that got new paint once in a while, a railway shelter, and a lunatic asylum and that was all. Only you didn't call it that these days, he'd think of the right words in a minute.

There now the train was full and he had a couple of kids sitting by him wearing plastic clothes, they were gog-eyed stretching their necks to see. One of them had a snotty nose and a wheeze.

On further it's the same—houses, houses—but people have to have houses. Two or three farms once, on the cold hills, and a rough road going through. By car along the old road you'd always see a pair of them at the end of the drive waving with their hats jammed over their ears. Fat one and a skinny one. Psychiatric hospital, those were the words to use these days, yes don't sound so bad. People had to have houses and the two or three farmers were dead now probably. Maybe didn't live to see it all. Maybe died rich.

The two kids stood swaying as they entered the first tunnel, their eyes stood out watching for the tunnel's mouth, waiting to pass out through the great mouth of the tunnel. And probably the whole of life was like that, sitting in the dark watching and waiting. Sometimes it happened and you came out into the light, but mostly it only happened in tunnels. Like now.

And between the tunnels they were slicing the hills away with big machines. Great-looking hills too and not an easy job cutting them away, it took pakeha determination to do that. Funny people these pakehas, had to chop up everything. Couldn't talk to a hill or a tree these people, couldn't give the trees or the hills a name and make them special and leave them. Couldn't go round, only through. Couldn't give life, only death. But people had to have houses, and ways of getting from one place to another. And anyway who was right up there helping the pakeha to get rid of things—the Maori of course, riding those big machines. Swooping round and back, up and down all over the place. Great tools the Maori man had for his carving these days, tools for his new whakairo, but there you are, a man had to eat. People had to have houses, had to eat, had to get from here to there—anyone knew that. He wished the two kids would stop crackling, their mothers dressed them in rubbish clothes that's why they had colds.

Then the rain'll come and the cuts will bleed for miles and the valleys will drown in blood, but the pakeha will find a way of mopping it all up no trouble. Could find a few bones amongst that lot too. That's what you get when you dig up the ground, bones.

Now the next tunnel, dark again. Had to make sure the windows were all shut up in the old days or you got a face full of soot.

And then coming out of the second tunnel that's when you really had to hold your breath, that's when you really had to hand it to the pakeha, because there was a sight. Buildings miles high, streets and steel and concrete and asphalt settled all round the great-looking curve that was the harbour. Water with ships on it, and roadways threading up and round the hills to layer on layer of houses, even in the highest and steepest places. He was filled with admiration. Filled with Admiration, which was another word he enjoyed even though it wasn't really a word for saying, but yes he was filled right to the top —it made him tired taking it all in. The kids too, they'd stopped crackling and were quite still, their eyes full to exploding.

The snotty one reminded him of George, he had pop eyes and he sat quiet not talking. The door would open slowly and the eyes would come round and he would say I ran away again Uncle. That's all. That's all for a whole week or more until his mother came to get him and take him back. Never spoke, never wanted anything. Today if he had time he would look out for George.

Railway station much the same as ever, same old platforms and not much cleaner than the soot days. Same old stalls and looked like the same people in them. Underground part is new. Same cafeteria, same food most likely, and the spot where they found the murdered man looked no different from any other spot. Always crowded in the old days especially during the hard times. People came there in the hard times to do their starving. They didn't want to drop dead while they were on their own most probably. Rather all starve together.

Same old statue of Kupe with his woman and his priest, and they've got the name of the canoe spelt wrong his old eyes aren't as blind as all that. Same old floor made of little coloured pieces and blocked into patterns with metal strips, he used to like it but now he can just walk on it. Big pillars round the doorway holding everything in place, no doubt about it you had to hand it to the pakeha.

Their family hadn't starved, their old man had seen to that. Their old man had put all the land down in garden, all of it, and in the weekends they took what they didn't use round by horse and cart. Sometimes got paid, sometimes swapped for something, mostly got nothing but why to worry. Yes great looking veges they had those days, turnips as big as pumpkins, cabbages you could hardly carry, big tomatoes, lettuces, potatoes, everything. Even now the ground gave you good things. They had to stay home from school for the planting and picking, usually for the weeding and hoeing as well. Never went to school much those days but why to worry.

Early, but he could take his time, knows his way round this place as good as gold. Yes he's walked all over these places that used to be under the sea and he's ridden all up and down them in trams too. This bit of sea has been land for a long time now. And he's been in all the pubs and been drunk in all of them, he might go to the pub later and spend some of his money. Or he could go to the continuous pictures but he didn't think they had them any more. Still, he might celebrate a little on his own later, he knew his way round this place without anyone interfering. Didn't need anyone doing his talking, and messing things up with all their letters and what not. Pigeons, he didn't like pigeons, they'd learned to behave like people, eat your feet off if you give them half a chance.

And up there past the cenotaph, that's where they'd bulldozed all the bones and put in the new motorway. Resited, he still remembered the newspaper word, all in together. Your leg bone, my arm bone, someone else's bunch of teeth and fingers, someone else's head, funny people. Glad he didn't have any of his whanaungas underground in that place. And they had put all the headstones in a heap somewhere promising to set them all up again *tastefully*—he remembered didn't matter who was underneath. Bet there weren't any Maoris driving those bulldozers, well why to worry it's not his concern, none of his whanaungas up there anyway.

Good those old trams but he didn't trust these crazy buses, he'd rather walk. Besides he's nice and early and there's nothing wrong with his legs. Yes, he knows this place like his own big toe, and by Jove he's got a few things to say to those people and he wasn't forgetting. He'd tell them, yes.

The railway station was a place for waiting. People waited there in the old days when times were hard, had a free wash and did their starving there. He waited because it was too early to go home, his right foot was sore. And he could watch out for George, the others had often seen George here waiting about. He and George might go and have a cup of tea and some kai.

He agreed. Of course he agreed. People had to have houses. Not only that, people had to have other things—work, and ways of getting from place to place, and comforts. People needed more now than they did in his young days, he understood completely. Sir. Kept calling him Sir, and the way he said it didn't sound so well, but it was difficult to be sure at first. After a while you knew, you couldn't help knowing. He didn't want any kai, he felt sick. His foot hurt.

Station getting crowded and a voice announcing platforms. After all these years he still didn't know where the voice came from but it was the same voice, and anyway the trains could go without him it was too soon. People.

Queueing for tickets and hurrying towards the platforms, or coming this way and disappearing out through the double doors, or into the subway or the lavatory or the cafeteria. He was too tired to go to the lavatory and anyway he didn't like. . . . Some in no hurry at all. Waiting. You'd think it was starvation times. Couldn't see anyone he knew.

I know I know. People have to have houses, I understand and it's what I want.

Well it's not so simple Sir.

It's simple. I can explain. There's only the old place on the land and it needs bringing down now. My brother and sister and I talked about it years back. We wrote letters. . . .

Yes yes but it's not as simple as you think.

But now they're both dead and it's all shared—there are my brother's children, my sister's children, and me. It doesn't matter about me because I'm on the way out, but before I go I want it all done.

As I say it's no easy matter, all considered.

Subdivision. It's what we want.

There'll be no more subdivision Sir, in the area.

Subdivision. My brother has four sons and two daughters, my sister has five sons. Eleven sections so they can build their houses. I want it all seen to before. . . .

You must understand Sir that it's no easy matter, the area has become what we call a development area, and I've explained all this before, there'll be no more subdivision.

Development means houses, and it means other things too, I understand that. But houses, it's what we have in mind.

And even supposing Sir that subdivision were possible, which it isn't, I wonder if you fully comprehend what would be involved in such an undertaking.

I fully comprehend. . . .

Surveying, kerbing and channelling and formation of adequate access, adequate right of ways. The initial outlay. . . .

I've got money, my brother and sister left it for the purpose. And my own, my niece won't use any of my money, it's all there. We've got the money.

However that's another matter, I was merely pointing out that it's not always all plain sailing.

All we want is to get it divided up so they can have a small piece each to build on. . . .

As I say, the area, the whole area, has been set aside for development. All in the future of course but we must look ahead, it is necessary to be far-sighted in these concerns.

Houses, each on a small section of land, it's what my niece was trying to explain. . . .

You see there's more to development than housing. We have to plan for roading and commerce, we have to set aside areas for educational and recreational facilities. We've got to think of industry, transportation. . . .

But still people need houses. My nieces and nephews have waited for years.

They'd be given equivalent land or monetary compensation of course.

But where was the sense in that, there was no equal land. If it's your stamping ground and you have your ties there, then there's no land equal, surely that wasn't hard to understand. More and more people coming in to wait and plastic kids had arrived. They pulled away from their mother and went for a small run, crackling. He wished he knew their names and hoped they would come and sit down by him, but no, their mother was striding, turning them towards a platform because they were getting a train home. Nothing to say for a week or more and never wanted anything except sitting squeezed beside him in the armchair after tea until he fell asleep. Carry him to bed, get in beside him later then one day his mother would come. It was too early for him to go home even though he needed a pee.

There's no sense in it don't you see? That's their stamping ground and when you've got your ties there's no equal land. It's what my niece and nephew were trying to explain the last time, and in the letters. . . .

Well Sir I shouldn't really do this, but if it will help clarify the position I could show you what has been drawn up. Of course it's all in the future and not really your worry. . . .

Yes yes I'll be dead but that's not. . . .

I'll get the plans.

And it's true he'll be dead, it's true he's getting old, but not true if anyone thinks his eyes have had it because he can see good enough. His eyes are still good enough to look all over the paper and see his land there, and to see that his land has been shaded in and had 'Off Street Parking' printed on it.

He can see good close up and he can see good far off, and that's George over the other side standing with some mates. He can tell George anywhere no matter what sort of get-up he's wearing. George would turn and see him soon.

But you can't, that's only a piece of paper and it can be changed, you can change it. People have to live and to have things. People need houses and shops but that's only paper, it can be changed.

It's all been very carefully mapped out. By experts. Areas have been selected according to suitability and convenience. And the aesthetic aspects have been carefully considered. . . .

Everything grows, turnips the size of pumpkins, cabbages you can hardly carry, potatoes, tomatoes. . . . Back here where you've got your houses, it's all rock, land going to waste there. . . .

You would all receive equivalent sites. . . .

Resited. . . .

As I say on equivalent land. . . .

There's no land equal. . . .

Listen Sir, it's difficult but we've got to have some understanding of things. Don't we?

Yes yes I want you to understand, that's why I came. This here, it's only paper and you can change it. There's room for all the things you've got on your paper, and room for what we want too, we want only what we've got already, it's what we've been trying to say.

Sir we can't always have exactly what we want. . . .

All round here where you've marked residential it's all rock, what's wrong with that for shops and cars. And there'll be people and houses. Some of the people can be us, and some of the houses can be ours.

Sure, sure. But not exactly where you want them. And anyway Sir there's no advantage do you think in you people all living in the same area?

It's what we want, we want nothing more than what is ours already.

It does things to your land value.

He was an old man but he wanted very much to lean over the desk and swing a heavy punch.

No sense being scattered everywhere when what we want. . . .

It immediately brings down the value of your land. . . .

. . . is to stay put on what is left of what has been ours since before we were born. Have a small piece each, a small garden, my brother and sister and I discussed it years ago.

Straight away the value of your land goes right down.

Wanted to swing a heavy punch but he's too old for it. He kicked the desk instead. Hard. And the veneer cracked and splintered. Funny how quiet it had become.

You ought to be run in old man, do you hear.

Cripes look what the old blighter's gone and done. Look at Paul's desk.

He must be whacky.

He can't do that Paul, get the boss along to sort him out.

Get him run in.

Get out old man, do you hear.

Yes he could hear, he wasn't deaf, not by a long shot. A bit of trouble getting his foot back out of the hole, but there, he was going, and not limping either, he'd see about this lot later. Going, not limping, and not going to die either. It looked as though their six eyes might all fall out and roll on the floor.

There's no sense, no sense in anything, but what use telling that to George when George already knew sitting beside him wordless. What use telling George you go empty handed and leave nothing behind, when George had always been empty handed, had never wanted anything except to have nothing.

How are you son?

All right Uncle. Nothing else to say. Only sitting until it was late enough to go.

Going, not limping, and not going to die either.

There you are old man, get your feet in under that heater. Got her all warmed up for you.

Yes young fulla that's the story.

The weather's not so good.

Not the best.

How was your day all told?

All right.

It's all those hard footpaths, and all the walking that gives people sore feet, that's what makes your legs tired.

There's a lot of walking about in that place.

You didn't use the buses?

Never use the buses.

But you got your business done?

All done. Nothing left to do.

That's good then isn't it?

How's your day been young fulla?

A proper circus.

Must be this weather.

It's the weather, always the same in this weather.

This is your last trip for the day is it?

A couple of trains to meet after tea and then I finish.

Home to have a look at the telly.

For a while, but there's an early job in the morning. . . .

Drop me off at the bottom young fulla. I'm in no hurry. Get off home to your wife and kids.

No, no, there's a bad wind out there, we'll get you to your door. Right to your door, you've done your walking for the day. Besides I always enjoy the sight of your garden, you must have green fingers old man.

It keeps me bent over but it gives us plenty. When you come for Minnie on Tuesday I'll have a couple of cabbages and a few swedes for you.

Great, really great, I'm no gardener myself.

Almost too dark to see.

Never mind I had a good look this morning, you've got it all laid out neat as a pin. Neat as a pin old man.

And here we are.

One step away from your front door.

You can get off home for tea.

You're all right old man?

Right as rain young fulla, couldn't be better.

I'll get along then.

Tuesday.

Now he could get in and close the door behind him and walk without limping to the lavatory because he badly needs a pee. And when he came out of the bathroom they were watching him, they were stoking up the fire and putting things on the table. They were looking at his face.

Seated at the table they were trying not to look at his face, they were trying to talk about unimportant things, there was a bad wind today and it's going to be a rough night.

Tamatea Whakapau.

It must have been cold in town.

Heaters were on in the train.

And the train, was it on time?

Right on the minute.

What about the one coming home?

Had to wait a while for the one coming home.

At the railway station, you waited at the railway station?

And I saw George.

George, how's George?

George is all right, he's just the same.

Maisie said he's joined up with a gang and he doesn't wash. She said he's got a big war sign on his jacket and won't go to work.

They get themselves into trouble she said and they all go round dirty.

George is no different, he's just the same.

They were quiet then wondering if he would say anything else, then after a while they knew he wouldn't.

But later that evening as though to put an end to some silent discussion that they may have been having he told them it wasn't safe and they weren't to put him in the ground. When I go you're not to put me in the ground, do you hear. He was an old man and his foot was giving him hell, and he was shouting at them while they sat hurting. Burn me up I tell you, it's not safe in the ground, you'll know all about it if you put me in the ground. Do you hear?

Some other time, we'll talk about it.

Some other time is now and it's all said. When I go, burn me up, no one's going to mess about with me when I'm gone.

He turned into his bedroom and shut the door. He sat on the edge of his bed for a long time looking at the palms of his hands.

Patricia Grace

BETWEEN EARTH AND SKY

I walked out of the house this morning and stretched my arms out wide.
Look, I said to myself. Because I was alone except for you. I don't think
you heard me.

Look at the sky, I said.

Look at the green earth.

How could it be that I felt so good? So free? So full of the sort of day
it was? How?

And at that moment, when I stepped from my house, there was no
sound. No sound at all. No bird call, or tractor grind. No fire crackle or
twig snap. As though the moment had been held quiet, for me only, as I
stepped out into the morning. Why the good feeling, with a lightness in
me causing my arms to stretch out and out? How blue, how green, I said
into the quiet of the moment. But why, with the sharp nick of bone deep
in my back and the band of flesh tightening across my belly?

All alone. Julie and Tamati behind me in the house, asleep, and the
others over at the swamp catching eels. Riki two paddocks away cutting
up a tree he'd felled last autumn.

I started over the paddocks towards him then, slowly, on these heavy
knotted legs. Hugely across the paddocks I went almost singing. Not
singing because of needing every breath, but with the feeling of singing.
Why, with the deep twist and pull far down in my back and cramping
between the legs? Why the feeling of singing?

How strong and well he looked. How alive and strong, stooping over
the trunk steadying the saw. I'd hated him for days, and now suddenly I
loved him again but didn't know why. The saw cracked through the tree
setting little splinters of warm wood hopping. Balls of mauve smoke
lifted into the air. When he looked up I put my hands to my back and saw
him understand me over the skirl of the saw. He switched off, the sound
fluttered away.

I'll get them, he said.

We could see them from there, leaning into the swamp, feeling for eel
holes. Three long whistles and they looked up and started towards us,
wondering why, walking reluctantly.

Mummy's going, he said.

We nearly got one, Turei said. Ay Jimmy, ay Patsy, ay Reuben?

Yes, they said.

Where? said Danny.

I began to tell him again, but he skipped away after the others. It was good to watch them running and shouting through the grass. Yesterday their activity and noise had angered me, but today I was happy to see them leaping and shouting through the long grass with the swamp mud drying and caking on their legs and arms.

Let Dad get it out, Reuben turned, was calling. He can get the lambs out. Bang! Ay Mum, ay?

Julie and Tamati had woken. They were coming to meet us, dragging a rug.

Not you again, they said taking my bag from his hand.

Not you two again, I said. Rawhiti and Jones.

Don't you have it at two o'clock.

We go off at two.

Your boyfriends can wait.

Our sleep can't.

I put my cheek to his and felt his arm about my shoulders.

Look after my wife, he was grinning at them.

Course, what else.

Go on. Get home and milk your cows, next time you see her she'll be in two pieces.

I kissed all the faces poking from the car windows then stood back on the step waving. Waving till they'd gone. Then turning felt the rush of water.

Quick, I said. The water.

Water my foot; that's piddle.

What you want to piddle in our neat corridor for? Sit down. Have a ride.

Helped into a wheelchair and away, careering over the brown lino.

Stop. I'll be good. Stop I'll tell Sister.

Sister's busy.

No wonder you two are getting smart. Stop. . . .

That's it missus, you'll be back in your bikini by summer. Dr McIndoe.

And we'll go water-skiing together. Me.

Right you are. Well, see you both in the morning.

The doors bump and swing.

Sister follows.

Finish off girls. Maitland'll be over soon.

All right Sister.

Yes Sister. Reverently.

The doors bump and swing.

You are at the end of the table, wet and grey. Blood stains your pulsing head. Your arms flail in these new dimensions and your mouth is a circle that opens and closes as you scream for air. All head and shoulders and wide mouth screaming. They have clamped the few inches of cord which is all that is left of your old life now. They draw mucous and bathe your head.

Leave it alone and give it here, I say.

What for? Haven't you got enough kids already?

Course. Doesn't mean you can boss that one around.

We should let you clean your own kid up?

Think she'd be pleased after that neat ride we gave her. Look at the little hoha. God he can scream.

They wrap you in linen and put you here with me.

Well anyway, here you are. He's all fixed, you're all done. We'll blow. And we'll get them to bring you a cuppa. Be good.

The doors swing open.

She's ready for a cuppa Freeman.

The doors bump shut.

Now. You and I. I'll tell you. I went out this morning. Look, I said, but didn't know why. Why the good feeling. Why, with the nick and press of bone deep inside. But now I know. Now I'll tell you and I don't think you'll mind. It wasn't the thought of knowing you, and having you here close to me that gave me this glad feeling, that made me look upwards and all about as I stepped out this morning. The gladness was because at last I was to be free. Free from that great hump that was you, free from the aching limbs and swelling that was you. That was why this morning each stretching of flesh made me glad.

And freedom from the envy I'd felt, watching him these past days, stepping over the paddocks whole and strong. Unable to match his step. Envying his bright striding. But I could love him again this morning.

These were the reasons each gnarling of flesh made me glad as I came out into that cradled moment. Look at the sky, look at the earth, I said. See how blue, how green. But I gave no thought to you.

And now. You sleep. How quickly you have learned this quiet and rhythmic breathing. Soon they'll come and put a cup in my hand and take you away.

You sleep, and I too am tired, after our work. We worked hard you and I and now we'll sleep. Be close. We'll sleep a little while ay, you and I.

Vincent O'Sullivan

DANDY EDISON FOR LUNCH

You could tell the Edisons were somebody not simply because their name made you think of the old geezer in the encyclopaedia (and of course they said they were relatives) but because Dick who was the father wore a little RAF moustache. It was because of that everyone called him Dandy. There wasn't another man within ten streets who wasn't as clean shaven as a bread board. And by the telephone table in the Edisons' hallway—we called that bit at home the front passage-way—there was a set of Winston Churchill's war histories, with gold writing on their fat blue spines.

The mother was taller, paler, than anyone else's. She kept to herself, and every evening she walked up the road, and round the top of the park, leaning on her husband's arm. Dandy smiled if you spoke to him, but anything he disagreed with made his mouth purse up as though he'd tasted a bit of lemon. The neighbours liked to say he reeked of sarcasm. This was a phrase I waited to hear when they spoke about him. Two or three women would sit round the kitchen table and the Edisons would come up. Then I'd sit with my hands beneath my thighs, pressing them flat against the chair, and look from one face to another, waiting for it to surface. 'Sarcastic though,' one of them would say at last. Another of the women would turn her cup about on her saucer or give a little snort. 'Reeks of it,' she'd say.

There were two children. There was a boy called Davie who was my age, and a girl five years younger. Another thing the neighbours said was that Janice was the apple of her father's eye, he couldn't see past her. The family had shifted next door while we were all at primary school, and I remember Davie because of two things. One was when he came round to our back porch and waited for me to open the high lattice gate to let him in. I was playing with a cousin so I told him he could get back home, he could scram. Then he began to bawl. I had my arm raised up to the metal catch on my side of the gate and kept snipping it as though any moment I might let him in. So he waited there and when he bellowed through the squares of the lattice I saw his opened mouth, and a pink lolly resting on his tongue. I watched him take from his pocket a white paper bag with the top screwed tight. I knew then he had come over to share the bag with us and on the way across he must have put one in his mouth. He handed the bag through one of the gaps in the gate. But he said nothing and he kept up his crying and I watched the pink lolly with the spit welling round it. I kept saying, 'You'd better get out of here, hadn't you? You better get back home.'

The second time was down the end of their yard. There used to be a creek running there before the state houses were built, so the grass was lush and tall. Davie's father also had this vegetable garden that made my own father say, 'Can't that man think of bloody anything else?' But there was this strip between the garden and the wire-netting fence where he let the grass grow.

'What's he do that for?' I asked Davie.

'He likes the look of it. He likes the colour and the way the wind moves it. Something like that.' So we used to sit in the grass and talk, and one day I told him he would probably go to hell. The next day his mother came over to see mine because Davie had been too afraid to go to sleep the night before. He was scared of burning forever the way I described it to him, how the flames are never burned out and when it seemed like a million years had passed it was only beginning, it was as if it hadn't yet begun. The nuns shieded off that kind of stuff by my time. I think I must have heard my father talking about what he had heard himself when he was a boy back home. But Mrs Edison stood there at the back door while my mother kept drying her hands on a tea towel.

'It's not what we believe,' Mrs Edison said. 'We'd rather not have your son instructing ours.'

Things were tense for a little, but then blew over. Dandy gave us a bag of nectarines and my father arranged to have firewood dropped off on the Edisons' front lawn. When the wood was piled there, the end-cuts and the scraps my father had spent ten minutes tossing from the back of his truck, Dandy walked down the road wearing his little cloth cap that would make anyone know he was an immigrant. He looked at the wood then said to Dad, 'All we need's Joan of Arc now, eh Jim?' That night none of us spoke while we had tea because the old man was so mad. Last time he'd do that sod a good turn, he kept saying.

'He mightn't have meant it,' my mother said. 'He needn't have been getting at Catholics.'

'Meant it!' Dad shouted. Then he began to cough and his breath caught and while my mother was holding a glass of water for him she said, 'I don't know why these things always have to come up.'

I remembered those things at my father's funeral as we came out of the church and I saw Dandy Edison standing at the back. I hadn't seen him for over twenty years. He was leaner, his hair was touch greyer, that was about the only difference. And he had shaved his moustache. With my arm round my brother's shoulder and the coffin resting between us, I glanced up and he looked across at me, and then nodded as though we were passing on a street. I remembered in a kind of flash as they say, the pink lolly in the dribbling mouth, and the way Davie looked at me while I told him about hell, he couldn't go away from me although he had wanted to, he squatted in the long grass beside me while I gave him terror for the first time in his life. And what he had given to me was the fact that words hold power, that saying 'No' to someone, 'You can't come in,' saying, 'Yes, there's hell all right,' is to put him in a cage, to be outside it oneself and run a stick along the bars.

We shook hands outside the church. The undertaker moved behind us, taking the wreaths from the church porch and arranging them on top of the coffin. We talked about Dad and the old days in Westmere and I said why not come round for lunch one Saturday? There was more to talk about than we could get through then.

He said, 'Yes, that would be nice, sometime.' I told him, 'Let's make it definite then. Let's say Saturday week?'

Karen demanded, 'Why in hell did you ask him?'

I said, 'He's a decent old bloke. He's probably a bit lonely.'

'Oh Jesus. Aren't you just the little chap for sentiment the moment you start sniffing the old incense.'

'He's not a Catholic.'

'Who said he was?'

'He's an old man. He turned up at my father's funeral. What's the crime in asking him to lunch?'

'Why not feed the multitudes as well?' she asked. 'Cure a few lepers for afters?'

When we get this far I can tell precisely where my wife's next thrust is going to be. As predictably as sunrise she said, 'Why not throw in your bit about the stars turning with love? You know, your little swotted up quote from that old dago? He was one of your boys.' She raised her hand and moved her fingers and rolled her eyes while she recited how divine love sets in motion such beautiful things. She had done languages at university and told me those lines before we were married. I had asked her to write them down for me. Then a year ago she found a letter of mine that said something almost the same, but to someone else. It was about love enduring anyway, about how it moves the spheres, etcetera. She had said, 'Nothing oils the odd screw like a bit of cultcha, eh?'

This is the last flourish that is supposed to take my breath away, the magician producing rabbits from his hat, a hippo from his arse, or whatever. I'm so used to it now I sit back and applaud when she brings it up. '*Very* good,' I congratulate her. 'Clever little read of a private letter and now all this as well.' As likely as not she'll go on then about secretaries without a brain in their heads and turning it on for the boss and I simply wait until she winds down, which she always does. She hasn't the stamina to be a total bitch. And it amuses me while she rages that I've never, but never been so bored with anyone in my life as I was with that little scrubber she is fuming about. *Raylene*, if you'd believe a human being could be called that. She was separated from her husband, she had blue eyes and curled blond hair like a child's doll, and she believed, as she put it, that true love was for keeps. She actually said so! (She went further down the line after I'd burned her off, down to one of the junior copy writers and she said exactly the same thing to him, after their first bash on the very same office couch. 'Love isn't just something you do for fun, is it?' she said. Ker-rist! I lushed up her beau with a touch of company scotch and it was like hearing the same record played over again. I said to him, 'She's a cross section of our market. Look at it that way and you might as well charge the company for overtime.' He was more pissed than I was and he thought he had to pay me a compliment in return. He said, 'If you'd written the press release for the first Easter there'd have been no doubting Thomas.' Then he said, 'Good tits though, eh?')

So Karen raised Raylene's ghost until she tired of it, then went back to Dandy. 'Why just him?' she demanded. 'We could always advertise. Old neighbours. Old school friends. The milkman when you were three. Your first Plunket nurse. Sister Mary Sanctuary Lamp from primer one. Get them all together for Kevin's M.S.P.'

She was sitting at her desk, working on the next morning's script. As she spoke she jabbed out the initials in the strong block lettering she uses these days. (Five years ago it was intertwining italics in purple ink.) I knew the game too well to ask her what she meant. 'What the hell's M.S.P.?' I was supposed to ask. It was an old trick on her broadcasts and her interviews. She would drop in some privately invented initials like that and throw someone completely. R.F. for Royal Family, that kind of brilliance. 'Top marks for S.E.,' she had complimented an aging visiting actor after his third marriage.

'S.E.?' he stumbled.

And Karen said 'Sexual Endeavour' and brought down the studio audience. She was ticked off by the Chairman himself over that one. She said he had sat there in his dark suit with his silver boyish hair glinting in the subdued lighting and his hands joined in front of him, as though he intended inviting her to prayer, or was simply waiting for the dove to descend.

The trick became a hallmark that viewers would wait for. You would hear her latest *mot* repeated at parties or in the pub. Once one of our brown brothers with a beard and the compulsory whalebone pendant, who didn't know me from the Maori Queen, orated as we waited at a bus stop, 'Call this a bus service? F.A. of that round here, as Karen would say.' Baby, I thought, that's fame! But when she came at it domestically I didn't rise to cue. 'There, there,' I told her. 'Back to letters, is it? Whole words too big for little Karen's tongue, is that it?'

We're good at being vile at each other. Often our sniping works up into something quite demanding—a kicked door, a poster ripped from the wall. Once I threw a rug on the fire and once Karen took my John Lennon spectacles, when they were the in thing, and folded them round themselves so they looked like some kind of perverted insect. I describe her outbreaks to her as a kind of emotional menstruation. Once a month, every six weeks at the latest, we simply have to brawl. Then we make it up and ask people to dinner who may have thought we were unhappy simply because they watched us slang each other at their place a week or so before.

Naturally, then, there was no asking her, 'Now tell me what that means, Karen.' Instead, I walked across the room and shut a window. I explained over my shoulder, 'The neighbours' children, you know?' Then I went to the bar beneath her McCahon. (*Lord, what shall we do in this darkness?* and other sundry slogans in a white, black, rat-grey mix. If the government could only commission posters like that, I say to visitors, we'd go back to candles overnight. We wouldn't waste power, we'd pay not to use it.) I opened a bottle of Russian vodka a client had given me and added the requisites. 'Real drink for you?' I asked her. 'Or your usual sherry?'

But Karen wasn't losing a good line because of my distractions. 'Where were we?' she said. 'Yes. Kevin's M.S. bloody P. Menopausal Senility Party.'

'Confusing me with your hack politicians aren't you?' I said. 'Your geriatric stick men?' I stepped aside when I saw her shadow raise its arm. The pad she heaved at me skidded across the top of the bar, then fell at the other side.

'N.F.M., that one,' I announced. 'Near Fuckin' Miss.'

'Oh, piss off,' she said. She ran her splayed fingers back through her long hair, raising it like a heavy mane.

All this, then, because I had told her Dandy Edison was coming to lunch. When Karen asked me the night before he came if we had to wear our Salvation Army hats, or was it permissible to have our old men's dinner in mufti, I smiled at her and said, 'Quite fancy a bit in Sally gear, actually. Don't you?'

On the credit side of our marriage is that we look so good together. I have very pale skin and dark straight hair that flops forward a little over my forehead—the same side as Hitler's did, Karen likes to point out. In a dark suit, and when I move my pale hands as I speak, I'm sometimes rather taken myself when I catch a glimpse in a mirror, in a reflecting window. When I'm with Karen, who even in winter looks as though she has just come in from the sun, we're the kind of couple people like to fuss over. 'Let them,' I always tell her. They recognise her voice first, because a lot of them hear it every morning of the week. Then after the voice there's her teeth, her figure, her sense of fun—they can't resist her. She is good with men in much the same way as we say some children are good with pets. She doesn't know how *not* to be. She has also had surprisingly few lovers, although she likes giving the impression that she knows the score, has been around, roots like a rattlesnake—whatever your patois is.

Last year she was tied up (literally, one wonders?) with a senior politician whose motto, as I told her, was if it moves, screw it; if it doesn't, tax it. And when she tired of trampling him, or whatever their number was, she repented and confessed to me with a few genuine little tears. She told me as she knelt in front of me in a long frock, after a champagne supper we'd been to. We had come home early and lit a fire. She told me while the pine logs flared and her head rested against my knee, and we both sipped scotch. It was pure *New Yorker*. (It actually came out later in one of my commercials. A similar fire, blonde woman, dark man, crystal glasses, on a rather crappy brand of carpet we were putting across. 'I've a confession to make,' she says. 'So have I,' he answers. Then together, 'We both love it.' A bar or two of melting Mozart, and the Voice-Over declares, 'We sell it by the roll.' A bit *risqué*, a bit cheap even, but we got away with it. I expect by now half of Otara spills its Kentucky Fried over inferior shagpile, thanks to Karen's line.)

'Why are you telling me?' I asked her. 'I'd never have found out.'

'Because it was wrong,' Karen said.

'Silly, don't you mean?'

'No, wrong.' So I patted her head and was understanding about it. We were caring and forgiving because that, quite simply, was what the role asked for. That's a feeling I have about our best times together, when we have the odd weekend away or we stroll through the Domain some quiet Sunday and I snap off a rhododendron and slip the stalk into her hair, it's as if we're watching a movie of ourselves being happy. Perhaps it's because when things go well between us it's like we've been scripted by a real pro. 'If life's not performance, then what is it?' I say some nights when we talk by ourselves, and I'm being what she calls especially H.P. (Heavy Philosophical). When we work as a team there's not much we're after that we don't get. It was teamwork for example that linked us up with California, the one LA–NZ connection that's not only viable but actually fully operative. We had already cut into the Sydney commercial market where they least expected it, you could hear the squealing from here. Then Hersch himself dropped down from LA and I told him, 'You'll only get where the opposition is from the corpses before long, Herschy.' He's an overweight tit of the Hebrew persuasion who wears magenta sports jackets and calls the tune in half the advertising we have. My kind of confidence makes him smile right back to his gold-stopped molars. Then when Karen got him on her morning show he was chuffed as a haemophiliac with a foolproof razor. She took him to lunch and when she introduced him to people in the corridor outside the studio she began with, 'You'll have heard of Mr Hersch, of course?' Later in the year when we got the call to LA I think it was as much her efforts as mine. As I tell her, when we dance in step, kid, you've really got footwork. When we were over there Herschy palmed us around like Beautiful People. (One night we drank with Jon Voight, among others, in the revolving bar of the Bonaventure. We saw the city sparkle out as far as your eye could reach. I remembered the nuns' story about J.C. up the mountain and Satan offering him the lot, I thought if it was anything like this and he didn't buy it, then they didn't have the right copywriter.) We picked up exclusive rights to one of their biggest cosmetic outlets. Back home I did a male deodorant clip shot in the changing rooms at Eden Park, it was the first commercial from here ever to sell in California.

'It was that parcel of lovely bum-meat that did it. Don't get swelled-headed,' Karen reminds me. 'That and my boobs in Herschy's face in the lift.'

'It's your way with old men,' I told her.

So I thought now, even if Karen didn't care for Dandy, he would take a shine to her. He'd see I did all right for myself there.

I phoned Dandy and offered to drive him round, but he insisted, No, if a man was too old to travel, he was too old to arrive. He dropped these wise saws into his conversation like saccharin pills into a coffee cup. So he took a bus to the bottom of the hill, then walked up. When Karen opened the door he stood there with his cap held in his hands at fly level. He wore a wine-coloured shirt, a pearl grey tie, and a cinnamon-coloured suit that was a little tight under his arms, a shade too loose at his waist. I thought he's had that handed down from someone.

I stood behind Karen and for a moment Dandy could see only my wife. He did this incline as though he was one of our Asian neighbours, a little bow because he was meeting a lady.

'Mr Edison, I presume?' Karen said.

'Do they still say that?' he asked her. 'Perhaps I'm not as old then as I thought.'

Karen turned to lead him in and I saw her eyebrows raised. I stepped forward and shook hands with him. I offered him a drink which of course he refused. This isn't going to be easy, Kevin lad, I told myself. Karen already had whipped off to the kitchen. I heard the blender suddenly burring, the clicking of plates.

'We'll have a look outside, shall we?' I proposed. 'Before the rain beats us to it?' There wasn't an earthly chance of rain, but one had to say something. I thought it was worth looking outside anyway, unless old Dandy's eyes were shot. The glimpse of sea we had down the end of the valley, the dip of the native trees beyond the edge of our section, there was nothing wrong with that, even if my old neighbour wasn't with it enough to admire how on one side our house hung out across the bank on poles. I mentioned the architect on the off-chance he may have heard of how class was actually spelled.

We had had the patio done a few weeks before. Karen dredged up some gifted little foreign chap from Parnell who worked wonders with old bricks. We had heard about a hall at a local convent that was going to be demolished, I was down there like one of my old aunts on Indulgence Day. I fed the good sisters the right line and next thing the yellow bricks were piled at the side of the house, at half the price I'd have got them anywhere else. ('You know I'm getting a bargain, now, don't you Sister?' The nun's lips did that classic convent moue. 'I'm sure you wouldn't offer us anything that wouldn't be a fair price, Mr Grant.') Once Karen's man got to work he chipped and fitted and buffed and we now had our own yellow brick road, as I tell her. I said that at the party we had to christen it and my senior partner did the whole bit, the Judy Garland routine I mean. 'He's pissed out of his tiny mind,' someone said. Anyway my partner did this take-off and all of us except my lady wife were in fits. Leary was so pleased with himself, the pathetic old bugger, so egged on by the clapping hands and the shouts from the rest of us under the fairy lights strung out between the trees, that he did this little dance where the bricks whirled into a circle. He made like he was going to undo his belt, to treat us to a down-trou, and someone shouted out, 'The Wizard of Ass.' Precisely where I stood now with solemn Dandy.

I said, 'We had a little party to launch it, a few weeks ago.' He kept up that smile which seems more for himself perhaps than for whoever he's talking to. I explained how by the end of summer we'd have a punga fence round the whole yard. Dandy was still looking down at the bricks. 'Made a nice job,' he told me.

'Come off it. You don't think I did it, do you?'

The old man tapped at the beautifully levelled bricks with his shoe. 'Pity,' he said. 'Do your own jobs like this and you get twice as much pleasure from it.' He walked across the lawn to examine the brickwork round the barbecue. He ran his palm along the sides. 'That's all right too. That's pretty good.' Karen came and stood beside us for a moment. She said, 'I'll set the lunch out, shall I?' Then before she went in, while Dandy was still above the bricks as though he were looking like a detective for some kind of clue, she said in a whisper, 'Polonius Mark II, eh?'

'A thousand bucks in that lot there,' I said. 'Pay through the nose for anything like that these days.' He was now touching the metal shield at the back. He seemed not to believe things until he had touched them with his hands. I'd noticed that when he first arrived, when he stepped inside and one hand moved along the brocaded back of a chair. He'd never have recognised it for what it was, of course, a new Belgian weave Karen had picked up in Sydney. And he told me now, as he left the brickwork to face me, 'It'll last you out, Kevin.'

That's rich, I thought, I wouldn't go in for too much of that talk if I were you, old cock. But I laughed to jolly him along. 'Not like that fence in Westmere, then?' I meant the one my father had put up at the end of the yard. It was a bush-carpenter's shambles, bits of wire that sprung loose, uprights that leaned off centre from the moment they were driven in. It was supposed to keep us in our own place, away from Dandy's nectarines, away from his lettuces where the ball kept falling every time we played cricket. There was a permanent sag in the wire where we balanced for a moment before leaping down to the other side. I brought the fence up now because I thought he'd like to be reminded of back there. (The line to play the oldies with is always the sentimental one.) I didn't tell him I drove down that way after Dad had died, the first time I'd gone back since we moved out. The state houses looked smaller, the streets drearier. The patch of park that used to be at the corner was gone, the big gum tree that stood at the end of the street and that I could see from my bedroom window, its grey strips of bark hanging down like unravelled bandages, that was gone too. It had grown at the end of Carpenters' section. The Carpenter girl had died of polio in the summer when we couldn't go back to school. I used to look at the tree in the night-time and it was the street's death tree, it was the closest I ever came I suppose to reverence. Of course it was bullshit, it was the dark regressive stuff our old mate Freud made light work of once and for all. But Christ, at the time I used to kneel on the bed and pull back the edge of the brown roller blind, and look at the spread arms, the tufts of foliage at the branches' ends. I could hear my parents talking in the kitchen and there was a bar of yellow light under my bedroom door. When someone moved in the kitchen the strip of light was broken. There was one night in February, a night when it was so hot that my father stood at the end of my bed in only his pyjama pants. I had woken up with pains in my legs and I had called out. My mother was crying and pretending not to, I knew they thought this was how it began with Doris Carpenter. Of course it was something else I had, I don't now remember what. But I told my father to make sure the sides of the blind were flat against the window. They thought my telling them that was some kind of fever, but it was the reality of the tree out there, dark against the sky. My father went in next door to Edisons and telephoned for a doctor. I heard his steps on the concrete path pass outside my window, and then his steps coming back. And now old Dandy was stepping across the patio and in the drift of my thinking, for the slightest fragment of time, his steps and my father's were the same.

He didn't answer me about the fence, so I presumed he hadn't heard. I stood closer to him, looking at the tuft of hairs that sprang from his ear, catching the light like a spray of fuse wire. I reminded him again because I thought at his age what else can there be except nostalgia? But he didn't rise to it. He turned quietly to look at the white-painted garden furniture, the hard lacy patterns in the cast iron.

'I think of those days quite a bit,' I told him. 'Isn't that curious? And the other families down the street, the Stoddarts, the Jeffreys, all that crowd.' I told him I'd seen one of the Jeffrey girls lately.

'Oh. Which one?'

'Valerie,' I said. I had seen her a month before in Queen Street. I was walking with one of the artistic design people from the office and I had turned almost full on towards him when I saw her coming. I didn't want her speaking to me, I didn't want her looking at me and perhaps not speaking either.

'She was the prettiest,' Dandy said. She had been tall as a girl, with lovely English skin. The sisters had long hair and a drunken old man who was mostly out of work. And their silence, that was it, their way of looking without answering back when most of our mothers thought of excuses why they couldn't play with us, had made them seem wild, defiant. They were the exotic ones amongst us. Davie Edison had crouched under the house with me one day, in the mixed odour of dry earth and firewood and a rotting canvas tent, and told me Valerie Jeffrey did.

'Did what?' I asked him.

'You know.' And in our newly learned jargon he told me she Father Uncle Cousin Kinged with the oldest of the Stoddarts, one of the other boys had told him down at the reef. The reef was the narrow strip of lava rock pushing out from the mangroves, across the shallows and the sometimes bitterly reeking mud where for some reason one always wanted to talk bad things, the territory of disorder and excitement behind the slope of houses, the tilt of streets, where the suburb leaned down towards the sea.

'His brother told me,' Davie repeated. 'Down the reef.' I thought of the two boys crouched and confiding while I waited for Dandy to speak, to step back towards me and to Karen who was at the opened doors. She watched him with arched amused eyebrows, tapping the front of her blouse just between her breasts, signalling me to note his jazzy tiepin with the red inset stone. I thought if you could only hit on some image to set people off as I had been, some slogan to dredge up instantly the old emotions, what you couldn't sell with that!

I now examined his old man's skin, that bloody awful pink tenderness around his eyes, the skin at his temples so thin you could see the soft blue branching of veins underneath. You're as good as dead when you're like that, I thought, your hands speckled and dry and already cold too, cold because I'd felt it when we had shaken hands, it's as though life is already drawing back. Then from my own little nostalgia gig I went into something darker, an unexpected anger with that careful old man who was now watching me. The feeling swept me so strongly that for several seconds I wasn't able to speak nor even hear him although I saw his prim mouth begin to move. At last I asked him, 'What? What are you saying?'

'I don't,' he said. He faced me with his bland level gaze as though I were under inspection. 'I don't think very much about them, those Westmere days.'

'I suppose a lot slips your mind,' I said. I knew that might sound offensive.

'No, you remember all right,' he corrected me. 'I mean you don't go out of your way to dwell on it.' Then he laughed, his new teeth grotesque in that dry, papery face. He put his fingers around my arm. We walked inside like that, pretty much as he led me round the side of the house when Davie and I cut up his daughter's doll, and the sawdust guts spilled out on the apron of concrete near the underhouse door. He now surprised me by saying, 'Live in the past, Kevin, you're good as dead already.'

As we came inside he did an odd thing. I hadn't noticed that he had picked anything in the garden, but he now opened his hand, holding it out towards Karen. There was a twig that branched into two or three pinkish tips. I didn't even know we had something like that growing. But Karen took it from his hand and raised it to her face. 'Yes,' she said, smiling at him. 'Daphne.' Then she was talking to him about that, about how it must be one of the loveliest scents there was.

'And verbena,' Dandy said. 'Daphne and verbena.' Karen told him how she had loved it when she first found out what that kind of bush was called. 'I was reading this book of Greek stories, you know, myths and things? It was a book I thought I should hide from my mother anyway because it had photos of statues that showed ladies' bosies, you know that kind?' Dandy was laughing with her, enjoying her casting back to when she was a girl. 'Anyway it had this story in it about Daphne. It was written in that stilted old style, *Apollo loved her, and as she would have none of him, pursued her.* I had only an inkling of what it was about, but once I knew she turned into a tree instead I thought well *anything* would have been better than that.'

'*Almost* anything,' Dandy wisecracked back at her.

'Exactly.' She was flirting with him now, she tapped her hand on his when she said that. I thought, Shit, you can't resist it, can you? See a corpse with a smile on it and you'd come on strong.

From then it might as well have been Karen who had lived next door to him when she was a kid. A couple of times I tried to bring the lunch back my way, he was eating my food after all, he was on a chair I'd paid for. When Karen went to bring the soufflé from the kitchen I said, 'Davie doing all right is he?'

'Still with Air New Zealand,' Dandy said. 'But I've told you that, you asked me earlier on.' He began to build a little tent from his table napkin and set it upright between his hands. He tapped at the side of it, balancing it, then took his hands away.

'Advertising doesn't have quite the same—well, the same thrills,' I tried to joke. 'I mean it has its moments but there's not the same glamour, is there, as flying those jets around?' I wanted him to say at least that we looked as if we were doing nicely too, to give some flicker that he saw you didn't buy furniture like ours in some bargain store in K Road, that the big picture with the writing on it probably cost more than he'd ever earned in a year at the Electricity Department. ('An inspector,' I'd explained to Karen when she asked what he used to do. 'Got trouble with your connections and old Dandy'd sort them out for you.') I knew even as I thought this that it was a bit vulgar, a bit downmarket. I don't mean that I wanted him to feel our gold, as my partner likes to say. Not quite. But I wanted him to know we had taste, and that taste wasn't cheap; that our imported glass-topped tables and Swedish lamps and Karen's collection of paintings were a far cry from Taihau Crescent. I wondered what sort of stuff Davie had. I expected that for all his wings and his flying hours he had wooden salad tongs from Fiji and carved Singapore tables. I suppose I didn't give a stuff whether I was crude about it or not, I wanted Dandy Edison with his Churchill histories and his prissy voice to know that I wasn't playing in the back yard of a state house any longer, scoffing a bar of chocolate before my sister came home. Because he'd seen me do that, fuck him. He'd come round with a phone message in those days before we had a phone of our own, and seen me ferret off into the wash-house with my mouth crammed. He had pushed open the door and looked down at me with his high quizzical stare.

'Mrs Mississippi wants your mother to phone sometime.' I looked up from where I stood edged in against the curved concrete surround of the copper. I felt my cheeks bulged out and the heat of embarrassment prickling up from the neck of my shirt. 'It's important she knows the name,' he said. 'What is it?' I remember how I repeated it, breaking up the word into its slippery syllables. He had told me, 'I need to know that you get it right.' So I had to say it to get rid of him.

'Mississippi,' I attempted. A dribble of chocolate saliva leaped in a dirty arc, I could feel the oozing at one corner of my mouth. Then Dandy laughed as he took a piece of paper from behind his back. 'Here, the number's on this.' The paper had some name on it as well, a name like our own, or like his, something as simple as that. I slammed the wash-house door and the tears danced in my eyes. I said whatever I could lay my tongue to.

I had that in mind now, watching the fastidious movement of his lips as he smiled at whatever Karen said, as he dabbed at his chin with the corner of the napkin he had unfolded from its temporary tent and laid again across his knees. They were onto cooking now, on how he managed by himself, the kind of dishes he found it most convenient to make. 'Time's never a factor you see,' he confided. 'I can take the whole after-noon preparing it, for all it matters.'

'More soufflé?' Karen was holding the dish in front of him, the server ready as though she were about to feed a child.

'No, I think I've had sufficient.'

'Go on,' she teased him. 'It'll build you up.'

'That's never worked before.' He raised both his arms from the table and his sleeves fell back. He showed her his skinny wrists, and the inch or two of thin forearm below his cuffs.

'But I love a challenge!' Karen opened her eyes wide so her eyelashes stood out like spokes, then they were goofing off together again, old mates, Jesus! I thought why push this little number any further, I've done my bit? I went and poured myself a decent-sized gin and clanked in ice from the fridge. Karen glanced across at me while she continued to dangle her geriatric fish (as I'd tell her later). Just to see if her lines still worked, was that it?

'Janice,' I interrupted when I returned to the table. They were onto talking about desserts by now, how to eat crap and save five dollars a year, that kind of recipe swapping.

'Guavas,' Dandy was telling her. 'So few people eat them and yet they're a joy. They're exactly that. A joy.'

'And the colour. That lovely deep pink.'

So I threw in, 'Janice.'

For once my spouse was startled at what I said. I had told her there was some kind of tragedy there somewhere, I wasn't sure of how the details went. But apparently no one ever spoke of it, it was something Dandy himself would never mention. So we wouldn't either, I had warned. Ask about Davie as much as you like, but leave Janice out of it.

'Oh,' Karen had said before Dandy arrived, 'but that's the only bit I want to know.'

'You haven't mentioned Janice.' I stirred the ice about in the glass and smiled across at Karen, then at Dandy. 'Or have I missed it?' I waited for what she calls the N.U. on occasions like this, the Nasty Upshot.

'We're onto recipes, love,' Karen pointed out. There's nothing like a touch of affection to show when she's close to panic.

I continued to smile at them. I lifted the glass and tapped it against my teeth. 'Funny,' I said, 'I seem to have kept up with Davie's movements over the years, but not Janice's. I met one of the Jeffrey girls lately, I think I told you, and she seems to have got through her net too.'

Karen was driven back to asking gaily, 'Janice?'

'Kevin must have mentioned her,' Dandy said. He pushed his plate away from him slightly and laid his dry speckled hands side by side on the cloth. I noticed one of his nails was dark blue, as if it had been jammed. When he looked up he held Karen's eyes, not mine. 'She was my daughter, you probably know that much.' Then he said, 'She used to be a stripper.' Without moving his hands, and in a voice that might still have been talking of guavas, he told us that she took her clothes off first in Wellington, then in Christchurch, because it was the easiest way she could make money. From time to time he smiled slightly while he was talking, when he said, 'She was lazy, you see, but she was also intelligent. I mean she could see the moral objections someone like myself might raise, but she could also talk herself out of them.' Then again, after telling us she had crossed to Sydney, he explained, 'They seem to pay more there for the same thing.' He went on with her career, almost laboriously. Although she was lazy, he repeated, that didn't mean she wouldn't rather do something else than have men look at her. So she bought a massage parlour she called 'Tropic Palms', and then another that was already named when she bought it. Finally there was one that we would probably call V.I.P. It catered only for the rich and was named very simply 'Lolly'. 'And so she led a life of what we call vice. She told me her one weakness in the business she had chosen was sentimentality.'

'What did that mean?' Karen asked.

'I don't know the details.' But he told us other things about her. That she wrote to him often, for example, and that he always knew, more or less, what she was doing. They agreed not to let her mother in on it. 'She always thought Janice had some office job over there. She knew she was doing well.' 'Davie,' I said at last. 'What did Davie think?' 'Oh, he wouldn't speak to her. Not even about her. Did you think he would?'

And again there was the slight smile, and the odd feeling he gave that for all his frankness what we were witnessing was only on the surface, some stirring of what went on far off. I felt I had been outmanoeuvred by the old man owning up that his daughter was some kind of seedy call girl. I could tell Karen was moved and that somehow Dandy was untouched, that saying all that filth about his own family seemed almost incidental to him, that because it was Janice it was somehow not so bad, was that it? I was unsure of everything about him. And then he was tapping the stone in his tiepin and saying, 'She sent this over to me once. It's not imitation either.' He moved the pin slightly for our benefit, so the light streaming in from the window opposite him glanced across the stone. 'Ruby,' he said. Then the old bastard threw his trump card, the one he can never be forgiven for because he must have known all the time he was setting it up, that Karen would go down in front of it like some whore in front of a customer with a hundred bucks, oh mustn't he just. Because Karen already had an expression on her face that I had never seen, not simply shock nor surprise nor wonder. It was like the look on some of those old women who used to go up to St Joseph's when I was a kid, who knelt during the long hours of Exposition when the host was stuck up on the altar in a glass disc and from the edges of the disc gold spikes rayed out, it was like they were gazing into the centre of a dulled sun. And these old hags would stare on and on and the look on their faces was this crazy mix, as if they saw and yet were blind at the same time, that what they looked at was a kind of veil and what they sought was on the other side. It bewildered me that I'd ever think of Karen like that, that I'd put her in that same clutch of mutter and superstition. I sat now without speaking, without any of us in fact moving until Karen tapped his hand and said, 'Is she dead?' And Dandy said, 'Yes, of course.'

We gave him coffee and got rid of him just after three. I'd put away a few more gins and thank Christ we'd got off the morbid line, we'd left the late-lamented Janice stroking the koozers of eternity and the last half hour was Karen's usual fund of chat, travel and work and a touch of politics about which she knows B.A., by which I don't mean Big Amount. But the moment he was gone and I stood beside her and my hand moved across her arse she said simply, 'Don't,' and she went out into the yard. She opened the door to the garden shed and took out the shears. Then she attacked a hedge at one corner of the section, a shaggy mound of a thing that I'd been meaning to ring someone to come and trim for weeks. She was so inept she was comic. I thought, she'll be inside in ten minutes, she'll want me to put band-aid across her angry little blisters. I was wrong about that one too. I don't know how long she worked because when she came in I had nodded off, I was sitting in the Ezyboy chair with the headphones on, listening to The Who.

'Time to dress up,' she told me. 'Not that I feel much like party times.' But of course she managed. Her gay station manager announced halfway through the night, ' Our Karen's nothing if not an old trouper.' He leaned within inches of my face to tell me, his breath rotten with halitosis. I know now why studio producers sit behind a pane of glass. And at midnight when we said we would have to go there were calls of 'Piker' and 'Off for a bit, eh?' and a general sigh of regret that I was depriving them of Life and Soul, as the fat hostess chided me.

'You'll survive without it,' I told her.

Karen put her head on my shoulder during the ride home. We covered the four or five miles without saying a word. Later when she leaned over me her hair fell across me in one broad brushing swathe, a kind of golden tent. It must have been all that old Westmere stuff being churned up earlier in the day, because I raised my hands to run them through her hair, I spread it to either side of us and said, 'Tabernaculum Dei.'

'Some of your old mick talk?' Karen teased. I lowered my hands from her hair and moved them to her tits.

'More a trade name than anything else.' Then I told her, 'Blame your visitor this afternoon.'

I felt her weight move across me, her nails run lightly across my neck. She said, 'Good old Dandy then.' Her hand stretched out and groped for the switch on the bedside lamp. Then it was dark as when we first pushed open the door to Edisons' under-house in the summer evenings, when we'd hide from Janice, and Davie would tell me 'Shhh!' We'd crouch until we heard her walk past, then begin to talk about our secrets, about the Jeffrey girls and the Stoddart brothers and the things we heard down the reef, and sometimes Davie opened his hand and gave me a badge, or some stamps, or once, a foreign coin he had taken from his father's desk upstairs.

Albert Wendt

CROCODILE

Miss Susan Sharon Willersey, known to all her students as Crocodile Willersey, was our House Mistress for the five years I was at boarding school. I recall, from reading a brief history of our school, that she had been born in 1908 in a small Waikato farming town and, at the age of ten, had enrolled at our Preparatory School, had then survived (brilliantly) our high school, had attended university and graduated MA (Honours in Latin), and had returned to our school to teach and be a dormitory mistress, and, a few years later, was put in charge of Boyle House, our House.

So when I started in 1953, Crocodile was in her fit mid-forties, already a school institution more myth than bone, more goddess than human (and she tended to behave that way!).

Certain stories, concerning the derivation of her illustrious nickname, prevailed (and were added to) during my time at school.

One story, in line with the motto of our school (which is: Perseverance is the Way to Knowledge), had it that Miss Willersey's first students called her Crocodile because she was a model of perseverance and fortitude, which they believed were the moral virtues of a crocodile.

Another story claimed that because Miss Willersey was a devout Anglican, possessing spiritual purity beyond blemish (is that correct?), an Anglican missionary, who had visited our school after spending twenty invigorating years in the Dark Continent (his description), had described Miss Willersey in our school assembly as a saint with the courage and purity and powers of the African crocodile (which was sacred to many tribes). Proof of her steadfastness and purity, so this story went, was her kind refusal to marry the widowed missionary because, as she reasoned (and he was extremely understanding), she was already married to her church, to her school and students, and to her profession.

The most unkindly story attributed her nickname to her appearance: Miss Willersey looked and behaved like a crocodile—she was long, long-teethed, long-eared, long-fingered, long-arsed, long-everythinged. Others also argued she had skin like crocodile hide, and that her behaviour was slippery, always spyful, decisively cruel and sadistic and unforgiving, like a crocodile's.

As a new third-former and a naive Samoan who had been reared to obey her elders without question, I refused to believe the unfavourable stories about Miss Willersey's nickname. Miss Willersey was always kind and helpful (though distant, as was her manner with all of us) to me in our House and during her Latin classes. (Because I was in the top third form I *had* to take Latin though I was really struggling with another foreign language, English, and New Zealand English at that!) We felt (and liked it) that she was also treating all her 'Island girls' (there were six of us) in a specially protective way. 'You must always be proud of your race!' she kept reminding us. (She made it a point to slow down her English when speaking to us so we could understand her.)

During her Latin classes, I didn't suffer her verbal and physical (the swift ruler) chastisements, though I was a dumb, bumbling student. Not for ten months anyway.

However, in November, during that magical third-form year, I *had* to accept the negative interpretations of Miss Willersey's nickname.

I can't remember what aspect of Latin we were revising orally in class that summer day. All I remember well were: Croc's mounting anger as student after student (even her brightest) kept making errors; my loudly beating heart as her questioning came closer and closer to me; the stale smell of cardigans and shoes; Croc's long physique stretching longer, more threateningly; and some of my classmates snivelling into their handkerchiefs as Croc lacerated them verbally for errors (sins) committed.

'Life!' she called coldly, gazing at her feet. Silence. I didn't realize she was calling me. (My name is Olamaiileoti Monroe. Everyone at school called me Ola and *translated* it as Life which became my nickname.) 'Life!' she repeated, this time her blazing eyes were boring into me. (I was almost wetting my pants, and this was contrary to Miss Willersey's constant exhortation to us: ladies learn early how to control their bladders!)

I wanted desperately to say, 'Yes, Miss Willersey?' but I found I couldn't, I was too scared.

'Life?' She was not advancing towards me, filling me with her frightening lengthening. 'You *are* called Life, aren't you, Monroe? That *is* your nickname?'

Nodding my head, I muttered, 'Yes—yes!' A squeaking. My heart was struggling like a trapped bird in my throat. 'Yes, yes, Miss Willersey!'

'And your name is Life, isn't it?'

'Yes!' I was almost in tears. (Leaking everywhere I was!)
'What does Ola mean exactly?'
'Life, Miss Willersey.'
'But Ola is not a noun, is it?' she asked.
Utterly confused, leaking every which way, and thoroughly shit-scared, I just shook my head furiously.
'Ola doesn't mean Life, it is a verb, it means "to live", "to grow", doesn't it?' I nodded furiously.
'Don't you know even your own language, young lady?' I bowed my head (in shame); my trembling hands were clutching the desk-top. 'Speak up, young lady!'
'No, Miss Willersey!' I swallowed back my tears.
'Now, Miss Life, or, should I say, Miss To-Live, let's see if you know Latin a little better than you know your own language!' Measuredly, she marched back to the front of our class. Shit, shit, shit! I cursed myself (and my fear) silently. Her footsteps stopped. Silence. She was turning to face me. Save me, someone!
'Excuse me, Miss Willersey?' the saving voice intruded.
'Yes, what is it?'
'I think I heard someone knocking on the door, Miss Willersey.' It was Gill, the ever-aware, always courageous Gill. The room sighed. Miss Willersey had lost the initiative. 'Shall I go and see who it is, Miss Willersey?' Gill asked, standing up and gazing unwaveringly at Miss Willersey. We all focused our eyes on her too. A collective defiance and courage. For a faltering moment I thought she wasn't going to give in.
The she looked away from Gill and said, 'Well, all right and be quick about it!'
'You all right, Miss To-Live?' Gill asked me after class when all my friends crowded round me in the corridor.
'Yes!' I thanked her.
'Croc's a bloody bitch!' someone said.
'Yeah!' the others echoed.
So for the remainder of my third-form year and most of my fourth year I *looked* on Miss Susan Sharon Willersey as the Crocodile to be wary of, to pretend good behaviour with, to watch all the time in case she struck out at me. Not that she ever again treated me unreasonably in class despite my getting dumber and dumber in Latin (and less and less afraid of her).
In those two years, Gill topped our class in Latin, with little effort and in courageously clever defiance of Crocodile. Gill also helped me to

get the magical 50% I needed to pass and stay out of Crocodile's wrath.

Winter was almost over, the days were getting warmer, our swimming pool was filled and the more adventurous (foolhardy?) used it regularly. Gill and I (and the rest of Miss Rashly's cross-country team) began to rise before light and run the four miles through the school farm. Some mornings, on our sweaty way back, we would meet a silent Crocodile in grey woollen skirt and thick sweater and boots, striding briskly through the cold.

'Morning, girls!' she would greet us.

'Morning, Miss Willersey!' we would reply.

'Exercise, regular exercise, that's the way, girls!'

In our fourth-form dormitory, my bed was nearest the main door that opened out to the lounge opposite which was the front door to Crocodile's apartment, forbidden domain unless we were summoned to it to be questioned (and punished) for a misdemeanour, or invited to it for hot cocoa and biscuits (prefects were the usual invitees!). Because it *was* forbidden territory we were curious about what went on in there: how Croc lived, what she looked like without her formidably thick make-up and stern outfits, and so on. As a Samoan I wasn't familiar with how papalagi (and especially Crocodile) lived out their private lives. I tried but I couldn't picture Miss Willersey in her apartment in her bed or in her bath in nothing else (not even her skin) but in her make-up, immaculately coiffured hair and severe suits. (I couldn't even imagine her using the toilet! Pardon the indiscretion which is unbecoming of one of Miss Willersey's girls!)

The self-styled realists and sophisticates among us—and they were mainly seniors who had to pretend to such status—whispered involved and terribly upsetting (exciting) tales about Crocodile's men (and lack of men), who visited (and didn't visit) her in the dead of night. We, the gullible juniors, inexperienced in the ways of men and sex, found these lurid tales erotically exciting (upsetting) but never admitted publicly we *were* excited. We all feigned disgust and disbelief. And quite frankly I couldn't imagine Miss Willersey (in her virgin skin) with a man (in his experienced skin) in her bed in the wildly lustful embrace of *knowing each other* (our Methodist Bible-class teacher's description of the art of fucking!). No, I really tried, but couldn't put Crocodile into that forbidden but feverishly exciting position. At the time I *did* believe in Miss Willersey's strict moral standards concerning the relationship between the sexes. (I was a virgin, and that's what Miss Willersey and my other elders wanted me to retain and give to the man I married.)

One sophisticate, the precociously pretentious and overweight daughter of a Wellington surgeon and one of Crocodile's pet prefects, suggested that Croc's nightly visitors *weren't* men. That immediately put more disgustingly exciting possibilities into our wantonly frustrated (and virgin) imaginations.

'Who then?' an innocent junior asked.

'What then?' another junior asked.

'Impossible. Bloody filthy!' the wise Gill countered.

'It happens!' the fat sophisticate argued.

'How do you know?' someone asked.

'I just know, that's all!'

'Because your mother is a lesbian!' Gill, the honest, socked it to her. We had to break up the fight between Gill and the Wellington sophisticate.

'Bugger her!' Gill swore as we led her out of the locker room. 'She sucks up to Miss Willersey and then says Croc's a les!'

'What's—what's a les . . . lesbian?' I forced myself to ask Gill at prep that evening. She looked surprised, concluded with a shrug that I didn't really know, printed something on a piece of paper and, after handing it to me, watched me read it.

A FEMALE WHO IS ATTRACTED TO OTHER FEMALES!!!

'What do you mean?' I whispered. (We weren't allowed to talk during prep.)

She wrote on the paper. '*You Islanders are supposed to know a lot more about sex than us poor pakehas. A les is a female who does it with other females. Savvy?*'

'*Up you too!*' I wrote back. We started giggling.

'Gill, stand up!' the prefect on duty called.

'Oh, shit!' Gill whispered under her breath.

'Were you talking?'

'Life just wanted me to spell a word for her!' Gill replied.

'What word?'

'Les—,' Gill started to say. My heart nearly stopped. 'Life wanted to know how to spell "lesson"!' Relief.

'Well, spell it out aloud for all of us!' And Gill did so, crisply, all the time behind her back giving the prefect the up-you sign.

After this incident, I noticed myself observing the Crocodile's domain more closely for unusual sounds, voices, visitors, and, though I refused to think of the possibility of her being a lesbian, I tried to discern a pattern in her female visitors (students included), but no pattern emerged. Also, there were no unusual sounds. (Croc didn't even sing in the bath!)

Some creature, almost human, was trapped in the centre of my head, sobbing pitifully, mourning an enormous loss. It was wrapping its pain around my dreaming and I struggled to break away from its tentacles. I couldn't. I woke to find myself awake (and relieved I wasn't strangling in the weeping) in the dark of our dormitory. Everyone else was fast asleep.

The I knew it was Miss Willersey. I knew it and tried not to panic, not to give in to the feeling I wasn't going to be able to cope. I wrapped the blankets round my head. It was none of my business! But I couldn't escape.

I found myself standing with my ear to Mrs Willersey's door. Shivering. Her light was on, I could tell from the slit of light under the door. The sobbing was more audible but it sounded muffled, as if she was crying into a pillow or cushion. Uncontrolled. Emerging from the depths of a fathomless grief. Drawing me into its depths.

My hand opened the door before I could stop it. Warily I peered into the blinding light. My eyes adjusted quickly to the glare. The neat and orderly arrangement of furniture, wall pictures, ornaments, and book-cases came into focus. Miss Willersey was enthroned in an armchair against the far wall, unaware of my presence, unaware of where she was and who she was, having relinquished in her grief all that was the Crocodile. She was dressed in a shabby dressing-gown, brown slippers, hair in wild disarray, tears melting away her thick make-up in streaks down her face, her long-fingered hands clasped to her mouth trying to block back the sound.

Shutting the door behind me quietly, I edged closer to her, hoping she would see me and order me out of her room and then I wouldn't have to cope with the new, fragile, vulnerable Miss Willersey. I didn't want to.

All around us (and in me) her grief was like the incessant buzzing of a swarm of bees, around and around, spiralling up out of the hollow hive of her being and weaving round and round in my head, driving me towards her and her sorrow which had gone beyond her courage to measure and bear.

And I moved into her measure and, lost for whatever else to do, wrapped my arms around her head, and immediately her arms were around me tightly and my body was the cushion for her grief.

At once she became my comfort, the mother I'd never had but had always yearned for, and I cried silently into her pain. Mother and daughter, daughter and mother. A revelation I hoped would hold true for as long as I was to know her.

Her weeping eased. Her arms relaxed around me. She turned her face away. 'Please!' she murmured. I looked away. Got the box of tissues on the table and put it in her shaking hands. I looked away. Tearing out a handful of tissues, she wiped her eyes and face.

I started to leave. 'It is Ola, isn't it?' she asked, face still turned away. In her voice was a gentleness I have never heard in it before.

'Yes.'

'Thank you. I'm . . . I'm sorry you've had to see me like this.' She was ripping out more tissues.

'Is there anything else I can do?' I asked.

'No, thank you.' She started straightening her dressing-gown and hair. The Crocodile was returning. I walked to the door. 'Ola!' she stopped me. I didn't look back at her. 'This is our secret. Please don't tell the others?'

'I won't, Miss Willersey. Good-night!'

'Good-night, Ola!'

I shut the door behind me, quietly, and on *our secret*.

Next morning there was a short article in the newspaper about her mother's death in Hamilton, in an old people's home. Miss Willersey left on the bus for Hamilton that afternoon.

'That Croc's mother's crocked!' some girls joked at our table at dinner that evening.

Yes, Crocodile Willersey remained married to her school and students until she died in 1982. By becoming a school tradition and a mythical being in the memories of all her students (generations of them) she has lived on, and we will bequeath her to our children.

Miss Susan Sharon Willersey, the Crocodile, I will always think of you with genuine alofa. (And forgive me—I've forgotten nearly all the Latin you taught me!) By the way, you were wrong about the meaning of Ola; it can also be a noun, Life.

Fiona Kidman

THE TENNIS PLAYER

1

On the leg from Bombay Ellen sat upright beside a cello which had had a seat booked for it because its owner said it was a Stradivarius. The cabin attendants seemed more gracious towards the cello than to the children who had joined the flight at Bombay. The lavatories were jammed with unflushed paper, service came less often than in the early part of the flight, and babies cried. Ellen offered to walk a child whose mother looked like a delicate Asian figurine.

She and the child stood and looked down at Turkey for a long time through the domed glass at the rear of the plane.

'Are you a missionary?' asked a woman across the aisle, when she returned.

Ellen shook her head and smiled politely. She had been travelling for nearly thirty hours. She had begun to think that she would like to be a cello.

2

In London she lugged her huge suitcase up five flights of stairs and found herself in a bedsit under the eaves of a building in Eccleston Square that looked elegant from the outside and was a dump on the inside. There was a fire escape out to the roof just like in *The Girls of Slender Means*.

Only Ellen was forty-five and the war was over.

3

She walked down the street until she came to a Mr Wimpy food bar. She was still unhealthily full of airline food, yet the cardboard-and-onion smell of packaged hamburgers was irresistible. It was like Friday night in Newtown, close to home. The restaurant was full, with black faces and white in about equal proportion, and she was certain that the black faces were friendlier than the white.

Afterwards, she went to the women's lavatory at Victoria Station and queued behind the barrier. The large black woman in charge shouted out, 'Which one of you ladies been and gonna done a wee wee on my floor?' Nobody answered and Ellen knew she thought it was her.

Her cheeks burned. She stepped over the puddle.

4

On the way home (for, for the moment there was no other, except Eccleston Square) she stopped to buy grapes from a fruit barrow, and fumbled with the unfamiliar coins.

'Doesn't know the bleeding time of day, does she?' the man who ran the fruit barrow said to a group of schoolgirls with cheeks like beastly English apples. She gave him money, took what he said was her change, and fled without the grapes. She heard the laughter of the girls as she hurried down the street. Stung, she turned and walked back, shouting at the fruit vendor, *fuck you, fuck you, ah fuck you.*

Then she ran for fear the bobbies would pick her up.

She felt better until she got back to Eccleston Square.

She spoke of herself as an ordinary woman. But she was used to living in a house with restored ceilings and pale walls that faced out to sea. She listened to classical music on the radio when she took her morning baths.

In the room, she sat on the bed and wondered if there would be a nuclear attack before she got back to New Zealand and what were the chances of seeing her family again.

5

The best part of every day was saying *fuck you* to the fruit vendor when she passed. You could almost say they were on nodding terms. In Wellington, the city she came from, she had observed a woman dressed in a yellow and red cloak, who ran from behind a door at the railway station to feed pigeons. This activity was strictly forbidden. She did it when she thought no one was watching. Only someone always was. She got chased by a station attendant with a broom. Ellen could not stop thinking about her.

6

She went to a communion service in Westminster Abbey. It was

Mothering Sunday and she began to cry. A woman in a good tweed suit and a slouched hat stood up in the middle of the service when the choir had just finished singing the Twenty-third Psalm. The woman shouted out to the congregation that they were all fools and hypocrites, and mistaken and misled. Ellen wanted to cheer when she was led away across the cold stones. Mostly because it might have been her getting caught but was not. Instead she drank the blood of Christ, and resolved to speak more forthrightly to the fruit vendor.

7

The next day she bought an Israeli avocado and a bottle of German wine at the corner store and took them back to the room. On a roof garden opposite to her, three men carried a garden up from the street, and she saw that it was full of flowering daffodils. In the square below, two men unlocked the gate and went inside to play tennis, locking the gate behind them, so that no one could get in.

It amazed her that nobody shook the bars. Rally, they cried, game love set.

On the day following that, she bought two cobs of bright gold corn. She had never eaten such sweet corn. It made her want to cry again, it tasted so much of home, and childhood, only better.

Outside snow had begun to fall, and the three men had appeared on the rooftop garden to take the daffodils away. She wondered how the corn had ripened in weather like this, and realised that of course it must have been imported. She rummaged through the rubbish tin and found the label on the packaging. The corn had been grown in South Africa.

8

She knew she was as nutty as a peanut slab when she got on the train at Charing Cross to go to Paris, but thought that maybe it wasn't showing. The thing was, she was getting out of it. She opened her phrase book. She had passed School Certificate French. She had meant to refresh herself but hadn't found the time. It felt as if it was thirty years since she had recited a French verb.

It was.

Exactly.

9

She sat for a long time watching the railyards turn to open fields, glimpsed grass and trees through mist. She was so afraid that now she would have been grateful for Eccleston Square. She had been running late and missed the *bureau de change*. Effectively, she was bound for Paris with no money. She passed her hand over her stomach where her travellers' cheques were strapped in her money belt. The belt had worked round and the zip chafed her skin. The lack of money was something to worry about, and she supposed it would preoccupy her all the way to Paris. Her husband would have said, if you haven't got something to worry about, you'll invent something.

Which was all very well.

But if there was no *bureau de change* at the station, how would she get a taxi? She must also go to the lavatory on the train, or the boat, or somewhere, because if she did not, maybe she would have to pay to go at the station in Paris, and then if she had no money, and they would not let her in, how would she take off her money belt to get the travellers' cheques out so she could change them anyway? There was so much to think about. Since she had been away she kept trying to cross things off lists she must do, if she was to survive alone in Europe, but instead she continually remembered more things to add. She did not know how she had ever looked after her children when it was so difficult to look after herself.

She pushed her gloved hand distractedly through her hair and avoided the feet of the young man sitting facing her, as they threatened to become entangled with hers. The feet were clad in fine soft leather boots.

10

She had observed the way people did not stare at each other in England, and the way that they did not make random comments to each other. Even though she had not spoken to anyone except the fruit vendor for several days she knew she should resist the urge to speak.

11

The young man pretended to be asleep whenever she looked at him. She knew he pretended by the way he moved his feet. He had started being tidy with them.

After a while he pretended to wake up and took out a book. She saw that it was a collection of Andrew Marvell's poems. She felt ashamed that she was only reading a novel, even though it was by Barbara Pym who was now rediscovered.

The young man wore designer jeans. He picked one of his feet up off the floor and placed it on the seat so that his very long leg was cocked along it, and his shapely crotch exposed towards her.

It was as good as a smile.

'Are you a student?' she said, looking at his book, and recalling English I.

'No,' he said, but he did smile. He had strong white teeth, and his face was lean and tanned. He turned the book a little so that she could appreciate the cover. 'It's a good read.'

'Have you been to Paris before?' she blurted.

'Not since last week,' he said.

He pointed to the luggage compartment. She saw then, two tennis racquets in frames. They looked shiny and expensive.

'I'm a tennis player. I play in tournaments. Most weeks I play somewhere in Europe. This week and last, it's been Paris.'

'How exciting,' she said, and heard herself breathless and a little tremulous. 'Are you famous? Should I know you? I'm from New Zealand, you see, we don't see all the games, well only the finals at Wimbledon, I might not have seen, you understand . . . ?'

'No, not so exciting, no truly. Of course, in New Zealand I can see you might not have . . . sometimes on television, yes, but in New Zealand, well I can understand that. I do win some.'

He smiled again. She recognised false modesty when she saw it.

12

He was kind though, generous with details. They told each other the story of their lives, listening carefully to one another. He came from Devon. His parents had thought he might do better than be a tennis player but he didn't understand their problem. It was a good job. It took a long time to tell her this. She, having had a longer life, took even more time.

They hurtled past fields she could barely see because the mist now hugged the edge of the railway tracks like white fur.

They discussed the agrarian patterns of Great Britain. In the fifth form, she had been taught about grain production in East Anglia. She could not understand its relevance to her life. She had wondered if, coming here to England for the first time, she would discover why it was important to her to learn about its grainfields when she had only a rough idea of where wheat was grown in New Zealand.

His tone was almost sharp. 'Of course it's important,' he said. 'It's a central factor in the British economy.' He paused, frowned. 'And New Zealand depends on Britain doesn't it?'

How curious, she thought, if, after all, an ear or two of wheat were to come between her and the consummation of what was clearly shaping up to be the most classic interlude in her life. A young man, in Paris, where despite the portents on this side of the Channel, it was officially spring and bound to be fine. A small subterranean voice begged her to remind herself that it was simply fucking in a general sort of way that she had in mind, rather than with this particular young man. She dismissed the voice. For a moment, she thought that if her husband were here, right at this minute, she would probably prefer the tennis player.

'Would you ever play in South Africa?' she asked him, holding her breath.

'Never,' he said with fervour. She breathed a long sigh of relief, forgiving him East Anglia. She saw his head on the pillow beside hers, and the index finger of her right hand sitting inside its new glove, purchased in Oxford Street the day before, traced his profile in her mind's eye. She knew already that she was bound never to forget him.

'In the mornings we eat breakfast outside at the sidewalk cafés. You must do that,' he was saying. 'It is the only way to have breakfast in Paris.'

13

At Dover she thought the white cliffs were a hill covered with birdshit. They had disappeared behind the hovercraft before she had time to appreciate them.

'Is that all?' she said to him. 'Is that all?'

At the terminal people had turned to look at them. He had bought her coffee and croissants, and refused to allow her to pay. 'In New Zealand,' he said. Already it had been decided that he must play the New Zealand circuit some summer soon.

She felt herself walking with the special pride of someone who has recently become one half of a new couple. It occurred to her that he might be very well known indeed. Look at him, she imagined the eyes that followed them were saying, he has a new woman. Perhaps it would get into the papers. Young tennis player woos mystery woman. Antipodean sweetheart—how long can this romance last? In praise, again, of older women.

'You'll be speaking French in a minute,' he said, and too late she realised that the English Channel was behind her.

She opened her phrase book at Arrivals and Departures. 'I have two hundred cigarettes, some wine and a bottle of spirits,' she said, frivolous in her mood.

'The children are on my wife's passport,' he said, running his finger down the list.

She laughed out loud. '*Non. Je ne suis que de passage.*'

He nodded approvingly. 'Passing through, eh? *Bon.*' He opened his hands, a mock Gallic gesture. '*Je n'ai rien à déclarer aussi.*'

He put his hand on her phrasebook. 'Don't worry about it so much.'

14

The train stopped often in the French countryside. The small towns all seemed to have rubbish tips for backyards. Their conversation became erratic. It was still raining.

'You must be privileged if you play tennis in England,' she mused, and aware already that he was. But she had been thinking of Eccleston Square.

His head was slipping sideways towards her shoulder. She could smell him. He smelled like a new racquet, gutsy and clean.

'Probably. Tell me some more about New Zealand,' he said drowsily, without minding whether she did nor not. She watched him. She thought of something special she would do for him.

15

The lock in the bedroom door worked by a number of turns in either direction. She could not work out the sequence. Not only could she not get in, but once in she could not get out either. She had to call reception three times before she had mastered it, and on the last occasion she was near to hysteria. The young man on the desk came upstairs on his own to explain it to her the first two times. His English was bad. The third time he brought another man, who spoke good English. He explained the lock in a slow and patient way as if she were simple. She considered leaving the hotel and going to another, but night had fallen and she did not know where to go.

When it seemed as if she understood the mechanism of the lock she sat in the room and shook. Several hours had passed since the tennis player had last bought her food, and the hotel had no restaurant. Even if it had, she was afraid to leave the room.

Still, at least she liked it. After Eccleston Square it was like a return to some other life where ease and comfort were again possible. The king-sized bed was covered with a frilled quilt with a pattern of pink and green peacocks, and there were rose-coloured lights on the wall. There were gold-coloured taps in the bathroom and a deep bath.

The louvre doors led out onto a wrought iron balcony overlooking Rue Pasquier. The life of the city stretched below her had she chosen to walk out onto the balcony, though for the moment the sound of traffic had caused her to close the doors so that she could hear herself think.

She knew she would not sleep if she did not eat, and maybe drink as well, and that the longer she left it the more difficult it would be to set out.

Carefully she tried the lock and this time the combination worked to perfection. Emboldened, she left the hotel and walked quickly along the boulevard in the direction of St Augustin. Her handbag was comfortably full of francs. 'You'll be all right now, won't you?' he had said when he left her at the counter of the *bureau de change*. 'I'm sorry I can't see you to a taxi.' He had become tense and athletic, fretting with his tennis racquets. He had explained on the first train, in England, that his game was on the other side of Paris. As it was, he would be cutting things to get there on time.

Traffic swirled past her. She could not see where the centre line of the road was, or indeed, if there were any true sides to the roads, as a car mounted the pavement and ran its left-hand tyres alongside her ankles. She leapt out of its path and watched it subside into the path of an oncoming car, which swerved in its turn.

Right up until the last moment she knew that she had been shamefully hoping. Even in the taxi, re-counting her money, which she had been short-changed the first time it was given to her, and she had had to demand in a loud high voice that it be counted again, she wondered if he had heard her tell him the name of the hotel, and regretted that she had not had the courage to repeat it when he was leaving.

It was after the second time that the lock on the door would not open that she admitted his expression. It was, she remembered, decent and perfectly nice, marred by a slight but growing sense of impatience.

She found a restaurant. The waiter was young. He did not speak any English at all. She pointed out a phrase in her small blue book. *Je ne parle pas bien le francais. Je viens de Nouvelle Zélande.* He brought her a carafe of wine without being asked. When she drank it thirstily he brought her another, and indicated to her what he had decided it would be best for her to eat.

Vous êtes très aimable, she wrote on her paper napkin when she left. She felt undone by such simple kindness.

Like the kindness of the tennis player. They had not talked about his aunts, but she knew without such a conversation taking place, that he was kind to them. He would be good to them if they were ever foolish enough to go to Paris alone. He might even try to dissuade them from going.

16

Inside the room she felt free, with a sudden odd delight that she was alone. She leaned against the door with her back to it. It was April, and she was in Paris. She had come from the other side of the world for this. She had transacted money. She knew the combination of her lock. She had bought a meal. In a minute or so she would run a large hot bath.

She had not drawn the curtains yet, and outside the night sky shone with reflected light.

Ellen walked to the doors leading out onto the balcony and opened them, breathing deeply and calmly. She stepped outside, and a fine rain was falling. She gripped the edge of the wrought iron balcony, and was happy.

As she stood there, a curious thing happened. The astonishing traffic began to grind to a halt beneath her. Two cars hit each other with a sickening thud. The drivers leapt out of the cars, and without looking at each other, raised their fists in her direction, as if it was she who was responsible for their misfortune.

More cars began to stop. Within moments Rue Pasquier was clogged with cars askew where their owners had abandoned them with their motors running. Behind the cars that had stopped, drivers in the oncoming wave who could not see what was happening began to sound their horns.

Ellen was increasingly bewildered by the commotion. But it was surely a phenomenon which, if studied, must give insight and meaning to the character of the French. She prided herself in a lively curiosity. The men who had first waved their fists at her were now shouting at each other. But other drivers, less hapless, still appeared transfixed by something at the point where she stood. She thought that it must be above her and looked upwards, putting her hand on the wall over her head.

A man headed towards the balcony then, laughing and shouting at the same time. She drew back, afraid. She was not so far above the street that a man could not scale the wall to where she stood.

She caught a word. She was sure it was not in her phrase book.

But she understood.

17

When the door to the balcony was double locked behind her she ran her bath. She took off all her clothes. She looked at herself in the steamed-up glass.

The wife who might pass for a maiden aunt or a missionary who might pass for a whore looked back though it was difficult to say whether she looked any more like one of these than the other.

Most likely, she thought, she resembled the cello.

Owen Marshall

VALLEY DAY

Every second month Brian went with his father on the Big Kick. They drove up the valley and the minister took services at the little church of Hepburn and at the Sutherlands' house. One midday service at Hepburn going up, one in the afternoon at Sutherlands', then the evening drive home. In the autumn the long sun would squint down the valley and the shadows blossom from hedges and trees, and slant from the woodwork of buildings in angles no longer true.

One sermon did the trick on the Big Kick, with only the level of formality altered to suit the circumstances. The minister was relaxed despite the hours of driving, and treated it as a gallant expedition for his son's sake. 'Off on the Big Kick again, eh,' he said. 'The Big Kick.' The scent of the hot motor, taste of finest, stealthy dust, sight of the valley floor paddocks all odd shapes to fit the river flats; and higher in the gullies sloping back, the bush made a stand. Few farmhouses; fewer cars to be met, and dust ahead a clear warning anyway.

Brian had his hand in the airflow and used it to feel the lift on his palm. He assessed the road. Each dip, each trit-trotting bridge, places he would set his ambushes. Hurons or Assyrians swarmed out to test his courage, while his father practiced parts of the sermon, or recited Burns and then murmured in wonderment at such genius. Brian made the air take some of the weight of his hand, and he kept his head from the window when a small swamp of rushes and flax was passed in case there were snipers hiding there.

'Will the one-armed man from the war be there?' he said.

'Mr Lascelles. Don't draw attention to it.'

'It happened in the war.'

'His tank was hit, I believe. The arm was amputated only after a long struggle to save it: not until he was back in New Zealand. I visited him in hospital I remember.'

'You can still feel your fingers when you've got no arm,' Brian said. 'They itch and that. If someone stood on where they would be then you'd feel the pain.'

'No,' said his father; but the boy kept thinking it. He saw a cloud a long way off like a loaf of bread, and the top spread more rapidly than the bottom and both were transformed into an octopus.

Hepburn was a district rather than a settlement. The cemetery was the largest piece of civic real estate, and the greatest gathering of population that could be mustered in one place. Mrs Patchett had nearly finished cleaning the church. She was upset because a bird had got in and made a mess, and then died by the pulpit. She said there were holes under the eaves. Even such a small church maintained its fragrance of old coats and old prayers, of repeated varnish and supplication, and insects as tenants with a life-cycle of their own. The air was heavy with patterns of the past: shapes almost visible, sounds brimming audible. An accumulated human presence; not threatening, instead embarrassed to be found still there, and having no place else to go. There were seven pews down one side, and six on the other. Down the aisle stretched two parallel brass carpet crimps, but no carpet in between. One stained window, all the rest were plain, a blood poppy amidst green and blue, dedicated to the Lascelles brothers killed within three days of each other in the great war.

Brian took the bird out on the dust shovel. It left just a stain on the boards behind the pulpit. He threw the bird above the long grass: it broke apart in the air, and the boy closed his eyes lest some part of it fly back into his face. He brought his father's bible, soft and heavy, from the car, and the travelling communion tray with the rows of small glasses set like glass corks in the holes, and the bottle full of the shed blood of Christ.

'Don't wander off then,' said his father. 'Don't get dirty, or wander off. Remember we'll be going with one of the families for lunch.' The boy was watching a walnut tree which overshadowed the back of the church, and ranks of pines behind. He found a place where Indian-like he was hidden, but could look out. He crossed his legs and watched the families begin to arrive. The Hepburn church no longer had a piano, and the man with the piano accordion came early to practice the hymns required. Rock of Ages, and Turn Back O Man. He was shy, very muscular, and prefaced everything he played or said with a conciliatory cough. Fourteen other people came as the piano accordion played. Fourteen adults and six children. Brian watched the children linger in the sunlight before trailing in behind their parents. The one-armed Mr Lascelles came. Even to Brian Mr Lascelles didn't look old. He wasn't all that many years back from the war, and he laughed and turned to other people by the cars as if he were no different. Brian got up and walked about in the pine needles as if he had only one arm. He looked back at the trees he passed, and smiled as Mr Lascelles had done. Without realizing it he walked with a limp, for he found it difficult to match a gait to having one arm.

The accordionist coughed and began to play, the families sang, and the boy stood still at the edge of the trees to see the valley and the bush on the hills. Rock of Ages cleft for me, let me hide myself in thee. He felt a tremor almost of wonder, but not wonder, a sense of significance and presence that comes to the young, and yet is neither questioned by them nor given any name. All the people of that place seemed shut in there singing, and he alone outside in the valley. He could see all together the silvered snail tracks across the concrete path, the road in pale snatches, the insect cases of pine needles drawn immensely strong, the bird's wing in the long grass, the glowing Lascelles poppy in the sunlit window. Rock of Ages cleft for me. Brian tipped his head back to see the light through the pines and the blood ran or the sky moved and the great, sweet pines seemed to be falling, and he sat down dizzy, and with his shoulders hunched for a moment against the impact of the trees. The church was an ark with all on board; it dipped and rolled in the swell of the accordion, and he alone was outside amidst the dry grass and shadows, a sooty fantail, gravestones glimpsed through the falling pines of his own life.

He saw cones. The old cones, puffed and half rotted in the needles were ignored. He wanted those heavy with sap and seed, brown yet tinged with green, and shaped as owls. When dislodged they were well shaped to the hand to be hurled as owl grenades against impossible odds across the road, or sent bouncing amongst the gravestones to wake somebody there. He gathered new stocks by climbing with a stick and striking them from the branches. At first he climbed carefully to keep the gum from his clothes, but it stuck to him anyway, gathered dirt and wouldn't rub away, and lay like birthmarks on his legs and held his fingers.

His father was preaching, for the church was quiet. Brian heaped up a mass of pine needles beneath the trees; working on his knees and bulldozing the needles with both hands out in front. He built a heap as high as himself, and jumped up and down on it. When he lost interest he left the trees and walked into the graveyard to search for skinks. Quietly he bent the grass from the tombstones, like parting a fleece, and after each movement he waited, poised in case of a lizard. He found none. He imagined that they were destroyed by things that came down from the bush at night. He picked at the resin stains on his hands. Deborah Lascelles, 1874–1932, Called Home. Brian forgot about the skinks. 'Called Home,' he said to himself. He thought about it as he went down the tree-lined margin of the small cemetery and on to the road. He was disappointed that there were no new cars, but one at least was a V8. He shaded his eyes by pressing his hands to the door glass, in an effort to see what the speedo went up to. He reasoned that anyway as it had twice as many cylinders as their car, it must do twice the speed.

Old now is Earth, and none may count her days. The final hymn. Brian went back into the trees and stood as king on his pine needle heap. He arced his urine in the broken sunlight as an act of territory, and checked the two balls in his pouch with brief curiosity. He jousted against the pines one more time, and brought down a perfect brown-green owl. He ran his hand over the tight ripples of his cone; he hefted it from hand to hand as he went back to the church.

His father stood at the doorway to shake hands and talk with the adults as they left. Those still inside showed no impatience. They talked amongst themselves, or listened with goodwill to what was said by and to the minister. There were few secrets, and no urgency to leave the only service for two months. Mrs Patchett showed Mr Jenkins the holes beneath the eaves, and he stuffed them with paper as an interim measure, and promised to return and do more another day. Things borrowed were transferred from car to car. Wheelan Lascelles stood unabashed, and on his one arm the white sleeve was brilliant against the tan. 'That poem you used,' he said to the minister. 'What poem was that?'

'One of my own in fact,' Brian shared his father's pleasure. They smiled together. The boy edged closer to his father so as to emphasize his affiliation.

'Is that so. I thought it a fine poem; a poem of our own country. I'd like some day to have a copy of it.'

From the sheets folded in his bible the minister took the hand-written poem, and gave it. It was found a matter of interest to those remaining: the minister giving his poem to Wheelan Lascelles. Others wished they had thought to mention it, and strove to recall it.

'We're going to the Jenkins' for lunch,' Brian's father told him when everyone had left the church. The Jenkins lived 20 kilometres up the valley. The minister preferred having lunch with a family living past the church, for then in the afternoon the trip to Sutherlands' was made that much shorter. He let the Jenkins drive on ahead because of the dust, and followed on. 'Mr and Mrs Jenkins eat well,' he said to his son with satisfaction.

On a terrace above the river were the house and sheds of the Jenkins' farm, and a long dirt track like a wagon trail leading in, and a gate to shut behind. 'What have you got on yourself?' said the minister as he checked appearances before entering the house.

'Gum.' Brian rubbed at it dutifully, but knew it wouldn't come off.

'And what's in your pocket?'

'Just a pine cone,' he said. His father flipped a hand as a sign, and Brian took the owl and rolled it away. It lay still warm from his body on the stones and earth of the yard.

'You realize old Mrs Patchett died of course and wasn't there today,' said Mrs Jenkins when they sat. Brian thought someday he might return and find his pine cone grown far above the Jenkins' home. 'Her mind went well before the end. She accused them of starving her, and used to hide food in her room. The smell was something awful at times.' Mr Jenkins smiled at Brian and skilfully worked the carving knife.

'She wasn't at the services the last time or two,' the minister said. 'I did visit her. As you say her mind seemed clouded, the old lady.' Mr Jenkins carved the hot mutton with strength and delicacy.

'She was a constant trial to them,' Mrs Jenkins said. Mr Jenkins balanced on balls of his feet, and gave his task full concentration. Like a violinist he swept the blade, and the meat folded away.

'I saw Mr Lascelles who's only got one arm,' said Brian.

'Yes, Wheelan Lascelles,' said Mr Jenkins without pausing.

'Old Mrs Patchett was a Lascelles,' said his wife. 'They only left her a short time, but she must have tried to walk back up to where the first house on the property used to be. She went through the bull paddock, and it charged, you see. She wouldn't have known a thing of it though.' With his smile Mr Jenkins held the gravy boat in front of Brian, and when the boy smiled back, Mr Jenkins tipped gravy over his meat and potatoes and the gravy flowed and steamed.

'The second family in the valley were Patchetts,' said Mrs Jenkins, 'and then Lascelles. Strangely enough Wheelan's father lost an arm. There must be long odds against that I'd say. It happened in a pit sawing accident before Wheelan was born.' Brian stopped eating to consider the wonder of it: two generations of one-armed Lascelles. On the long sill of the Jenkins' kitchen window were tomatoes to ripen, and a fan of letters behind a broken clock. And he could see a large totara tree alone on the terrace above the river.

'And which was the first European family?' said the minister as he ate.

'McVies. McVies and then Patchetts were the first, and now all the McVies have gone one way or another. McVies were bushmen of course, not farmers, and once the mills stopped they moved on.'

'I haven't seen a McVie in the valley for thirty years,' said Mr Jenkins, as if the McVies were a threatened species, fading back before civilization.

'If your father has only one arm then you're more likely to have one arm yourself,' volunteered Brian.

'Play outside for a while,' his father said. 'Until Mr and Mrs Jenkins and I have finished our tea.'

'There's a boar's head at the back of the shed,' said Mr Jenkins. 'We're giving the beggars something of a hurry up recently.'

'There you are then,' said the minister.

The boar's head was a disappointment; lopsided on an outrigger of the shed. It resembled a badly sewn mask of rushes and canvas. False seams had appeared as if warped from inner decay. Only the tusks were adamant in malice; curved, stained yellow and black in the growth rings. Brian reached up and tried to pull out a tusk, but although the head creaked like a cane basket, the tusk held, and only a scattering of detritus came down. The vision of the bull that murdered old Mrs Patchett was stronger than the defeated head of a pig. The boy sat in the sun and imagined the old lady escaping back to her past, and the great bull coming to greet her.

'What happened to the bull?' he asked his father as the minister topped up the radiator.

'What's that?'

'What happened to the bull that killed Mrs Patchett?'

'I don't know. Why is it you're always fascinated with such things? I don't suppose the bull could be blamed for acting according to its nature.'

As they left amidst the benevolence of Mr Jenkins' smile, and the persistent information from his wife, Brian saw his cone lying in the yard: green and turning brown, and he lined it through the window with his finger for luck, and saw it sprout there and soar and ramify until like the beanstalk it reached the sky. 'A substantial meal,' said the minister.

'There was too much gravy,' said Brian.

'I was born in country like this,' said his father. The bush began to stand openly on the hillsides, and on the farmland closer to the road were stumps which gripped even in death. 'It's awkward country to farm,' said the minister. 'It looks better than it is.' There would be a hut in his pine, and a rope ladder which could be drawn up so that boars and bulls would be powerless below. Tinned food and bottles to collect the rain. Mr and Mrs Jenkins wouldn't realize that he was there, and at times he would come down to the lower world and take what he wanted. 'They tried to make it all dairy country, but it didn't work,' his father said. Brian was willing to be an apparent listener as they went up the valley; mile after mile pursued only by the dust.

Dogs barked them in to Sutherlands'. The Oliphants and more Patchetts were already waiting in the main room. There was a social ease amongst them, arisen from a closeness of lifestyle, proximity and religion. The Sutherlands had no children left at home; the last Patchett boy was at boarding school; only the Oliphant twins, six-year-old girls, were there to represent youth. They sat with their legs stuck out rebelliously because they weren't allowed to thump the piano keys. The Sutherlands had a cousin staying who was a catholic. Brian watched him with interest. There was a mystery and power in catholicism he thought; a dimension beyond the homespun non-conformism that he knew from the inside. Surely there was some additional and superstitious resource with which to enrich life. 'Absolutely riddled with cancer,' Brian heard Mr Oliphant tell the minister.

When the minister was ready the service in the living room began; there was no more exact timing necessary. Mrs Sutherland played the piano, and Mr Oliphant enjoyed singing very loudly and badly. The Oliphant twins refused to stand up with the adults, remaining in a sulk with their legs stiff before them. Their eyes followed Brian past the window as he went from the house. He thought the piano disappointing in comparison with the accordion; more inhibited and careful, less suited to the movement of leaves and water, to the accompaniment of birds.

Brian remembered a traction engine from previous visits. Once it had been used in the mills, but since left in the grass: heavy iron and brass, and great, ribbed wheels. It was warm from the sun, and Brian scaled it and sat there. The traction engine had been built to withstand enormous pressures, and before an age of planned obsolescence. It was a weathered outcrop; the rust only a film which didn't weaken, and the brass solid beneath the tarnish. A land train cast there amidst the barley grass and nodding thistle. He shifted what levers were not seized, and rocked to suggest the motion of the engine on the move.

'You get tired of all the services, I suppose?' said the Sutherlands' cousin. He stood in his carpet slippers, and wore a green woollen jersey despite the heat. He was almost bald, with just a rim of coarse, red hair, like the pine needles the boy had heaped up in the morning. Brian came down to talk. It seemed discourteous to remain raised up. 'I'm in charge of the afternoon tea. I'm a catholic, you see.' His eyes were deeply sunk, like the sockets of a halloween pumpkin. 'I've nothing against your father.' They watched heavy, white geese trooping past the sheds. 'There's cake of course, but you know there's water-cress sandwiches as well. Can you imagine that.' Brian thought it rabbit food, but the cousin was from the city. 'She went and collected it from the creek, just like that. There's wonder still in the world,' he said. 'Did I tell you I'm a catholic?' The cousin began to cry without making any noise, but shedding tears. Brian gave him some privacy by taking a stick and beating a patch of nettles by the hen-run. But the cousin wiped his tears away and followed him. He didn't seem interested in maintaining an adult dignity any more. 'Is that gum on your legs?' he said. The boy told him that he had been playing in the trees at Hepburn.

'There's graves there. One said "Called Home" on it.'

'"Called Home", did it really.' The cousin shared Brian's fascination with the phrase. 'Called Home.' He began to laugh: not a social laugh, but a hoarse laugh, spreading downwards and out like a pool. A sound of irony and fear and submission.

Mr Oliphant began shouting 'Earth might be fair, and all men glad and wise.' The cousin listened with his mouth still shaped from the laughter.

'I'd better see to the afternoon tea,' he said. 'There are lesser rendezvous yet. I'll crib another water-cress sandwich if I can hold it down.'

'Peals forth in joy man's old undaunted cry,' they heard Mr Oliphant singing.

'These things are at the end of my life,' the cousin said, 'and the beginning of yours. I wonder if they seem any different for that.' The cousin turned back from the house after a few steps, and came past Brian. 'Jesus,' he said. 'I'm going to be sick again.' He rubbed the flat of his hands on the green wool of his jersey as if in preparation for a considerable task, and he walked towards the sheds. He gave a burp, or sudden sob.

The Sutherlands, Mr Oliphant and the minister came out in search of him when their afternoon tea wasn't ready. Brian could see the Oliphant twins looking through the window. 'Have you seen Mrs Sutherland's cousin?' Brian's father asked him. The boy told him about the crying and the sheds.

'I hate to think—in his state of mind,' said Mr Sutherland. He and the minister began to run. Mr Oliphant saw his contribution best made in a different talent. He filled his lungs. 'Ashley, Ashley,' he cried: so loud that birds flew from the open sheds, and the Oliphant twins pressed their faces to the window. The echoes had settled and Mrs Sutherland had prevented him from further shouting when Mr Sutherland came back.

'It's all right,' said Mr Sutherland. 'He's been sick again that's all. He's got himself into a state.'

'Who can blame him,' said Mrs Sutherland.

'He was going to make the afternoon tea,' said Brian. 'He started to cry.'

'He's a good deal worse today, but the Rev. Willis is with him.' Mr Sutherland was both sympathetic and matter of fact. 'They're best left alone,' he said. 'Come on back to the house.' Mr Oliphant was disappointed that it wasn't the end; not even a more dramatic approach to the end.

'A sad business,' he said in his lowest voice which carried barely fifty metres. Brian was left to wait for his father. He thought that in that quiet afternoon he could hear Ashley's sobs and his father's voice. He climbed back on to the throne which was the engine, and rested his face and arms on the warm metal.

A column of one-armed Lascelles was moving back up the valley from the war, each with a poem in his hand, and the accordion played Rock of Ages as they marched. Mr Jenkins deftly knifed a wild pig, all the while with a benevolent smile, and in his torrent voice Mr Oliphant Called Home a weeping Ashley: deep eyes and woollen jersey. A host of pine owls, jersey green and brown, spread their wings at last, while old Mrs Patchett escaped again and accused her kin of starvation as she sought an earlier home. Behind and beyond the sway of the accordion's music, and growing louder, was the sound of the grand, poppy-red bull cantering with its head down from the top of the valley towards them all.

Owen Marshall

MUMSIE AND ZIP

Mumsie saw the car coming at five, as she had expected. The general noise of homeward traffic was at a distance: but still the desperation was apparent in the pitch of it. Zip always turned off the engine when in the gate, and coasted on the concrete strips until he was parallel with the window. The grass was spiky and blue in the poor light of winter. Mumsie had cacti on the window sill, and the dust lay amid the thorns of *Mammillaria wildii*.

Zip undid his seat belt, and stepped out. He took the orange, nylon cover from the boot, and began covering the car for the night. He spread the cover evenly before he began to tie it down. Zip always started at the same corner and worked clockwise round the car. He didn't bend to tie the corners as a woman would bend, with backside out, but crouched agile and abrupt, balanced on his toes. Sometimes when Mumsie was close to him when he crouched like that she would hear his knees pop. Mumsie wondered if there would be a day when she would go out and ask Zip not to cover the car because there was something of significance she had to attend: a premiere perhaps, or an apparently trivial summons which would become This Is Your Life, Mumsie.

Mumsie knew Zip wouldn't look up as he came past the window: they always reserved recognition for the kitchen when Zip came home from work. Zip would go to the lavatory, and then to their bedroom to take off his jacket and shoes. Mumsie heard him flush the bowl, and go through for his other shoes.

Zip came to the stove. He stood by Mumsie's shoulder. 'How's things,' he said. The mist of the winter evening was strung through the poles and gables; the thinning hair of a very old woman. Toby McPhedron tried to kick free a flattened hedgehog from the surface of the road.

'Fine,' said Mumsie. 'And you?'

'Busy as usual,' said Zip. 'Just the same, Mumsie. You know how it is.'

'Casserole,' said Mumsie as Zip lifted the lid, 'with the onions in chunks the way you like it. Chunky chunks instead of sliced up thin.'

'Good on you, Mumsie, good on you,' said Zip. 'You know what I like all right.' He rubbed his forehead and circled the sockets of his eyes.

'So the usual day?' said Mumsie.

'You know how it is. Busy of course; always the same.'

'So Mumsie's got a casserole,' said Mumsie.

'You know I like a casserole all right,' said Zip. Mumsie noticed how the pupils of his eyes jittered the way they often did, although his face was flat and still. He stood beside her and looked at the casserole while his pupils jittered.

'You know I couldn't get hardly a thing to dry today. There's no wind and no sun. Hardly a thing dried. I had to take most of it off the line again and put it in the good room with the heater.'

'It's that sort of day,' said Zip. He placed the butter and salt and pepper on the table, and cork mats with the picture of a kitten halting a ball of fluffy wool.

'Mr Beresford died,' said Mumsie.

'Mr Beresford?'

'The place with the new roof; two down from the corner. I heard Mrs Rose talking about it in the shop.'

'Ah,' said Zip.

'So nothing of interest at work today.'

'Uh-huh,' said Zip. He sat down at his place, which was facing the stove and the bench. He laid his hands one each side of his cork mat, as a knife and fork are laid.

'They haven't found the murderer yet,' said Mumsie.

'Murderer?'

'Who murdered those two girls in the boatshed in Auckland. Shaved their heads I think it said. There's a lot of sick things.'

Zip left his hands resting on the table and he looked at the floor by the bench where the pattern on the lino had been worn away. Mumsie's legs plodded this way and that around the kitchen, but always came back to that worn place, on which she shuffled back and forth from stove to table to bench. Zip seemed absorbed: as if that worn patch were a screen and Mumsie's splayed shoes played out some cryptic choreography. But his black eye spots continued to jiggle, and the focus wasn't quite right to hit the worn lino, but aimed deeper, at something behind. Zip sat still, as if conserving energy for a final effort, or as if that final effort had been made to no avail. Mumsie looked at him from time to time. 'Mumsie's done peas shaken in the pot with butter,' she said, 'and baked potatoes in their skins.'

'You're a winner, Mumsie, that's for sure.'

Tears began to form on the windows, and the light outside was fading quickly. 'I like to be in my own house when it gets dark,' said Zip. They could hear persistent traffic noise from the corner, and Toby McPhedron ran a stick along the tin fence next door.

'You don't mind about the heater on in the good room?' said Mumsie. 'There's no drying at all.'

'We can go there ourselves later,' said Zip. 'We'd have to heat one room.'

'Now why would the murderer shave those girls' heads?' said Mumsie.

'Kinky sex, Mumsie. You want to watch out.' Zip watched his casserole with the chunky onions being served, and the potatoes blistered grey-brown, and the peas in butter glistening as emeralds.

Mumsie talked about Mrs Rose's visit to the dentist, about the manner of Mr Beresford's dying third hand, about the boatshed murderer and the good room doorknob which just came off in her hand. The tears made tracks down the windows, and those tracks showed black, or spangled back the kitchen light. Mumsie talked of a party at the Smedley's which they weren't invited to, and how either a niece or a cousin of Debbie Simpson's had a growth in her ear which might be pressing on her brain. Zip said, 'Is that right, Mumsie,' and nodded his head to show that he was listening, and in satisfaction as he crunched the casserole onions done in chunks as he liked them: and he kept looking at things deeper than the worn lino by the bench. Mumsie wondered if she should take some pikelets along to Mrs Beresford, or whether she would only be thought nosey because she hadn't really known him. A dog had torn Mrs Jardine's rubbish bag open again, and Mrs Jardine had to clean it up in her good clothes when she came home at lunchtime, Mumsie said.

The winter night, the lizard voice of the traffic at a distance, the condensation on the windows, all intensified the artificial light of the kitchen where Mumsie and Zip ate their casserole, until it was a clear, yellow space separate from the rest of life; independent even from the rest of their own experience, and isolating them there—Mumsie and Zip.

'Mumsie,' said Zip, 'now that was a real casserole, and don't worry about the door knob, because I can get that bastard back on later.'

'I knew you'd like it, being winter and that. And there'll be enough for you tomorrow.'

Zip lit a cigarette as he stood by the bench and waited to help with the dishes. He pulled the smoke in, and his eyelids dropped for a moment as the smoke hit deep in his lungs. In a long sigh he breathed out. The smoke drifted, the colour of the condensation on the window, and Zip had the tea-towel folded over his arm like a waiter and stood before the plastic drip tray as he waited for the dishes. 'I'll put the rest of the casserole in something else,' said Mumsie, 'and then the dish can be soaked. There's always some bubbles out and bakes on the rim.'

'Let it soak then, Mumsie,' said Zip.

'Don't let me miss the start of the news. Maybe they've found the boatshed murderer.' Mumsie liked everyone to be brought to justice. Zip dried the forks carefully, pressing a fold of towel between the prongs. He tapped the ash from his cigarette into *Chamaecereus silvestrii* on the sill.

'It's just as well we're not in the boatshed belt,' he said.

'But it could be anyone, Zip.'

'Except Mr Beresford, Mumsie. I'd say he must be in the clear.'

'No, I meant it could be any woman. It said on the talkback that these things are increasing all the time.'

Zip spread the tea-towel over the stove top, and shuffled the cork mats into symmetry so that the images of the kittens and the wool were in line. He stood by Mumsie as she wiped the table, and then he sat there and put down a plastic ash tray. Mumsie told him not to pick at the contact because it was already tatty, so Zip rotated his cigarette packet instead; standing it alternately on the end and side, over and over again. His fingers were nimble, and the packet only whispered on the table as it turned. 'We'll go through to the good room soon,' said Mumsie, 'seeing the clothes are already in front of the heater there.'

'That's right,' said Zip. He sighed, and the smoke came like dust from deep in his lungs, and drifted in the yellow light. 'Another day another dollar,' he said.

'Just another day, you said.'

'That's right. Another day,' said Zip. He tapped with his finger on the cigarette above the ash tray; a column of ash fell neatly and lay like a caterpillar.

'How many of those have you had today?' asked Mumsie.

'Five or six.'

'Mumsie's going to have to hide them, or you'll be up to a packet a day again.'

'You're a tough lady all right,' said Zip.

'Well Mr Beresford was a heavy smoker, Mrs Rose said, and he wouldn't be told; just kept on. Mrs Rose said in the shop she wouldn't be surprised if that was it.'

'But you don't know it was smoking Beresford died of.'

'It can't have helped,' Mumsie said. Zip continued to turn the packet with his free hand, head over heels it went again and again. Mumsie said that she'd heard that a lot of drugs had been found in the fire station, but it was all being hushed up. Mumsie enjoyed her delusion of occasionally sharing privileged information. 'It'll all be swept under the carpet because they know each other, all those people, you see if they don't.'

'They'd bloody well come down on you or me though, Mumsie, that's for sure,' said Zip.

Mumsie was talking about the food specials at Four Square when the phone rang. She was comparing for Zip the large coffee with the giant and the standard. Standard meant small, but nothing in supermarkets is labelled small. Zip remained still, apart from turning the cigarette packet. He paid no attention to the phone: he had no hope of it. He was unlucky enough to know his own life. But Mumsie was quite excited. She wondered who that could be she said, and she tidied her hair as she went into the passage. Zip didn't alter just because Mumsie had gone. He stayed quietly at the table as if relaxed, turning the cigarette packet. He did work his mouth; pulling his lips back first on one side then the other, as a horse does on a bit. Zip looked at the table, and the worn lino by the bench, and Mumsie's cactus plants which could survive her benign forgetfulness, and at the windows decked with tears; and his eyes jiggled.

Mumsie was happy when she bustled back in. She felt things were going on. There were decisions to be made and she was involved, and someone had taken the trouble to phone her. 'It's Irene and Malcolm,' she said. Zip let out a dusty breath. The tears of condensation left black trails on the windows, and a small rainbow bubble winked as Mumsie shifted the detergent flask. 'They're going to stay for a few days next week,' said Mumsie. 'Malcolm's got some management course again.'

'No,' said Zip.

'Why's that?'

'I don't want them here. I don't want them here next week, or next year, or ever. I don't want other people in my house Mumsie. Got it? I don't want Malcolm and his moustache telling me how well he's doing, and your sister making you look like Ma Kettle all the time.' Zip didn't raise his voice, but there was in it a tone of finality.

'But they're family,' said Mumsie. She turned the water on and off in the sink for no reason.

'They're not coming. You're going to tell them that they can't come, or I'm going to. You'll do it nicer than me.'

'How often do we have people?' said Mumsie. 'We never see anyone.'

'I don't want to see anyone, and I don't want anyone to see me. People are never worth the effort, Mumsie, but you never seem to learn that.'

'I get sick of no one coming. I get sick of always being by ourselves,' said Mumsie.

Zip spread the corners of his mouth in one grimace of exasperation, and then his face was flat again. 'You're stupid,' he said. 'What are you?'

'Maybe I am,' said Mumsie, 'but I've got a life too. I'm not too stupid to have my own sister to stay am I.'

'You're a stupid, old bitch, Mumsie, and I'm as bad. In a way I'm worse because I'm just bright enough to see how stupid we both are, and how we're buggered up here like two rats in a dung hill. We've got to keep on living our same life over and over again.'

'Oh, don't start talking like that, and getting all funny.' The windows were black eyes shining with tears, and the custard light of the room grew brighter in contrast with deep winter outside. The table legs cast stalks of shadow across the floor, and high on the cupboard edges the fly dirt clustered like pepper spots. 'Anyway, I've told them they can come, and so they can,' said Mumsie. She pretended that by being emphatic she had made an end of it, but her face was flushed and her head nodded without her being aware of it.

Zip eased from the seat, and took a grip of Mumsie's soft neck. He braced his body against hers and he pushed her head back twice on to the wall. Mumsie's jowls spread upwards because of the pressure of Zip's hand, and trembled with the impact of the wall. Their faces were close, but their eyes didn't meet. The sound of Mumsie's head striking the wall echoed in the kitchen; the mounting for the can opener dug in behind her ear. Mumsie began to weep quietly, without any retaliation. 'Now I tell you again they're not coming,' said Zip. He sat back at the table, and began to turn the cigarette packet top over bottom. Mumsie put her hand to the back of her head for comfort, and her fingers came back with a little blood.

'I swept out the storeroom today, Mumsie,' Zip said. 'I swept out the bloody storeroom when I went to that place twenty years ago, and today I swept it out again. I was doing it when the buyers came and they all went past me and into Ibbetson's office. Ibbetson didn't say anything to me, and neither did any of the buyers. I'm the monkey on a stick.'

'I thought you liked my sister,' said Mumsie. She dabbed at the blood with a paper towel, but Zip didn't seem to notice.

'I'd like to screw her, Mumsie, you know that, but she wouldn't let me, and there's nothing else I want to have to do with her apart from screwing her. She's up herself, your sister.'

'You're just saying it.'

'I'm just saying it and it's the truth. We make a good pair, you and me, Mumsie. We don't take the world by storm. Two stupid people, and if we stopped breathing right now it wouldn't mean a thing.'

'It would to me,' said Mumsie.

'We're dead, Mumsie,' said Zip.

'Don't say that.' Mumsie watched Zip, but he didn't reply. He seemed very relaxed and he looked back at the watching windows, and his eyes jittered. Mumsie didn't like silences: talk was reassuring evidence of life moving on for Mumsie.

'You're that proud,' said Mumsie. 'You're so proud, and that's the matter with you. You'll choke on your pride in the end.'

'You might be right there, Mumsie,' said Zip. 'Most of us could gag on our own pride.'

'You hurt my head then you know. It's bleeding.'

'You're all right. Don't start whining. I'll have to hit Ibbetson's head one day. Mumsie, and then there'll be hell to pay.'

'Oh, don't talk about things like that.'

'It's going to happen. Some day it's bound to happen, and there'll be merry hell to pay.'

'Why can't you just be happy, Zip?'

'I'm not quite stupid enough, more's the pity. I can watch myself; and I don't bloody want to.'

'Let's go into the good room,' said Mumsie. 'We'll push the clothes out of the way and sit in there in the warm.'

'Sure, but first Mumsie we'll have a cuddle in the bedroom. I quite feel like it, so you get your pants off in there and we'll have a cuddle.'

'It's cold in there,' said Mumsie.

'You get your pants off, Mumsie,' said Zip. 'You know what your murderer did to the boatshed girls—shaved their hair all off, so you want to watch out.'

'It's awful. I meant to watch it on the news to see if they've found him.'

'You can't trust anyone but your family, Mumsie. You've got to realize that.'

'I suppose so.'

Mumsie kept on talking so that Zip would forget to tell her again to go into the bedroom and take her pants off. She told him that after Mr

Beresford died the blood came to the surface of his body, so Mrs Rose said, and his face turned black and his stomach too. 'Maybe it was the tar-brush coming out,' said Zip. She told him about Mrs Jardine claiming the family care allowance even though their combined income was over the limit. She told him again that the doorknob had come off in her hand, and about the niece or cousin of Debbie Simpson's who had a growth in her ear and they might have to operate because it was pressing on her brain and making her smell things that weren't really there. 'What a world,' said Zip. He ran his thumb and forefinger up and down the bridge of his nose, and his eyes jittered and their focus point was a little beyond anything in the kitchen. He lit another cigarette, and Mumsie didn't say anything about that, but went on talking about who did Mrs Jardine think she was just because they both worked and she could afford plenty of clothes.

The light was banana yellow, and the windows like glasses of stout, beaded with condensation. Mumsie had a magnetic ladybird on the door of the fridge, and the one remaining leg oscillated as the motor came on. Zip had no question on his face, and his hands lay unused on the table before him. 'Mumsie's going to tell you now that I made some caramel kisses today as a treat,' said Mumsie.

'You're a Queen,' said Zip. 'You're a beaut.'

'And we'll have another cup of tea, and take it through to the good room with the caramel kisses.' Mumsie brought the tin out and opened the lid to display the two layers of kisses. 'They've come out nice and moist,' she said.

'They look fine, Mumsie,' said Zip. 'You know I like a lot of filling in them.'

'I made them after I'd been to the shop,' said Mumsie. 'It'll be warmer in the good room, and the clothes should be dry.'

When the tea was made, Mumsie put it on a tray. She was pleased to be going at last to the good room. She paused at the door. The blood was smudged dry behind her ear. 'Bring in the caramel kisses for me,' she said.

'Sure thing, Mumsie,' said Zip. He heard Mumsie complaining about there being no knob on the good room door.

'This bloody door, Zip,' said Mumsie. Zip cast his head back quickly and made a laughing face, but without any noise.

'All right, Mumsie,' he said. 'I'll come to do it now,' but he stayed sitting there; his hands on the table, his face still once more, and only his eyes jit jittering as bugs do sometimes in warm, evening air.

Michael Morrissey

JACK KEROUAC SAT DOWN BESIDE THE WANGANUI RIVER AND WEPT

Late on Christmas Day Jack Kerouac was hitching through Putaruru with a Maori driving a 1967 Falcon Ute. The town was so quiet—even the Takeaways were closed—that Jack said, 'Are they making a film here?'

'Not in Putaruru,' said the Maori laughing. 'They made an ad here once.'

'They did!'

'Yeah,' nodded the Maori, 'about the end of the world,' his body shaking so violently Jack Kerouac could hear the forty-five cents in his pocket begin to jingle.

'The world isn't going to end,' said Jack Kerouac, 'even though it feels like it.'

'Hang-over?' asked the Maori.

Jack Kerouac stared forlornly at the empty street. 'Any girls in Putaruru?'

'Lots of them,' said the Maori, 'but not this time of year.'

'I'm looking for a grave,' Jack Kerouac said.

'On Christmas Day?—you got it wrong, Pakeha—that's the day he got born—he got buried at Easter.'

'His name's James K. Baxter. I heard he died around these parts.'

'Not in Putaruru,' said the Maori. 'Never heard of him.'

'He wrote a lot of poetry before he died.'

'But not much after he died, eh?' the Maori laughed again.

'I don't think death should stop us doing anything,' said Jack Kerouac.

'There's no red lights on Christmas.' The Maori roared through an amber one. 'What are you doing for a feed?'

'Bottle of Coke, takeaway—that's all I need.' Jack Kerouac looked down at the holes in his blue canvas crêpe shoes.

'You look thin, Pakeha,' the Maori grunted, 'haven't you got anyone to look after you?'

'Course I have,' said Jack Kerouac, 'but mémère isn't here.'

'Who's mémère? A racehorse?' The Maori shook with laughter.

'My mother,' Jack Kerouac's voice froze over.

'O.K.,' said the Maori, 'but you listen to me, Pakeha. I got chicken, eggs, plenty of kai—and lots of beer—how about a feed?'

'I've got to find Baxter first,' said Jack Kerouac.

'He won't feed you though, will he?'

'He'll feed me,' Jack Kerouac flicked his hair, 'he'll feed me.'

The Maori dropped Jack in Taupo.

Jack went into a Takeaway and ordered a Giant burger without the pineapple.

The girl behind the counter was six feet four inches tall and wore unrimmed glasses. As she bent over the vats of bubbling fat her glasses misted over.

Jack Kerouac wondered if she would look beautiful without her glasses.

He imagined her naked with just the glasses on.

Then he took the glasses off.

The muscles of his imagination had to flex, for it was hard work picturing *large* girls naked.

While waiting he noticed the machine in the corner. Walking over, Jack Kerouac peered into the cloudy glass. He saw three plateaus, heaped with ten-cent pieces, grinding slowly back and forth. The stated object was to drop a coin so as to successfully overload the first plateau, thereby nudging a further coin on to the next plateau and so on. The end result was an avalanche of ten-cent pieces.

Jack dropped a ten-cent piece in.

The plateau moved but nothing happened.

Jack Kerouac dropped in a second coin.

Again, no jackpot.

'Honey,' he said to the giant with fogged glasses. 'I need some change.'

'I could do with one myself,' she smiled down at Jack.

'Don't get fresh with me, honey,' snapped Jack Kerouac, 'remember what happened to Primo Carnera.'

'Who?'

'You don't have to worry—he won't come back.'

The girl gave him five more ten-cent pieces.

Jack dropped the coins in one by one without causing a single avalanche.

Then he noticed a sign which read. 'DO NOT TILT OR BANG THE MACHINE.'

'Yippie,' cried Jack Kerouac, banging the machine with his fist.

The lights went out and a bell started ringing.

The giant looked at him through her fogged glasses.

Jack Kerouac felt nervous. He had been beaten up in New York but this was Taupo. He'd heard they were killers in small towns. They blew your head off first and asked your name afterwards. He heard a car outside. Two cops came through the door.

The larger, younger cop looked questioningly at Jack.

Jack wished Neal Cassady was here.

'How are the Russians tonight?' the cop asked.

How are the Russians tonight. Jack Kerouac was terrified. They must think I'm a Communist, he thought. They must be a special squad. They would bundle him into a helicopter and give him a joyride over Tarawera. He would say, 'You can't do this to me, I'm Jack Kerouac. Wait till I tell Neal Cassady.' But that wouldn't cut any ice. They would slide open the door of the helicopter and shove him out. 'Merry Christmas Jack!' On the way down he would think about mémère and his little cat Tyke and feel sad. When he hit the Tarawera she would open her giant belly and Jack would go out like a letter on Caesar's Palace.

But nothing happened.

The cops talked to the giant, got their Whoppaburgers and left.

Jack played for the jackpot again with no luck.

Then a young guy dressed in patched jeans and jandals came reeling in. The whites of his eyes were poultice-yellow. He began telling the giant how he had ton-upped down the wrong side of the road at midnight, tyres ribboning and how when the cops had stopped him, he had laid them out cold as frozen hams . . .

Jack put in another ten-cent piece.

Poultice-eyes came over. 'You want to get rich, mate?'

Jack Kerouac nodded.

'Here's what you do.'

Poultice-eyes banged the machine with his fist.

There was a hard clinking sound that reminded Jack Kerouac of the subways of New York, then several coins came sliding down the chute.

'That's the way you do it, mate,' said Poultice-eyes, collecting the coins.

'Say,' Jack Kerouac flicked back his hair, 'that's my money you've got there.'

'You want to make something of it?'

'No—I just want a few coins back.'

'Get lost pal!'

'I am lost,' said Jack Kerouac, 'I'm looking for Baxter.'

'Who?'

'Baxter.'

'Never heard of him.'

'Have you heard of Jerusalem?'

Poultice-eyes had, but he told Jack Kerouac that there was a lot more action in Taupo.

He reckoned they should have a drink.

They went to the nearest pub and got drunk.

Later on, the giant with fogged glasses joined them.

She took off her glasses and started singing dirty songs, her voice a razzy contralto that made Jack Kerouac's knees tremble.

Afterwards, reeling over the streets of Taupo — no cops in sight—they all lurched back to her flat and made love.

Jack was in the middle.

'This isn't helping me find Baxter's grave,' Jack Kerouac told the mirror next morning.

The mirror winked right back.

Poultice-eyes dropped Jack in the heart of a green nowhere.

By midday he was sitting beside a river.

Not far away he noticed a girl dressed in white overalls. On her hips she carried a bunch of keys, the kind that janitors used to carry.

She did not turn when Jack Kerouac sat down beside her but simply went on staring down into the slowly turning river as though she was totally Nirvana-ed and in a private ecstasy to which no one else was invited.

No one spoke.

But Jack Kerouac was sure their silence was warming up.

He began picking daisies and trying to split their stems to make a chain, but he had bitten his nails down trying to hitch through Hamilton.

'How are your fingernails?' he said at last to the girl.

'Why do you want to know?' she frosted him with her eyes.

'I want to join these fuckers up.'

'They look all right to me,' said the girl.

'Yeah, everything's all right,' said Jack Kerouac softly. He lay back and tickled his throat with one of the unchained daisies. Turning his head he looked at the girl with such vast, dark desolation that even her private river-turning ecstasy was broken into. She seemed to soften a little, her legs bending at the knee.

'I guess those keys unlock many doors,' Jack Kerouac was imagining the girl without her overalls, naked, the big metal keys swinging from her hips.

'Yes,' she said.

'And what's through those doors?'

Rising to her feet and zipping up her overalls the girl led Jack Kerouac to a large white house, half hidden behind trees, ferns and vines. It was cool inside the house, where there were big iron pots and grandfather clocks and little laced cradles devoid of living children.

'Ghost town?' asked Jack Kerouac.

'No,' the girl laughed, her throat was full of muscles.

'God, your neck is beautiful,' said Jack, 'it's full of—'

'The house is well over a hundred years old,' the girl went on.

'Yeah, I know that feeling,' Jack Kerouac said. 'But I'm on fire now. You feel me.'

The girl wheeled at the dark wooden staircase. 'Where are you from?'

'The world— Lowell—but that's not important now. It's where I'm going that's what counts. I'm looking for a grave of a man who never died. He wrote a lot of poetry. His name was Baxter.'

'He could be in the cemetery up the river. I'll drive you there.'

They left the house, got into her car and snaked off down the winding metal road. The ride was full of terror. The road hung over a sheer drop to the river. The girl, driving as though eager to test her theory of reincarnation, told Jack how she had never been inside a city longer than a day. 'So how do you like New Zealand?' she asked nearly skidding the car over a two hundred foot drop.

'I just came through Putaruru,' said Jack Kerouac. 'They were making a film there about the end of the world—I couldn't get a hamburger, no Coke, nothing—so I went on down to Tokoroa and ordered a thickshake and felt sad.'

'Why did you feel sad?'

'I thought about Christmas and Gerard and when I tried to hitch back from Bixby Canyon and couldn't get a ride on Highway No.1, and how I got known as the Buddha who was the Great Quitter—I thought about all that and got sad.'

'Wasn't Buddha always smiling?' the girl asked.

'Yeah, you're right,' said Jack Kerouac, 'but when he was me he cried.'

The girl shot him a Tantric look.

'Why don't we stop the car,' Jack said.

The girl stopped the car on the edge of a cliff and kissed him.

She had a stronger tongue than Jack's so when they parted he felt as though the top of his head had been hit with a tyre mallet from the inside.

Then they got out of the car, lay in the warm grass over the river and made love.

Jack was underneath.

Coming into Jerusalem from the Raetihi side Jack Kerouac didn't get the picturesque view. In the middle of the dusty narrow road was a huge sow.

As Jack climbed out of the car, the sow snorted.

'Okay mother,' Jack Kerouac murmured. 'I know you're a big one.'

He made a mental note that there were no takeaways in Jerusalem. Looking upward he saw the small white wooden church high on the hill. He began walking towards it. As there was no direct path he walked in a zigzag, seemed to get lost, even though he never lost sight of the church. Passing two sheep he got on to a track that led into undergrowth, lost sight of the church, came round to the road again. The sow was about three feet away. She charged. Jack Kerouac vaulted a barbed wire fence and ran straight up towards the church. Again a hedge blocked his way. He wondered what to do next.

'Looking for someone,' said a female voice.

Glancing up Jack saw a woman entirely dressed in white.

'Sister Magdalene,' she said. 'Would you like a cup of tea?'

Jack Kerouac smiled, raising his hand to his brow to shade out the sun that dazzled behind her.

Sister Magdalene took Jack Kerouac inside the convent and gave him a cup of tea, a lamb roast with five different kinds of vegetables, a plate of blood plums, a slice of apple and blackberry pie covering one hundred and ten degrees, then another cup of tea and a dozen date-impregnated scones.

He was scared that the nun was going to ask him if he was Catholic. But she didn't.

'I know what you've come for,' she said.

'You're wise,' said Jack.

The nun looked so satisfied Jack started to feel uncomfortable.

'Okay,' he said rising to his feet, 'where is he?'

'Don't worry,' Sister Magdalene said, 'he isn't far away.'

She took Jack outside and pointed him in the direction of the cemetery.

'He's beyond the graveyard. You go back down there where you came, and come up the path.'

'There's a huge pig down there,' said Jack Kerouac.

'Don't worry,' said Sister Magdalene, 'she hasn't killed anyone yet.'

'Mam, you gave a condemned man the best meal he could have.'

Jack Kerouac went down the path, walking past the sow so coolly the pig took no notice, then up a winding path to where James K. Baxter was buried. Passing car corpses, rusted and overgrown with apple trees, Jack picked an apple and bit into it. It was sour.

He heard a noise behind him.

It was the sow, following him.

'Get along, old mother,' said Jack Kerouac softly.

The sow snorted.

'Okay, watchpig, you come too.'

At the top of the path there was a tethered black goat and a house. On the verandah a group of Maoris sat motionless in the evening twilight. The air was so still that an unbroken pencil of smoke rose from the chimney and went ramrod straight into the pale indigo sky.

The Maoris watched Jack Kerouac as he walked up toward their house.

No one spoke.

Reaching the top of the path, Jack Kerouac saw the solitary gravestone with the single word HEMI written on it.

A dog came over from the verandah and barked at him.

'Watch out,' one of the Maoris called, 'he might take a bite.'

'I taste of blackberry pie and blood plums,' said Jack Kerouac patting the dog's head.

'He wasn't recognised till he died,' said the Maori. 'We lectured together, Hemi and I—you see that stone?—we pulled it out of the river, carried it up here—hand-carved the name out—there was no charge.'

The Maori continued to talk about James K. Baxter as Jack Kerouac sat down in the grass beside the headstone, lay back and looked up at the darkening sky.

From his pocket he drew out *The Rock Woman* and began reading aloud some of the poems.

Jack Kerouac felt something tug at his eye.

It was a tear.

'Merry Christmas,' he said, and once more bit into one of the sour apples, the tears from both eyes running down into a white stream that shone silver in the last rays of the sun as it flowed into the black heart of the Wanganui River.

'Merry Christmas, Jim.'

Witi Ihimaera

BIG BROTHER, LITTLE SISTER

He burst out of the house and was halfway down the street when he heard Janey yelling after him, her cry shrill with panic. He turned and saw her on the opposite pavement, appearing out of the night. As she passed under a street light her shadow reached out like a bird's wing to ripple along the fence palings toward him.

—Go back, Janey, he called.

She cried out his name again, and pursued her shadow across the street. A car screamed at her heels and slashed her with light as she fluttered into her brother's arms.

—I'm coming with you.

She wore a jersey and jeans over her pyjamas. In her hands she was carrying her sandals. She bent down and began strapping them on.

—You'll be a nuisance, Hema grunted. Go home.

He pushed her away.

—No.

She wrapped her arms and legs round him. He wrestled her off and she fell on the pavement.

—Hema, no.

He began running, down that long dark street of shadowed houses towards Newtown. Behind, he could hear Janey chasing after him again.

—Don't leave me, Hema.

He turned. His face was desperate.

—You're too small to come with me, he yelled. Go home, Janey.

In desperation, he picked up a stone and pretended to throw it at her. She kept on running. He picked up another stone.

—Go back, he raged.

—No. No.

She gritted her teeth, closed her eyes with determination and launched herself at him. Hema felt her trembling in his arms. She seemed to shake his rage apart.

—You'll just be a nuisance, he growled.

—Where you go, I go, she said.

Then she looked trustfully at him.

338

Hema had been asleep when Janey began to peck at his dreams. He had turned on his side away from her. She began to shake him.

—Hema.

The two kids slept in the same bed in one of two bedrooms in the flat.

—Hema, wake up.

There was the sound of a crash. Hema sat up. He saw a crack of light under the closed door. Mum and Dad were back from the party. They were quarrelling again.

—Don't be scared, Hema said to his sister.

He went to the door and pushed it open. How long Mum and Dad had been fighting he didn't know. He'd never heard them as violent as this and he had to close his mind against the pain. He went back to the bed and sat on it. Janey crawled into his arms. They watched the light stabbing past the edge of the door and listened as their parents fought.

—Don't you talk to me like that, Wiki, Dad was threatening Mum.

—I'll talk to you any way I like, you rotten bastard.

—And don't you answer me back, Wiki.

—You don't own me, Mum screamed. You and your black bitch, you and her were made for each other. And keep your hands off me. They stink of her. Get away. Get out.

Hema could hear his mother panting and struggling in the bedroom. There was a ripping sound, a helpless woman-cry and a sudden crack of an open hand against her face.

—You bastard, she cried.

She spat into Dad's face. He slapped her again and threw her against the wall. Janey gripped Hema with fright.

—Damn bitch, Dad swore.

Hema saw Dad's shadow cut through the lighted crack of the door. He heard his father walk down the passage to the front door. And he heard his mother's voice, filled with fear.

—No, John, don't leave me. Don't.

Dad laughed. Their mother cried out, ran to the bedroom and began to pull open drawers and throw clothes at Dad, her breath exploding with grief.

—Here then. And here. See if I care.

Dad began to turn the handle to leave. Their mother looked up at him, pleading. Her body became limp.

—You bastard. Well, two can play your game.

She picked up the telephone in the passage. She began to dial a number.

—Taxis?

—Can't wait to get rid of me, ay! Dad was laughing.

Then Mum dialled another number.

—Hullo? Is that you Pera?

Dad's laughter stopped. There was the sound of scuffling in the passage and shapes flicked across the crack in the doorway.

—You been playing around, ay Wiki?

—You're hurting me.

—You and Pera? Ay? Ay?

Hema ran to the door and opened it. Dad had forced Mum against the wall and his hands were squeezing her throat.

—Dad. Mum. Don't.

Dad yelled at him and pushed him back into the bedroom.

—Get back to bed, you damn kid.

The door cracked shut against the faces of his father and of his mother—her face wide with agony and blood streaming from her mouth.

—Leave them alone you bastard, she screamed.

On the other side of the door, Hema and Janey heard her clawing at their father. Then they heard her fall heavily to the floor.

Hema opened the door again. Dad was standing there, his fists clenched, kicking at Mum. Hema tried to shield his mother and lay over her. For a while, his father kept on kicking. Kicking. Until he was exhausted.

Mum leant against the wall. Her face was bruised and covered with sweat and tears. She beckoned Janey. She cradled Janey and Hema close to her.

—You bastard, she whispered to Dad. Don't think we'll miss you. Get out. Get out.

Dad looked at them. His face was grim. He was silent for a while. Then he lurched out of the flat.

Uncle Pera had come to stay.

Janey tugged at Hema's hand. He looked down at her. She was squirming and fidgeting and holding her other hand across the front of her jeans.

—I knew you'd be a nuisance, Hema growled.

—Can't help it, Janey answered lowering her head.

They were just passing Wellington Hospital. A taxi swerved into the kerb in front of them. Hema could see a man inside with a smashed face. As the taxi driver and a woman took the man into the main entrance he began screaming through a red hole where his mouth used to be. Hema pulled Janey away through the crowd of fear-filled bystanders.

—There was a lav a few streets back, he said to Janey. Why didn't you tell me then?

—Because you were in a hurry. And I didn't want to have a mimi till *now*.

—Well you'll just have to wait, Janey.

Newtown was busy. Cars had double-parked all along the main shopping centre impeding the stream of traffic. A trolley bus had snapped its poles, and the showering blue sparks made it appear like a giant red beetle writhing in pain. Along the crowded pavement echoed the voices of people talking in strange languages. The shops spilled their crates of fruit, bolts of cloth and other wares almost to the street. Two small children sold evening newspapers. A Salvation Army band exhorted the passers-by to come to God. A man in a fish shop swung his cleaver and cut off the gaping head of a large grey fish. Crayfish seethed in a tray near him.

A woman haggled over the price of an old cabinet stacked with other junk outside a second-hand mart. Her face was wan and desperate.

—Hema, Janey wailed.

—Hold on just a bit longer, he said.

He pulled her after him through the littered pavement towards the lights at the corner of John Street. He glanced back at the hospital clock. It was still early. Not half past seven yet. Mum and Uncle Pera would be in the pub till ten and afterwards they would go to a party. So there was still plenty of time to get away—even if Janey might slow him up. Not that Mum would miss them. She'd probably be glad they'd gone.

The traffic punched to a stop as the lights turned red.

—Come on, Hema said to his sister.

Car motors revved and roared at them and unblinking headlights watched them cross. Then the lights turned green and the traffic leapt through the intersection into the crush of Newtown's main street.

For a moment, Hema stood undecided on the opposite pavement. No, better not keep to the main road for that would take them past the Tramway Hotel, and Mum and Uncle Pera might be there. Be safer to go up John Street.

—Hema, Janey cried again.

—All right, he answered. Look, there's some trees over there. You better have your mimi there.

Janey rushed into the shadows. Hema kept a look-out. Across the road, fading billboards announced an industrial fair of a month before. Emerald lights were strung across the dead facade of the Winter Show Building.

—Hema, you still there?

—Just hurry up, Janey. Quick, before some people come and catch you.

She hurried out of the trees, hitching up her pants. Hema brushed her down and tucked her clothes in. There were stains on her jeans.

—Eeee! he smiled.

—Well, you told me to hurry, she said.

Quickly they walked along the road. Cars slewed past in a steady stream. A few yards ahead people were arguing on the pavement. They began to fight and a beer bottle smashed on the asphalt. Hema and Janey skirted them, their sandals crunching on broken glass. They hurried on. All along the street the lights from the houses shone down on them.

—Where we going, Hema? Janey asked.

—You'll see.

His mind was working fast. He'd previously planned to make for the railway station and get a ticket for Gisborne. That was where his Nanny George lived. Now that Janey was with him he knew the money he'd saved wouldn't stretch to two tickets. Perhaps he could put just her on the train. Somehow, he would follow after her.

He made up his mind. Yes, that's what he'd do. He couldn't think of anything else to do or anywhere else to go. He told her they were going to the railway station. Her eyes widened.

—Are we going to walk all the way? she asked.

He nodded.

—You said you wouldn't get tired, he said.

Her face set with determination.

—No, I won't get tired, she answered.

Hema grinned at her and she grinned back. They walked on, past the lighted windows, the row of singing windows, toward the city.

When Uncle Pera had come to stay Mum began pushing Hema and Janey away from her. It happened slowly and with only small things at first— Hema, dress Janey for me, ay? Janey, go out and play for a while? You kids do the dishes for Mum? Go away now, kids, because Pera and I want to be by ourselves. Go away. Away. Go.

Janey would be hurt and puzzled. For a time she asked Mum when Dad was coming back. She was confused about the strange man who'd come to live with them. As time went by, she stopped asking her mother about Dad. He was never coming back. Mum had Uncle Pera now.

Actually he was quite nice at first, was Uncle Pera. He seemed to like the kids or be amused by them anyway, as if they were a novelty in his life. But he wasn't interested in them really; only in Mum. Sometimes, when he was fondling her, he would dart them a look of irritation and whisper in Mum's ear.

—Go away, kids, Mum would say. Uncle Pera and I want to be alone now.

Her anxieties about pleasing Uncle Pera began to affect Hema and Janey. They became careful when he was around, treating him with as much caution as their mother did. Trying to please him. Trying to please Mum. Because she seemed happy with this man and wanted him to stay with her.

But he was much younger than Mum. His lips were moist for pleasure and his eyes reckless for fun. Hema felt that one day this man would leave Mum too. Watching her lying in his arms, he would feel sad. Sad enough to hate Uncle Pera. For Hema could see from Mum's eyes and the little nervous things she did that even she knew that one day this man might walk away from her; and Uncle Pera, knowing her fear, would play on it and twist their mother round his finger whenever he wanted to. As the weeks went by he began to twist her tight like a rope. He became bored with the children.

He frowned one night when Janey clambered into Mum's arms. Mum pushed her away. From then on, Janey only went to her mother when Uncle Pera was not around.

—Do these kids have to eat with us? he asked at dinner.

The kids began to have dinner before he came home. Afterwards, watching television in the sitting room, Hema would be aware of his mother's anxious glances at her children. He would take Janey by the hand and lead her to bed.

The happiest times for the children were during the mornings after Uncle Pera had gone to work when Mum was getting them ready for school. In the mornings their mother always kissed them.

—Look after your sister, she would tell Hema.

Once, in a moment of truth, she said to him:

—I'm sorry, son. Your mother was always lousy at picking her men.

She was strong-willed, but not strong enough with Uncle Pera. She was passionate; she needed a man. Perhaps she was frightened of being left alone with her kids. Whatever the case she began doing whatever her man wanted her to do.

—Let's go to the pub, he would say. Let's go to a party. Let's go to the pictures. Let's just go somewhere.

—All right, she would answer.

The long nights of being left at home began for the kids again. They weren't any different from those nights when Mum and Dad would go out except that now, every time Mum walked out the door, the kids felt as if she was leaving them. Mum had Uncle Pera now. They only had each other and could depend only on each other.

Sometimes, while Janey was asleep, Hema would creep to the window-sill and look out. Across the road, he would see people sitting behind lighted windows. He would glance at Janey where she fluttered in her dreams. No. For them there were no lighted windows.

The night cracked open. Through the gap the bikies rode like helmeted harpies with high silver-chromed wings. Their bodies were carapaced with leather and studded with silver and as they shrieked through the dark they trailed black scarves from their necks like clotted blood.

—My feet are sore, Hema.

Hema watched the bikies as they passed. He and Janey had come down Taranaki Street and were at Pigeon Park.

—We'll go and sit over there, he said.

They ran across the busy road. The bikies rumbled into the concrete canyons of the city. Janey sat on a bench and began unstrapping her sandals.

—Let me have a look, Hema said.

He found a small sharp stone in one of the sandals. It had bruised his sister's heel. He rubbed it.

—No wonder your feet are sore, he told her. Never mind. All better now. Why didn't you tell me before?

—I've already been a nuisance.

—Well, we'll have a little rest, Hema said. I'm feeling tired too.

They sat there, watching laughing people walk past and the traffic glittering in the streets. Further along, on another bench, an old man sat with his head hunched between his legs. The ground was stained with his vomit. A group of girls walked past the old man and giggled at him. They giggled again when they passed Hema and Janey.

—I like your maxi coat, one of the girls laughed through her thin painted lips.

Hema flushed, but he didn't really care. The park seemed littered with people like him and he had a strange sense of being part of them.

Then he saw a policeman coming, jabbing at others in the park, hustling them on.

—We'll go now, he said to Janey.

As they hurried away, Hema saw the policeman shake the old man on the nearby bench. The old man fell to the ground. The children passed beneath trees where pigeons cramped themselves tight against one another.

Janey pointed to a bus standing at the corner of Cuba Street.

—We haven't got enough money, Hema said.

—I've got some, Janey answered.

She reached into the pocket of her jeans and showed her brother some coins. Hema smiled at her. Her money would never get them on a bus.

—Better keep it for later, he said to her. Just in case we need it for something else. Okay?

—Okay, she answered.

She grinned proudly and put the coins back in her pocket. At the corner, while waiting for the lights, Hema saw a man thumbing through green notes and stuffing them carelessly into his wallet.

—Now hold on tight, he said to Janey as they crossed the street. I don't want you to get lost. If you lose my hand you stop right where you are and don't move. I'll find you.

Ahead, the pavement was crowded with people. Thrusting through them was like struggling through a land of giants, of people who did not look down or see the boy and his sister.

—Are you holding on tight? Hema asked.

His sister nodded back, scared. Her fingernails dug into his arm. Heavy bodies slammed into Janey as her brother dragged her after him, and loud voices boomed about her.

Along Manners Street the children went. Into Willis Street. From a movie billboard a grim-faced man pointed a gun at them. In a television set in a shop a woman was being stabbed to death. A gaunt youth staggered into them out of a hotel, shouting loudly.

—Hema? Janey cried.

Couldn't people see her down here?

—Just keep holding tight, he said.

They came to another intersection. A thick crowd was waiting to cross. For a brief moment Hema's eye was caught by a beautiful shop display—a family table laid with silverware.

Then the lights changed and the crowd began to move. From the four corners of the crossing they came to merge in the middle and jostle, shove and push their way across the road. Hema felt Janey's hand wrench away from his.

—Hema, she yelled.

He looked back and glimpsed her fluttering in the crowd. He tried to get back to her but the rush of people pushed him along to the pavement. Stragglers were dashing across the street. The lights were changing. The cars were beginning to move. Janey was still standing there, turning round and round looking for him, alone, in the middle of the street. Round and round. As if she was a bird in a cage. Looking.

—Janey.

She heard him calling and saw him. Her eyes lost their frightened look and filled with trust. He rushed out from the pavement and put his arms tightly round her. The traffic roared on both sides of them and drivers were shouting and horns were booming but he didn't care. Then a car braked in front of them. The traffic came to a stop.

—Get your sister off the road, boy, a voice called.

He picked Janey up in his arms and carried her to the pavement. He heard a bystander mutter something about mothers who let their children roam the streets at night. He felt eyes piercing him like sharp needles.

—You told me to stay right where I was if I lost your hand, Janey said.

Hema looked down at her. He nodded.

—Come on, he said. Not far to go now.

They hurried down Lambton Quay. Department store windows gleamed with rich brilliance. Behind the glass-paned window of a coffee bar a man jabbed at a blood-red steak with a fork.

It happened slowly at first, their mother pushing them away from her, but it increased as Mum's life twisted more and more around Uncle Pera. Her kids were her own—she owned them—but she did not own her man. Some need for security made her attempt to possess him and, in the attempt, she pushed her children further into the background of her life. They became as unsure of her as they were of Uncle Pera, trying to read the signs that flickered across her face. Once they thought they'd known everything they needed to know about Mum. The signs became strange, clouded and opaque. It wasn't that she didn't love them anymore; it was just that possessed as she was with Uncle Pera she became more and more like him. Her moods were inconsistent. Sometimes she would laugh and play with her kids; at other times she would growl them or appear not to notice them. At one moment she would kiss them; the next moment she would lash out at them with a harsh word or hand. They could never tell with their mother now.

Once, Hema had returned home late from school. He'd asked his mother where Janey was. She said that Janey was probably sulking somewhere. Mum had given her a thrashing.

Hema had known instantly where Janey would be. He'd gone into the bedroom and looked under the bed.

—Come out, Janey, he had said. No use crying.

—Mum hit me.

—She didn't mean to.

—Yes she did. She hit me.

He'd crawled under the bed and put his arms round her. Although Hema consoled her, he'd felt Janey was comforting him too. He had thought of his mother and realized he and Janey were secure only in each other.

—Look after your sister, Mum would say.

Always those words even when Mum and Uncle Pera were home.

—We're having a party tonight, Hema. *Look after your sister.* Uncle Pera and I want to watch television. *Look after your sister.* We want to be by ourselves. *Look after your sister.*

His mother had always been careless about keeping the flat clean. After Uncle Pera came she was more careless. Hema had begun making the breakfast for himself and Janey, washing their clothes, doing the dishes and sweeping the floor. Sometimes his mother noticed, sometimes she didn't. Not that it mattered. It had to be done. Mum was too busy enjoying herself. As long as she was happy, Hema was happy too.

Yet he could not help wondering whether or not she was really happy. He wondered constantly what his mother really meant to Uncle Pera. Whenever parties were held at the flat Uncle Pera would often flirt with other women—kissing them, fondling them—and treat Mum with amusement. Mum would drink more, sit on other men's laps and her eyes would glitter with despair. Hema would watch her sometimes through a crack in the bedroom door. She was very pretty and gay. Yet when she danced by herself while everyone else clapped and told her to dance faster she looked so desperate and haggard—her hair swinging free, sweat dripping down the neck of her dress, thighs grinding and face given to the passion of the dance—that he would feel ashamed of her. He would look at the others in the room and wish they would go away and leave Mum alone. That Uncle Pera would go away and leave her alone too.

The morning after, the children would clear up the debris of the party. They would sweep the floor, wash the glasses, stack all the flagons downstairs in the hall, set the chairs in their places and open the windows to get rid of the smell of stale cigarettes and spilt beer. More and more often they would find their mother flaked out wherever she'd fallen—on a chair, on the floor or across the sofa. Uncle Pera, he always made it between the blankets.

—Come to bed, Mum, Hema would whisper. Come on.

He would shake her gently. Her eyelids would flicker and then shut again.

Sometimes Hema and Janey would be able to pull her to bed. Other times she'd be too drunk to move, so they would get some blankets and tuck them in round her. If she'd been sick, Hema would wipe the stains from her lips with a towel.

—Poor Mum, he would say.

Once, she had heard him and looked at him and her face had screwed up with sorrow.

—You're good kids, she'd whispered. Too good for a rotten thing like me. I'm sorry.

She wasn't rotten; she should never feel sorry for the way she was. She was Mum. Her children loved her. If anyone was rotten it was her man. He did not love her the way they did.

Fists thudded in a sudden fight outside the main entrance of the railway station. Two men argued over ownership of a taxi at the rank. Within the pillared shadows thin faces gleamed.

—At last, Janey said.

The station was crowded. It was half past eight. Late night shoppers rushed to catch their units to the Hutt or Porirua. Above the clamour, the loudspeaker announced departure times, platform numbers, welcomes and farewells to passengers. Everyone seemed to have a place to go, a destination.

—You wait here, Hema told Janey.

He sat her on a bench next to a middle-aged Maori woman. The woman looked at them with eyes shattered by tiredness.

—What are you going to do? Janey asked.

He told her. Her eyes glistened.

—I'm not going on the train without you, she said.

—We've only got money enough for one ticket, he answered.

—I don't care, she said stubbornly. I won't go without you.

He pulled her out of the railway station. He shook her and tried to explain to her why she had to go on the train by herself. Then he took her back to where the Maori woman was sitting. Janey put an arm around his neck.

—You got to do what I say, he said.

He walked towards the ticket office and joined one of the queues. Every now and then he looked back at Janey. Would she be all right travelling by herself? Would she? What if. . . .

—Yes?

The voice boomed at Hema from behind thick glass. A bored face looked down at him.

—Please, can I have a ticket for Gisborne, please.

—For where? the face asked.

—Please, Gisborne.

—When for?

—Tonight, please.

—No trains go to Gisborne tonight.

The concourse shuddered beneath his feet. A unit roared into the station. An old man tripped and fell. Two youths swore at a woman who had bumped them.

Hema looked back at the man behind the thick glass. The man's face was curious.

—Where you sitting, sonny?

—Over there.

The face looked towards Janey and the woman sitting next to her. It became thin.

—Why didn't your mother come to get the ticket herself? I've better things to do than muck around with kids.

He waved Hema away.

—No trains tonight, he told Janey.

She tried not to smile too much.

—What do we do now? she asked.

—I'll think of something, he answered. Are you hungry?

Janey gave him a guarded look.

—Have we got enough money? she asked.

—Enough.

—Are *you* hungry?

—A bit.

—Well, I'm a bit hungry too then, Janey said.

They went into the station cafeteria. Hema bought a pie to take away. They went outside the main entrance steps. People ebbed and flowed around them. Then they returned to the seat they had left and sat down.

Hema closed his eyes. Nowhere to go. Nowhere.

—I wouldn't have gone without you, Janey whispered. You could have hit me but I wouldn't have gone. Where you go, I go.

Hema grinned at her.

—I knew you'd be a nuisance, he said.

He saw a couple dragging a stubborn child towards the train. The man muttered to the boy and then raised his hand and hit him.

And Hema felt as if Uncle Pera was hitting him again and put his hands across his body to protect himself from the blows.

Last night. Hema, Janey and Mum, sitting in the kitchen having tea. Mum's face was tight and her hands kept smoothing down her dress, moving down her thighs and up again, brushing the room with tension.

—Mum . . . Hema had begun.

—Just eat your kai, she answered.

The night before, she and Uncle Pera had argued. He was tired of her, he said. He was pissing off.

Yet he'd rung up that day to say he was coming back. Tonight. He'd just wanted to teach Mum a lesson, he'd said. Just to let her know he was boss. Did she want to see him? Oh yes, she'd crooned. Yes. Yes.

Now, they were waiting for him. Hema was feeling sick at his mother's weakness for this man.

The door opened downstairs. Mum gave a cry and ran down the steps to her man. He was drunk. She didn't care. He saw Hema and Janey sitting in the kitchen.

—Go to bed now, Mum said. Look after your sister, Hema.

Her voice was deep-throated with happiness.

—Didn't you hear your mother? Uncle Pera growled.

The kids hadn't finished their dinner. Hema began clearing the table. Behind him, he could hear Mum kissing this man, and when he turned he saw Uncle Pera's hand squeezing her buttocks. Tears spilled in his eyes.

—Why didn't you just stay away, he yelled. You don't love my mother. You'll never look after her.

—Get to bed, Mum hissed. Take Janey with you.

He turned on her.

—Why don't you look after Janey yourself, Mum. And me, too. Tell him to go, Mum. Tell him.

His mother recoiled from his words.

—We don't want you, Hema yelled at Uncle Pera. Janey. Mum. Me. We can look after ourselves.

But Mum had not understood. She had not seen Hema or Janey. Her eyes were filled only with the man standing next to her.

—Get out, she'd screamed at Hema.

—No.

—Do as your mother says.

—You're not my father. I don't take orders from you.

Uncle Pera had pulled him along the passage. Mum was saying to him:

—The kid doesn't mean it, Pera. He doesn't mean it.

Janey ran to Mum and hid her face in Mum's dress.

—Pera, no, Mum pleaded.

—He needs a lesson, Uncle Pera answered. He needs to know who's boss around here.

Uncle Pera had taken off his belt. Just before he began to thrash Hema with it, he kicked the door closed.

—Mum, Hema had called.

The door was closing on her face. She did not come to stop this man. She did not come to her son. She did not. . . .

The *pain*. He held his body tight against the blows. All he could think of was his mother, standing there, not helping him. Only two hours afterwards had she come, from the bedroom she shared with her man.

—Don't interfere, she said. You only get hurt if you interfere.

She'd reached out to caress him.

—Don't touch me.

—Try to understand, Hema.

—Don't touch me.

They'd gone out later, Mum and Uncle Pera. Janey had crawled into Hema's arms. Hema had cradled her softly.

—Mum doesn't need us any more, he'd said. She doesn't need me. She let that man give me a hiding. She let him.

They had sat there, watching train after train pull out of the station, carriage after carriage of lighted windows flowing past like dream after dream. Now, a newspaper scraped across the concourse floor. The station was becoming a derelict place strewn with cigarette butts, spilled food, lolly wrappers, ripped magazines—all the rubbish discarded by people during their passage through the station. The stalls in the concourse had closed for the night. Only a few people remained—an old man, three youths, and a young girl with her boyfriend in the darkness of a railway platform. A late night porter whistled his way across the concourse. He cast a curious look at Hema and Janey.

—We can't stay here, Hema said.

—I'm cold, she answered.

Mum had just stood there. She'd let that man give him a thrashing. She'd let him.

—Do you think Mum will be home yet? Janey asked.

—Too early, Hema answered.

And when she got home and saw they weren't there she would cry out their names and run from room to room and down into the street looking for them, looking, looking. . . .

—Where shall we go, Hema?

She got off the bench and began rubbing her legs.

There was no place to go. There was no use running away.

—We can't stay here, ay Hema?

He began to think of his mother. Love for her overwhelmed him. Their mother was a weak woman. She needed people. One day, when all others had left her, she might need Hema and Janey again.

—We'll go back. Hema said.

—Home?

Home. Yes, life with Mum was home. He and Janey would have to make the best of it. Home was here, in this place, now.

He took his sister's hand. They walked out of the railway station. Janey shivered. The city was not yet dark but it was so quiet—a waste land punctured with street lights. Just outside the station was a police car.

Janey clutched Hema tightly. She was like a little bird seeking his shelter.

—You'll never leave me, ay Hema?

—No, he answered. Not now. Not ever.

They hurried through the night. A patrol car screamed along the street. A star burst across the sky. The lights of the city tightened round them.

Bill Manhire

THE POET'S WIFE

The poet looks at the poet's wife and says: You are my best poem. Did I ever tell you that?

The poet's wife looks at the poet. And you are my best poet, she says. Giving a little laugh. Thinking a little thought.

The point is this, he says.

*

Years ago, before the poet's wife was, strictly speaking, the poet's wife, she wrote a little poem. She was so sick of holding open refrigerator doors. She was so sick of it all.

> dedum dedum dedum dedum
> out where Kapiti lies
> like a dark mummy on the horizon
> forever unwrapping its bandages
> into the future . . .

She took it to the poet, who read it aloud in that special voice of his.

When I put in the bandages, she said, I was thinking of clouds.

The poet said: Would you like to move in with me and we could talk about books and stuff?

*

She is sick of his talk of Douglas Bader's legs. She thinks: Probably some people might be impressed. But I know better.

*

Would their life together be significantly better if the poet's book royalties were put towards an annual holiday? A holiday for them both.

No it would not be better.

Last year, the poet's royalties were $43.75.

*

In fact, holidays aside, the poet has a job that brings in plenty of money.

She has no idea what kind of job it is. It takes him out of the house each day, the way jobs do, and sometimes he wears walk-shorts.

*

The poet is working on his opera libretto, CARNAGE ON THE ROADS.

Don't hover! he says to his wife.

Am I hovering? says the poet's wife

Yes, you are. Hovering.

Sorry, says the poet's wife.

It's just that it's extremely difficult with you hovering like that. I had something really good coming and I lost it.

*

He is actually a geography teacher and assistant careers adviser in a large North Auckland school. All he can do is warn.

*

The poet's wife reads a magazine at the hairdresser's. An article catches her eye: DANGEROUS LOVERS.

You could be looking for love in all the wrong faces. You could be ignoring the warning signs that you're romancing Mr Wrong.

I wonder, wonders the poet's wife, if he is a Don Juan or a Mother's Boy, an Obsessive Possessive or a Danger to Shipping? Or are poets different, like they say?

*

She watches a television documentary about lighthouse keepers. The loneliness. The isolation. The children taking correspondence courses. She tries to feel God in her muscles, but there is no sign of him.

*

The poet judges a poetry competition. He awards the $150.00 first prize to a poem about refrigerators written by an entrant with the pen name, Rumpelstiltskin. The poet receives a $500.00 judging fee. It is good the way everything is getting on to a proper professional basis he thinks. He spends his fee on personalised number plates. Now the number plates on his car say: POET 7.

Six other poets have had the number plate idea before him. They all live in Dunedin. The Dunedin school.

The poet does not live in Dunedin. He lives in his imagination.

*

The poet's wife watches a television programme about two brave elderly stroke victims. One has lost the use of her left arm, one her right. They play the piano together, each using her one good arm. They are helping each other to turn adversity into harmony.

*

Reach for the Sky. Still one of the great titles. This is only the poet's opinion, but he thinks it is a good one.

*

In the newspaper she reads about a two-headed baby which has been born in Tehran. The baby's body is outwardly almost normal, except for a third short arm. Internally, it had two hearts and four lungs, a main stomach and a sub-stomach. Each head has its own neuro system. The baby's movements are not harmonious. While one head cries, the other may be sound asleep.

*

Well, wonders the poet's wife, AM I romancing Mr Wrong?

*

The poet's wife once had a job as a woman opening refrigerator doors. It was on television advertisements mostly, in the early days of television, though also some magazines, and sometimes there were trade displays, up on a stage, it was quite hard work actually, though it did take you round the country. This is how the poet first saw her—on television, opening a refrigerator door, in the days before colour.

*

The poet's wife hums and puts on the kettle. The poet is at a literary festival in Hamilton—reading his poems, and presenting the winning cheque to 'Rumpelstiltskin'. Soon he will be home again.

A small cloud on her horizon. What if 'Rumpelstiltskin' turns out to be a woman and not a grotesque little man? What if 'Rumpelstiltskin' is . . . beautiful?

*

The telephone rings. It is a journalist who is writing an article on poets' wives—from the angle of the wife, of course. He has come to feel a lot of sympathy for poets' wives in the course of his researches. He wonders if they can set up an interview?

How do you mean, says the poet's wife.

Just talk and that, says the journalist. He has a soft Irish brogue.
Will I or won't I? thinks the poet's wife.

*

He writes: 'There's a tree, one of many, of many one . . .' Then scores out
the line with a practised scoring movement.

*

He reads Osip Mandelstam. In his sleep he cries: Nadezda!

*

She looks out of the window. Grey day. The grey before rain, the grey
after rain.
    The whole garden seems to sag, like a hammock sunk in the earth,
slung between two stumpy lemon trees. Neither of them exactly covered
with fruit.
    A simile, thinks the poet's wife.
    She claps her hands in excitement. A simile!

*

He tells the pretty girl that he likes to rescue words—take them by the
arm and lead them to some unlikely place, where they tend to look more
interesting.
    How do you mean? says 'Rumpelstiltskin'.
    Like putting a boy from Dunedin on the streets of New York, says the
poet, in a voice which indicates this is his final word on the matter.

*

Riff-raff: he cannot get the word out of his head. Dunedin riff-raff. He
looks it up in the OED. Persons of a disreputable character or belonging
to the lowest class of a community. Persons of no importance or social
position. Unlearned rifraffe, nobodie. There were a good many riff-raff
in the upper gallery. The riffe-raffe of the scribbling rascality. The Rabble
or Scum of the People, Tagrag and Long-tail. A collection of worthless
persons. Odds and ends. Trumpery; trash; rubbish. A hurly-burly, a
racket; a rude piece of verse.
    Ah, thinks the poet, there is the title of my next book.

*

He has become interested in Douglas Bader's legs because Douglas
Bader's widow wants to sell one of them. It says so in the newspaper.

*

One day the poet's wife writes a poem:

> Out where Soames Island
>   like a dark tape recorder
>   endlessly unwinds its reels
>   into the unrecorded storm

Stepping the lines down like that. Covering several pages.

*

The poet reads one of his recent poems in the foyer of the Founders Theatre in Hamilton:

> Out where Rangitoto lies
> like a dark breast
> forever bearing its nipple
> to the insatiable city . . .

The applause, he guesses, is somewhere between perfunctory and reluctant. He catches Rumpelstiltskin's eye. Ah! Would it be fair to call that an adoring gaze?

*

I hope he is not a TRAVELLING MAN, thinks the poet's wife.

Away from home a married man becomes a travelling man. He can take off his wedding ring. A salesman can become a company president, a company president can become a poet, a poet can become an All Black. The warning signal is seen through fog. By falling for this fellow, you are seduced by a phantom: he is no longer visible when he leaves town.

The Travelling Man can be a particularly Dangerous Lover.

*

Toynbee. The poet is on fire for her. Toynbee is Rumpelstiltskin's real name. The poet's lines flame with her being. She is the match which sets imagination alight.

He starts a little poem:

> Here she comes, with her
> Douglas Bader eyes,
> scanning the clouds
> & wild enemy skies.

But he will probably throw it away. Something tiresome about the rhyme.

*

Why only one, anyway? What has happened to the other leg? Is it lost? Is she hanging on to it for some reason? These are the sort of questions which pass through the poet's head.

*

The poet leaves his wife and goes to live with Toynbee. A big decision, but he makes it. He writes romantic passages about clouds and a few somewhat bitter lines about his wife. None of it much good. All I can do is warn, he thinks. All I can do is warn.

*

The poet's wife joins a support group for poets' wives. There are hundreds of members in the larger organisation, with branch offices all over the country.

*

She meets a woman who is now married to a stockbroker. And then there is another woman who goes around with a man who owns a whole chain of boutiques in the South Island. Her mind drifts off on the cloudy winds of envy . . .

Begorrah! (She has just remembered the Irish journalist.)

*

The poet receives an invitation to a writers' festival in Dunedin. All expenses paid. Just after the August holidays.

*

'Throw your heart over the bar, and your body will follow.'

The poet's wife reads this in a book. Because she is the kind of person who fumes and frets a lot, she keeps turning to a chapter called 'Stop Fuming and Fretting'. It tells her that she needs the peace of God in her muscles, in her joints. Then she will stop fuming and fretting.

The book says: Speak to your muscles every day and to your joints and to your nerves, saying: 'Fret not thyself' (Psalm xxxviii.i.) Think of each important muscle from head to feet, and say to each: 'The peace of God is touching you.'

*

The point is this, the poet says to her on the telephone.

But then he says nothing.

*

That wasn't you in those refrigerator ads, was it? says the journalist. Back in the 60s when television was just starting up? I was straight off the boat. By God, you were the first good thing I saw.

*

The journalist moves in with the poet's wife. The first good thing I saw. His word processor comes with him. Several nights a week they go to the pub. One day the journalist writes a poem:

> Dedum dedum dedum dedum
> Out where Stewart Island lies
> like an old refrigerator
> opening and opening its door
> upon the vastness of Antarctica. . . .

He looks her straight in the eye. So there you are then, he says. You are still a poet's wife.

*

The poet travels to Dunedin. He steps up to the podium—his eye in a fine frenzy rolling. I am the prince of clouds, he thinks, I ride out the tempest and laugh at the archer. He thinks: The Burns Fellowship. He thinks: Riff-raff. He thinks: All I can do is warn.

*

They make love, a strenuous bout.

Afterwards, the poet's wife draws a rectangle; in it she draws two lines which intersect to form a cross. Guess what it is, she says.

A window? says the journalist.

No.

A parcel?

No.

What, then?

A short story, she says. With a trick ending.

*

The poet's wife sits at the word processor. Her fingers fly over the keys. Now what is that? A simile? Of course not. Perhaps a cliché? Or—an image of transcendence?

*

The poet explains how he used to be fascinated by the idea of a poop deck—phrase itself seemed naughty. He imagined a deck covered in . . . well, not to put too fine a point on it . . . poop. But looking back . . . looking back, he can see the first stirrings of the poet there. That interest in language—the young boy sniggering in the playground—in love with the sea, in love with his native tongue . . .

Stop me, he says, if this is boring you. Or if it isn't the sort of thing you want.

No, says the *Landfall* interviewer. No not at all. She smiles behind her hand.

*

The journalist stands on the roof of the house. For a while he stares down at the garden: one rhododendron, two lemon trees. Other houses in the distance. Is he going to jump? Of course not. He is going to fall. My beautiful one! he cries. My icebox girl! My mistress of the lonely voice . . .

Ian Wedde

THE GRINGOS

The Gringos, a former rock and roll band of the nineteen fifties, seldom met these days. When they did it was by accident. Though none of them now played professionally they'd all kept their gear, with the exception of Nigel who'd sold his kit after the band's break-up because he'd felt stupid playing the drums by himself especially when his wife was listening.

But he still had his suit and since his attachment to performing days had increased over the years he'd also guarded those potent accessories: two pairs of blue suede ripple soles, a couple of chunky rings set with huge fake rubies, some velvet Mississippi string ties.

He was pretty sure the other Gringos had hung on to their clobber too. In their heyday they'd had a band suit: a midnight blue three-quarter length jacket shot with silver lurex, shoulders padded right out, wide scarlet silk lapels plunging to a single button at navel level, a scarlet Edwardian waistcoat with a rich paisley pattern, pegleg pants with a zipper on the inside of each ankle, blue silk shirts with a foam of blue lace on the front and scarlet piping on the cuffs. The Gringos had been good enough to afford this number and they'd played anywhere there was a hop between Christchurch and Invercargill, though Dunedin was their base and summer at Caroline Bay in Timaru what really took care of the brass.

There, they'd got the cops out more than once as local bodgies and yahoos packed dances to pick fights with kids on holiday at Caroline Bay. Of course The Gringos got the blame, or rock and roll did. But they played four summers anyway. In those days there was no bullshit. The lead guitar's pickup went straight into the amp and the metallic music came straight back out again. The two saxophones blew right in the faces of rock and rolling kids. The Gringos' bass went electric long before that was common, but he still marched it up and down, solid and even, that split-second ahead of the beat, the notes sliding out from under the guitar's syncopation.

From time to time they used a second guitar, but they found it complicated the music too much. Then there was Nigel with his basic kit: snare, foot-bass, hihat, one tomtom to the side, and one cymbal, a pair of seldom-used danceband brushes, and a rack of hickory clubs. The rim of the snare was battered, the paint and chrome flaking off down the side. But he wasn't just a walloper. If Pete had the knack of keeping his marching bass just an eyelid-bat ahead of the beat, Nigel had an equally necessary talent for staying that split-second behind: this was what gave the music its truculence: 'shootin' the agate'.

After the old rock and rollers stopped being heard—those endlessly interchangeable pros who blasted away behind Chuck Berry and Bo Diddley and even Elvis Presley—Nigel thought the only rock drummer who got close was Charlie Watts of the Rolling Stones. But he didn't listen to much 'modern' rock music. After The Gringos stopped playing there didn't seem to be much point in listening either. And after about two and a half minutes of any rock track he listened to these days he kept hearing a coda asking to be played, some final chop, a chord that would stamp down like a shoe on a cigarette butt. But the music went on, *nah nah nah*, like jazz. He didn't like jazz, never had. Years back a friend had tried to get him to listen to Charlie Parker.

'That's bullshit, mate. The bastard doesn't know shit from clay.'

It was Chuck Berry from the start and it was still Chuck Berry as far as he was concerned when the band broke up. A few years later he'd listened in disbelief as a new English group called The Beatles sang 'Roll Over Beethoven'. The music had been ironed out a bit, he could hear how the equipment had changed, but it was the old Chuck Berry number all right.

Only it wasn't the same. Why he felt like this he didn't know. When he thought about it he decided it was because he wasn't playing any more. When he talked to the band they said the same. Also Lorraine didn't like rock and roll any more. She said it was all right when you were a kid, but. . . .

But *he* could remember her dancing back then in 1959.

It had occurred to him that The Gringos lasted only a short professional time: '56 to '59. It was a thought whose meaning he couldn't catch. The *real* time was more than four years. Here he was in '73, he had one kid who'd be leaving school soon, and two more as well, he had a house up Brockville and an okay job with Cooke Howlison, it was fifteen years since The Gringos had played 'Maybellene', the last song they played as a band, Chuck Berry's first hit, their homage to Chuck. But *then* was still the most important time in his life.

'It was okay when we were kids,' said Lorraine.

And his son, who was fourteen, said he liked the old records but it made him laugh to think of his dad playing in a rock and roll band at Caroline Bay in Timaru.

'I can't imagine it.' Ha ha.

All the same the boy would skite to his friends. Sometimes a bunch of them would turn up, look at Nigel, and listen to some of his collection: 'Maybellene', 'Johnny B. Goode', 'Sweet Little Sixteen', 'Memphis'. Then he'd play them Little Richard, Elvis, and even Muddy Waters. The records were scratchy and worn. Down in the basement rumpus room of his house he longed to put on his gear and show them what it had been like. They stood around, amused, *listening*. He played his collector's item, a recording of Chuck Berry from the film *Jazz on a Summer's Day* at the 1958 Newport Jazz Festival, a performance of 'Sweet Little Sixteen' with Jack Teagarden's trombone blasting in behind. It made him sweat. He wanted to say, 'It took over, see?' They jigged awkwardly, shifting their feet. Then he'd play 'Rock and Roll Music' or 'Roll Over Beethoven', knowing what was going to happen, and sure enough one of the kids would always say, 'But that's a Beatles' song. . . .'

When he went back upstairs with his records carefully under his arm they'd put on Osibisa or The Moody Blues or Grand Funk Railroad or for fucksake Simon and Garwhatsit. It was rubbish. He'd hear the *clok* of pool balls on the miniature table and from time to time the fizz of aerosol freshair as they doused their cigarette smoke with Pine Fragrance.

At fifteen he'd been a chippy's apprentice and smoking a packet of cigarettes a day. He couldn't afford it. But like everything else it had to be done with style. You spent hours practising, letting the smoke dribble from your lips and back again up your nostrils. You practised lighting matches inside the open half of a matchbox. Kidstuff. . . .

It was no coincidence that The Gringos all had similar jobs. Nigel was a warehouseman. So were two of the others. The other two were clerks. They were all married. They all lived in suburbs near Dunedin. So it was natural that they all got home on a certain day and saw a photograph of Chuck Berry on the front page of the evening paper, and all reached to ring each other up for the first time in months or in some cases years. It took a while before any of them was able to get through the scramble of lines. And then, as if by telepathy, there was nothing to say.

'D'ja. . . .'

'Yeah it's. . . .'

'When I got home. . . .'

No sooner had Nigel hung up, heart thumping, than the phone rang again.

'Hey, d'ja see. . . .'

'Yeah Chuck. . . .'

'Inna paper. . . .'

'Fuck me dead. . . .'

They met in the pub. What had happened? Where had the time gone? They went over a half-forgotten litany of names and dates and places. They remembered songs. They swallowed tears.

The day before the concert Nigel gave in to a nagging temptation. In the bedroom he took a large box down from the top of the wardrobe and from it he carefully lifted out The Suit. It was wrapped in tissue and then polythene and had been impregnated with thymol crystals. The Shirt was there too. He hadn't got it all out for so long he'd forgotten the texture and feel of the heavy cloth. It was perfectly preserved. He held the jacket up by the shoulders. He felt furtive and exalted. Quickly he buttoned himself into The Shirt with its chemical smell and its frenzy of lace. The neck button wouldn't do up. No matter, he'd. . . .

Sitting on the edge of the bed he undid the inside zips of the trousers and stepped in pointing his toes like a dancer. In spite of their generous forward pleats he couldn't get the trousers past the tops of his thighs. They'd have to be altered.

Spreading his legs to hold the pants up as far as they'd gone, he grunted into The Jacket. Though cut to drape full and free, tapering not to the waist but to a point below his backside, The Jacket crushed his armpits and wouldn't button. Lorraine could let it out for sure.

Keeping his legs spraddled, his arms held out from his trunk by the crushing jacket, he pushed his feet into the Blue Suedes. They fitted.

He shuffled sideways to the wardrobe mirror. There he saw a fat-faced man of forty with a shit-eating smile, whose hair, still black, had receded from his temples along the path the comb still took it, straight back. The fat man's hornrim glasses had slipped a little down his nose. He was standing with his trousers half up like someone caught having a nasty in a bus shelter. Between the straining buttons of a lacy blue shirt came tufts of black chest hair. The man's arms were held out sideways. The bottoms of his trousers were concertina'd against the insteps of blue shoes whose scarlet laces trailed on the floor.

Skip the waistcoat.

'Jesus Christ. . . .'

But he stood outside the town hall with a dry mouth and a pounding happy heart. The other Gringos were there too with their wives. That made ten altogether. They felt like a club. It was a cold spring evening. The rest of the crowd was mostly young. The Gringos felt conspicuous but proud. They exchanged derisive glances as the crowd whooped it up. Some of *them* had got dressed nineteen fifties style: there were kids of nineteen and twenty with makeshift duck's-arse hairstyles and there was even one beautiful girl wearing pedal pushers, a sweater and a pony tail, and bright red lipstick. Nigel's eyes wandered her way. He wondered if she could rock and roll. It was certainly news to him that Chuck Berry was still appreciated or was being appreciated again. Lots of these kids were only a few years older than his own son! What did they know about the old style?

'The old style . . .': he caught at the phrase as it sidled through his mind. Then they were going in. He was still examining the phrase as they took their seats. The ten of them sat in a row. All around was the racket of a young excited audience. But no dance floor. A *town hall*. Like for concerts, the symphony orchestra.

He was still thinking 'the old style' when the backing group came on: guitar, bass, drums, electric piano. They powered straight into some standards beginning with 'Johnny B. Goode' and going without a pause into Little Richard's 'Awopbopaloobop'. It was deafening. The amps were six feet high. There was wire all over the stage. The bass player kept getting off licks like cracks of thunder which jabbed at Nigel's ears. He could *feel* it in his guts. The guitarist and singer had beanpole legs. He banged his knees together as he sang and played. He appeared to be chewing at the micro-phone. You couldn't really hear what he said. The audience sat somewhat sullenly.

Then there was a pause. There were groups chanting 'Chuck Chuck Chuck!' It just wasn't like rock and roll. The Kiwi backing group came on again and began tuning up. They looked scared. The phrase 'old style' was still whining away in Nigel's ears which he felt had been damaged by the preceding hour of noise. He watched the drummer up there as he straightened out his kit. He had about twice as much gear as Nigel had ever played with. For a start he had two tomtoms mounted on the foot-bass and another to the side as well. Then he had a total of four cymbals including a sizzle and not counting the hihat. What for? You didn't need it. Nigel admitted the joker was quick and fancy. But he couldn't play rock and roll. He was whipping the music along like a jockey taking his nag away in the home straight but what you wanted to get into rock and roll was slouch, you had to shoot the agate. You had to feel the slug of it like the sexy split-second between the thud of a girl's heart and the squirm of the artery in her neck, her breath gasping as she swings back under your arm, catching her flying hand as she goes past again, then rocking back in close. Or it was like not letting a fuck accelerate away with you before the lights changed, yeah. . . .

This thought struck him as original. Leaning sideways to confide it to another Gringo he missed Chuck Berry's entry. When he heard the crowd go mad he looked up and saw a lean wolfish Negro wearing a check shirt and narrow peglegs grinning back over his shoulder as he slung his guitar and moved across to the electric piano to tune. This he did with such care and absorption, moving from member to member of the backing group, that the audience thought it was a put-on and began to howl.

But The Gringos knew better. Nigel was sweating but he sat like a boulder. The wolfish man struck a few elegant licks off his guitar. The sound was simple and familiar. The amps had been turned right down but he waved to turn them down further.

Then he cracked off a couple more licks with a bit more velocity behind them, grinned, rode rubber legs to the front of the stage and all at once was into 'Reelin' and Rockin'' while The Gringos sat petrified in their seats three-quarters of the way back from the stage of the town hall with all around them a howling audience of kids not much older than their own.

At one point as Chuck lolloped into 'Too Pooped to Pop' a group in front of The Gringos struggled out into the aisle with a banner which read 'We love you Chuck'. They ponced round the front of the stage with it and back down the next aisle. Chuck Berry acknowledged this gesture with an ironical double-take. But the music rode on. He swung his gat arm knocking the steely chords off the instrument as though brushing lint from a coat. He rode one heel across stage, the other leg stretched out in front. He did a pretty good splits and never stopped playing. Lowering the guitar between his legs he shot wads of sound into the audience which was by now dancing wildly in the aisles, not rock and roll, just. . . .

But The Gringos sat without moving, as though turned to stone. They didn't miss a thing. They noted the glances Chuck shot at the electric piano player who couldn't rock the instrument. Nigel noted with satisfaction the looks Chuck sent from time to time in the direction of the drummer who was sweating blood. The bass player had been briefed.

He marched it up and down.

And Chuck Berry, lean as a knife, lazy as calm water, mean as a wolf, sang and strutted and rubber-legged and licked away at that guitar whose pickup went straight into the amp while the music came straight back out again, no bullshit, metallic, 'in the old style', as though Chuck could never get old, as though rock and roll could never die, and The Gringos sat there with their wives while their Suits stayed at home with the real Gringos folded up inside somehow with the thymol crystals.

Oh Maybellene
Why can't you be true?

sang Chuck Berry. The Gringos had been a good rock and roll band for four years and that had been a lifetime. It was fifteen years since they'd played 'Maybellene' for the last time at Caroline Bay in Timaru in the summer of '59, and that had been even longer.

Colleen Reilly

JIM'S ELVIS

Jim's problem was so obvious and so simple I don't see how all the psychologists and therapists could have missed it. It was Elvis Presley.

Some women will know immediately what I mean, and some men, those who don't have an Elvis problem, will think they know what I mean, but they don't, because these are the kind of men who wouldn't recognise Elvis if he stared them in the face. They dismiss his music and him as too much, too obvious.

I am talking about the young Elvis. The old one should have acted as a warning to Jim, but of course Jim couldn't see an old Elvis. That is, he could and did make sad, pitying comments about time passing, idols falling, but I could tell he didn't really connect this fat, drug-doped, faltering slob with Elvis.

Elvis is young, he pulsates with endless unexplored energy, he is music, he is male sexuality, he is the place where music and sex meet, he is Icarus whose wings never melt, he is the dancer and the dance. All he has to do is let go—and he is there—and you can hear that place in every one of his early songs, and watch it happen in every one of his early performances. He doesn't always stay there long, but so what? He gets there, which is more than most of us do.

I knew that was Jim's Elvis. Not right away—after all, the psychologists never knew, and all I was was a woman in love.

A woman who falls in love with a man whose problem is Elvis has two choices. She can stay with this man, because when with him there is always the possibility that he will take her to the place where Elvis lives. The rest of the time he will be a child, spoiled, or a bitter old man, intractable. Or he will be with other women, not because he loves them like he loves her, but because Elvis doesn't stay still. He won't apologise for this when she finds out, he won't make any promises, because he is in his own way, Elvis's way, innocently honest.

So she can stay with him, on those terms. Or she can leave him, which is what I did. Everybody told me I should leave him, but that wasn't my reason for doing so. My reason was simple: I wanted a normal life, I wanted to watch Elvis in old clips in a cinema or on television, with my partner by my side squirming a bit uncomfortably, then trying his best later that night to excite me with something new. I hate these men who don't know Elvis, I like to watch their pitiful small souls reaching out through their unable bodies for Elvis. This is my revenge on Jim. Perhaps that doesn't make sense, but I can't get my revenge on him, not in that place where all his power lies, where he hurt me so much and gave me so much, and I can revenge myself on his sex, with sex. It doesn't heal the wound, but it toughens it. A callus is better than nothing.

I've had perhaps six or seven lovers since Jim—that was over ten years ago now. In this decade, I've seen him four times—twice from afar, and he didn't see me, and twice face to face. We had coffee and a talk each of these times. Once, as we got up from the table to leave the coffee shop, he put his hand very lightly on the small of my back to steer me through the narrow aisle. I can feel it now.

He hadn't changed. He is nearly fifty now, he is almost completely grey, he had a middle-aged paunch, and he wears glasses for reading. He said he hadn't met anyone important since me, he said it with no self-pity, just fact. I said that had been true for me too for a while, but now I'd finally found someone. He knew I was lying. He is still having trouble managing his affairs, still in debt most of the time, drinking too much, hates all authority. He still walks the same, a slow dance, and his eyes still look straight at you.

The psychologists were my idea. He went along with it, because he wanted to have more of the kind of life people around him had. He wanted to be able to enjoy his job, to feel like a good and faithful lover, to be happy, to make me happy. The psychologists diagnosed alcoholism, a mother problem, a father problem, middle-aged man's performance anxiety, delayed adolescence, chronically low self-esteem, compensatory inflated high self-esteem, slight paranoia, a reality problem. I agreed with all of the diagnoses, as did Jim more or less. You could see they really had little effect on him. He said in those offices—I know this because I was there too for some of the therapies and he told me about the others—he sat there and he played the game, not cynically, but because why not? Maybe they would be able to cure him, he thought, and so did I.

Of course what was needed was an old-fashioned exorcist, someone who could summon Elvis from the depths of Jim's psyche and kick him out the door. Or at least put him in his place, where Jim or I could use him only when we wanted to. Where he was under some kind of control, preferably mine.

Jim didn't dress like Elvis or anything like that. He dresses like any man his age, with a good eye for casual wear. And although he has all the early Elvis records, he rarely listens to them. His taste is more baroque, particularly Bach. He is also quite successful in his field, freelance photography. He always turns in a good product, sometimes a brilliant product, but he himself can't tell the difference. He can make good money, but he is always worrying about not making enough or spending too much. Or he was. I am using the present tense, as if I knew. Well, I do know. It has been over two years since I saw him last, but I know he is still the same.

My last few lovers have been very young, fifteen to twenty years younger than me. I thought maybe I'd find in a young man's energy something like Jim had. It took me a while to realise that would be like expecting Mick Jagger or Bruce Springsteen or Simon Le Bon to be Elvis. It's not my age which makes me realise how ridiculous that is. In fact, I was the Beatles era, and I never really thought about Elvis until I met Jim. It is simply, as Jim would say, that there is not and never will be another Elvis.

I remember the day Jim told me about the first time he heard Elvis. We were lying in bed one afternoon, the outside world slowly coming back to me. I remember the sound of a dog barking far away and a jet engine noise even further away. That slow awakening, that drowsy reluctance, all that. Jim lay there too like that and then he told me the story. He was in a milk bar—these too were before my time—he was in a milk bar, feeling unhappy, drifting, like any adolescent. Someone put on the jukebox and That's Alright Mama filled the room. Jim says absolutely everything changed from that moment on. I believed him, he is not the kind of man who plays with symbols of revelation or indeed with any symbolic experience. He says he just suddenly knew that this was real, that life was real, that he was real. He bought all the records, he learned to play and sing the songs, he perfected the pelvic thrust, the leg strut, he had found himself. And he lost himself too, every time he listened, sat still and listened, to Elvis.

It strikes me as more of an imprinting than a revelation. Forever and ever Jim would be attached to this Elvis, this state of being. He tried marriage, then later he loved me, and as I said he has also been able to achieve some worldly successes, but none of it measures up. How could it? For him, there is this world—wives, lovers, work travel food wine books Bach, and there is Elvis. Elvis gives Jim enough cool to make a show of it in this world, sometimes a good show. Elvis is always there to go back to, come out from, live in for a while. Nothing and no one changes that place, you can meet Jim there, you can't stay there and neither can he, and it is the rest of life that counts in the end.

I find it hard to end this. At least I've named Jim's problem and this is at least some accomplishment. That is what one does in this world, and Elvis is dead.

Keri Hulme

ONE WHALE, SINGING

The ship drifted on the summer night sea.

'It is a pity,' she thought, 'that one must come on deck to see the stars. Perhaps a boat of glass, to see the sea streaming past, to watch the nightly splendour of stars . . .' Something small jumped from the water, away to the left. A flash of phosphorescence after the sound, and then all was quiet and starlit again.

They had passed through krillswarms all day. Large areas of the sea were reddish-brown, as though an enormous creature had wallowed ahead of the boat, streaming blood.

'Whale-feed,' she had said, laughing and hugging herself at the thought of seeing whales again. 'Lobster-krill,' he had corrected, pedantically.

The crustaceans had swum in their frightened jerking shoals, mile upon mile of them, harried by fish that were in turn pursued and torn by larger fish.

She thought, it was probably a fish after krill that had leaped then. She sighed, stroking her belly. It was the lesser of the two evils to go below now, so he didn't have an opportunity to come on deck and suggest it was better for the coming baby's health, and hers, of course, that she came down. The cramped cabin held no attraction: all that was there was boneless talk, and one couldn't see stars, or really hear the waters moving.

Far below, deep under the keel of the ship, a humpback whale sported and fed. Occasionally, she yodelled to herself, a long undulating call of content. When she found a series of sounds that pleased, she repeated them, wove them into a band of harmonious pulses.

Periodically she reared to the surface, blew, and slid smoothly back under the sea in a wheel-like motion. Because she was pregnant, and at the tailend of the southward migration, she had no reason now to leap and display on the surface.

She was not feeding seriously; the krill was there, and she swam amongst them, forcing water through her lips with her large tongue, stranding food amongst the baleen. When her mouth was full, she swallowed. It was leisurely, lazy eating. Time enough for recovering her full weight when she reached the cold seas, and she could gorge on a ton and a half of plankton daily.

Along this coast, there was life and noise in plenty. Shallow grunting from a herd of fish, gingerly feeding on the fringes of the krill shoal. The krill themselves, a thin hiss and crackle through the water. The interminable background clicking of shrimps. At times, a wayward band of sound like bass organ-notes sang through the chatter, and to this the whale listened attentively, and sometimes replied.

The krill thinned: she tested, tasted the water. Dolphins had passed recently. She heard their brief commenting chatter, but did not spend time on it. The school swept round ahead of her, and vanished into the vibrant dark.

He had the annoying habit of reading what he'd written out loud. 'We can conclusively demonstrate that to man alone belong true intelligence and self-knowledge.'

He coughs.

Taps his pen against his lips. He has soft, wet lips, and the sound is a fleshy slop! slop!

She thinks:

> Man indeed! How arrogant! How ignorant! Woman would be as correct, but I'll settle for humanity. And it strikes me that the quality humanity stands in need of most is true intelligence and self-knowledge.

'For instance, Man alone as a species, makes significant artefacts, and transmits knowledge in permanent and durable form.'

He grunts happily.

'In this lecture, I propose to . . .'

> But how do they know? she asks herself. About the passing on of knowledge among other species? They may do it in ways beyond our capacity to understand . . . that we are the only ones to make artefacts I'll grant you, but that's because us needy little adapts have such pathetic bodies, and no especial ecological niche. So hooks and hoes, and steel things that gouge and slay, we produce in plenty. And build a wasteland of drear ungainly hovels to shelter our vulnerable hides.

She remembers her glass boat, and sighs. The things one could create if one made technology servant to a humble and creative imagination . . . He's booming on, getting into full lectureroom style and stride.

'. . . thus we will show that no other species, lacking as they do artefacts, an organised society, or even semblances of culture . . .'

> What would a whale do with an artefact, who is so perfectly adapted to the sea? Their conception of culture, of civilisation, must be so alien that we'd never recognise it, even if we were to stumble on its traces daily.

She snorts.

He looks at her, eyes unglazing, and smiles.

'Criticism, my dear? Or you like that bit?'

'I was just thinking . . .'

> Thinking, as for us passing on our knowledge, hah! We rarely learn from the past or the present, and what we pass on for future humanity is a mere jumble of momentarily true facts, and odd snippets of surprised self-discoveries. That's not knowledge . . .

She folds her hands over her belly. You in there, you won't learn much. What I can teach you is limited by what we are. Splotch goes the pen against his lips.

'You had better heat up that fortified drink, dear. We can't have either of you wasting from lack of proper nourishment.'

Unspoken haw haw haw.

> Don't refer to it as a person! It is a canker in me, a parasite. It is nothing to me. I feel it squirm and kick, and sicken at the movement.

He says he's worried by her pale face. 'You shouldn't have gone up on deck so late. You could have slipped, or something, and climbing tires you now, you know.'

She doesn't argue any longer. The arguments follow well-worn tracks and go in circles.

'Yes,' she answers.

> But I should wither without that release, that solitude, that keep away from you.

She stirs the powder into the milk and begins to mix it rhythmically.

> I wonder what a whale thinks of its calf? So large a creature, so proven peaceful a beast, must be motherly, protective, a shielding benevolence against all wildness. It would be a sweet and milky love, magnified and sustained by the encompassing purity of water . . .

A swarm of insectlike creatures, sparkling like a galaxy, each a pulsing lightform in blue and silver and gold. The whale sang for them, a ripple of delicate notes, spaced in a timeless curve. It stole through the lightswarm, and the luminescence increased brilliantly.

Deep within her, the other spark of light also grew. It was the third calf she had borne; it delighted her still, that the swift airy copulation should spring so opportunely to this new life. She feeds it love and music, and her body's bounty. Already it responds to her crooning tenderness, and the dark pictures she sends it. It absorbs both, as part of the life to come, as it nests securely in the waters within.

She remembers the nautilids in the warm oceans to the north, snapping at one another in a cannibalistic frenzy.

She remembers the oil-bedraggled albatross, resting with patient finality on the water-top, waiting for death.

She remembers her flight, not long past, from killer whales, and the terrible end of the other female who had companied her south, tongue eaten from her mouth, flukes and genitals ripped, bleeding to a slow fought-against end.

And all the memories are part of the growing calf.

More krill appeared. She opened her mouth, and glided through the shoal. Sudden darkness for the krill. The whale hummed meanwhile.

He folded his papers contentedly.

'Sam was going on about his blasted dolphins the other night dear.'

'Yes?'

He laughed deprecatingly. 'But it wouldn't interest you. All dull scientific chatter, eh?'

'What was he saying about, umm, his dolphins?'

'O, insisted that his latest series of tests demonstrated their intelligence. No, that's misquoting him, potentially high intelligence. Of course, I brought him down to earth smartly. Results are as you make them, I said. Nobody has proved that the animals have intelligence to a degree above that of a dog. But it made me think of the rot that's setting in lately. Inspiration for this lecture indeed.'

'Lilley?' she asked, still thinking of the dolphins, 'Lilley demonstrated evidence of dolphinese.'

'Lilley? That mystical crackpot? Can you imagine anyone ever duplicating his work? Hah! Nobody has, of course. It was all in the man's mind.'

'Dolphins and whales are still largely unknown entities,' she murmured, more to herself than to him.

'Nonsense, my sweet. They've been thoroughly studied and dissected for the last century and more.' She shuddered. 'Rather dumb animals, all told, and probably of bovine origin. Look at the incredibly stupid way they persist in migrating straight into the hands of whalers, year after year. If they were smart, they'd have organised an attacking force and protected themselves!'

He chuckled at the thought, and lit his pipe.

'It would be nice to communicate with another species,' she said, more softly still.

'That's the trouble with you poets,' he said fondly. 'Dream marvels are to be found from every half-baked piece of pseudo-science that drifts around. That's not seeing the world as it is. We scientists rely on reliably ascertained facts for a true picture of the world.'

She sat silently by the pot on the galley stove.

An echo from the world around, a deep throbbing from miles away. It was both message and invitation to contribute. She mused on it for minutes, absorbing, storing, correlating, winding her song meanwhile experimentally through its interstices—then dropped her voice to the lowest frequencies. She sent the message along first, and then added another strength to the cold wave that travelled after the message. An oceanaway, someone would collect the cold wave, and store it, while it coiled and built to uncontrollable strength. Then, just enough would be released to generate a superwave, a gigantic wall of water on the surface of the sea. It was a new thing the sea-people were experimenting with. A protection. In case.

She began to swim further out from the coast. The water flowed like warm silk over her flanks, an occasional interjectory current swept her, cold and bracing, a touch from the sea to the south. It became quieter, a calm freed from the fights of crabs and the bickerings of small fish. There was less noise too, from the strange turgid craft that buzzed and clattered across the ocean-ceiling, dropping down wastes that stank and sickened.

A great ocean-going shark prudently shifted course and flicked away to the side of her. It measured twenty feet from shovel-nose to crescentic tailfin, but she was twice as long and would grow a little yet. Her broad deep body was still wellfleshed and strong, in spite of the vicissitudes of the northward breeding trek: there were barnacles encrusting her fins and lips and head, but she was unhampered by other parasites. She blew a raspberry at the fleeing shark and beat her flukes against the ocean's pull in an ecstacy of strength.

'This lecture,' he says, sipping his drink, 'this lecture should cause quite a stir. They'll probably label it conservative, or even reactionary, but of course it isn't. It merely urges us to keep our feet on the ground, not go hunting off down worthless blind sidetrails. To consolidate data we already have, not for example, to speculate about so-called ESP phenomena. There is far too much mysticism and airy-fairy folderol in science these days. I don't wholly agree with the Victorians' attitude, that science could explain all, and very shortly would, but it's high time we got things back to a solid factual basis.'

'The Russians,' she says, after a long moment of non-committal silence, 'the Russians have discovered a form of photography that shows all living things to be sources of a strange and beautiful energy. Lights flare from finger tips. Leaves coruscate. All is living effulgence.'

He chuckles again.

'I can always tell when you're waxing poetic.' Then he taps out the bowl of his pipe against the side of the bunk, and leans forward in a fatherly way.

'My dear, if they have, and that's a big if, what difference could that possibly make. Another form of energy? So what?'

'Not just another form of energy,' she says sombrely. 'It makes for a whole new view of the world. If all things are repositories of related energy, then humanity is not alone . . .'

'Why this of solitariness, of being alone. Communication with other species, man is not alone, for God's sake! One would think you're becoming tired of us all!'

He's joking.

She is getting very tired. She speaks tiredly.

'It would mean that the things you think you are demonstrating in your paper . . .'

'Lecture.'

'Work . . . those things are totally irrelevant. That we may be on the bottom of the pile, not the top. It may be that other creatures are aware of their place and purpose in the world, have no need to delve and paw a meaning out. Justify themselves. That they accept all that happens, the beautiful, the terrible, the sickening, as part of the dance, as the joy or pain of the joke. Other species may somehow be equipped to know fully and consciously what truth is, whereas we humans must struggle, must struggle blindly to the end.'

He frowns, a concerned benevolent frown.

'Listen dear, has this trip been too much. Are you feeling at the end of your tether, tell us truly? I know the boat is old, and not much of a sailer, but it's the best I could do for the weekend. And I thought it would be a nice break for us, to get away from the university and home. Has there been too much work involved? The boat's got an engine after all . . . would you like me to start it and head back for the coast?'

She is shaking her head numbly.

He stands up and swallows what is left of his drink in one gulp.

'It won't take a minute to start the engine, and then I'll set that pilot thing, and we'll be back in sight of land before the morning. You'll feel happier then.'

She grips the small table.

Don't scream, she tells herself, don't scream.

Diatoms of phantom light, stray single brilliances. A high burst of dolphin sonics. The school was returning. A muted rasp from shoalfish hurrying past. A thing that curled and coiled in a drifting aureole of green light.

She slows, buoyant in the water.

Green light: it brings up the memories that are bone deep in her, written in her very cells. Green light of land.

She had once gone within yards of shore, without stranding. Curiosity had impelled her up a long narrow bay. She had edged carefully along, until her long flippers touched the rocky bottom. Sculling with her tail, she had slid forward a little further, and then lifted her head out of the water. The light was bent, the sounds that came to her were thin and distorted, but she could see colours known only from dreams and hear a music that was both alien and familiar.

(Christlookitthat!)

(Fuckinghellgetoutahereitscomingin)

The sound waves pooped and spattered through the air, and things scrambled away, as she moved herself back smoothly into deeper water.

A strange visit, but it enabled her to put images of her own to the calling dream.

Follow the line to the hard and aching airswept land, lie upon solidity never before known until strained ribs collapse from weight of body never before felt. And then, the second beginning of joy . . .

She dreams a moment, recalling other ends, other beginnings. And because of the web that streamed between all members of her kind, she was ready for the softly insistent pulsation that wound itself into her dreaming. Mourning for a male of the species, up in the cold southern seas where the greenbellied krill swarm in unending abundance. Where the killing ships of the harpooners lurk. A barb sliced through the air in an arc and embedded itself in the lungs, so the whale blew red in his threshing agony. Another that sunk into his flesh by the heart. Long minutes later, his slow exhalation of death. Then the gathering of light from all parts of the drifting corpse. It condensed, vanished . . . streamers of sound from the dolphins who shoot past her, somersaulting in their strange joy.

The long siren call urges her south. She begins to surge upward to the sweet night air.

She says, 'I must go on deck for a minute.'

They had finished the quarrel, but still had not come together. He grunts, fondles his notes a last time, and rolls over in his sleeping bag, drawing the neck of it tightly close.

She says wistfully,

'Goodnight then,'

and climbs the stairs heavily up to the hatchway.

'You're slightly offskew,' she says to the Southern Cross, and feels the repressed tears begin to flow down her cheeks. The stars blur.

Have I changed so much?

Or is it this interminable deadening pregnancy?

But his stolid, sullen, stupidity!

He won't see, he won't see, he won't see anything.

She walks to the bow, and settles herself down, uncomfortably aware of her protuberant belly, and begins to croon a song of comfort to herself.

And at that moment the humpback hit the ship, smashing through her old and weakened hull, collapsing the cabin, rending timbers. A mighty chaos . . .

Somehow she found herself in the water, crying for him, swimming in a circle as though among the small debris she might find a floating sleeping bag. The stern of the ship is sinking, poised a moment a moment dark against the stars, and then it slides silently under.

She strikes out for a shape in the water, the liferaft? the dinghy?

And the shape moves.

The humpback, full of her dreams and her song, had beat blindly upward, and was shocked by the unexpected fouling. She lies, waiting on the water-top.

The woman stays where she is, motionless except for her paddling hands. She has no fear of the whale, but thinks, 'It may not know I am here, may hit me accidentally as it goes down.'

She can see the whale more clearly now, an immense zeppelin shape, bigger by far than their flimsy craft had been, but it lies there, very still . . .

She hopes it hasn't been hurt by the impact, and chokes on the hope.

There is a long moaning call then, that reverberates through her. She is physically swept, shaken by an intensity of feeling, as though the whale has sensed her being and predicament, and has offered it all it can, a sorrowing compassion.

Again the whale makes the moaning noise, and the woman calls, as loudly as she can, 'Thank you, thank you' knowing that it is meaningless, and probably unheard. Tears stream down her face once more.

The whale sounded so gently she didn't realise it was going at all.

'I am now alone in the dark,' she thinks, and the salt water laps round her mouth. 'How strange, if this is to be the summation of my life.'

In her womb the child kicked. Buoyed by the sea, she feels the movement as something gentle and familiar, dear to her for the first time.

But she begins to laugh.

The sea is warm and confiding, and it is a long long way to shore.

Fiona Farrell

THE GIFT

Alt. F1. Type/Edit
Kempe, Margery. (Born c. 1373) . . .
Outside a bird calls, over and over.
Kathie types, bowed before the screen, hot in her quiet room.
Alt. F4. Get/Save/Remove
Save the working copy as . . .
Enter.
The bird calls.
Escape . . .

Her mother was in the sitting room one night reading her Bible as she did every night after they had gone to bed, when she saw Jesus. Not all of Him, you understand; just His feet and the hem of His white robe, from the knees down. She didn't look up, couldn't look up, but she felt His hand on her head and was comforted. Kathie can't remember now if He said anything. Probably He spoke a bit from the Bible, in the language of the Authorised Version. Probably something about being of 'good cheer'. She told the children about it in the morning over breakfast while they ate their toast by the kitchen range since the frost was heavy and feathered all the windows. 'I was sitting there on the sofa,' she said, 'feeling sorry for myself and suddenly, there He was.' 'Did He have shoes on?' asked Kathie, who then as now requires the reassurance of tangible fact. And her mother said no, he wore sandals. And Tessa, who was the youngest, saw two shining heavenly feet, very clean, in a pair of the pink plastic sandals all the girls except her had had at school last summer. Vonny and Trish saw sensible brown leather sandals such as Neil wore to school. And Kathie and Neil came closest with the sort the Romans wore in their battered Arthur Mee's Encyclopaedia, with bits up the leg. 'And I felt His hand on my head and this wonderful soft feeling all through, like . . .' Their mother stopped, sat stirring and stirring her tea for no words could describe the soft feeling. The children sucked the butter from their toast and tried to imagine.

It came as no surprise that Jesus should choose to spend a few minutes in the sitting room with their mother. She had heard Him before, of course, when her mother died, Grandma Simms. On that occasion He had been present in a gust of wind which blew the windows of the sick room wide, bearing the scent of magnolias though there were none in flower and He had whispered, 'Weep no more, Milly. Weep no more.' And Grandma Simms had smiled a little though her eyes were weighted down with pennies and she was two hours dead.

Then there were the other smaller miracles. When Kathie nearly drowned at school after Mervyn Jones pushed her in the deep end, Milly had known and rang the school office before they could ring her. They would sing 'The Lord's my Shepherd' at church which was her Auntie Bobbie's favourite hymn and sure enough, before evening, there'd be a phone call from her up in Wellington, just to say hullo. And the day the organist stopped too soon, pumping out 'Aaaaaamen' before the last verse, that had been the bad day. The day Auntie Bobbie had her stroke in the tea rooms at the Botanical Gardens and died.

The air was full of noises. Other people seemed to exist without noticing, but they were all around if you had the gift of perception. In the way the bus would arrive just as their mother did at the stop, in the convenience of rain after she had planted out young seedlings or the sun when she was ready to put out the washing. And if it didn't rain, or the bus was very late, or the wind gusted and tore the wet clothes in amongst the potatoes then it was simply Not Meant To Be and one should leave the shopping or the washing for another day and try to recall sins not fully repented.

Milly had not always been on Christ's visiting list. Long before the children and the miracles she was a large, round young woman in a check pinny left behind by her sisters to look after Mother and Artie. Mother had married late, and had her children in middle age. Artie, the last, was born three months after her husband fell to his death at the quarry, and he was born simple, a noddy drooling baby who grew slowly into a shambling young man who rode through the streets on his large-wheeled tricycle pretending to be a cowboy pyow pyow and sucking his way through bags of peppermints. It broke Mother's heart. She became morose, grew fat. And in her fifties began to forget names, to wander. Bobbie got out as soon as she turned sixteen and went to Wellington to be a typist. Alison married young, a farmer from Tuatapere. Which left Milly. Milly was not clever or pretty so she accepted her lot philosophically, until one morning soon after the war when she was sitting on the verandah shelling peas. The postman came. A new young man. He pedalled unsteadily up the hill to the gate, put two letters in the box then went very white and fell off his bike. Milly ran to the gate and gathered him to her pinafored chest. He was tall, taller than her by several inches, but thin and light as a feather. She carried him without effort up to the house and laid him on the verandah couch. He was Clem Bush, just back from overseas. He had volunteered, set off briskly a solid brown young man, and returned four years later from a POW camp, weighing seven and a half stone and with a chronic bowel disorder. All this she learned later. On that first morning when Milly looked at him lying on the couch, black hair glued to a white and sticky forehead, the skin drawn blue over cheek and nose bone, all she knew was that she felt passion for the first time. 'Have a cup of tea,' she'd said, and brought out the tin of gingernuts and buttered four scones. And that was that. A few months later, Grandma Simms went to Eventide, Artie went to Seacliff, and Milly took up the task of 'getting Clem right again'.

It took more than buttered scones. At first they got on well. She fed Clem, warmed his gloves in the oven on cold days, packed him a thermos of soup for his lunch. He began to recover weight and something of the vitality he had once had, though he was never strong. Then the babies started coming. Neil, then Vonny, Trish, Kathie, Tessa. Five children in seven years and an income of £6 a week. They moved into an old villa house just over the town boundary where the rates were cheaper and they could run a cow. They economised, made do, got by . . . The sixth pregnancy miscarried at five months after Milly had wrung out the week's washing. Blood all over the wash-house floor, spots on the clean shirts and a trail of it to the phone in the hall. She didn't die. But she became frightened. The next time Clem turned to her in bed on a Saturday night, she stiffened and said 'Not yet'. She developed headaches, blinding headaches, after tea, when diamonds and stars jostled before her eyes and she had to lie with a damp cloth on her forehead until sleep. She felt her body, once round and sturdy, grow tight and resistant. She sickened with panic when Clem so much as put his arm around her waist. His hands alarmed her. Clem for his part became mean. He took to teasing Neil, the oldest, who was scaly with eczema, asthmatic, until he was roaring and tearful. 'What's the matter with you?' Clem would snap.

'Thick as two short planks, that's what you are. And stop that bloody snivelling.' Then Milly would intervene. 'Eat your tea, Neil,' she'd say, fury making her voice thick and fuzzy. 'Now just listen to you, Clem, ruining all our dinners.' The other children would eat steadily, eyes down, letting the voices roll over their heads, sausages, silver beet and potatoes dry in each mouth. 'God damn it,' Clem would say then, 'he may have his problems but it won't help if he's turned into a pansy.' Milly would slam out into the kitchen and Clem would leave saying he knew where he wasn't wanted and off to the 2nd NZEF for the evening. Within a year of the miscarriage Milly had exchanged the double bed for two singles at the Auction Mart and moved out to sleep in the sun room.

When Kathie was six an evangelist came to town. There were posters everywhere advertising the crusade. 'The Healing Fire Crusade' it was called. The posters showed a lantern-jawed man like Clark Gable whose piercing eyes looked straight at you. 'Bring Me Your Sick and Let Jesus Make Them Whole!' said the large print. Neil's eczema made his face look as though it had been roughly peeled. After a row with his father he wheezed and Milly panicked inwardly watching his chest puff up, his breath shorten, while outwardly she went through the drill, calming, pacifying, getting him back to normal. On the night of the Crusade she said to the children, 'Come on. Get your coats, we're going out.' It was a Friday. Clem wouldn't be home till late. They set off walking down the gravel road as the sun sank.

It was a calm evening, a pink and grey wash over hedges and hills and trees. They walked without talking, Tessa and Trish put their hands in their mother's, Vonny and Neil swished at the tall grass with sticks, and Kathie walked in front kicking a stone and reciting to herself Chicken Licken from her new school reader ' . . . the sky is falling and I'm off to tell the king . . . '. They took the short cut through the cemetery, past the shops and the school to the park where a huge marquee covered what was normally the soccer ground. There was an organ inside, a dais with flowers and a choir dressed in blue and white. The seats were like circus seats and they sat us as near the front as they could while the place filled. The organ sounded, and a small spotlight focused on Clark Gable on the dais. He leant over above the chrysanthemums and looked straight at Milly. 'Are you weary?' he asked. 'Are you weighed down with trouble? Do you feel there must be a better way?' To all of which Milly whispered, 'Yes, yes'. When it was time to come forward, she rose with the children and they joined the queue. Clark Gable's assistant gave each of them a white vinyl Bible and Clark Gable blessed Neil, who was not, as the girls hoped, immediately divested of his scaly skin like the lizard they had caught once and kept in a jar, but stayed just as he was: weak-eyed, given to wheezing. But from that day, nevertheless, the miracles began, the visions.

Milly stopped worrying. Each morning she opened her Healing Fire Bible at random, letting the heavy pages flop as they would, shut her eyes and dabbed at a verse. Then she'd read. 'And their camels shall be a booty and the multitude of their cattle a spoil: and I will bring their calamity from all sides saith the Lord. And I will scatter unto all winds them that are in the utmost corners.' 'Now . . . I wonder what that will mean?' And by evening it would have been made clear, fulfilled in some mysterious fashion (the cow out again through the weak place in the fence). It drove Clem wild if he caught her at it at breakfast though he never challenged her directly. He spoke, instead, to Kathie or Tessa or the table itself, avoiding her eye. 'Simpleminded superstition. She's bloody daft and what's worse, she's teaching you kids to be daft.' Milly didn't answer, drifted through the days in her rattling house, humming hymns, petticoat dangling, comfy slippers. On Sundays, she combed her hair and went to the Baptist chapel she had attended as a girl. She took the children with her while Clem slept in. When they returned Clem ignored her, pouncing instead on Neil. 'Now,' he'd say, sitting at the kitchen table, pyjamas loose about his thin body, 'what did you learn today, eh? What did the bible bashers try to teach you, eh?' Neil stood, pink, his eyes shifty. 'Look at him, will you? Not the full quid, wouldn't you say? He wants some of that testing. We'll have to get him some of that psychological testing.' Milly cut the children slices of bread with butter and sugar. 'Take no notice,' she'd say. 'He's in one of his moods. Now off you go.' And they'd go, fast, into the free Sunday air with sweet sticky mouths.

One Sunday Clem did look at Milly straight. 'If you'd seen what I've seen,' he said suddenly, 'you'd not believe in a good God either. If He is out there He's a tough old bugger who leaves the weak to go to the wall. I know, I've seen Him do it.' 'What do you mean?' asked Milly. But he wouldn't say any more. He never talked about the POW camp, and only once about the war—on the day Kathie did her project. She had a big piece of cardboard with THE WAR printed at the top in red crayon, and she was turning each downstroke into a gun with a puff of blue smoke at one end. 'What's all this then?' said her father coming in from work. 'It's for school,' said Kathie. 'We have to find a true story about the war and Mr Tripp's going to give a Crunchie bar for the best one so tell me a true story, Dad.' 'A Crunchie bar?' said Clem, rinsing his hands at the sink. 'Go on, Dad,' pressed Kathie. So Clem, just this once, told her about running over some German trenches in the desert, a bayonet charge, all of them running in the blazing sun and in the sand a sudden black hollow where two young men were huddled, two Germans, two blondies. They had their arms round each other and didn't move. 'So what did you *do*, Dad?' said Kathie, who then as now liked her stories to have a proper conclusion, a finishing point. 'Left 'em,' said Clem wiping his hands, grey streaks on the towel. And 'But *why* did you leave them?' asked Kathie who then as now needs to make sense of people, who hates imprecision. Clem stood by the sink. 'Mahleesh,' he said. 'It's a long time ago.' He opened the back door. 'I hope your Mr Tripp thinks that's worth a Crunchie bar,' he said and went out to the garden. Kathie knew Mr Tripp wouldn't. He wanted gallantry and the Battle of Britain and fighting them on the beaches. Proper stories that they could pin up on the wall for Anzac Day when other people's fathers put on their suits and medals and marched to the memorial. Their father didn't even march. On Anzac Day Clem went round instead to his mate Alf's place and stayed all day, returning in the evening with a slam of the front door, stamping up the hall. 'Ferdinand, Ferdinand,' he'd sing, 'the bull with the delee-cate ego . . . '. The house on its rotting piles shuddered. 'But he didn't want to FIGHT FIGHT FIGHT!' He'd try to draw Milly on to his knee but she'd be gentle, fetch him his tea and watch while he ate, for he still needed his strength. Then she'd cover him with a blanket and leave him to sleep it off on the sofa.

However strong his proof, whatever bitter examples of divine malice Clem could draw from his past, he kept them to himself. He refused to argue. Instead, that Sunday afternoon he fetched a pen and the writing pad from the sideboard and wrote the first of what became weekly letters to the paper. 'Dear Editor, How can anyone seriously quote the Bible as moral authority,' he'd ask, 'when its major figures include a man like Abraham who acted as pimp to his own wife?' Or, 'Dear Editor, Recent research proves that many hands contributed to the writing of the New Testament and that . . . ', signing himself 'Rationalist' or 'Unconvinced'. Then on Wednesday nights, when the letters were published, he'd cut them out and pin them to the mantelpiece above the range where they turned yellow and crackly like so many dry skins.

One day Neil forgot to shut the road gate and the cow got out. She was hit by a truck and the children found her, legs in a loose tangle in the barberry hedge on their way home from school. That night, Clem cut a willow stick and took Neil out to the shed. But he tired after only four strokes and sat instead gasping, 'Bloody clown idiot boy useless bastard never amount to anything daft it's in the blood.' That night Kathie woke suddenly. It was late, pitch black still outside but there was light in the hall and a soft murmuring. She got out of bed and went down to Neil's room. He is wheezing, scarlet-faced, eyes popping and her mother stands beside the bed leaning towards him in her big white nightie, gripping his hands, eyes shut, saying over and over 'Help him, help him'. Neil lies looking up at her, drawing breath through her fingers in a circle of torch light. Behind her, Kathie hears her father, sleepy 'Is it bad?' and her mother turns. Milly looks at Clem with such sudden rage that Kathie steps back, though the eyes are directed well above her head. 'I hope you're pleased with yourself,' says Milly. 'If it were you here on this bed I'd not come two steps to help you.' Her father stands very still, wavers a moment, then shuffles slowly to bed.

Neil didn't die that night and the verse next morning was 'Blessed be the Lord my strength which teacheth my hands to war and my fingers to fight', which was Further Proof. Neil told Kathie that he had felt as though he were flying unaided over their house, but happy, airy, seeing them all looking up as he flew and waving. Neil often saw such things and dreamt such dreams. Kathie tried often to hear the voices he and her mother heard, to see the patterns they saw, but something held her back, a sense of the improbable, the absurd. Once she saw an angel, but he was not Milly's gentle guardian. He was a huge figure, a gleaming giant on the misty hillside behind the house who dwarfed the pines and the power pylon and drove her into a panic-stricken run back down the gully home. Neil was Extraordinary. Neil had inherited The Gift. Once he prayed over Tessa's sick kitten and it shuddered and revived. Once he prayed over Clem's homebrew and it soured. He alone could lay his hand on his mother's forehead while her headaches raged and clear them. The other children were in awe of him. They were all, Kathie included, more harum scarum, pre-occupied with making friends at school, getting on as best they could, playing Sardines in the long grass in the cemetery, pinching lollies from the shop on the way home. Neil existed apart, tall and thin with his raw red face. In his school shoes, Kathie knew, he had placed small sharp white stones. 'Pain,' he said to her, 'is sort of clean. It's the only really true thing. That's why Jesus let himself be crucified.' He stuck barberry thorns from the hedge into the soft flesh under his arms. And as he walked he spoke with Melchior, his angel, who stood always at his right shoulder.

On another afternoon Milly brought down from the wardrobe where she kept her treasures—her wedding dress, the silver, a chocolate box of pale pressed flowers—a violin. 'It was Grandad Simms's,' she told the children, unwrapping the case carefully from a length of faded green cloth. 'He wasn't a bad player when he was young. He could pick out all the tunes By Ear. He used to play for the pictures.' Neil lifted the violin to his shoulder. 'No,' said Milly. 'This way.' Neil drew the bow across the strings, scratching at first, then a single true note. The children liked the violin, its curves, its special golden shininess, but Neil was the one who played it, picking out tunes as Grandad Simms had done, By Ear, and with fierce concentration. Milly wanted him to have lessons. 'Waste of time,' said Clem. 'And where's the money to come from?' But Milly said she had a bit put away at the Post Office and besides, she could use the Child Allowance so it wouldn't cost him a penny, so Neil had his lessons. He never played when Clem was home, but he learned quickly nevertheless. He was often sick and away from school. Then he sat on his bed and practised. Milly left all the doors open, so she could hear him wherever she was in the house and after he'd done his scales and pieces she'd call '"Abide With Me", Neil. Play "Abide With Me".' And Neil would play, slowly, just for her. When the girls were walking up the road from school they'd hear Neil's violin from as far away as the corner, a pure ribbon of sound threading through the barberry hedge. Mr Spencer, the trim little English man who taught Neil, told Milly he had a 'talent for the violin which must be fostered'. But Neil told Kathie in secret that it was not him but Melchior who held the bow and they played together to the glory of God.

When Neil was sixteen he fell in love. Jillian Brassett worked in the Power Board office where Neil was serving his apprenticeship. She was small and blonde with tiny even teeth and high breasts, like a pigeon pecking and bobbing and bright. She went to the same Bible Class and Neil told Kathie that they were going to marry and go to the Islands together as missionaries. The two of them. In pure white clothes, bringing the Word of God to His children. Neil had prayed and the vinyl Bible had replied, 'Get thee out of thy country and from thy kindred and from thy father's house into a land that I will shew thee.' It was A Call, as plain as daylight. On Saturday nights now, Neil went out, his red skin dabbed with an aftershave which smelled exactly like vanilla ice-cream, off to Teen Fun, or a bonfire or a Beetle evening or a barn dance arranged by the church for the Young People. Kathie, who was too young yet to be Young Person, looked on with astonishment, envy and embarrassment. In Jillian's company Neil seemed even more gangling and awkward, his neck too thin inside his shirt collar, his hands too wild. She watched him one morning after church, standing on the edge of the group of Young People. Jillian was teasing Malcolm Johnston and the group laughed and jostled closer, Neil craning from the edge to hear and smiling. 'You look silly,' said Kathie to Neil that night as they washed the dishes, not knowing why she wanted so much to needle and hurt but it had something to do with blonde hair and being at the centre of a laughing group and wanting to protect those who stood on the edges of such seductive sweetness. Neil dried a cup carefully and didn't hear her. Her mother didn't like Jillian either or this new vanilla-scented Neil. One Saturday night she lay on the sofa, her head splitting into fragments. 'Smooth my hair, Neil,' she said. And Neil sat beside her as he had done before, often, hands resting on her face, but with one eye on the clock, one leg jiggling to run. At a quarter to eight he leaned over. 'Got to go, Mum,' he said. 'I'll be late.' Milly gripped his wrist suddenly, eyes screwed tight with pain. 'You've lost it all,' she said. 'You never play for me, you never see or hear any more. You are becoming ordinary.' Neil kissed her forehead, and she lay quiet till the door slammed and his footsteps, at a run, silenced. 'I'll get you an aspirin,' said Kathie. 'You're a good girl,' said Milly as she did and undid the top button of her cardigan.

That October Jillian married Malcolm Johnston after a three-week engagement and people said they had to. And Neil, extraordinary once more and muttering, was cutting kindling one evening while Kathie watched from the window where she sat to do her homework. The wood fanned out into neat straws and from time to time he stopped and straightened, his lips moving, talking again across his right shoulder. From where she sat she could see his lips and Clem coming round the house to put his bike away in the shed, could hear him. 'Cut out that silly blethering,' Clem said, weary and bent down to take off his bike clips. Neil looked up at him. 'Do you want to be put away? Cut it out.'

Neil turned, hatchet in hand, and walked toward his father. 'What the hell do you think you're up to?' asked Clem. 'I've known sheep with more guts than you.' Neil stood still a few feet away, then turned as suddenly and walked back to the block. He spread his left hand, looked up at Clem, and chopped. Kathie saw his fingers skip like little pink minnows and land on the pile of white kindling. 'Precious shall their blood be in His sight,' said Neil.

Mr Spencer was distraught. 'The only able student I've had in this place,' he said, 'and look what happens.' The family said nothing, not to one another, not to their friends. Milly took the violin and wrapped it in its green cloth and put it back on top of the wardrobe. She went up the gully through the pines to the power pylon, where the earth buzzed under your feet and the air was charged with God and prayed for guidance. The Lord spoke from a gorse bush blazing and told her that human hopes are frail things and that only faith is sure.

So here is Kathie, years later, sitting in her office while a bird calls and now as then she tries to make out a pattern, to finish the story properly, to decide who to forgive, who to accuse. Or are blame and accusation irrelevant? What shape do all these tiny pieces create? She is good at finding shapes, after all, detecting patterns. She turned out to be the clever one in the family and now lectures in history. She is a professional tracker of connections.

Far to the north, her brother lives alone. He is, officially, a sickness bene-ficiary, a quiet and unremarkable person, patient with animals. He gathers in birds and rabbits, diseased cats, injured dogs, and makes them whole. He walks on still days up through the bush behind his house on the mountain to the snow line.

Her sisters Trish, Vonny, Tessa, live in other places, selling air tickets or cosmetics, having babies and playing tennis on Saturdays, carefully marking their doors with such ordinary signs that any angels will pass safely overhead.

To the south their mother lives alone. Clem died one Sunday morning just after she had come in from church. He looked up, pen in hand, while she was making a cup of tea. 'Milly,' he said, 'there's a couple of young men come to the door.' 'Those Mormons again,' said Milly, tugging her dress neat at the front and opening the back door. 'That's funny. They've given up easily for a change. No sign of them.' And she turned in the sudden cold draught to Clem, who was sitting very straight at the table then falling slowly forward. So she put her hand round his and signed his last letter to the editor in full: 'C. F. Bush', and after the funeral when it was published, she pinned it with the others above the range. Then she shut up the front part of the house, moved her bed to the sitting room to be near the heater and lives there still. Vonny, who is doing well in real estate, wants her to come up and live with them in Timaru. She has written asking Kathie to help persuade their mother. 'It will be more comfortable for her now she is getting on. And the old house is so isolated I worry about her, what with all the crime you read about these days.' But Milly says no, nothing can happen to her which is not Meant to Happen. The sudden fall, the blocked heart valve, the midnight prowler are no threat to her at all. They are part of His Plan.

The curtain flaps in the breeze at the open window. It is quiet, a contemplative quiet compounded of muffled sound, people talking outside, a tui calling over and over in the trees by the car park, the hum click tick tack of the word processor. This summer Kathie is writing her book: The Female Visionary. *For some years now she has gathered them in, those women blessed and cursed with the gift. The ones who led armies, the ones who saw their angels in the smoke of their own flaming skin, the ones who argued with theologians, who drew about them believers and moved to distant countries. Their names are ranked in alphabetical order in the filing cabinet at her elbow and now she is transferring them to disk.*

Kempe, Margery. Born c. 1373 (in torment for six months after child-birth . . . 'and in this time she saw as she thought devils opening their mouths all in flames' and then Christ comes, not in white but in purple silk to sit on her bed and she is calmed and asks for the keys to the buttery that she might eat and drink as she had done before . . .).

Lee, Ann. Shakeress. Born c. 1773 (her four children dead in infancy, her vision of Adam and Eve in the garden and her sudden perception that this was iniquity and the only salvation total chastity . . .).

The screen shimmers and Kathie looks up at the blue curtain to rest her eyes, thinking about patterns and repetitions, about the ordinary extra-ordinariness of people, about the past and how it is always in lockstep with the present, about gifts and blame and purple silk and three fingers and paper yellowing in the heat. And she is thinking too that it must be nearly time for coffee in the staff lounge.

The bird calls
She types Alt. F4. Save the working copy as. . . .
The screen replies.
Enter.
Escape.

Peter Wells

OUTING

'Why is fate always so fucking inscrutable?' queried Perrin McDougal as Eric knelt at his feet, guiding his dead toes into his shoes.

'I suspect,' said Eric rather too tartly, because he hadn't actually thought he'd be acting as nursemaid, 'it means, that way, the old fraud is never quite caught out.'

They were in Perrin's exquisitely muted bedroom, with its frosty Viennese chandelier reflected in perpetuity in the floor-to-ceiling mirror. This now returned an image of themselves, ironically, in poses of almost biblical simplicity. Though Eric thought he caught a faint ammoniacal pong from Perrin's socks. 'Isn't it time, darling, these putrescent articles were, well,' Eric tried to sound noncommittal, '*substituted* for something more savoury?'

They used the telegraphese of old friends, accentuated by the frequently sharp, sometimes hilarious, even acid appendage of '*dear*.' Though in the present situation, with Perrin so ill, the *dears* had taken on a warmer, more amber hue.

'Can you find me my walking-stick?'

Perrin had phoned up that afternoon and commanded Eric—the tone was properly regal and brooked no contradiction—to take him off to the Remuera Garden Centre. Eric thought ironically—though fondly too, because in the contradiction lay the quintessence of his character—that here was Eric almost certainly going to be absent in the flooding spring yet he, Perrin, was planning a lavish bouquet for his 'spring' garden.

'What I see,' Perrin had announced over the phone in that way that had the faint edge of the visionary to it, 'is a mixture of marigolds, blue violas and delphiniums. Don't you remember . . . ?'

Eric didn't, but it didn't matter.

'Don't you remember how Aunt Priscilla down in Te Awamutu always had a daphne bush by her front steps and the way it always used to *invite* you—yes, *invite* is the right word—' Perrin kept his legal precision intact, a careful weapon against the unknown, 'so that as you ascended the stairs into her hall, the scent was *incroyable*!'

Perrin now rose to his feet unsteadily. His once fleshy form had been stripped by the disease to a frightening gauntness. His stylish garments—once bought in Melbourne or 'inexpensively' run up in distant Bangkok—clothed his skeleton in a simulacrum of 'health'. To the outside world—that crowd of on-lookers who instantly became extras in the cinema reel of Perrin's declining life—he probably looked only frail, possibly suffering from cancer.

Eric clung to these illusions as he handed Perrin his elegant malacca cane. He was still getting used to the shock of being seen with Perrin in public.

He had told himself as he drove over to Perrin's Epsom bungalow (a clever pastiche of Frank Lloyd Wright, via his Napier disciple, Louis Hay) that the public gaze simply didn't matter, that it was more important to simply help Perrin, that this accompanying him a little along the road was the very least he could do. But the truth was he had gone into a state of near shock when he thought he'd left his sunglasses behind.

He realised when his fingers touched bakelite—they connected with the impact of a lodestone—that he was sweating uncomfortably, not even watching the road. His heart was banging away, in a mocking Judas dance.

'Give us your arm, dear.' Perrin now stood at the brow of his front steps whose very sweep and height had once signalled power. Now they simply spoke danger: Perrin's grasp of Eric's arm was surprisingly tight. Eric registered Perrin's frailty as he leant into him.

He watched the almost random—yet hesitant, hesitant—fall of Perrin's numbed feet.

Suddenly Perrin lurched to a halt. 'This!' he cried in a voice full of emotion.

Shit, thought Eric, stopping back his alarm, *the bugger's going to cry*.

'This is where I want to have a whole *flowery mecca*,' Perrin waved his wand towards a dug circle of dirt. Even though he was facing financial ruin he'd hired a student to create a new flowerbed. 'When people come to see me, I want them—to—feel *welcomed*.' The last in a breathless rush. Then Perrin took off suddenly, as if blown along on the coat-tails of his inspiration. Eric hurriedly shadowed his movement, getting ready to catch, hold, balance. But Perrin had miraculously connected with gravity.

'The scent of marigolds!' he cried out in something like rage.

'This is the whole fucking trouble,' Eric said to himself in an aggrieved way. You can never tell with Perrin what tangent he's going to hare off on next. He thought of the long somnolent telephone conversations they had each night while Perrin waited for his sleeping pills to take effect. Eric would sit in his armchair, armed with a glass of gin, half watching the televisual fantasy of reality while Perrin's voice purred away in his ear—sometimes thin as cellophane, occasionally close as a voice in a dream: his needs, emotional, physical, his dreams; his plans for the future. To sell the house and go to Venice. A week later to offer the house to people with the disease. Another week and he is planning to repaint the hall a Polynesian shade of blue. 'Sea-blue, just that shade of light at dusk—the moment before the sun sinks.'

Shit, and I'm only one of his friends, Eric often said to himself. Not even his oldest. What about his *family*? But Perrin's family in faraway Te Awamutu were in disarray. They were busy tending to their own emotional wounds: they would leave Perrin alone to attend to his actual torment.

Yet, if Eric were honest with himself—and he occasionally was, by dint of necessity rather than pleasure (he was old enough now to realise that honesty, though cruel, was the best policy in the end)—Eric's truth was, silently and subtly, he himself had come almost to depend on Perrin's presence: his closeness. The fact of the matter was Perrin's reality had become the ballast in Eric's somewhat unsteady life.

Ahead of them, as if a testimony, lay Eric's blue, shockingly dented Renault.

Eric's boyfriend was 14 years younger than him. He was a student of architecture who had never heard, thankfully, of aversion therapy as a 'cure' for homosexuality. He could not imagine a city in which there were no bars, saunas or nightclubs. Matthew, handsome, athletic like a basketball player, with an engaging sweep of hair that never quite managed to stay down, had pranged Eric's car in fury one night because, as he yelled out for the whole street to hear, 'You care more about Perrin's dying than *loving* me.'

It was unfair, it was emotional blackmail: it was true.

Eric needed Matthew, his beautiful boyfriend, for the warmth of his flesh, the passion of his kisses: the way he connected him back to life. In the middle of the night he could reach out and let his hand just roll down Matthew's flank and find that softly sweating crease in his knee. This soothed away the phantoms which hid in the dark: Matthew's body was so tangibly real.

Yet for Eric his experiences with Perrin—Perrin sick, Perrin dying— were almost like a pre-vision into the future, a kind of warding off of evil spells so that he would at least know the path of the disease if it should ever strike near him. This was his private truth. And Perrin, who never for one moment doubted Eric's presence by his side, communicated the full phalanx of his illness to him so that Eric's daily equanimity was conditioned by Perrin's. They moved in uneasy duality, two friends linked like horses on a circus merry-go-round, ceaselessly rising and falling together till that final moment when one horse would rise alone.

'Now my funeral,' Perrin took up as the car moved along the streets.

This is what is so odd, thought Eric, as he drove along. When he was with Perrin it was as if that became the centre of reality in the world. Even driving along it was as if the streets of Epsom outside, with their casual realities—a father pushing his babycart into the drycleaners, a woman ducking into the wineshop in broad daylight—became like a moving cyclorama which streamed past them: Eric and Perrin were at the storm-centre, stilled.

'For my funeral,' Perrin was saying in the matter-of-fact, 'now take note of this' voice he used for the important formality of his funeral. He was planning it as he had planned his famous dinner parties, with the exquisite silver, linen and flowers acting as courtiers, nervously anticipating the throwing back of the gilded doors, the regal entrance of the food. Now the unpalatable truth was that Perrin's body would be the main course: and Eric, as a friend who had come forward—and for who came forward and who fell back there were no rules—was to act as courtier, arbiter of Perrin's final feast.

'I only want flowers picked from people's gardens. I don't want *one*— *one* !' Perrin tapped the floor with his stick vehemently, 'of those embalmed creations dreamt up by florists! And fruit should be whatever is freshest in the shops. Vegetables of the season—organic. And definitely kai moana. That shop in K Road, you know the one. Only the freshest. Can I rely on you for that?'

'You can rely on me for that.'

A slight pause. Eric turned and looked at his old friend. 'Your Celestial Highness,' he said.

Perrin smiled but did not laugh.

Going through the Domain, they were suddenly accompanied by a flock of graceful runners. Eric slowed down in appreciation. There was one man, sweating in the silent chiaroscuro of sport which echoes so closely the fury of sex. They both watched him silently.

Suddenly Perrin wound down his window. 'You beautiful man!' he yelled out in the voice of a healthy male. 'You're the most beautiful flower in the whole fucking Domain today!'

Eric blessed the presence of his sunglasses while inwardly shrieking.

Fortunately the runner turned towards them and, in his endorphin bliss, showered an appreciative smile at them. The other men pulled away. They passed in a blur of sequined sweat on muscular flesh, with frolicsome cocks beating to and fro like agitated metronomes inside their tiny shorts.

Swiftly the runners became manikins in the rear vision mirror.

'Thanks, darling,' said Perrin in a small voice of exhaustion. 'I really appreciated that.'

Eric felt a surge of exhilaration as he moved closely behind Perrin through the gates of the garden centre. Already queues were forming, with well-heeled Aucklanders guarding trundlers full of merchandise. Eric realised he hadn't felt so good—dangerous would be the wrong word to use—since the very early days of Gay Liberation, when to hold hands in public with another man was a consummate—if inevitably provocative—act.

Now time had shifted the emphasis somewhat—but Eric felt a shiver of pride at Perrin who, once so socially nuanced and named, could now lurch—almost like a toddler in reverse, Eric thought with a saving sense of hilarity. He was completely oblivious to the reactions of people around him. Indeed, as he stopped to pass a cheery word with the middle-aged housewife acting as a trundler-guard, he was actively engaging everyone in his act of dying.

Behind his shades, Eric was aware of people staring. They looked on silently, hit by the stilled impact of thought.

'Perrin!' Eric called out, because it suddenly seemed imperative to keep up contact, 'it's marigolds you're looking for, isn't it?'

He moved over to Perrin and, in a movement he himself had not contemplated, hooked his arm through Perrin's frail, bird-like bones and clung on. That was the mystery: it was he who was clinging to Perrin, not the other way round. But Perrin was off, putting all his suddenly furious energy into pushing the cart along. He was calling out the names of the plants as he went, voice full of glee: 'Pittosporum! Helleborus! Antirrhinum! Cotoneaster!'

Now people *were* staring.

But Perrin was unstoppable. It was as if he were gathering in energy from the presence of so many plant forms which, embedded in earth, nourished, watered and weeded, would continue the chain of life: just as his dust would one day, soon, oh soon, too soon, be added to the earth, composting.

Eric felt an uneasy yet piercing sense of happiness, a lyrical rapture in which he conceived the reality of how much he loved Perrin: of how Perrin was, at that very moment, leading him on a voyage of discovery so that they were, as in the dream, two circus horses together rising, leaping wonderfully high, almost far enough above the world, so that for one moment it was as if Perrin and he were experiencing in advance that exhilarating blast of freedom as they surged away from the globe on which all of life was contained, and beyond which there lay nothing—at least nothing known.

The plants were loaded into the boot. Eric had, at the last moment, tried to modulate Perrin's buying frenzy but, as if in testimony to his mood-swing, Perrin had impetuously bought too much, ordered Eric to shut up, and had sailed past the cash register issuing a cheque which Eric felt sure, with a lowering degree of certainty, would bounce. But Perrin, like a small child now, exhausted, almost turning nasty, threatened to throw a tantrum in front of the entire queue. 'I must have what I want,' he had cried. 'You don't *understand*. I *must*!'

And now, thankfully safe inside the car, Eric began breathing a little easier. He shook off his sunglasses, which now weighed heavy on his nose. He felt the beginning pincers of a headache. Perrin was saying to him that he wanted—he *needed*—to take Eric's car for a drive. He needed to be on his own. He could drive still. Did Eric doubt him? Why was Eric always doubting him?

'Trust me,' said Perrin in a small voice, like a caress.

Eric looked at his old friend. How much longer would he have him with him, to trust, not to trust, to doubt—to be astonished by. He did not know. So, doubting everything, doubting his own instincts to be firm, to say no, Eric allowed himself to be dropped off outside a mutual friend's townhouse, a refugee, and, standing on the pavement, about to go in, he watched Perrin drive away in his car, faltering out into the middle of the road, hugging the centre line. And seeing Perrin move off, odd, slow and cumbersome, trying so hard to control his own fate, Eric watched his dear love, his friend, turn the corner, with as much grace as possible, attempting to execute his own exit.

John Cranna

ARCHAEOLOGY

We lived that summer of the war in a house that looked down over a dry valley to the low blue wall of the Tasman Sea. Between the house and the sea was a riverbed in which the stones gleamed like polished skulls in the sun, and beyond the riverbed, a grove of apricot trees, and when in the late morning the wind came down from the hills behind the house, the trees would stir quietly as though touched by the ghosts of the gold-diggers who a century before had left the valley. Apart from the apricot trees there was little in the valley but tussock grass and the occasional ruined shack with its iron roof adrift and moving cautiously with the wind.

We lived there, he and I, with his mother, who in the mornings sat among the skulls in the riverbed weeping, and in the afternoons crept silently through the cool rooms of the house in search of insects. The house had stood now for a very long time, and along the side facing down the valley to the sea was a wooden veranda from which the white paint peeled and flaked with the sun and the wind. In the evenings we sat on the veranda and watched the dusk settle into the Tasman, and imagined, a thousand miles beyond, the red disc of the sun hanging low over the Australian deserts. We talked on these evenings of the war, of which we knew almost nothing, and discussed our theories about how it might have begun, about whether the exchanges had stopped, but we had no hard facts on which to base our theories, there had been no travellers on the coast road for months, and our small plastic radio had for some time now given us no news.

During the day we worked on the ground beside the house, extending the small garden to several times its previous size and constructing an irrigation channel to bring water from a stream in the nearby hills. The channel had enabled us to grow a number of vegetables in the barren soil of the valley, and had been put together from the remains of a sluice run we had found in one of the gold workings in the hills. On the day of its completion we held a small ceremony, for which Chris's mother dressed in her best clothes and made a short, incomprehensible speech, but when the clear water of the stream started on its new course between the timbers of the channel she began to weep and we had to cancel the rest of our little ceremony and return to the house. She lived between two rooms at the back of the house, every few days moving her possessions from one to the other, so that one of the rooms was always quite empty, the floor-boards dusty and bare and the drapes removed from the windows. When I asked Chris about this he shrugged and grinned in his nervous way, Maybe she gets bored in one room, he said, unembarrassed by the madness of his mother. He was seventeen, older than I was, and little taller, we had been friends now for a long time, and when our fathers were taken by the navy because they were fishermen and the war seemed inevitable, I had come to stay with him on the coast. Each day we went to the beach and took shellfish from the pale yellow sand for the evening meal, varying our method of preparation from night to night to avoid tiring of our constant diet of food from the sea. Afterwards, on the veranda, we listened to the radio, aware of the need to conserve the batteries, but there was nothing to be heard except the uninterrupted buzz of static, as though the waveband was being jammed by unseen electrical storms beyond the horizon. I watched the sea at dusk, searching for the flicker of distant lightning, but nothing disturbed the dissolving line of sea and sky.

The lack of news did not appear to worry Chris, he was concerned more with day-to-day matters, such as the condition of the water channel and his plan to build a boat so that we might catch larger fish offshore. We sat on the veranda one evening and he spoke about the boat in his quiet, sure voice. He had found some sound planks and a few pit-props in a working up the valley, he said, and he would carve the props into ribs and fashion a clinker hull from the planks. When I sat and listened to Chris talk in this way, I found it hard to believe that our time in the house was anything but a long holiday, and although I had not yet made the connection between the war and the behaviour of his mother, I felt sometimes that her strange ways were all that prevented this from becoming a permanent delusion. Earlier we had heard her moving with her insect jar through the distant rooms of the house, and now she appeared beside us on the veranda, holding the top down rigidly on the jar, as though afraid that its contents might escape. Two grey moths lay on their backs in the bottom. Chris looked at her solemnly, Are you sure they're dead, Mum? he said. His mother examined the fragile shapes through the glass, holding the jar up to the lamp overhead, then abruptly disappeared down the steps into the dark. We heard her making her way to the riverbed, where each night she buried her catch on the bank above the smooth white stones.

When I could no longer hear the sound of her steps I said, What will she do when there are no insects left to catch? and Chris grinned, Maybe we can persuade her to come to the beach with her jar and catch fish instead. His mother had lost interest in the ordinary things of life, she did not have it in her to help with finding food or with cooking, and when, on Sunday mornings, I took her down to the beach to wash, she resisted me strongly, not so much from fear of the sea, but rather because she held something against it. When eventually I got her to the beach, she stood stiffly in the shallows while I scrubbed her with sand, she said nothing, but it was plain that she hated the sea water on her body. The ocean that month was a glassy green, there had been no storms and the debris along the beach had remained undisturbed now for as long as I could recall. When I sat with my line in the sand, I could close my eyes and conjure in my mind the exact pattern of debris along the tide-line, from the scattering of bone-white pumice to the position of the last desiccated twig. They were long, empty afternoons, with just the burning sky and the flat green sea, afternoons, spent locked into a trance that would be broken only by the jerk of the line around my wrist—and then I was alert, touched by a startling invisible life, a life I could never believe existed until the nylon was taut and running, sending back its message of terror from the swarming bed of the sea.

And the sky to the west did not change, I watched it as I fished, neutrally and without expectation, and at the end of the day I took the fish back up to the house to fry on the iron stove in the kitchen, and we sat at the table and ate and joked with Chris's mother. Sometimes she smiled and we would pretend that she understood our jokes, but we knew that in reality she smiled because of some unimaginable event in the other distant world that she inhabited. She had begun to look thinner and more pale of late, so that we pressed food upon her, we gave her the largest portions of fish, but she would often leave her food unfinished and no amount of urging would persuade her to eat any more.

One afternoon Chris and I went up the valley to the gold workings to search out wood for the boat he was planning. A century before, the upper valley had been well populated with men looking for gold, and above the stream bed we came upon a collection of derelict huts and their complicated arrangement of wooden parapets and sluices. We worked on a sluice run until we could free its boards with ease, digging to loosen the framework from the earth. Then Chris stopped and stood up, he held in his hand a long tapered bone from which he shook the remaining traces of soil. What's this? Leaning forward, he pointed the bone at my chest, he was frowning heavily, You are condemned to take this boat we build, and sail in her to the west for all eternity, he said, and I said, Don't joke, what kind of animal is it anyway?

We scraped at the earth at the base of the frame and came upon other bones, they were laid out in a pattern that twisted in under the frame posts, and after a while Chris said, I think it's a man. Maybe the miners buried people alive under their buildings for luck, like the Melanesians. But the skeleton was too large to be human, the bones of the legs were exceptionally long, and as we uncovered more of it, we could see that the creature had a thin, curved neck like a swan, but much longer and more powerful. Then I said, It's a moa. We both stopped digging and sat back from the skeleton. We shouldn't move it, I said, and Chris said, But who is there to show it to? We sat and looked at the bones for a while, a little afraid, aware that the great bird had remained undisturbed for a thousand years. Then Chris said that we should collect the bones and take them to the house, where we could piece the skeleton together again, it would be safer there, though safer against what, he did not say. That evening we sat on the veranda and tried to remember what we knew about the great flightless birds that had ruled the country before man arrived from the north and hunted them into oblivion. We argued about their size and colouring, and finally agreed that they had been as high as twelve feet, with powerful, scaly legs and a plumage of deepest blue. Chris was certain that they were predators, able to catch their victims through their great speed across the ground, but I was sure that they did not kill, that they were stately birds who were able to live quietly among the rich grasslands of the time.

In the days that followed, we laid out the bones in a shed beside the house and began to fit them together. I had made a sketch of how they lay and Chris had glued a piece of paper to each bone and numbered it according to my drawing, the way we imagined scientists did. Because the skeleton had been twisted where it lay in the earth, our attempt to arrange it in its true shape was based partly on how we imagined the bird must once have looked. We worked on the moa late into the evenings, the two of us crouched in the shed under an oil lamp with the bones scattered around us, arranging, adjusting, fitting and matching the pieces we had taken from the earth, until we were light-headed with the effort of it, and still the great bird lay stubbornly misshapen on the floor, less clear now in its form than when we had uncovered it first at the head of the valley. We had been working on the bird now for more than a week, and we sat defeated in front of the skeleton, looking down at the bones, which showed ashen white in the dull light from the lamp. Are you sure you didn't make a mistake with the numbering? I said. Chris stared at me for a moment without speaking, then turned back to the bird, and I wished that I had said nothing. We went up to the house and switched on the radio. That evening the static seemed a little more subdued than usual, and as Chris carefully turned the dial, I thought I caught the fragment of a human voice. I grasped his arm, Turn it back. We found the spot almost immediately, and for the first time in many months a broadcast filtered out of the night, a voice that was infinitely fragile, as though exhausted by continual battle against the static that choked the waveband. We could catch only occasional words and could make no sense of them, until without warning a clear phrase emerged, '. . . windsheer across the equator . . . cloud projected south . . .' before the voice faded and was submerged once more in the relentless surf of static. Chris looked up and shrugged, Just a weather report, he said. We discussed the static and what might be causing it, but as on previous occasions we could think of no explanation that sounded at all convincing and eventually we lapsed into silence. Chris's mother sat bent forward beside us, the insect jar on the table next to her unfinished meal. Chris said, Aren't you hunting tonight, Mum? It pained him to see her like this, hunched forward as though paralysed, he preferred her to be occupied with her inexplicable rituals of capture and burial, he felt responsible for her when she was still. His mother made no response, she was watching the night outside in the particular intent way she did from time to time, and I knew that she would remain like this until after we had gone to bed.

   Next day the weather changed, and for the first time since the beginning of summer a haloed sun shone through high cloud. At the beach, where I sat fishing in the sand, the colours were bleached from the land and a dull wind blew in off the sea. I sat all afternoon without a bite on the line, day-dreaming of a port in the north where the days, the weeks and the months had been marked out by the coming and going of a rusted trawler in which men shouted and joked, and where the catch was tumbled still living onto a quay that smelled of bilges and diesel. Towards evening the shoals had moved offshore and I wound in my line, as the onshore wind strengthened and whipped the tussock on the dunes behind the beach. By the time I reached the house the wind was funnelling up the valley to lift dust from the hills beyond and slamming the door to the skeleton shed. Chris was in the kitchen preparing sea-eggs and had filled a huge bowl with their translucent pulp. I looked at the bowl and he laughed at my expression, Have you seen Mum? he said. I shook my head and turned away from the bowl of pulp to the window, You left the shed door open, I said. Chris started up from the table, That must have been her.

We went to the shed and pulled open the door against the wind, inside the skeleton lay inert in the dust, the great neck curved towards us, as though straining towards the light. We had kept the discovery of the creature from his mother, not knowing quite why, and now for an insane moment I thought, She's found it and pieced it together for us, and then I saw that the creature was the same as we'd left it the day before, misshapen and incomplete. Chris bent down to examine the skeleton, then looked around the shed. Some of it's gone, he said. One of the long bones that made up the legs of the bird had been removed, and although we searched the shed and went through the pile of bones that we had failed to fit into place, we could find nothing. Then distantly, from down the valley, came the sound of his mother's voice. At first we could not place it as we hurried towards the sea, and then we saw her, a slight figure standing beyond the apricot trees, the great leg bone of the moa clenched in her hand, screaming her incomprehensible accusations at the Tasman Sea as the wind blew in out of the chaotic dusk.

The wind blew steady and warm all night without a break, and in the morning it was still high when I went to check on the irrigation channel, which was vulnerable to wind where it crossed a gully as a raised bridge. Chris could remember nothing like it on the coast, it came now from the west at a constant speed, so dry that it wilted the crops and cracked the mud in the riverbed. The water in the irrigation channel had slowed to a trickle, as though the wind had sought out the stream that supplied it and dried it off at its source. Since her discovery of the skeleton, Chris's mother had taken refuge in her room, and she would not come out, even for meals. She lay on her side in a corner, her knees drawn up to her chin and her eyes fixed on a wall, oblivious to the food that we left for her on the floor beside her mattress. She held in her hand the moa bone, which she would not let go of, and she gripped it so tightly that I could see the sinews in her forearm stand out beneath the skin. We tried to get her to eat, but she would not hear us, instead she moved closer to the wall, holding the bone against her breasts, as though afraid we would take it from her. We worked silently on the skeleton now, for several days the steady wind threw up so much dust that work outside was impossible, we spent all our time in the shed with the bird, shuffling the remaining bones through an endless series of patterns that made no sense, we did not talk, somehow we could no longer think of very much that we wanted to say to each other.

And then the wind dropped and on the same day we had a visitor. She came along the coast track in the late afternoon, she was about our own age, and her hair was cropped very short on her head. We had seen no one in months, and we watched in surprise as she came up to veranda and threw her bag on the steps. She looked dirty and tired. Do you have any water? she said. Later we sat together around the table and ate, and she told us that she had been travelling for five days up the coast, and in that time she had seen no one at all. She had come across a number of deserted houses, the occupants it seemed had gone inland to the mountains, though she did not know why. After telling us this she was silent, and we watched her eat the sweet potatoes and shellfish we had cooked. She ate awkwardly, her jaw moved at a slight angle to her head, as though her jaw-bone had once been broken. It was clear that she was very hungry so we did not ask her more questions, we let her eat undisturbed. When she had finished the meal she looked up and spoke: In the south they said that Australia was caught in the exchanges. There was a silence, I looked at Chris, then indicated the transistor radio. Could that be causing the static? She picked up the radio, listened to a burst of static, then placed it back on the table and shrugged. I dunno, she said, then, Where can I sleep? I put a mattress in the room next to Chris's mother and left the girl to her exhaustion. Chris and I sat up late that night arguing about our visitor and what she had told us. Chris was inclined not to take her news seriously, he said that she did not look very trustworthy, and that the word of a total stranger should be treated with caution. But what if she's right? I said. Chris got up tiredly from the table, You think too much, he said, and went in to bed. Next morning, before the others were up, I walked down to the beach to look at the horizon. The morning was still and quiet beneath a burnt-out sun, and to the west a haze covered the sea. Nothing showed in that western sky, it was as blank as it had been all summer, an empty gateway to the continent a thousand miles beyond, and after a time I went back up to the house for breakfast.

I found Chris in his mother's room, crouching by her mattress, a plate of cold toast beside him on the floor. He was speaking to her in a new, urgent voice. You've got to eat, Mum, you'll get ill if you don't. She did not even look at him, she remained with her face to the wall, the bone still gripped firmly in her fist. He tried again. We have a visitor, she's from the south. If you come and have some breakfast, you can meet her. His mother pulled her knees into her body and huddled closer to the wall. Chris got up and we went out into the kitchen where the girl was finishing her breakfast. She glanced up as we came in and continued eating, carefully cleaning the last scrap of food from the plate. Who was that? she said without interest. My mother. She's ill, said Chris. The girl looked suddenly uneasy. What's she got? There was a long pause, and then I said, She seems to have lost her appetite. The girl said she planned to continue up the coast that day, she did not want to speak of her eventual destination, and in the afternoon she went off up the coast path with a wave, and did not look back. Later we found our last cheese and a tin of honey missing, and Chris said, What did I tell you?

We worried about his mother now, it had been three days since she had eaten, she lay frail and thin on her mattress and her eyes were dark holes in a white face. I put the insect jar beside her on the floor and sat with her that evening, a lamp by the open window to attract the night insects, hoping that this might help her to rediscover her old obsessions. When she slept, her breathing came in shallow gasps, as though she did not trust the air to enter her lungs when she was not awake. I dozed in a wooden chair beside her mattress, half listening to the ocean and dreaming of the creature that once walked its ancient shore. The bird was very clear now in my dreams, its curved beak and bulbous, searching eyes, and in those eyes was an intelligence that spoke to me out of the past, there was some knowledge there that I strained towards but could not grasp, and in the moment that I felt I might understand, a subtle shift in the rasping breath of the sleeper propelled me awake, my palms moist with sweat and my heart pounding in my chest.

The keel of the boat we were planning lay in the garden, but the enthusiasm I felt for the project was gone, and I only half believed now that the craft would ever be completed. We disagreed over the way in which the hull should be fixed to the ribs, we seemed now to be opposed on the smallest of issues. I told Chris that the method he proposed was dangerously fragile and the fixings might part in a heavy sea, but he insisted that as the originator of the plan to build the boat he had the final word in matters of design. I had not seen him like this before, the old diffidence was gone and had been replaced by a hardness that was quite new. The house, which had seemed so large when I arrived in the spring, now seemed small and cramped, we could no longer escape each other there, and I spent more time away on long walks in the hills and along the beach. We continued to leave food for his mother but mechanically now, without much hope, for she had lost all contact with the outside, and I knew that only some change within the sealed world of her madness would free her to eat. She would not even let us wash her and gradually the odour of her body crept through the house until it was so sharp that it took away the breath, like a thin strong hand at the throat.

Often on my walks I would find myself at a place I recognised as being miles from the valley, without being conscious of how I had arrived there. One afternoon I found myself above the sluice run where we had discovered the moa. I sat on the step of the shack and stared at the mound of earth still fresh beside the hole we had dug. It seemed an age since we had found the skeleton, but in reality it had been only a few weeks. And then I was on my feet. Of course, how stupid we had been. Some of the bones were still in the ground! I was in the trench, scrabbling with my hands at its sides and sifting through the loose earth in the bottom, each pebble a lost fragment of the bird, I was certain that a few more inches would reveal the vital bones we had missed. Eventually I sat back against the side of the trench and examined my hands. I had driven a wood splinter into my palm and my nails were torn and bleeding. There was nothing in the trench, not even the smallest shard of bone, and as I sat there beneath the sluice run I thought suddenly how foolish we had been to remove the creature from the dry earth of the gold-field where it had lain undisturbed for so long.

When I returned to the house Chris was standing at the door to his mother's room. He was half turned away from me and did not move when I came in. What is it? I said. He turned as if to speak, his face drained of colour, but in the end he said nothing. I went to the door and looked into the dim room. The insect jar lay shattered on the floor, and with one of the pieces his mother had carefully cut both her wrists. The blood had dried to a crust that spread out on the floor before her in a crisp red sheet, and although she sat upright in her chair and looked across the room at us with round, interested eyes, it was clear that she was quite dead. She was dressed in her best clothes, the ones she had last worn at the ceremony we held to open the irrigation channel, and as I stood there in my shock, I thought, At least she looks like someone's mother again now. Later that afternoon we combed her hair and pinned it back the way she had once worn it, then we cut her fingernails, which had become ragged and bitten. When we finished we took her down to the river bank and buried her beside the smooth white stones, she was very light and either of us could have carried her there alone. The moa bone was still clasped in her hand and I suggested that as a mark of respect for her last obsession we should bury it with her, but in the end we could not bear to do it, to sacrifice in this way such an important piece of the bird, and before we lowered her into the trench we had dug in the flinty soil, Chris gently prised her fingers loose from the bone.

Somehow our work on the moa now became something over which we had lost control. We were drawn each day to the shed as surely as we were drawn each day to the sea for our food, there was some larger imperative involved that we did not even try to talk about, but which was as real as our daily routines of survival. We did not seem to be any closer to a solution, but we knew now that there was no question of not finishing what we had begun. Sometimes, after hours of work, we would find that we had entered a cul-de-sac we had left some weeks before, we were repeating our mistakes, and it was at these times that our task seemed most hopeless. We blamed each other for these errors, though little was openly said. Each of us now saw the other as an obstacle to progress on the bird, and often we would work for hours without a word passing between us, locked into the bitter isolation that our work had brought us. Chris had developed a rash that began on his back and spread to his neck, his face and his arms, until his upper body was covered with raised weals. I said that we should eat separately in case it was contagious, and that I should work in the skeleton hut alone, but he maintained that the rash was caused by the dry wind, which blew in off the sea every few days.

I was dreaming every night now, harsh vivid dreams that were more real than the days themselves. I dreamt of a beach from which the ocean has withdrawn so that the seabed is exposed to the horizon, a naked plain of sand on which stranded creatures struggle for breath in shallow pools. And I dreamt of a harbour where a young girl with close-cropped hair sits beneath a yellow canary in a cage. She is absorbed in her task, which is to cut with a pair of scissors a perfect circle from the sheet of paper she holds in her hand, and as it is completed, the circle becomes a disc that glows first red, then whitens to an incandescent heat, until it burns itself into the retina of my dreaming eye.

Parts of the irrigation channel had begun to collapse and we could no longer find the energy to repair the damage. The early summer had become a distant time with no connection to the present, the projects we had planned seemed to be little more than futile exercises that had diverted us from the more important business we were not engaged in. Everything was sacrificed to the creature, to the hut where the dry scrape of bone on bone, the scuffle of some emerging pattern on the dirt floor and the magnified whisper of our own breathing were the sounds that marked out the boundaries of our waking hours. By now our stocks of food were running down, we had no more sugar or flour, and although Chris talked vaguely of an expedition down the coast to one of the abandoned houses the girl had seen, I knew we would never go. At the beach, the shoals seemed to have moved away from the land, and on some days I caught nothing at all. Then one morning I found that the tide had marooned a huge swarm of jellyfish on the beach and in the shallows, and for three days fishing became impossible. They were a type I had seen very occasionally in the nets of trawlers that had been fishing in the tropics, their bodies a pale mauve flecked with pink, and I wondered how they came to be many hundreds of miles south of their home waters. After a few days they began to rot, and the wind blew the stench up the valley so there was no escaping it, it hung there in the house as it had once before, and I woke up that night with the sweat cold on my body, certain that Chris's mother was back with us, that she lay with her bone and her rasping breath on the floor of the room next door.

For three days we survived on rice and a little dried fruit, and on the fourth day the stench from the beach was so great that I did not even bother to check whether fishing was possible. Instead I sat on the veranda and repaired my floats. Chris came up from the shed and watched me for a time. Then he said quietly, Are you going to the beach? We had not spoken that day, and I shook my head without looking up from my work. He watched me for a while longer, then went over to my fishing tackle and began loading it into its sack. What are you doing? He threw the sack over his shoulder and started towards the beach, down the slope to the riverbed, picking his way among the stones, an arm extended for balance. I got up and leant against the veranda rail, a point of hot metal seemed to press up against my ribs and my vision blurred a little so that I had difficulty in following him as he continued down the valley. Then I was down the steps and after him, slipping and scrabbling in the riverbed, I could hear myself shouting, but what I heard made no sense to me. By the time I reached the beach he was wading out through the shallows with the line in his hand, the jellyfish a grey carpet that folded in behind him. I ran into the sea and felt the creatures cling suddenly to my legs, they had been dead for days but now they came alive in opposition to me. I struggled towards Chris, he glancing back over his shoulder, then turning and wading on towards the outer edge of the blobbing carpet. The creatures disintegrated as I forced my way among them, I was up to my waist in a soup of jelly and tangled filaments, I was getting no closer to Chris, but my blind anger drove me on through the stench that rose choking around me and through the insects that hung in clouds over the grey sea. There was no escaping the insects, they bit my neck and arms and lodged in my ears and in my nostrils, I was inhaling them, spitting their bitter taste from my tongue and wiping them clear of my stinging eyes. And then suddenly I was free of the swirling bank of insects and wading into open water.

Chris stood motionless a few yards ahead of me, gazing out to sea, and as I made my way towards him he let go of the line he was carrying so that it spun away into the clear water, the skein of invisible nylon unravelling as it sank. We stood there very still, up to our waists in water, and looked at our new horizon, a horizon across which stretched a shimmering band of palest green. It lay in a continuous arc that appeared to touch the coast to the north and south, but this was an illusion brought on by the scale of the thing and by the curve of the horizon, and I knew that it must still be far out to sea. Despite its distance I could see that it had an internal life of its own, it was illuminated from within by a flickering that appeared to be due to electrical storms and which disturbed its surface like the movement of eels beneath the surface of a pond. The beauty of the thing took the breath away, we stood there hypnotised for a long time, watching its imperceptible progress across the face of the ocean, until eventually I touched Chris's arm and we made our way back to the beach.

At the shed the bird waited for us in the dim light, its bones laid out as we had left them in clumsy imitation of its lost form. We knelt there in the dust of the floor of the hut and began to work, we handled the creature with a new care, weighing each bone with a patience that had previously escaped us, testing our patterns against a fragile image of a living form that seemed somehow to have clarified in our minds. At first we had the impression of a small advance, but the further we pushed the advance the faster we found the puzzle giving way before us, pieces of the skeleton that had lain awkwardly together all summer were dovetailing smoothly; rib, joint and socket began now to match with ease, until the coupling of bone on bone acquired an effortless momentum of its own, and the outline of a new, vital pattern began to take shape in the dust. There was no stopping us now, we were the agents of a mechanism that moved with some older and deeper logic, and which now that it had been set in motion swept aside the trivial errors and false starts of the past months. . . .We were laughing and shouting as we worked, the long summer which had seemed to disintegrate around us outside the dim confines of the shed, the abandonment of our crops and our plans to build the boat, the decline and final madness of Chris's mother and now the cloud that had appeared out to sea . . . all this was a distant irrelevance when set beside the intoxicating power of the process that we had become part of, the rebirth of the great creature that had once ruled the shores of our ancient ocean.

When we had finished, we sat very quiet and very still beside our completed work. The skeleton expressed a perfection of form that reached out of the past and silenced us with its beauty. It was much more than the proud creature of my dreams reborn into the present, it was the vehicle for a form of knowledge that had previously been denied us, and which was linked to the dry wind that had sprung up outside and was rattling the windows of the distant house. Chris knelt beside the creature and gently stroked the great bone of the leg. I stood behind him, my hand on his shoulder, and felt the slow flex of muscle beneath his skin. We were very close again now, we belonged there together in the gloom with the creature, and I knew then that we would never leave the hut, we could not abandon the bird at such a time. I heard the wind rising in the apricot trees beyond the stream bed, but all sound had somehow become external to the hut, and even later, when the wind was howling up the floor of the valley from the sea and beginning to pry with steady insistence at the door to the shed, it did nothing to disturb the deep, clear silence inside.

Lloyd Jones

WHO'S THAT DANCING WITH MY MOTHER?

We were living in Napier at the time. My father pulled the keys down from the hook in the kitchen and my mother asked where he was headed.

'Up the coast,' he said, and my mother went on slicing the ends off the beans for the meal she now knew he wouldn't be around to eat.

'Allie,' my father said by the kitchen door. 'I feel like being alone for a while.'

My mother quietly emptied the colander of beans into the sink. She turned around to face us both.

'Just say where it is you are going.'

My father looked at the keys in his hand, and turned down the challenge. He crossed the lawn to the Hunter parked in the driveway. My mother followed as far as the porch. There she stopped, as if the lawn was a slippery area she would rather not cross, and yelled out: 'Why can't you say it, you lousy stinking coward!' My father settled behind the wheel and backed down the driveway. My mother raised her hands to her face. Then she noticed me; and that seemed to be the last straw.

'What are you looking at . . . . goddammit!'

From being hurt, she wanted to be forgiven. It was a confusing moment. Her faced screwed up with anger, and she drew me over and said, 'Hug your mother, Charlie.' I was happy to, of course, but when I looked I noticed she had drawn herself into two parts: one I hugged, and the other—her proud face—had already turned with a thought to something inside the house.

I followed her inside, through to the living room. She walked directly to the bookcase, where she pulled out a thick book on flora. Most of our books were on plants, lichen and mosses. My father worked in the ecology division of the DSIR.

The book fell open, and the photo of my father fell out. It was taken near the snowline. There was no snow in the photo but you could tell from the rocks and the lichen grown over them that snow was not far off. My father had on his hiking boots. His arm was draped around a woman, an Australian. She was a plant illustrator, who had come here for dinner one night, a long time ago.

My mother studied the photo. She seemed to be trying to prise a bit more from it than the contents were prepared to tell. I couldn't say what she found. Perhaps it was because the photo was deliberately vague that she got so angry. She tore the photo into quarters and watched them settle over the carpet. My father's head was now severed; his whiskery smile even more a mystery.

My mother stepped back and almost fell over. She had forgotten I was there. She swore, then, she smiled bravely. 'Know what we're going to do, Charlie? No. Second thoughts I'm not going to tell you. Let's make it a surprise.'

Our town held few surprises, although it was useful to pretend otherwise. I was just as happy not knowing in any case, because we ended up at Chee's.

Some of the pub crowd had wandered across the road and were trying to chat up the Chinese girl behind the counter. The girl blushed and smiled out of politeness, but you could see she didn't know what the men were on about, and I thought it just as well.

We took the table by the window. Cars were leaving spaces outside the hotel. One of the men at the counter came over and sat at our table. 'Hello beautiful,' he said.

My mother turned and looked straight into his face the way it is said to be cruel to do with dogs. The man said 'Jeeeesus' and got up as quickly as he had sat down. Our meals arrived. My mother hardly touched her fillet.

She counted out the money on the table. She had enough, clearly more than she had thought, because she appeared to be relieved.

'Now is the real surprise,' she said, and we started towards the beach.

The sea breeze was on the way out and the leaves in the trees along the esplanade had stopped rustling. It was growing dark, and sure enough the storm clouds were bunched inland over the ranges.

'I feel like dancing,' my mother announced. She looked at me, then burst out laughing. We walked briskly. The music from the roller skating rink grew louder, and my mother pulled the sides of her cardigan to cover her chest. We could hear Cadillac Jack trying to hustle the crowd onto the rink. He spoke in rhyming couplets—so my mother said, and word had it he was brother of a famous American DJ. My mother always said, it was worth believing anything so long as it wasn't harmful. So little happened around here anyway.

My mother fussed over the skates like they were vegetables from the cheap bin.

She glided out onto the rink. She did a lap. Her lips were pursed, kind of hard-looking without lipstick. She usually wore lipstick when she went out. Her eyes were concentrated, as if trying to find a way back to some partially lost feeling. She came down off the high shoulder at the beach end and overtook a bunch of kids from the high school. You could easily be fooled, but if you forgot the rest of her and watched the skates you saw she was in complete control. The third or fourth lap she came soaring down and picked me off the rail.

'Push off your toes, Charlie. Push. Push. Push. You're much too stiff.'

She glided out ahead, and started to do skater's goose-step, holding one skate out front about knee height and alternating with the other. She came past the crowd and turned the heads on half a dozen cowboys. Her face glowed. She knew what she had done. She took off her white cardigan and tied it about her waist. Some of the slower skaters moved out of her way and found the sides as she barrelled down the straight past the hot dog stand. Cadillac inside his glass dome let go a gi-normous hooooeeeee. My mother went into a speed crouch and shot up high on the end bend.

Just short of the cowboys, a guy in black jeans and a bush shirt tied at the throat with a length of string pushed off the wall. There were twenty metres in which to decide whether she would go around him. He held his hand out like a ballroom dancer. My mother dug in the toe of her back skate. The stranger's hand collected her around the waist; she spun round once, then again, this time under her own steam to show she enjoyed it.

They pushed off together. The cowboy holding her hand, and my mother bothered by a strand of damp hair that kept falling across her face.

I had stopped trying to skate. I leant against the rail in front of some spectators. I was wondering where my father was right this moment. What he was doing. And what kind of person the Australian woman might be getting to know. I suppose I had taken over my mother's thoughts for the time being—caretaking while she skated.

My mother and her partner seemed none the wiser that a lot of attention was on them. The people behind me had begun to mutter. Something about the 'prison-escaper'. Cadillac had gone quiet.

At the town end of the rink they rose together up the shoulder; the escaper hoisted my mother into the air. She threw her head back and used one leg to clamp his shoulder; the other leg she clasped behind the knee and held it straight out front. In this formation they swept down off the bend. By the hot dog stand some of the pub crowd began to clap. I caught a glimpse of the escaper's face; it appeared caught halfway between a big loony grin and serious concern.

'I thought he had gone bush forever and a day,' a voice said behind me.

Somebody else said he had slipped out of the bush this morning. 'Robbie Hale seen him sniffing on the edge of town at daybreak.'

This time as the skaters came barrelling down the straight before the crowd my mother threw her head all the way back until her skates were over the escaper's head, which brought a gasp from the crowd. Then she brought her skates overtop, as if she were doing a backward roll. Over she went until her skates touched the rink. The escaper reached between his legs and drew her through until my mother was the lead skater. She turned to face him, now, and he lifted her so she had her legs splayed either side of him and they were joined at the waist. People had stopped talking and were just staring. My mother's head was well tossed back and she held onto the escaper's shoulders. She started to move up and down with her hips. Neither of them seemed concerned for skate speed. The escaper managed to steer them both up the end shoulder to see them down the straight. On the far side of the rink they moved through the pool of light from the overhead lamps, into shadows, then light again. My mother's face turned a fluorescent colour; now the escaper's head fell back. They were locked together with another movement that had nothing to do with skating.

I heard Cadillac come on over the sound to get more skaters onto the rink. But no one was listening. And there was no heart in the message because Cadillac did not repeat it.

What happened next had nothing to do with Cadillac, or the crowd looking on. From the esplanade a police siren could be heard. The escaper's head turned a fraction. I believe it was the only intervention he would have heeded. He and my mother had virtually come to a standstill in a shadow at the end of the rink. Some of the crowd had moved there to get a better look. The sirens were close, now. My mother was lowered on to her skates. She and the escaper stood straight and near to each other, like lovers in a park.

He kissed her once—on the cheek. Then he split. He pushed off and was nearly in a speed crouch when he passed me.

I heard someone bitch that the escaper hadn't returned his skates.

'Typical' from someone else.

He leapt the turnstile for the esplanade and skated through the first set of lights. One violation after another, cast behind like discarded clothing.

My mother was buttoning her cardigan, as if it was the most important thing in the world. Her cheeks were still flushed. She knew I was nearby, but she looked up in her own good time. She said, 'You enjoying yourself, Charlie? Not too much I hope because I feel like going home now.'

The drunks near the hot dog stand called out things, but she took no notice. 'Look at that, Charlie,' she said, and very deliberately she pointed over the heads of the cowboys, to a fairly ordinary sunset.

While we were getting out of our skates Cadillac came out of his glass dome. I had never actually seen him. He had a pointed beard—like the famous record-spinner—but he only just cleared the top of my head. He looked frightened, and in a quiet voice I never imagined might be his, he said the police had sent through word that they wished to speak with my mother.

He mentioned the man being an escaper, and my mother, still cool as a cucumber, said, 'What, you mean that nice young man?'

Two blocks away from the skating rink she permitted herself to say something, and I realised she was shaking like a leaf.

'I feel like singing,' she said to the trees. Then she stole a quick look at me. 'Charlie, you're not angry with me. Are you, Charlie? Don't be. I haven't skated like that for years.'

We came to our street and from here we should have been able to see the house lights. The car wasn't in the driveway, and I worried that it would have some effect. But she didn't appear to notice. Or, if she did, she didn't care. At the door she said she thought she might have a bath. As it happened we pushed through to the living room, where her eyes went straight to the torn quarters of the photograph. She crossed her arms, and thought.

'Charlie,' she said. 'Go get that glue from the top of the fridge. Let's not disappoint your father.'

Vivienne Plumb

THE WIFE WHO SPOKE JAPANESE IN HER SLEEP

In the winter the nights become long and cold. In Honey Tarbox's house all is hushed on a frosty midwinter night.

Then slowly, slowly, Honey rolls over in her bed and starts to wake. She is speaking Japanese.

'Kyoo wa samui desu ne.'

'What . . .?' she thinks.

'Ohayo gozaimasu,' she says out loud. The words echo around the cold, still bedroom. Her husband groans,

'Huh, wozzat?'

She stops speaking but her mind keeps turning, rolling around. What did I say, she thinks. She doesn't know it was Japanese. She's the wife who spoke Japanese in her sleep.

* * *

At first she didn't speak much Japanese.

Her husband, Howard, stayed awake one night and described what he saw happen. He watched her go to bed. Gradually she fell asleep, then after an hour she started speaking in another language. She spoke for a little time.

When she woke in the morning Honey was amazed to hear Howard's description.

She never felt tired. She was always rested, relaxed. But Howard often looked exhausted.

'The talking keeps me awake,' he said.

At first they couldn't understand which language it was. Neither of them had ever spoken any language themselves other than English. Honey had once gone on a holiday to Fiji but Howard had never travelled.

So one night Howard said he would tape Honey talking in her sleep. The next day they took the tape to the School of Languages which was very close by. They asked to see a teacher. While they sat waiting they watched six goldfish swimming in a large tank.

'Mr and Mrs Tarbox?' said the teacher. She wore spectacles and a maroon cardigan. Her hair was pulled back into a bun. To Honey and Howard she looked very educated.

'How can I help? What would you like to learn? Arabic? Spanish? Lithuanian? Mandarin? We offer them all.'

'Please listen to our tape,' said Howard, his face slightly flushed. He switched on his pocket machine.

'Nan desu ka,' said the voice on the tape. It didn't sound like Honey at all.

'What language is that?' asked Howard. The teacher listened.

'Why it's Japanese,' she said. She listened some more, then laughed. 'Good grief,' she said.

'What is it?' asked Honey.

'Well it's rather rude,' said the teacher. 'I don't think I could give you a direct translation. Where did you get this from?' Howard and Honey looked at each other.

'Umm . . .' they both said. Honey looked at her shoes, and Howard looked at the ceiling.

'Wait a minute,' said the teacher. 'Now what's she saying?' She leaned forward, concentrating on the tape recording.

'Wow, incredible. Who is this woman? I'd love to meet her. What a wonderful woman she is, she seems to know so much.'

'Why, what did she say?' said Howard. He wriggled on his chair. Honey watched the fish flipping around the tank and waited to hear what the teacher would say next.

'Well it's a kind of speech, about mankind,' said the teacher. 'Sort of prophecies . . . it's hard to describe.'

They all stood staring at each other. The voice on the tape had stopped.

'She says things. She's like a kind of . . . oracle,' said the teacher. 'I'd really like to meet her. Is she a friend of yours?'

Howard giggled. Honey looked at the fish. One really big goldfish swam right up to the glass, it's mouth opening and shutting at Honey. 'Oh! Oh! Oh!' it looked like it was saying.

'It's me,' said Honey in a flat voice. 'That tape recording is me.'

'You?' said the teacher. She was obviously surprised. She took her spectacles off and polished them and put them back on again.

'I don't understand,' said the teacher. 'If you speak Japanese, why don't you know what you're saying? Also, excuse me if I appear rude, but that voice doesn't sound like you at all. Hajimemashite. Watashi wa

Florica desu. Doozo yoroshiku.' She bowed low towards Honey.

'No, no!' whispered Honey. She backed away. 'I don't understand you!
. . . Tell her Howard. Tell her what happens.'

Howard moved closer to Miss Florica and lowered his voice.

'When Honey goes to sleep at night, she speaks like that.' He nodded
his head towards the tape recorder. Miss Florica gasped.

'She speaks in her sleep?' Howard nodded.

'And in a language she doesn't understand?'

'Yes,' said Howard. 'We don't know what to do.'

'But do you realise what she's saying?' asked Miss Florica.

'This voice on the tape is making prophecies. On the tape she made
some predictions about the government of our country.'

'No!' said Howard. Honey looked away. She was feeling so
embarrassed. She wished they'd never come.

'You must have a very special power,' said Miss Florica, 'to be able to
perceive things that we cannot. A clairvoyant power.' She smiled at
Honey.

But Honey said to Howard, 'Howard, let's leave, I just remembered I
left the heater on at home.'

Howard came straight away. He'd never encouraged large electricity
bills. Was in fact quite a penny pincher when it came down to it.

'Which heater?' he kept asking all the way back. 'The big one or the
little?'

'Oh, Howard, shut up,' said Honey. She withdrew to the bathroom
where she ran a long hot bath. She didn't come out until she heard
Howard leave for his afternoon class at the Community Institute. (He
was learning how to make patchwork.) Now he was retired he had
nothing else to do with his time. As for herself, the children had all grown
up long ago. She had no hobbies, no pastimes, no job, but now she had
this.

She looked at herself in the bedroom mirror. She saw a short, stout
woman, with blonde hair. A fleshy, plump body. She pinched the flesh
on her face. When she pulled her fingers away, a white mark was left on
the sagging pink skin.

She thought she knew what a clairvoyant was.

It was a woman, dressed with a scarf on her head, and wearing rings
and jewellery. She had a rich plummy voice, and she waved her hands
around in an artistic manner. She'd seen them in old Sherlock Holmes
movies. The lights would be dimmed and then, the spirits would come.
They would fill the room, knocking over lamps and tables in an effort to

make their presence known.

Was she a clairvoyant?

She laughed. She shook her head and her blonde hair fluffed around her head like a halo. What a preposterous idea!

Or in the newspaper. Sometimes she'd seen them in the newspaper. A woman would be called in to assist the police in finding a dead body. CLAIRVOYANT HELPS POLICE it would shout across the front page. And there'd be a photo of her, hand outstretched, eyes shut. Could that be Honey?

Or at school, many years ago. She remembered they had learnt about the Oracle at Delphi. A woman had sat on a sacred tripod over a deep fissure in the earth. The mists of the inner earth would rise and send her into a trance. Then she'd speak, tell everyone all manner of things. She might talk for hours, then collapse exhausted. A priest interpreted her messages. People would come from everywhere to ask her questions. And often her answers were correct.

Honey considers herself. Looks at her hands, not artistic, but capable.

She glances at her bed, smoothly made, her fuchsia pink nightdress rolled up and slipped under the pillow. And she wonders what the night will bring.

*   *   *

At nine o'clock that night there is a knock at the door. Howard answers it. Miss Florica is standing on the step, her eyes shining.

'Good evening Mr Tarbox,' she says. She has someone else with her, a friend, another woman. She introduces her as Mrs Brunt.

'Mrs Brunt knows a little of these matters,' says Miss Florica. 'She once had a psychic experience herself.'

Mrs Brunt wears short, black rubber boots, and a thick woollen coat. A black beret is balanced on her large square head.

Honey enters the lighted hall. Howard is excited. He is gabbling to the two ladies. It is apparent to Honey that Howard skipped his patchwork class and went instead to ask Miss Forica here tonight. Honey's shadow falls across the rose patterned carpet. All three stop talking and turn quietly towards her. Howard clears his throat.

'Honey, I know you won't mind if Miss Florica and Mrs Brunt stay to listen to you. It's in the interest of Science, I'm sure you'd agree.'

The two woman smile and nod their heads. Their heads look strangely loose on top of their wooden necks. Honey stays quiet, she doesn't smile back.

Please themselves, she thinks. She feels in control. All her life she's had nothing. But now, she has this. And this is becoming important, making her important.

'Have they brought me anything?' asks Honey.

'Brought you anything?' says Howard.

'Yes, a gift, a present. They must have something.'

The hall light hangs behind her, lighting up her body in silhouette, but they cannot see her face.

'I did bring something,' says Mrs Brunt. She pulls a rectangular object out of her crocheted shopping bag.

'A box of chocs.' She beams.

'That's good,' says Honey. 'If any more people come, Howard, you must ask them for their gift.' She turns away. 'I'll go and make a pot of tea.'

Howard is embarrassed.

'Really, she's never acted like this before . . . Come in. Come in.' He leads the two visitors into the lounge.

The fringed lamp shines a soft glow over the room. The television is on with the sound turned down and Honey's knitting lies on the sofa.

It isn't long before Honey brings the tea.

'I'll get ready while you all have a drink,' she says. She goes into the bedroom and changes into her nightdress. She sits waiting on the edge of the bed. Howard comes in. He says,

'You go to bed Honey. I won't ask anyone in until you're asleep.'

'Howard,' says Honey, 'what do they want?'

'I think they want to ask you some questions,' he says.

*   *   *

Howard, Miss Florica, and Mrs Brunt, stay waiting in the lounge. The clock ticks on. They make small talk. Mrs Brunt examines Honey's knitting.

'She's dropped a stitch ten rows back,' she says.

Suddenly they hear a voice talking in the bedroom. Miss Florica is on her feet straight away.

'That's Japanese!' she says. Howard leads them at a trot down to the back bedroom. He turns on a bedside lamp.

Honey is lying on her back in the bed. Her arms are folded across her chest. Her face is smooth, wiped of all expression. She is apparently fast asleep.

'Komban wa,' says Miss Florica. She bows towards the bed.

'Komban wa,' replies Honey. And a torrent of Japanese follows. She still looks like Honey but she doesn't sound like Honey. The voice is higher, more penetrating.

Miss Florica introduces Mrs Brunt. She presents the box of chocolates and says,

'Tsumaranai mono desu ga, doozo.'

Mrs Brunt smiles.

'Now she'll explain my problem,' she whispers to Howard. Howard pulls over another chair and they both sit down. There is a pause, then Honey says,

'Doomo arigatoo gozaimasu. Watashi wa ureshii desu.' Miss Florica smiles. She talks to Honey for about five minutes explaining Mrs Brunt's problem.

Honey replies, she talks on and on, hardly stopping for breath. The Japanese syllables sound strange to Howard. He crosses and recrosses his legs.

Finally Miss Florica turns back to them both.

'It's wonderful,' she says. 'It's all so clear. Her answer is simple.'

'What did you ask?' says Howard. Miss Florica and Mrs Brunt exchange looks.

'I don't mind if you tell,' says Mrs Brunt. 'I think we can trust Mr Tarbox.' Miss Florica explains.

'Mrs Brunt has a lovely miniature poodle, only three years old. His name is Schnookie. Schnookie is suffering terribly from arthritis and he may have to have plastic ligaments inserted in his front legs. Mrs Brunt was worried about the pain this operation may cause Schnookie, but now I have the answer.'

'And what is that?' asks Howard.

'It has been suggested Mrs Brunt finds a hypnotherapist.'

Mrs Brunt grins. 'What a terrific idea!'

'I'm so glad Honey helped you find the answer to your problem,' Howard says. Miss Florica and Mrs Brunt prepare to leave.

'Do you think Honey could help other people this way?' asks Howard. Miss Florica's face shines. She comes forward and places her hand on Howard's arm in a warm, caring way.

'Without doubt,' she says. 'Without doubt, I think I could say that Honey's advice and predictions could be the light at the end of the tunnel for many people. And I would make myself available any night to translate . . . for a small donation. Think about it, Mr Tarbox, and let us keep in touch.' She squeezes his arm. He opens the front door for them and says goodbye.

The sound of their footsteps fades away into the still, deep night.

The stars hang, glittering fiercely in the cold midnight sky. Howard hears a noise and swings around. It's Honey. She's wearing her fluffy lilac dressing gown.

'Did I do it?' she asks.

'Yes,' says Howard. His voice is low. 'They were very pleased. You were very successful. Miss Florica thinks you could help even more people.'

'I see,' says Honey. 'Tell her she can have thirty percent.' She turns and goes back to the bedroom. Howard comes inside. He's surprised. Honey seems so different, so business-minded, it's not like her. He frowns at the lock, pulls the chain across and slips it into it's tiny slot. Tomorrow he'll ring Miss Florica and make her an offer.

*   *   *

During the next few months the Tarbox home becomes famous. Word gets around, and every night many people arrive at Honey's with a little hope in their hearts. Some have simple questions written on a tiny scrap of paper. Others come escorted by note-taking secretaries who read their questions out for them.

They ask so many things. How to become rich, how to look more beautiful, how to become loved, and how to love. How to be good, to be received into heaven, to die happy. Honey answers them all.

Now Honey wears a beautiful peach pink nightie. She has her hair styled during the day so she will look her best every night. Reporters come and go. Honey is a popular personality to interview. They adore her combination of mystery and modesty. They ask her opinion on everything, her favourite colour (peach), and her favourite food (watermelon). She's even been on daytime chat shows, and has been photographed with many of the famous and well known people who now pass through the portals of her house in search of advice and predictions.

Her predictions are often correct. Her advice, politely and kindly offered, is always well accepted.

The Japanese ambassador has visited several times. The last time he came they talked at length about the future of Japan.

'Are wa sakura desu ka,' he'd said, peering out of Honey's window into the dark night.

'Hai,' Honey had answered. 'Haru desu.'

Waiting outside the door in the shadows, Howard had thought to himself how much Honey had changed.

To Howard, she now appears controlled, never flustered. She's always well dressed, her make up well applied. She offers her opinions even when they've not been asked for. And she expects Howard to keep accounts that add up.

Howard thinks he liked the old Honey better. She pottered around the house in her fluffy dressing gown. She always looked to Howard for advice about the way to dress, besides everything else. She was warm, caring, and she looked after me, thinks Howard. Now he thinks she's a Dragon Woman.

The business of the accounts upsets him the most. Maths was never his forte and he often makes mistakes. Sometimes, when it all gets too much for him, he seeks Miss Florica's help. In her old cardie and smudgy pink lipstick and her dishevelled bun and glasses, she reminds Howard of the old Honey.

She is pleased to help Howard. She pats his hand and sometimes makes him a pot of tea. She calls him Howard now, not Mr Tarbox.

* * *

During the day Honey often likes to sit in the garden. Howard used to look after it. He would mow a flat square in the middle and clip back the rest.

But it's all different now. A young Japanese man, Kenta Yamashita, has offered to build a real Japanese garden for Honey. Honey's advice to Kenta about his problems with his mother has so touched him that he comes back all the time just to visit. Now he has offered to build the Japanese garden.

He has planted a cherry tree and wants to pull up all the grass and replace it with raked gravel.

He is setting three large stones in their geomantic positions. The large stones are covered with lichen. They are the mountains, says Kenta. The gravel will be the water. All the elements of life. Honey loves watching the transformation of the garden. She sees it somewhat representative of what has happened to herself. She's looking forward to the complete removal of Howard's dusty geraniums and proteas and the installation of the raked sand. Smooth, flowing, meditative.

* * *

One Monday morning Honey wakes earlier than usual. She walks up the hall and into the kitchen.

Howard and Miss Florica are pushed against the sink bench grappling with each other's bodies. Howard's hands are up Miss Florica's blouse. Miss Florica's hands are down Howard's trousers. Their mouths are squashed against each other's. It makes Honey remember the goldfish.

She coughs gently and they both spring apart. Miss Florica blushes. 'I don't know what came over me,' she says.

Howard looks smug. He says nothing. Instead, he leans across Miss Florica and takes two pieces of toast out of the toaster. He butters them evenly and eats them straight away. Miss Florica excuses herself and hurries out of the kitchen.

'Would you like some toast?' asks Howard.

'No,' says Honey. She prefers to eat fish for breakfast these days.

'You're so different now,' says Howard. It's the first time he's ever talked to Honey about the changes in their lives.

'You're not the same Honey I married.'

'We all change,' says Honey. 'From decay grows new life. From the old is born the new.'

'How poetic,' says Howard. Honey pauses, she then replies,

'I must now take this opportunity to thank you for starting me on this path.'

'No worries,' mutters Howard.

*   *   *

That night Honey dons a white sateen nightie. She pins her hair up, adding a flower or two to the arrangement. She applies a little lipstick to her mouth and climbs into bed. She lies still, waiting for Miss Florica to arrive. This is the way they always do it. When Miss Florica comes, she sits over near the window and Honey slowly falls asleep.

Tonight Honey is more voluble than ever. She is funny and witty, and very likeable in this mood. Her *joie de vivre* breaks the language barrier. When her visitors leave they are smiling and laughing. Miss Florica is kept busy. Honey talks at such a rate, she can hardly keep up.

Then suddenly Honey sits up in her sleep. She has never done this before. Everyone stops what they're doing.

'Howardsan wa doko desu ka,' she says.

'Quick! Call Howard!' shouts Miss Florica. 'This is for him!'

'Watashi wa megami desu. Me ga mienai. Kiri ga mieru. Howardsan ga kiete iku!'

'I can't see. I see a mist,' translates Miss Florica quickly. Her face flushes. 'A disappearance!'

Honey falls exhausted onto her pillows and goes into a deep sleep. Howard cannot be found until the next morning. (He was down at the all-night service station talking to his friend.)

* * *

The next week Howard disappears.

No one sees him leave, nor can anyone remember for sure what happened. One day he was there, the next day—zilch! No one had ever taken much notice of him anyway (except Miss Florica).

She is allowed to move into his old room. She touches the razor on his dresser and carefully runs her finger along the blade. The terylene curtains wave in the breeze coming through the open window. Miss Florica opens the drawers and wonders why Howard never took any spare underwear with him when he left.

Kenta Yamashita has finished Honey's Japanese garden. Ten tons of white gravel and sand was delivered and raked into uniform patterns. Only Miss Florica can remember the particular day that the gravel arrived.

Yes, she can remember the day, the month, and the year (in case she's ever asked). It was the day before Howard disappeared.

Anne Kennedy

A VEIL DROPPED FROM A GREAT HEIGHT

Her weight is nothing to be alarmed about
An angel is her heaviest possession, apart from a piano which has hired
carrier pigeons to take its notes heavenwards.

A funeral attended by a truckload of hippies (this in 1973) was
followed in quick succession by its own death. Since then every day in
Wellington has been a public holiday—a Good Friday, a Christmas Day,
the day after.

She is leaving this city of sudden bereavements, taking her two
heaviest objects and also her two lightest; one, an ecstasy, the other, her
happiness seen from above.

A whiteness becomes black
When she was sixteen she took up sleep. She took to sleep like a duck to
water. Before that there had been no sleep to speak of. This is how E. J.
Byrne entered sleep:

Her brother, a storeman for a pharmaceutical firm, was paid in kindness, a plastic bag full of all sorts of states. The one he offered here was
embossed on one side with a pair of closed eyelids, on the flip side with
the letter M.

'M for Mogadon, eyelids for sleep,' said E. J. Byrne. She swallowed
the white tablet with a glass of milk, its cylindrical likeness, a stack of
itself. She called through the crack in her bedroom door: 'E. J. Byrne
has taken sleep!'

E. J. Byrne sleeps. She has not slept since sleep was spoken of. Now
every night she creeps into his room. 'I must just steal forty winks.' Every
night without fail E. J. Byrne sleeps.

Everyone says sleep becomes her
In the morning there is nothing that does not match Mogadon; sheets,
shirt, knickers, socks, a dotted line on the road to school, a lined refill
that will one day make landfill. Everything is white. In the midday glare
E. J. Byrne takes three white isosceles sandwiches from a plastic bag and
inspects their fillings with her protractor. They contain ninety-degree

heat. 'This is the end of the white,' says E. J. Byrne, moving into the shade. Mogadon vanishes without trace—except perhaps for a half-life of speed and colour.

Now it is the afternoon and everything is very fast and colourful.

Her afternoons contain her mornings
The class is considering its centre of gravity. 'I am it!' says E. J. Byrne, putting up her hand. Her mornings, her evenings have accumulated here, about the pull of her activity. E. J. Byrne does everything there is to do at a furious pace.

In the late afternoons she plays scales prestissimo up and down the piano until there are no more keys, all twenty-four have been used up. If there was another key, E. J. Byrne would play its scale, the twenty-fifth state, but unfortunately there is no such thing.

Instead she swallows a tiny white bead, one of a decade prescribed for her unhappiness, should it arise—half of it, saving the other 2.5 milligrams for an hour later to make sure it is absolutely necessary (also that it will last until 11 pm).

E. has learned ecstasy
This is the Simplicity pattern for E. J. Byrnes's happiness. She can use it over and over again, fitting the pieces on a size ten dummy, the size of a very small woman.

At first she thinks she must have a light body to achieve her most preferred state, the state of weightlessness (later she realizes it is not her body which has weightlessness among its possessions). She diets rigidly, living on Mogadon and the white wafers of the body of Christ.

She is not a great eater but her report card describes her as a high achiever and everyone is very pleased.

Music shop assistant (Wellington) knows a veil
In another age she would have been a jongleur. She spends her days demonstrating bamboo saxophones imported from Indonesia, but to no avail. The notes she plays carry no weight. ('They have no say-so la ti do,' says the frivolity of E. J. Byrne, amusing itself while she is not there, she is away in despair). The notes are gone before they can be sold. She has more success selling sheet music, a thin film noir.

A blackness (she does not see)
She tried to keep track of the beds she slept in and this was possible until

the age of twenty-one. Now she has lost count—also of the dead people she knows, and she can no longer remember how each Christmas has been spent. It is quicker to count down. She reads a thermometer and keeps a chart to gauge the largest ovulation of her life, whether it has passed yet.

The paradox, according to E. J. Byrne, is that when you are young nothing happens, and that is precisely the time in your life when something happening is what you want most in the world. When you are older—just a little bit, the difference between one day, its close of trade, and the next—when you are quite capable of making things happen, they happen of their own volition.

The parallax is, there is nothing that does not match

She is drawn to women and she is drawn to men, but more so to the symmetry of herself drawn either way. She wears a dress with a line down the middle, black on one side, white on the other, forming herself in an image to attract likenesses. At all costs she must have one or the other.

She once went to a ball, 'Le blanc et le noir,' held on a public holiday in the foyer of a public library in New York City. To this she wore flaming red. A splash of colour in black and white will not be seen, as on a screen, thought E. J. Byrne. She dropped into bed on the vanishing line between night and day.

Falling for the cause of her weightlessness

A light flickering in a darkened room she has just entered, E. J. Byrne assumes it signifies a presence, and she genuflects, then looks round quickly, ready to explain it was just a slip of the knee. She sees the light comes from a television set. The image of a woman shines upon a man watching from a low chair opposite. Caught in the light between these two gazes, there is nothing E. J. Byrne can do, deflecting, but summon a great Passion for one of them.

A documentary about RSI

E. J. Byrne now believes that is what the women in her family have been suffering from—too many years all the same, and injurious action between Christmases. Following the advice of a television documentary, she turns her head to one side when serving customers in the music shop. She stands on tiptoe to prevent fallen arches, and rotates the wrist that once faced the sky. The coins in the palm of her hand fall to the floor.

A folk song at night
Die Lorelei, sung by a siren in a major key as it approaches, becomes minor once it has passed the fixed object, E. J. Byrne. If there was a key between major and minor, E. J. Byrne would play its scale, but there is no in-between.

A telephone rings few changes
A white telephone ringing in the middle of a dark night, a black one ringing in sunlight on a bright morning (an afternoon)—the voice E. J. Byrne answers with is the same for each, even though she knows one call announces; he turned his palm to the sky for a last injection of ecstasy; the other, the pharmaceutical firm offers a pall bearer. Why else does a telephone ring at these hours? As in dreams she knows the outcome but she does not know it. She is leaving this city.

Why E. J. Byrne can never leave
An angel fallen from a tombstone (life-size, the size of an angel or a four-year-old child) lost its arm and part of its wing under a bulldozer. A man she knew once found it and now it is her stability (it takes four people to lift it), also the reason she must leave.

What she does with her days still is sleep
They are throwing a little cutlery around the room. An 8 am start is the time they go to bed. They have reversed night and day, retrieving the outlines of sleeves, the inner circles of neckbands from the cutting-room floor. A length of film she makes use of for a false hem on a dress she once wore to a black and white ball—this to match the negatives she glimpses at the corners of her eyes when she is tired. Before she can get a proper look the negatives disappear. That is their nature. She suspects they may be the blackness of what is here (but she does not see).

Her bête noir is the thing she most desires
She is the mother of three pregnancy scares and that is more than enough.

'There is no need to bring any more blood tests into this world,' says E. J. Byrne.

Utopia seen from a distance
Once from the eleventh floor of a building in New York it was difficult for E. J. Byrne, drawn to the window, to identify a mass of falling objects.

When she looked up they appeared to be part of a tickertape parade—looking down she saw the tiny flutter of pinstriped stockbrokers. The moment of her great sadness is also her happiness seen from above. She must have one or the other.

An injection calms her nerves
A Dystopia she once packed up and moved to by the picking of a fight, leaving soon afterwards for its opposite, a seduction. Now she need not search for these states, they fall into her lapdog. She takes an injection of passion at bedtime like a tablet with drawn eyelids. This is her bliss, the despair of which is a lover who once held her in the palm of her hand.

If she is wearing black, well, E. J. Byrne must wear white.

Anthony McCarten

BABY CLARE

The wind was drowning out the sound of everything else. A group of travellers stood in heavy flapping coats watching the light of the 8.55 train, still one mile off, coming slowly towards them through the night. Soon there was activity on the platform—kisses and firm handshakes were given, parcels picked up, and suitcases drawn against legs. But the light in the distance seemed to remain a fixed point in the darkness, barely growing larger at all.

Havilland Smith pulled the coat collar up around her daughter's neck and helped her onto the train.

On board, there were few spare seats because of the number of Auckland travellers trying to get home for New Year's Day, and Clare was unable to follow her mother's instructions to find two empty ones so that she could lie down during the night.

By the time the train began to pull out of the station, Clare was still looking for a seat, so she missed her chance to reach a window and wave to her mother. Instead, she swayed about in the passageway, trying to hold onto her bags and a parcel and some short stories by Truman Capote she liked to read but could not fully understand. The train increased its speed, and abandoning her mother's plan, she hurried right to the back, where she dropped her luggage with a clatter.

Clare Smith, or as her family called her, Baby Clare, never travelled alone, although she was almost seventeen. She was cripplingly shy and quiet. Her hair was thin and fell flat on her head, parted in the middle. But her complexion was good, and her eyes would have been quite stunning if she could have learnt to stop looking down at her shoes. And even her dreary clothes couldn't completely conceal the fact that she was a woman, not a child.

There were two other people at the back of the car, a woman and a man, lying spread out along two seats. Clare put down her bags. 'Do you mind if I sit down?'

The woman lifted her head from the seat. 'What?'

'Do you mind if I sit down?'

The woman did not reply, but seemed amazed to be asked this

question. It also inspired the man on the other seat to lift his head. 'What
did she say?'

'Wants to sit down,' said the woman.

'You blind or what?' the man asked Clare.

'The other seats are full.'

'So are these,' the woman answered. She appeared to be in her mid-
thirties. Her companion looked older, probably forty-five. Clare could
smell the booze in the air. The woman lay her head back down.

Clare stood there for several minutes, holding onto the back door
handle, her bags against her legs, trying to think this through. The train
was now travelling at full speed. Could she try other cars? Yes. She had
just decided to do this when the woman lifted her head once more and
said, 'You still here? What's the matter with you? You a total drongo or
what? Well?'

The man on the other seat stirred again at this. 'What's that?'

'She's still here,' said the woman. 'She's still here.'

The man propped himself up on his elbow to look at Clare. For a few
long seconds he stared at her. He was large, better dressed than the
woman, with an evident pride in his looks. His black hair was combed
back with some sort of grease. Together they seemed like one of those
couples often seen in holiday resorts who appear united by a temporary
situation such as a train strike or the cancellation of a bus.

Clare could feel his gaze and avoided looking at him at all. But she
did glance once or twice at the woman. Whereas the man was big and
oily, the woman was slim and fine-featured. She was a fake redhead and
wore her pale make-up so thickly that it lay in grains on her face. And
she was drunk. The mood between them suggested they'd had a big
argument earlier, which she had lost, so she'd hit the bottle, losing
interest in her appearance and wanting to let every lousy aspect of herself
show.

The man was still looking at Clare. She decided they were not
husband and wife. Then he swung his eyes onto Clare's cases—the big
new one of her mother's and a hard-top travel bag. She was also holding
a parcel. He looked at each of these in turn, rubbing the flat of his hand
over his mouth. Clare just stood there.

Then the man said to the woman, 'Hey, get up! You! We've got
company!' He slowly slipped his legs off the seat. 'Move it!'

The other woman lifted her head. 'Yeah? So what? Forget it. First
here, wasn't I? First in, first served.'

'Move!' repeated the man.

'Go to hell!'

'I *said*, didn't I?'

'Go to hell!' she replied with some heat.

At this the man got to his feet, stepped across the compartment, slipped his hand under the resting woman's ankles, and roughly swung them onto the ground. 'There—now move it!' Turning to Clare, his mood suddenly changing, he said almost politely, 'OK, you can sit.'

'Thank you,' said Clare, promising herself that she'd change carriages at the next station and look for another seat.

'But it's just you. No-one else. Just the three of us in here. There's too many already.'

They both sat down, Clare next to the woman, who had pushed herself into the corner by the window as if she needed to prop herself up. Clare could smell the booze more strongly now. None of this had improved the woman's temper.

Nobody said anything for a while. The carriage swayed and bounced, and shadows flashed past the windows in the darkness. Clare looked at her hands folded in her lap and at her cases gathered around her feet. Twice she glanced up and caught the man looking at her out of the corner of his eye. He was not quite as old as Clare's father, but almost. His eyes were clear and his good looks made Clare even more uncomfortable.

As for the woman, she seemed to be trying to stay awake, but her eyes kept closing and her head knocked rhythmically on the glass. After a bit of this, she would shift and complain. 'What the hell's the time?' He would never answer her.

Clare glanced at her watch, which she always kept freshly wound up to the last quarter-turn and never more. 'It's ten past nine,' she said.

The woman turned to look at Clare, squinting as though it were hard to see. 'What?'

'It's ten past nine.'

The squint continued. 'Who are you?'

'I beg your pardon?' asked Clare, giving a smile to make sure she didn't offend. But her fingers began to fidget in her lap. She was hardly ever confident with strangers, and the first signal would always be her fingers.

'Who the hell are you? I said.'

'Clare Smith.'

'Clare who?'

Clare glanced at the man and caught him a third time with his eyes on her. 'Smith,' she said.

At this the man leaned quickly forwards. Clare jumped backwards in her seat. He put his hand on her suitcase and flipped over the tag tied to the handle. 'Baby Clare,' he said, looking up at her, surprised.

Clare felt herself blush and her stomach tighten.

'What's it say?' asked the woman, who hadn't heard.

'Ba–by . . . Clare,' the man told her, rechecking.

'Baby what?'

'Clare.'

The woman turned to Clare again. 'That your name?'

Clare tried to smile at both of them. 'No.'

'Is that your name?'

'No. Not really,' she said. 'It's just . . . it's just a nickname, sort of. It's Clare. I've got an older cousin—'

'It's not your name?'

' . . . I've got an older cousin, that's all. Called Clare. So in the family I got called . . . sometimes . . . '

'Baby,' finished the man, a serious look on his face.

'But only when I was younger.'

For some time the couple did nothing but stare, possibly wondering whether this thin young woman was pulling their leg. They weren't sure.

Then the drunk woman offered her opinion. 'That's weird shit. That's weird shit, that is. How old are you, anyway? Fourteen? That's weird shit.'

'I beg your pardon?' asked Clare.

'I said how old are ya?'

'Sixteen'.

The woman kept squinting. 'Sixteen? Then why don't you wake your ideas up? Jesus! What a twerp!' Then she began to laugh. 'What a twerp!' She laughed for a good thirty seconds, as a drunk will do.

When the woman stopped laughing, she looked at Clare again. 'So what's in the bags?'

'I beg your pardon?'

'You got a hearing problem? What's in the bags?' The woman turned to the man. 'She's deaf too.'

'Just my things.'

'So why aren't they in the baggage car? We haven't got room in here for all these bags. This is ridiculous! That's what it is. It's ridiculous. There's no room in here already and you bring in all these bags!' The woman's eyes were bloodshot and her words were slurred. 'So what have you got to say for yourself? Or do you just like to sit there and be a complete waste of space?'

'The train is full,' said Clare. 'There was nowhere else—'

'There was nowhere else,' mimicked the woman. She started laughing again.

Clare was too unsettled to say anything. She just clutched her hands, moving her fingers, twisting them slowly but with enough slow pressure to break, say, a chicken bone. Whereas most people might try to be courageous, Clare did not. She told herself two things only, over and over: she was wearing two quite stylish clips in her hair, and her neat dress was precisely pressed.

'What's the matter with you, anyway?' asked the woman. 'Hey, I'm talking to you! You retarded or something? Hey, Baby Clare. Ha-ha-ha!'

'Leave her alone,' said the man, looking out the window.

'What?'

'Leave her alone, I said.'

The woman considered this option for a minute and then disregarded it. 'Why the hell should I? She's the bloody troublemaker. Did I ask her to come and sit down here? No.' She leaned very close to Clare and said quietly but very deliberately into her ear, 'You're a proper little bitch, aren't you? Well, don't mess around with me. Get it? You understand that one, honey?'

Clare looked up the carriage. The conductor had not yet checked the tickets. He would be coming soon. She longed to see him heading down the aisle.

'That's it, honey, you keep your mouth shut. Or I'll shut it for you.' The woman returned to her corner and after a couple of glances moved her attention off Clare.

In the next half-hour Clare looked up only twice. The first time she noticed that the woman was staring at her companion with a kind of anger, and the second time she noticed the man was looking out the window.

Eventually, sitting so still became painful; she tried not to move or attract attention, but there were certain movements she couldn't stop. Her ankle began to twitch and this caused her knee to move slightly. She rested her hand on it. A pain developed in her shoulder blade. But then the conductor entered the carriage from the other end, clipping tickets. It seemed to take him forever to make his way down the crowded car.

'Are there any more seats further up?' Clare asked.

'Full load.'

He clipped the tickets of the man and the woman and turned to go back up the carriage.

'Excuse me,' said Clare.

'What is it?'

'Toilets. Are there toilets?'

'Yep. Right up the front. But you'll be waiting quite a while tonight.' At this point the conductor must have observed the strain on the girl's face. He softened. 'I'll tell you what. If you're just gonna be quick, you can go into the guard's van behind you. There's one in there. But you'd better be quick. I'll get shot.'

'Thank you.'

Clare got to her feet right away, picked up her jacket, and without looking at anyone, fearing a hand might grab her, stepped to the door, opened it as quickly as she could, and went through.

On the other side, she slipped on her jacket, feeling tremendously relieved. The deserted van was unlit past the toilet cubicle. Feeling her way along the handrail, she moved out of the light towards the racing wind at the far end, where she did up all her buttons.

The shapes of trees and hills flashed by outside. Lights from farm houses drifted in and out of view. Clare's hair swept about on her head. But it was OK. She breathed in the air, telling herself she hadn't been in any real danger. At any time since boarding she could have raised her voice and thirty heads would have turned. Why hadn't she? Because it was easier to pretend those things weren't happening, and she was looking so nice tonight with her new dress and shoes. Her aunt would meet her at the other end off the train. It would have been crazy to yell out in a public carriage.

She stood in the dark at the end of the van with her hand against the wall, breathing short breaths, seeing the land roll by, and taking in the cold air. Out on the hills were the lights of a few isolated homes. These passed slowly behind and were not replaced. The train was many miles from the town now, sweeping into remote parts of the Wairarapa. The moon had drifted behind the hills, leaving them a midnight blue, and the sight of it calmed Clare, allowing her to think over her arrangements with her aunt. Clare had phoned three times that week to make sure there would be no confusion. She had wanted to have what her mother would call Peace of Mind. 'There is no price you can put on Peace of Mind.' This was something her mother loved to say whenever she had the chance.

Suddenly the door of the guard's van opened. There was an outline in the doorway, lit from behind so that Clare could not see the face. The figure did not move.

Clare immediately pushed herself back into the dark corner. Not wanting to be seen, she stood quietly, gripping the rail. At first she didn't recognise the man but remembered other outlines in other doorways, when she was younger, the shadows that children see when it's dark and the wind is blowing and they're too afraid to sleep because a branch is scraping against the window.

The man's head turned this way and that, looking. The door to the toilet was open, and he looked from there into the blackness where Clare his holding the rail with both hands behind her back.

Looking towards her, he shut the door and came through. Clare did not move as he groped his way along the handrail.

'So.' He placed his hand lightly on her shoulder.

He was so close she could smell the grease he wore in his hair and feel his breath on her cheek. 'This is where you are. I was looking for you. When you didn't come right back, I wondered where you'd got to. Well, how about this?' he chuckled. 'How about this?'

Clare didn't reply. She hardly seemed to acknowledge his arrival, and he could have been forgiven for thinking she was simply snubbing him. The smile remained on his face as he spoke in a friendly, soothing way. 'What's the matter? Don't wanna talk or something? And you're shaking too. Well, that's because it's freezing back here with the door open. Or are you frightened of something? Are you? Well, don't be frightened. You've got nothing to be frightened of with me. Some types you might, but not me.'

Clare tried to ignore every word, but the odd one broke through: *freezing, frightened, are you?* 'I'm not frightened,' she said, so faintly he could hardly hear her.

'What's that? You're frightened? You shouldn't be either. Nothing to be frightened about, is there? Just you and me having a wee chat down the back of this here guard's van, aren't we? That's right.' His face seemed very close to hers and she expected at any moment to feel it touch hers.

'I can hardly see a thing. Hell, it's cold back here. You smoke?' he asked. 'You wanna fag? They're mentholated. I said, you wanna fag?'

She didn't move. She wasn't listening. She wanted to look out at the trees or anything, but he moved in front of her.

'Do you smoke?'

Clare looked into his face. He was eyeing her, but then he started to shake his head slowly, as is disappointed in the way she was carrying on.

He stepped away from her to light his cigarette. The wind blew out two matches before he got it. Clare watched his face glow and fade with the match.

'She shouldn't drink,' he said. 'She gets mean. There's something wrong with her tonight. I don't know what it is. She's passed out and snoring her head off now.' He blew some smoke out the open door, but the draught blew it back. 'Nice, back here.'

He stood a few feet away from her, looking out at the trees and the hills and the occasional lights. 'I used to work around this area. Out there.' He motioned with his head. 'Driving. That's right. Matamata. Arlington. You can see Arlington over there. I've worked over this whole bit of country. Driven every type of vehicle you could think of too.'

The wind lifted the glow of his cigarette. He sighed and turned to face Clare again, moving closer. The smell of menthol was strong. He had a strange look in his eye, as if something had made him angry all of a sudden. 'Y'know,' he said, after studying her face and looking down at her dress, 'you're not bad-looking, if you didn't try to hide it.' His breath upon her was baby-warm. 'If you didn't wear your mother's dresses, you wouldn't look so gloomy. If you brightened yourself up a bit, put on a decent sorta dress, no, you wouldn't look too bad.' His hand was on the small of her back. 'I bet you're eighteen, anyway. That right? I bet you're older than you look. I bet you're at least eighteen.' His hand moved to her rump, tracing slow circles as he drew the whole of his body up against her, pressing, pressing with sudden intimacy. Then he slowly, gently bent forward and touched his lips to her cold cheek, holding them there for a long moment. It was the action of a supremely confident man alone with a timid woman. She pulled her face back swiftly.

'I know what you are. You're one of those quiet ones, aren't ya? One of those plain Janes. You've hardly even kissed yet, I'll bet.' He wore a slightly amused smile on his face and stared at her for a few moments as if considering his next move.

But instead of kissing her again, he released his hand and stepped back, letting her go. She withdrew back against the wall, grasping the handrail again. 'OK. OK.' he said. 'Forget it. Let's just forget it. But I'll tell you something for nothing. You stop wearing your mother's dresses and you'll be a lot better off. I've seen plenty of women with no more than you've got and they make the most of it. They don't have much, but they know what to show off and they do all right too. I've been with a hundred of 'em. Take that from me and you'll do a lot better for yourself. A lot better than you think you could too. And then you should learn to kiss.'

Clare was trying to hear none of this, but she could still smell the menthol and feel the pressure of his hand on her backbone as if he were still pressed up against her. Trying to keep her mind on all the things she had to do tomorrow was not working any longer. His words kept breaking her concentration and frightening her in a deep way. His smell, his touch. The impression of his outline in the doorway.

'Yep,' he said. 'I've worked all round that country, and you wanna know something? The funny thing was I never got tired of it.' He exhaled in the open doorway, looking out there, and the smoke blew in a rich plume over his shoulders. 'This is nice. You wanna know something else? This is like old times.' He sighed. 'I'm gonna tell you something interesting now, and I hope you're listening. Well, *I* reckon it's interesting, anyway—'

But in an instant it happened, and it was over. Clare took a step forward. Her hand went into the centre of his heavy back, and somehow he was gone. Out the open door without a scuffle. She had pushed him from the train.

The doorway was empty. The outline, the cigarette, the voice.

Clare steadied herself at the edge, where just a second ago he had been standing, almost falling out herself, amazed at how easily such a big man had vanished. The noise of the iron wheels beneath her was deafening. The wind was tearing at her hair. She could see nothing but the track falling away. He had tumbled out without a shout or the slightest noise and was gone into the night.

She stepped back out of the wind, doing her coat up tight around her neck, and listened for his voice. But there were no more descriptions of the country where he had worked and nothing about what was to have been interesting. There was only what seemed to be the echo of his voice in her head under the noise of the wheels, but even that was fading as Clare's thoughts returned to her travel arrangements. She thought how convenient it was going to be for everybody that her aunt had been able to borrow the car to drive her down. and with each passing moment the train put a distance on everything outside that had been there before.

Clare stood there until her fingers became numb. Then she turned and made her way back up the van to the carriage door. She opened it and went through.

The redhead was asleep on the seat, but she awoke as Clare sat down. 'So you're back,' she mumbled, groggy with drink.

Clare didn't reply. She sat down and drew her bags up closely and uniformly against her legs, as she would always do, holding the parcel in her lap. She didn't hear what the woman was saying or notice her looking around for her friend. 'Say, where the hell has he gone? Hey you, I'm talking to you! Did you see him? My fiancé? Hey you!'

Clare still didn't answer.

The woman leaned closer, breathing alcohol and whispering with sinister calm. 'Hey! What's the matter with you? You're stupid, or what? I'm talking to you, so listen to me!'

Clare just sat upright in her seat, clutching her bags, her hair set back in place, her dress as neat as ever, ready to meet her aunt at the other end, knowing that a bed would already be made up for her in the clean guest room and that perfect towels would be laid out on the dresser.

And all the pitch-black shapes outside the train window slipped away.

Biographical Notes

Renato Amato (1928–64) was born in Potenza, Southern Italy. The early years of the Second World War he spent in Turin, and was obliged to serve in the notorious *Brigate Nere* until his escape to the Allies. He began learning English in 1950, while working for the International Refugee Organisation, and emigrated to New Zealand in 1954. 'One of the Titans', first published in *Mate* in 1961, was included in his one posthumous volume, *The Full Circle of the Travelling Cuckoo*, 1967.

Barbara Anderson was born in Hawke's Bay in 1926, graduated from the University of Otago in science, and worked for many years as a science teacher and technician. She followed this thirty years later with an Arts degree at Victoria University, Wellington, when she also began writing. Her short stories and her two novels, particularly *Portrait of the Artist's Wife*, 1991, have met with critical acclaim. 'Up the River with Mrs Gallant' is from the collection *I think we should go into the jungle*, 1989.

Lady Barker (1831–1911), born Mary Anne Stewart in Jamaica, was educated in England, and at the age of twenty married George Barker, an officer in the Royal Artillery. He was knighted for military prowess, and died soon after the Mutiny in India. As the wife of Frederick Broome, poet, journalist, and later colonial administrator, she came to New Zealand in 1865, and for three years lived on a sheep run in Canterbury. Back in England she published, as Lady Barker, the highly successful *Station Life in New Zealand*, 1870, and went on to write over a dozen books, ranging from children's stories to cooking. The extract from 'Christmas Day in New Zealand' is from *A Christmas Cake in Four Quarters*, 1872.

Amelia Batistich was born in Dargaville, North Auckland, in 1915, where her parents were Dalmatian settlers, and has spent most of her life in Auckland. With Yvonne du Fresne, hers is certainly the strongest voice in New Zealand writing from a non-English-speaking emigrant community. She has published two novels and two collections of short stories. 'A Dalmatian Woman' is from *An Olive Tree in Dalmatia*, 1963.

Clara Cheeseman (1852–1943) is remembered for her one surviving story, 'Married for his Money', published in the *Australian Ladies'*

Annual, 1878. She also wrote with critical perception about New Zealand social mores in her novel *A Rolling Stone*, 1886.

Joy Cowley was born in 1936 in Levin, and lives in the Marlborough Sounds. A prolific and highly successful writer of children's books, she has also published five novels and a collection of short stories. Her short story 'The Silk' appeared in the *New Zealand Listener*, 5 March 1965, and has been included in several anthologies.

John Cranna was born in Te Aroha in 1954, and grew up in the Waikato. After living for some years in London, he returned to Auckland and published his first collection of stories *Visitors*, 1989, from which 'Archaeology' is taken, and a novel, *Arena*, 1991.

Dan Davin (1913–90) was born in Invercargill, whose Irish Catholic community, along with military life in the Second World War, were the constant interests of his fiction. He went to Oxford as a Rhodes Scholar in 1935, and returned there, after a distinguished war career, to the Clarendon Press. He wrote seven novels, three collections of short stories, memoirs, the volume on *Crete* for the New Zealand War History Branch, and incidental criticism. His story 'Coming and Going' is from *Breathing Spaces*, 1970.

Jean Devanny (1894–1962) was born into a mining family in Collingwood as Jean Crook. Already a committed political activist, she married Francis Devanny when she was seventeen. Conventional society found it difficult to accept either her Marxism or her sexually frank novel, *The Butcher's Shop*, 1926. She settled in Australia in 1929, took a prominent part in the affairs of the Australian Communist Party, and added nine Australian novels to her eight New Zealand volumes. 'The Perfect Mother' is from her collection *Old Savage and Other Stories*, 1927.

Yvonne du Fresne was born in the Manawatu in 1929 and now lives at Makara, near Wellington. Her fiction reflects the Danish-Huguenot community in which she grew up. She has combined a career in teaching with writing radio plays, two volumes of stories, and two novels. 'Morning Talk' is taken from *Farvel and Other Stories*, 1980.

Maurice Duggan (1922–74) was born in Auckland, briefly attended

Auckland University and visited Europe where his ill health began. He earned his living as a sardonically successful advertising executive, while writing his intricately crafted stories. 'Along Rideout Road that Summer' is from the second of his three collections, *Summer in the Gravel Pit*, 1965. He also wrote children's fiction.

Fiona Farrell was born in Oamaru in 1947. After Otago University she studied drama at Toronto University, and has written for theatre as well as teaching drama. A volume of her poetry was published in 1987, and her first novel, *The Skinny Louie Book*, in 1992. 'The Gift' is from her short story collection, *The Rock Garden*, 1989.

Roderick Finlayson (1904–92) was born in Auckland and followed early architectural training with his life-long commitment to Pacific life and affairs. His fiction reflects his extensive experience in Maori farming districts after rejecting a 'ruthless and technological and acquisitive society'. 'Another Kind of Life' is from *Sweet Beulah Land*, 1942, the second of several collections of short stories.

Janet Frame was born in Dunedin in 1924, and has told the story of her childhood and education in *To the Is-land*, 1982, the first of three acclaimed volumes of autobiography. Her brief attempt at schoolteaching was followed by the disturbed years in psychiatric hospitals that furnished so much for her fifteen books of fiction, from *The Lagoon and Other Stories*, 1951, to *The Carpathians*, 1988. Although she has travelled extensively, most of her writing life has been spent in small towns in New Zealand. The recipient of numerous honours and awards, she has created what is virtually a unique narrative method, and produced a vast, disturbing, and coherent *oeuvre*. 'The Reservoir' is the title story from *The Reservoir: Stories and Sketches*, 1963, and 'The Bath' is from her selected short stories, *You Are Now Entering the Human Heart*, 1983.

A. P. Gaskell was born in 1913 in Kurow, Otago, as Alexander Gaskell Pickard. His father's work in the Railways took him in his boyhood over much of the North Island, before he attended the University of Otago, where he took his MA in French and English. His life has been spent in secondary school teaching in several areas of the country. His story 'School Picnic' is from *The Big Game and Other Stories*, 1947, which was reissued with six new stories as *All Part of the Game*, 1978.

Maurice Gee was born in Whakatane in 1931, and grew up in Henderson. After taking his MA at Auckland University he taught for a short time, worked at a number of jobs in Australia, but has now been living mainly as a writer for thirty years. He has written television scripts and children's fiction, and his many novels have been much praised, especially the *Plumb* trilogy. 'A Glorious Morning, Comrade' is the title story from his short story collection published in 1975.

G. R. Gilbert was born in 1917 in Greymouth on the West Coast. He went from school into broadcasting, but was to lose this job for his pacifist convictions. He chose, however, to serve in the RNZAF during the Second World War. He published two collections of stories. 'A Girl with Ambition' is from the first of these, *Free to Laugh and Dance*, 1942.

Patricia Grace was born in Wellington in 1937, and is of Ngati Raukawa, Ngati Toa and Te Ati Awa descent. She grew up in the King Country, Northland, and Porirua, where she still lives. A teacher as well as a writer, her *Waiariki*, 1975, was the first collection of stories by a Maori woman. She has written children's stories in Maori and English, three volumes of stories, and her third novel, *Cousins*, has just been published. 'Journey' and 'Between Earth and Sky' are from *The Dream Sleepers and Other Stories*, 1980.

Alexander Guyan (1933–91) was born in Aberdeen, came to Dunedin when he was sixteen, and returned to England in the 1970s. He was a significant figure in drama and early television writing, as well as a short story writer. His novel *Exciting, Isn't It?* appeared in 1989. 'An Opinion of the Ballet' was published in *Mate*, June 1960.

Russell Haley was born near Leeds in 1934, and served in the RAF before settling in Auckland in 1966. Since his MA at Auckland University, he has taught there in the English Department, and published two volumes of short stories, two collections of poetry, a novel, and a biography of the painter Patrick Hanly. 'Fog' is from his collection *Real Illusions*, 1984.

Noel Hilliard was born in Napier in 1929, and followed a degree at Victoria University with a career in journalism, as well as spells as a schoolteacher and farm worker. His strong leftist convictions and his rapport with Maori life are the driving forces of his three collections of stories, and his five novels. His work has been translated into several East European languages, Russian, and Chinese. 'Corrective Training' is from his collection *Send Somebody Nice*, 1976.

Keri Hulme was born in Christchurch in 1947, of Kai Tahu, Orkney Scots, and English descent, and lives at Okarito on the West Coast of the South Island. She has published three volumes of poetry, one collection of short stories, and *the bone people*, 1983, which won the Booker Prize. 'One Whale, Singing' is from her collection *Te Kaihau: the Windeater*, 1986.

Witi Ihimaera was born in Gisborne in 1944, as Witi Tame Ihimaera Smiler, of Ngati Mahaki descent. After a range of temporary jobs he took his arts degree at Victoria University, and was living in England when he completed *Pounamu, Pounamu*, the first volume of stories by a Maori writer, and also the first Maori novel, *Tangi*. For several years he served in Australia and the United States with the Ministry of External Relations and Trade, and has published three collections of stories, three novels, has written for children, and edited Maori writing. 'Big Brother, Little Sister' is from *The New Net Goes Fishing*, 1977.

Lloyd Jones was born in 1955 in Wellington, where he still lives. Since attending Victoria University, he has given most of his time to writing. As well as two novels, he has published *Swimming to Australia and Other Stories*, 1991. 'Who's that Dancing with my Mother' is from that collection.

Anne Kennedy was born in Wellington in 1959, and now lives in Auckland. She has written for television and film, her short novel *100 Traditional Smiles* appeared in 1988, and in 1993 the University of Queensland Press and Auckland University Press bring out *Musica Ficta*. 'A Veil Dropped from a Great Height' is from *New Women's Fiction*, edited by Aorewa McLeod, 1988.

Fiona Kidman (b. 1940) grew up in Northland and Rotorua, and lives in Wellington. Although trained as a librarian, she has worked mainly as a journalist and writer. She has written extensively for radio and television, published seven novels, two collections of stories, several volumes of poetry, and drama. 'The Tennis Player' is from *Unsuitable Friends*, 1988.

Rudyard Kipling (1865–1936) visited New Zealand in October 1891 'for a loaf and to see pretty things'. Already a literary celebrity, he was in the country for less than three weeks, but his 'One Lady at Wairakei' managed to touch on key issues of colonial writing and national aspirations. It appeared in the *Saturday Supplement* of the *New Zealand Herald* on 30 January 1892, the story presumably sent on from Australia. It remained uncollected and virtually unknown until republished with an introduction by Harry Ricketts in 1983.

G. B. Lancaster (1873–1945), the pseudonym of Edith Lyttelton, was born in Tasmania and came to New Zealand as a child. She wrote over a dozen novels of the 'popular romance' genre, and many short stories that have never been collected. 'Hantock's Dissertation' is from *Sons o'Men*, 1904.

Henry Lawson (1867–1922) was born on the goldfields at Grenfell, New South Wales, received scant education, and went on in his short stories to shape the dominant Australian conception of life in the bush, and the values of mateship. In the 1890s he spent three periods in New Zealand, the longest for seven months as a schoolteacher near Kaikoura, in the South Island. 'Stiffner and Jim (Thirdly, Bill)' was published in the *Pahiatua Herald*, 9 March 1894. The revised version of the story appeared in his collection *The Country I Come From*, 1902.

Bill Manhire was born in Invercargill in 1946, grew up in Southland and Otago, and attended Otago University and University College, London. A Reader in English at Victoria University, he has published several collections of poetry, including the prize-winning *Milky Way Bar*, 1991, two volumes of fiction, a study of Maurice Gee, and with his wife Marion McLeod, *Some Other Country*, an anthology of New Zealand stories. 'The Poet's Wife' is from *Sport* 4, March 1990.

Katherine Mansfield (1888–1923) was born in Wellington, and spent half her life in New Zealand, half in Europe. New Zealand's best known and most influential writer, she published three volumes of short stories, and two long short stories in private editions. John Middleton Murry edited two further posthumous volumes of uncollected and incomplete stories. These various volumes have been republished, and her stories anthologized, numerous times. *The Stories of Katherine Mansfield*, 1984, edited and annotated by Antony Alpers, is now the essential text. 'The

Wind Blows' was first published as 'Autumn II' in *The Signature*, No. 1, 4 October 1915, a magazine edited by D. H. Lawrence and John Middleton Murry. It was substantially revised before taking its place in *Bliss and Other Stories*, 1920. 'An Indiscreet Journey', although written out of her visit to the war zone in early 1915, cannot be dated with any certainty. It was not published in her lifetime, and appeared in *Something Childish but Very Natural*, 1924.

Owen Marshall was born in 1941. After his degree at Canterbury University, he took up a career in teaching, and is now deputy principal at Craighead Diocesan Girls' School, Oamaru. A short story 'specialist', and a 'South Islander by choice', his work is admired for its regional as well as artistic strengths. He has published six collections, including *The Divided World: Selected Stories*, 1989. Both his stories in this anthology are from *The Lynx Hunter and Other Stories*, 1987.

Anthony McCarten was born in New Plymouth in 1961, worked as a journalist, took his BA at Victoria University, and is now a full-time writer. His several plays, especially *Ladies' Night*, written with Stephen Sinclair, have met with wide success. Also a poet and short story writer, his 'Baby Clare' is from *A Modest Apocalypse and Other Stories*, 1991.

Ronald Hugh Morrieson (1922–72) lived all his life in the small Taranaki town of Hawera, and yet created a bizarre and funny world which constitutes one of the most distinctive contributions to New Zealand fiction. Two of his novels, *Scarecrow* and *Came a Hot Friday*, have been made into feature films. 'Cross my heart and cut my throat' first appeared in *Landfall* in 1974.

Michael Morrissey was born in 1942 in Auckland, where he has spent most of his life. He has written eight books of poetry, and three collections of short stories, as well as writing for film, and editing *The New Fiction*, 1985, an anthology of postmodern New Zealand fiction. His story in this volume is from *Octavio's Last Invention*, 1991.

Vincent O'Sullivan was born in Auckland in 1937, attended Auckland and Oxford universities, has lived mostly in New Zealand, and mostly as an academic. He has published nine volumes of poetry, five collections of stories, written several plays, and edited a number of anthologies. His story in this volume is from *Dandy Edison for Lunch*, 1981.

Vivienne Plumb was born in Sydney in 1955, and came to Wellington as a teenager. Recently she has begun to write for the theatre, and to publish short stories. 'The Wife Who Spoke Japanese in her Sleep' is from the anthology *Between These Hills*, 1991.

Colleen Reilly was born in Nebraska in 1946, took degrees in Nebraska and the National University, Dublin, and worked as a journalist after coming to New Zealand. She teaches at Victoria University, Wellington, writes a national TV column, and has published two novels. 'Jim's Elvis' is the title story of her new collection.

Frank Sargeson (1903–82) was born and grew up in Hamilton and the Waikato. After a law degree at Auckland University and a year's visit to Europe, he returned to New Zealand. His life was devoted almost entirely to writing, supported by casual labouring jobs. His first stories in the 1930s appeared in the journal *Tomorrow*, and he was awarded the first prize in the Centennial Literary Competitions in 1940. As well as three collections of short stories, he wrote eight longer fictional works, essays, and autobiography. The selection *The Stories of Frank Sargeson* was published by Penguin in 1982. Both 'Old Man's Story' and 'A Great Day' are from *A Man and His Wife*, 1940.

Maurice Shadbolt was born in Auckland in 1932, and continues to live there in the Waitakeres. The most prolific of contemporary New Zealand novelists, he has published over twenty volumes, including biography and drama. His last novel, *Monday's Warriors*, 1990, is the second of a trilogy on the Land Wars of the last century. 'The People Before' is from the second of his volumes of short stories, *Summer Fires and Winter Country*, 1963.

C. K. Stead was born in Auckland in 1932, and after degrees at Auckland and Bristol universities, spent twenty years until 1986 as a Professor of English at the University of Auckland. Now a full-time writer, he has published nine collections of poetry, several critical books, and four novels. 'A New Zealand Elegy' is from his volume of short stories, *Five for the Symbol*, 1981.

Greville Texidor (1902–64) lived in New Zealand between 1940 and 1948, and during that time wrote most of her fiction. Born in Wolverhampton as Greville Foster, and educated at Cheltenham Ladies

College, she travelled widely as a young woman, worked as a professional dancer in variety shows, and married Manuel Texidor, a Catalonian businessman. After joining the Anarchist Centurias during the Spanish Civil War, she and her second husband settled in Auckland. 'Home Front' was published in *New Zealand New Writing* No. 1, 1942, and her short stories were collected and edited by Kendrick Smithyman as *In Fifteen Minutes You Can Say a Lot*, 1987.

Ian Wedde was born in Blenheim in 1946, attended Victoria University, travelled extensively, and now lives in Wellington. He has published ten books of poetry, three novels, including *Symmes Hole*, 1986, and edited two Penguin anthologies of New Zealand verse. 'The Gringos' is from *The Shirt Factory and Other Stories*, 1981.

Peter Wells was born in 1953. He has worked for over a decade as a film-maker, and his *Death in the Family*, 1986, on the death of an AIDS sufferer, won the American Film Festival prize for Best Drama. 'Outing' is from his first book of fiction, *Dangerous Desires*, 1991.

Albert Wendt was born in Samoa in 1939, graduated from Auckland University, and for many years taught at the University of the South Pacific before taking up a Chair in English at Auckland. He has published five novels, two volumes of short stories, and two of poetry. His story 'Crocodile' is from *The Birth and Death of the Miracle Man*, 1986.

Glossary of Maori and Samoan Words

ae yes
alofa love
aroha love
haere mai welcome
he mea Maori a Maori thing
hori Maori (derogatory)
hoha fellow (slang)
kai food
kai moana seafood
kainga village, home
kehua ghost
mahita schoolteacher
manuka a shrub or small tree with aromatic leaves, also known as tea-tree
Maori an indigenous New Zealander; their language
marae courtyard of Maori meeting-house, the focus of social life in a Maori community
mimi (to have a mimi) to urinate
moa large extinct flightless bird
pa fortified Maori village or, by extension, a settlement
Pakeha New Zealander of European descent
papalagi European
pipi a kind of shellfish
pohutukawa large coastal tree with crimson blossom in summer
puriri a kind of forest tree
rangatira chief
rata vine or tree with bright red blossom
raupo bulrush
Tamatea a Ngana, Tamatea Aio, Tamatea, Tamatea Whakapau days 6–9 in the traditional Maori lunar calendar
tangi funeral
tapu ritual restriction
tena koe hello
'tenaa koe e hine' hello young lady
toitoi tall tussocky grass with long creamy plumes
wahine woman
whakairo wood carving
whakapapa genealogy
whanaunga relative

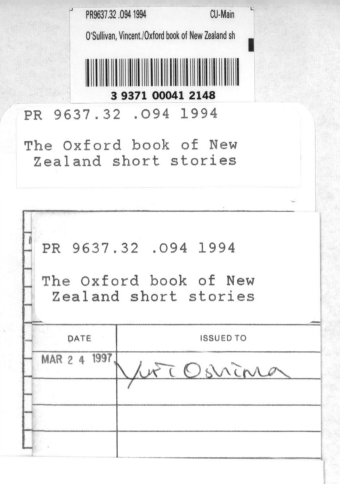